Deploying iPads in the Classroom

Planning, Installing, and Managing iPads in Schools and Colleges

Guy Hart-Davis

Apress®

Deploying iPads in the Classroom: Planning, Installing, and Managing iPads in Schools and Colleges

Guy Hart-Davis
Barnard Castle, Durham, United Kingdom

ISBN-13 (pbk): 978-1-4842-2927-9   ISBN-13 (electronic): 978-1-4842-2928-6
https://doi.org/10.1007/978-1-4842-2928-6

Library of Congress Control Number: 2017958049

Cover image designed by Freepik

Managing Director: Welmoed Spahr
Editorial Director: Todd Green
Acquisitions Editor: Aaron Black
Development Editor: James Markham
Technical Reviewer: Martin V. Minner
Coordinating Editor: Jessica Vakili
Copy Editor: Corbin Collins
Compositor: SPi Global
Indexer: SPi Global
Artist: SPi Global

Distributed to the book trade worldwide by Springer Science+Business Media New York, 233 Spring Street, 6th Floor, New York, NY 10013. Phone 1-800-SPRINGER, fax (201) 348-4505, e-mail orders-ny@springer-sbm.com, or visit www.springeronline.com. Apress Media, LLC is a California LLC and the sole member (owner) is Springer Science + Business Media Finance Inc (SSBM Finance Inc). SSBM Finance Inc is a **Delaware** corporation.

For information on translations, please e-mail rights@apress.com, or visit http://www.apress.com/rights-permissions.

Apress titles may be purchased in bulk for academic, corporate, or promotional use. eBook versions and licenses are also available for most titles. For more information, reference our Print and eBook Bulk Sales web page at http://www.apress.com/bulk-sales.

Any source code or other supplementary material referenced by the author in this book is available to readers on GitHub via the book's product page, located at www.apress.com/978-1-4842-2927-9. For more detailed information, please visit www.apress.com/source-code.

Printed on acid-free paper

Contents at a Glance

Contents

About the Author

Guy Hart-Davis is the author of more than 100 computer books, including *Learn Office 2016 for Mac*, *Learn Excel 2016 for Mac*, and *Pro Office for iPad* (Apress).

About the Technical Reviewer

Martin V. Minner is a technology publishing consultant and historian. He has a Ph.D. from Indiana University and an M.A. from the University of North Carolina. Marty's home is in Bloomington, Indiana, but he lives at the intersection of technology and the humanities. He's on Twitter as @MVMinner.

Acknowledgments

My thanks go to the many people who helped create this book:

- Aaron Black for signing me to write the book

- Jim Markham for developing the manuscript

- Martin V. Minner for reviewing the manuscript for technical accuracy and contributing helpful suggestions

- Jessica Vakili for coordinating the book project, keeping things running, and being very patient

- David Pasqua of TabPilot Learning Systems for kindly providing help with TabPilot

- SPi Global for laying out the chapters of the book

- [PROOFREADER] for proofreading the book and making suggestions

- SPi Global for creating the index

Introduction

Apple's iPad is the most successful tablet computer ever. Almost as easy to use as it is to damage (you'll want to protect your iPads with cases), the iPad is great for computing anywhere and everywhere. iPads are also terrific in schools, enabling you to put in each student's hands an easily-manageable but powerful tablet on which the student can do everything from learning Internet use to developing essential office software skills, from recording live audio to creating backing tracks and producing CD-quality music, and from taking photos and shooting video clips to creating high-quality movies.

Who Is This Book For?

This book is for anybody who's looking to deploy iPads in a classroom or lab situation. Most likely you're a teacher or educator in a school or college, and that's the scenario this book and its examples aim at. But even if your situation and aims for deploying multiple iPads are different, you'll find useful information in this book. For example, you might run a community computing club providing Internet access, or you might offer private computing lessons to small groups.

What Does This Book Cover?

This book contains nine chapters that take you from planning a classroom deployment of iPads to managing the classroom and troubleshooting the iPads when things go wrong.

Chapter 1, "Planning Your Classroom Deployment of iPads," discusses how to plan your deployment of iPads in the classroom. The chapter starts with a quick reality check about your school's plans to add computers to the classroom and then move along to practical matters. After that, the chapter makes sure you know the capabilities of iPads and how they compare—both favorably and unfavorably—to laptops and desktops. The chapter also goes through what you'll need to do to plan the deployment, starting with choosing a deployment model; moving along through choosing which iPads to get, deciding whether to supervise them, and choosing how to manage them; and finally making sure that your school's network and Internet connection have enough bandwidth to handle the additional traffic that the iPads will generate.

Chapter 2, "Choosing iPads and Accessories," explains how to choose the right iPads for your school's needs and how to select suitable accessories—chargers, cases, screen protectors, mounts, stands, and so on—to enable yourself, your students, and your colleagues to make the most of the iPads.

Chapter 3, "Essential iPad Skills for Administrators and Teachers," teaches you essential skills for using an iPad as an administrator or as a teacher. The chapters with the basics: you learn how to set up an iPad, how to perform basic power operations, how to navigate the interface, how to connect to Wi-Fi networks and so on. Once you know those moves, the chapter covers how to configure an iPad's essential settings manually: Notifications, Do Not Disturb, Restrictions, and Accessibility. Toward the end of the chapter, you learn about connecting keyboards to the iPad; updating the operating system; installing, removing, and organizing apps; and managing both local storage and iCloud storage.

Chapter 4, "Managing iPads with Apple Configurator," walks you through using the Apple Configurator app to configure iPads automatically. The chapter starts with a quick overview of what you can do with Apple Configurator. You then download the app and install it on your Mac, configure the app itself, and then work through the actions it offers: connecting and updating iPads, organizing and sorting them, and backing them up and restoring them; preparing the iPads for deployment; building configuration profiles and applying them to iPads; and creating templates called blueprints and applying them to iPads.

Chapter 5, "Managing iPads with Apple School Manager," teaches you about Apple School Manager, Apple's turnkey service for managing Macs and iOS devices in schools and similar institutions. The chapter explains what you need to know about Apple School Manager to use it effectively, starting with the fact that you may not need to use Apple School Manager directly at all if your school uses an MDM solution that integrates with Apple School Manager.

Chapter 6, "Managing iPads with Mobile Device Management," tells you how to manage your school's iPads with Mobile Device Management (MDM) solutions. MDM enables you to automate many aspects of deploying, configuring, and controlling iPads, so if your school has any serious deployment of iPads, you'll likely use MDM to manage them.

Chapter 7, "Accessing Files and Printing Documents," explains how to connect your school's iPads to local storage and online storage for accessing existing files and creating new files. You also learn how to print from iPads to your school's printers.

Chapter 8, "Controlling a Lesson with Classroom for iPad," shows you how to use Apple's Classroom app to manage your students' iPads directly from your own iPad. Classroom is a great tool for running iPad-based lessons, giving you the power to do everything from launching the app the students will use for the class to monitoring what each student is viewing—or doing—on screen at any moment.

Chapter 9, "Troubleshooting iPads in the Classroom," takes you through troubleshooting the problems you're most likely to experience with iPads in the classroom. The chapter starts by looking at how to locate a missing iPad—and how to erase it remotely if necessary. It then moves on to resetting an iPad in different ways, which can clear up everything from minor ailments to lost passwords. After that, you learn to troubleshoot apps, network connections, Bluetooth issues, display issues, audio problems, and problems connecting to AirPort devices and Apple TVs.

CHAPTER 1

■ ■ ■

Planning Your Classroom Deployment of iPads

This chapter discusses how to plan your deployment of iPads in the classroom. We'll start with a quick reality check about your school's plans to add computers to the classroom and then move along to practical matters. You'll get to know the capabilities of iPads and how they compare—both favorably and unfavorably—to laptops and desktops. We'll then go through what you'll need to do to plan the deployment, starting with choosing a deployment model, moving along through choosing which iPads to get, deciding whether to supervise them, and choosing how to manage them. Finally, we'll discuss making sure that your school's network and Internet connection have enough bandwidth to handle the additional traffic the iPads will generate.

Making the Decision to Computerize Classrooms or Classes

To deploy iPads or other computers successfully in your school, you should have the agreement and cooperation of your colleagues, your students, and perhaps also the students' parents. Although it's certainly possible to make in isolation the decision to computerize and then impose the decision, you'll typically get much better results if you get each group involved in making the decision and supporting its implementation.

Given that you're reading this book, you've perhaps already gotten past this stage in the planning process. If so, skip ahead to the next section, "Understanding iPad Capabilities." If not, you'll probably want to take the following steps, not necessarily in exactly this order:

- Research the costs and benefits of computerizing one or more classrooms or classes

- Convince your colleagues of the merits of adding the computers

- Get input from students

- Build a budget for a pilot scheme and get it approved

© Guy Hart-Davis 2017
G. Hart-Davis, *Deploying iPads in the Classroom*,
https://doi.org/10.1007/978-1-4842-2928-6_1

- Select a classroom or a class for a pilot scheme

- Run the pilot scheme

- Review the success or challenges of the pilot scheme and the feedback you get from it

- Scale up your pilot scheme for full deployment

- Budget for the full deployment

- Execute the full deployment

- Build in a review cycle to gauge successes, failures, and improvements needed

DEVELOPING FAQS AND ACCEPTABLE USE POLICIES

As you plan and build out your deployment, you should develop a FAQ—a list of *frequently asked questions*—that you can make available on your school's website as an information resource for students, parents, teachers, and support staff.

The FAQ needs to cover everything from the school's purpose in deploying the iPads through straightforward issues such as startup, login, and basic skills like running apps and accessing resources. You should also cover more advanced topics such as understanding the restrictions the school has applied to the iPad and the ways in which the school can monitor iPad usage. Make sure to publicize the FAQ in the school and provide an easy-to-use mechanism for users to submit questions for adding to the FAQ. Add a shortcut to the FAQ on each iPad's Home screen to encourage students and teachers to use the FAQ.

You will also need to create two *acceptable use* policies. The first policy should explain the rules under which students use the iPads—what they're allowed to do, what isn't permitted, and who is responsible for lost or broken iPads. The second policy should do likewise for teachers. Students and teachers should sign the acceptable use policies to confirm that they accept the rules. For younger students and for one-to-one deployments (in which the students typically take the iPads home), the students' parents should also sign the policies.

Understanding iPad Capabilities

As you know, the iPad is a series of tablet computers made by Apple. Since Apple launched the first iPad in 2010, it has released various models with faster processors, more storage, and higher-resolution screens.

Apple has also constantly updated iOS, the operating system used by the iPad, iPhone, and iPod touch, issuing a major update each year. Version 11 of iOS was released in September 2017.

■ **Note**   The first three versions of what became iOS were called iPhone OS—iPhone OS 1, iPhone OS 2, and iPhone OS 3. At version 4, in June 2010, Apple changed the name to iOS. At version 4.2.1, in November 2010, Apple added iPad support to iOS.

---

iPad Models and Screen Sizes

As of this writing (Fall 2017), the iPad comes in three different models, which have four different screen sizes among them:

- *iPad mini*: As its name suggests, this is the smallest iPad. It has a 7.9-inch screen.

- *iPad*: The iPad takes over from the iPad Air as the midpoint in the iPad range. It has a 9.7-inch screen.

- *iPad Pro*: The iPad Pro is a more powerful iPad. It comes in two sizes, one with a 10.5-inch screen and the other with a 12.9-inch screen.

■ **Note**   See Chapter 2 for more specifics on the iPad models.

---

iPad Apps

The iPad runs apps built for Apple's iOS operating system. The primary source of apps is Apple's App Store, which you can access either directly through the App Store app that comes with iOS or indirectly via either the Apple Configurator deployment tool that Apple provides or a third-party mobile device management (MDM) tool. It's also possible to install third-party apps, such as apps that your school has developed.

The iPad as a Consumer Device

At the consumer level, the iPad can work as a standalone device, but you can also sync data either directly from a Mac or PC or through an account on Apple's iCloud service. For example, iCloud enables you to sync contact and calendar data, notes and reminders, e-mail accounts and photos, and other items. You can also back up some of an iPad's contents to your iCloud account.

The iPad as an Education or Enterprise Device

For education, business, and other organizational uses, the iPad works as a managed client. By using the free Apple Configurator app or a third-party tool, you can configure an image file containing the operating system set up the way you want it and then apply the image file to your school's iPads. You can also create policies to automatically configure the iPads. For example, you can create Wi-Fi payloads to enable the iPads to connect to the appropriate Wi-Fi networks at your school, and you can apply restriction payloads to impose restrictions on the iPads (such as preventing installation or deletion of apps, forbidding the use of specific apps, and so on).

Comparing iPads to Laptops or Desktops

This section looks at how iPads compare to laptops and desktops, given that these are typically the most likely alternative technologies for classroom deployment.

COMPARING IPADS TO OTHER TABLETS

You may also need to compare iPads to Windows tablets and Android tablets. Many different models of Windows tablets and Android tablets are available, offering a wide range of sizes and form factors.

Both Windows tablets and Android tablets offer similar benefits of portability and ease of use as iPads—and are equally easy to remove if not secured. Android tablets also provide instant on and quick login, whereas Windows tablets turn on quickly but typically take somewhat longer to log in because Windows is a larger operating system.

Both Windows tablets and Android tablets have apps available for most needs—as of this writing, the Play Store, Google's main source of apps for Android tablets, carries more than 3 million apps. Windows tablets have the advantage here, as they can typically run any of the full-featured Windows apps that laptops and desktops can run, though less powerful tablets may struggle to run complex apps at an acceptable speed.

Both Windows tablets and Android tablets enable you to set up multiple user accounts on a device, just as you can on desktop and laptop computers. Each user has their own storage space and custom settings, and the operating systems allow for quick switching among users.

Some Windows tablets and Android tablets are available in ruggedized designs suitable for use in schools—or outdoors—without a case. For non-ruggedized devices, you will normally want to use cases.

Prices of Windows tablets and Android tablets vary considerably, but in general, you can get similar functionality for a lower cost than with an iPad.

Advantages of iPads Compared to Laptops and Desktops

The iPad has several advantages compared to laptops and desktops for use in schools:

- *Portability*: The iPad is designed for handheld use, so students and teachers can easily use iPads while at desks or tables and while moving around the classroom. The iPad's portability can encourage or facilitate students working in groups.

- *Ease of use*: The iPad's operating system, iOS, is designed for ease of use, and you quickly can bring students (and teachers) up to speed with its essentials. Given the popularity of the iPhone, it's likely that some (perhaps most) of your students will possess or at least have used iPhones; these students will already know how to navigate and use iOS on the iPad.

- *Apps available for most needs*: Apple's App Store offers more than 2.2 million apps, a range that covers most known computing needs and many others besides. Unless your school and your students have extremely specialized needs, your challenge probably won't be finding apps with the capabilities you need; it will be finding the *best* apps with those capabilities.

- *Instant on and quick login*: The iPad wakes up from sleep at the press of a button, and the login process is much quicker than most laptops and desktops, enabling students to get to work in a short time.

- *Ease of configuration and administration*: As you'll see later in this book, Apple and third-party manufacturers provide tools for configuring iPads automatically and for running classes on iPads. For example, you can apply profiles to iPads to configure specific settings and prevent users from customizing certain categories of settings while still allowing users to customize other settings.

■ **Note**   Similar configuration and administration tools are available for laptops and desktops, so although this capability makes it easier for you to deploy iPads in the classroom, it doesn't score significantly over the competition.

- *Volume Purchase Program for apps and e-books*: Apple's Volume Purchase Program simplifies the process of distributing apps and e-books to your school's iPads. You can also reclaim the apps and e-books afterward if necessary—for example, when a student leaves the school.

Disadvantages of iPads Compared to Laptops and Desktops

If you're considering iPads as an alternative to laptops or desktops in the classroom, you'll also need to evaluate the disadvantages of iPads compared to laptops or desktops. These are the main disadvantages:

- *Single-user device*: Unlike PCs, Macs, and even Android tablets, the iPad is a single-user device, not a multiuser device. You can't configure an iPad with multiple user accounts and switch among them. This makes it harder to have iPads as shared devices in the same way you can share Macs, PCs, and Android tablets (but see the nearby Note on Shared iPad). If you're planning for each student to have an iPad as a personal device, this isn't a problem.

■ **Note** To help work around the limitation of the iPad being a single-user device, Apple introduced a feature called Shared iPad in January 2016. Shared iPad quickly sets up an iPad for a user by copying that user's environment and data files from the network when the user logs in to the iPad. See Chapter 5 for more information on Shared iPad.

- *Easy to damage*: Apple has designed the iPad as a slim and lightweight device that's dominated by its screen—it's hardly the heavily armored, industrial-style device you might prefer in the classroom or out in the wild. (For example, HP's ProBook x360 Education Edition laptop, which is designed to survive student use, is built ruggedly enough to meet the MIL-STD-810G military standard.) As a result, the iPad is all too easy to damage, accidentally or otherwise, and you will normally need to protect your school's iPads with protective cases. Chapter 2 reviews some of your options for protecting iPads.

- *Easy to remove*: Being portable and small enough to slip into a school bag, iPads are easy to remove from the classroom. You may need to tether your school's iPads using cases that lock onto the iPad or secure the iPads with stands. Laptops are similarly portable and removable, but many models include a built-in Kensington slot that enables you to lock them easily using a standard cable. Desktops tend to be far less portable and are generally easy to secure.

■ **Note** Chapter 2 discusses some of the hardware you can use to secure iPads.

- *Cost*: Even the least expensive iPad model typically costs more than alternative devices, such as Android tablets, Chromebooks, or laptop or desktop PCs. Any case or other accessories you add to the iPad brings the cost up further.

- *No hardware keyboard*: The iPad doesn't include a hardware keyboard, although you can add one easily enough via the Smart Connector built into the iPad Pro models or via Bluetooth. The iPad's on-screen keyboard could hardly be easier to use, but it's adequate only for lightweight text input; few people can touch-type satisfactorily on it. So if your students will need to enter large amounts of text on the iPads—whether for taking notes or for original writing—you'll almost certainly need to add keyboards. This means extra expense and effort.

- *Some key apps and power-user apps are not available*: Even though the App Store offers a vast range of apps, some of the most important apps are not available for the iPad or are available only in more limited versions. For many people, the Microsoft Office apps are the epitome of this limitation: Even though Microsoft has built versions of Word, Excel, PowerPoint, and OneNote for iOS (and for Android), these versions lack the features and power of the Windows and Mac versions. This same limitation applies to various power-user apps such as database apps, apps for manipulating photographs and editing video to a professional standard, and other apps too complex or too specialized to be ported to iOS.

■ **Tip** If you rely on an app that's available for Windows but not for iOS, you may be able to run the app via a remote-desktop app such as Microsoft Remote Desktop (which is free). This can be a good solution for specialized but crucial apps, though it's typically less effective than running a suitable app on the iPad itself. You may also be able to use web versions of some apps, although such versions tend to have fewer features than the desktop versions.

Analyzing Your Needs and Making a Plan

Once you've decided that you'll be deploying iPads rather than another technology, you'll need to work out the best way to deploy iPads. This section covers the main questions you should consider to establish your needs and plan the deployment. Consider the following:

- What deployment method will you use? Will you get iPads to issue to students, iPads to equip a classroom or classbound computer carts, or both? Will you get iPads for teachers?

- How many iPads will your school get?

- If you will equip the teachers with iPads, how will the teachers use the iPads?

- Will you need to train the teachers to use the iPads? If so, what kind of training will you run?

- How will you manage the iPads?

- How will the iPads fit into your school's IT system and connect to its resources?

- Does your school have adequate network and Internet bandwidth to handle the increased traffic the iPads will bring?

What Deployment Model Will You Use?

Usually, your first decision is which deployment model you will use. Typically, this means choosing between a one-to-one deployment model and a model based on classes or classrooms:

- *One-to-one*: In the one-to-one deployment model, you issue an iPad to each student in a class or other group. Each student keeps that iPad and can store their own files on it. Normally the student gets to take the iPad home at the end of the school day so they can use it for homework and other study. However, in some cases, the iPad is restricted to the school's premises, so the student checks it out at the beginning of the school day and checks it back in at the end.

- *Class or classroom*: In the class or classroom deployment model, you outfit a class or a classroom with enough iPads for the largest number of students the class or classroom will contain. (*Class* here refers to the group of students; *classroom* refers to the room.) The teacher issues an iPad to each student at the beginning of a lesson, and the student logs in to the iPad using a Managed Apple ID, causing the iPad to retrieve the student's files from the network. At the end of the lesson, the student saves the files to the network and returns the iPad. In this deployment model, the iPads may live in the classroom or in another secure location, such as a charging and storage cart that you can move from one classroom to another as needed.

Whether you decide to issue iPads to students or to classes, you'll likely want teachers to use iPads as well, especially if they're using Apple's Classroom app to run lessons (see Chapter 8 for more on Classroom). For each teacher who needs an iPad, you can choose between issuing an iPad on a permanent or semi-permanent basis and having the teacher use an iPad that's assigned to the class or classroom in which they'll be teaching. There are good arguments for and against both approaches, but issuing iPads to teachers enables them to do much more with the iPads and generally delivers greater value.

How Many iPads Will Your School Need?

After deciding which deployment model to use, you next need to establish roughly how many iPads your school will need. You should be able to determine the number easily enough based on the deployment model you've chosen:

- *One-to-one deployment*: Plan to get one iPad for each student involved, plus iPads for teachers or assistants, plus a reserve of extra iPads to cover for when students break their iPads, leave them at home, or incapacitate them.

- *Class or classroom deployment*: Plan to get one iPad for each of the maximum number of students who will be in the class or in the classroom, plus an iPad for each teacher or assistant who will lead the class. Again, you'll want a reserve of iPads to handle contingencies such as iPads getting damaged or misconfigured, or visiting students or teachers requiring extra iPads.

GETTING AND MAINTAINING YOUR RESERVE OF IPADS

How many iPads do you need as a reserve? There's no hard-and-fast answer, because it depends on your situation and your students, but between 10% and 20% of the base number generally seems to work well. For example, for a class of 30 students, a reserve of 3 to 6 iPads would normally cover absentee iPads and attrition. But as usual, more would be better.

If money is tight, you may find it hard to get the budget for an adequate reserve of iPads in your initial deployment. And you may find that having the iPads do double duty as *teacher training* iPads or *instructor* iPads gets you further than simply calling them *reserves*.

You should also include at least some new iPads in your IT budget each year. Assuming you can buy some new iPads, you can then downgrade some of the surviving older iPads to reserve status. This way, you can gradually build up enough of a reserve to handle extra demand when it occurs.

Which Models of iPad Will You Get?

Next, you'll need to decide which models of iPad to get for your deployment. Chapter 2 looks at the current iPad models in some detail, but at a basic level, your choice will be based on the physical size (and screen size) of the iPads and by their power:

- *iPad mini*: The smallest iPad tends to be the best choice for younger students with smaller hands and for older students who need portability rather than screen size or power.

- *iPad or 10.5-inch iPad Pro*: The mid-size iPad models tend to be the best choice for most students and for many teachers. The screen size is large enough to display plenty of data, but the iPad itself is light enough (even with a protective case) to be easily portable. Unless students will need to run apps that require the extra power of the iPad Pro, or apps that require the Apple Pencil stylus (for example, art apps), choose the iPad model simply called *iPad*.

- *12.9-inch iPad Pro*: The larger iPad Pro model is too large and too vulnerable to damage for typical student use—not to mention too expensive for most budgets. But teachers may benefit from the greater screen size, especially for multitasking and for running classes with Classroom.

Will You Have Supervised iPads or Unsupervised iPads?

The next big choice you have to make is between supervised and unsupervised iPads. Here's what those terms mean:

- *Unsupervised iPad*: The iPad's user controls the iPad's configuration. For example, when a consumer buys an iPad, they can set it up to work the way they prefer.

- *Supervised iPad*: You retain administrative control. You can configure the iPad using mobile device management (MDM) tools and limit the actions the user can take on the iPad.

For most school deployments, you'll want supervised iPads because supervision lets you manage iPads centrally, saving time and effort. Supervision also lets you impose extra restrictions on an iPad, such as disallowing the use of specific apps or features (for example, you might disallow iMessage or Apple Music, or prevent the user from changing the passcode) or placing the iPad into Single App Mode (which limits the iPad to running an app that you specify).

■ **Note**   If you're deploying only a handful of iPads, you may choose to keep the iPads unsupervised and configure them manually, setting restrictions by working directly on each iPad, rather than making the iPads supervised and configuring them via policy. But for more than a few iPads, manual configuration quickly becomes a waste of time and effort, both of which supervision can save.

How Will Your School's Teachers Use the iPads?

You'll also need to consider how the teachers will use the iPads. There are many different ways of using an iPad for teaching, but the following tend to be the main uses:

- *Use the Classroom app to lead lessons*: Apple's Classroom app is designed to enable a teacher to organize and manage a class. For example, using Classroom the teacher can open a web page or a document on all the students' iPads to ensure that everyone is literally on the same page. Classroom also lets the teacher work with existing groups of students, such as those using a particular app, or create custom groups of students on the fly, switching from group to group as needed.

- *Demonstrating techniques*: The teacher can quickly demonstrate iPad skills and gestures, app usage, and so on using their own iPad to enable a student to perform those moves on their iPad.

- *Displaying information on a TV or monitor*: The teacher can share content from their iPad to a TV or monitor connected to an Apple TV, enabling all the students to see the content.

- *Communicating with students*: The teacher can communicate with students via various means, ranging from communication within the Classroom app to standard instant messaging and e-mail.

- *Collecting and grading papers and homework*: The teacher can collect work from students easily, grade it, and return it.

How Will Your School's Students Use the iPads?

Students can use iPads to perform a wide range of tasks both at school and (in a one-to-one deployment) outside it. The following list gives examples of typical tasks that students may perform using iPads:

- *Reading textbooks*: Many textbooks are available in electronic formats, reducing what students need to carry to and from school.

- *Researching topics online*: Students can access a vast array of information resources on the Internet, depending on restrictions you've applied to the iPads.

- *Taking notes*: The iPad is a great tool for taking notes, either in Apple's lightweight Notes app or in a fuller note-taking app such as Microsoft OneNote.

- *Creating and editing documents, spreadsheets, and presentations*: Students can use apps such as Apple's Pages or Microsoft Word to create and edit documents, Apple's Numbers or Microsoft Excel to build spreadsheets, and Apple's Keynote or Microsoft PowerPoint to develop presentations.

- *E-mailing and communicating:* The iPad comes equipped with Apple's Mail app for e-mail, the Messages app for instant messaging, and the FaceTime app for audio and video calls. If necessary, you can add other communications apps that you permit the students to use.

- *Completing and submitting papers and homework*: Students can use the iPad to complete papers and homework and submit them to teachers for marking.

- *Social networking*: Social networking is notorious as a time-sink, but it can be useful for organizing and coordinating school-related events.

- *Shooting and editing videos*: Students can use the iPad's built-in front and rear cameras to shoot video clips and then edit them into projects by using Apple's iMovie app or another app.

- *Composing, recording, and editing music*: Students can use Apple's GarageBand app or another app to compose, record, and edit music directly on the iPad.

Which Apps Will You Need to Get?

The iPad comes with plenty of apps to get you and your students started with iPads. You can add other apps easily, and you can prevent students from using most of the included apps.

Table 1-1 briefly summarizes the apps normally included with iOS on new iPads, presenting the apps in alphabetical order and summarizing their main uses.

Table 1-1. *Apps Normally Included with iOS on New iPads*

App Name	Uses
App Store	Browsing, buying, and getting apps for the iPad.
Calendar	Tracking events, such as lessons, lectures, and other commitments.
Camera	Shooting photos and videos.
Clock	Tracking time in different locations with World Clock, getting reminders with Alarms, timing events with Stopwatch, and getting a countdown with Timer.
Contacts	Collecting and using data about people, organizations, companies, and so on.
FaceTime	Making audio and video calls to other users of iPads, other iOS devices, and Macs.
Find Friends	Locating friends and contacts who share their locations.

(*continued*)

Table 1-1. (*continued*)

App Name	Uses
Find iPhone	Locating an iPad (or iPhone or iPod touch) that has gone missing.
GarageBand	Composing, recording, and editing music.
Home	Automating home electronic equipment.
iBooks	Reading books (including textbooks) and PDFs, and listening to audiobooks.
iCloud Drive	Storing files online in an iCloud account.
iMovie	Creating movies by importing, editing, and arranging video clips.
iTunes Store	Buying music, movies, and TV shows online.
Keynote	Creating and delivering presentations.
Mail	Sending, receiving, and managing e-mail messages and attachments.
Maps	Getting directions and exploring locations.
Messages	Communicating via instant messaging with other users of iPads, other iOS devices, and Macs.
Music	Playing and browsing music and listening to Apple Radio.
News	Reading news stories from the Internet.
Notes	Taking, editing, and sharing notes. Notes can include text, sketches, documents, and photos.
Numbers	Creating spreadsheets.
Pages	Creating word-processing and layout documents.
Photo Booth	Taking self-portraits and other informal photos and applying entertaining effects to them.
Photos	Importing photos and videos from digital cameras, organizing them, and editing them.
Podcasts	Watching video podcasts or listening to audio podcasts online.
Reminders	Tracking tasks with reminders lists.
Safari	Browsing the Web.
Settings	Configuring the iPad. You can disable many of the settings by applying restrictions.
Tips	Getting tips on how to use the iPad.
Videos	Organizing and watching video files.

■ **Tip**   Spend some time exploring the included apps to evaluate which of them will address your students' needs and which other apps you will need to get. For example, if your students will create reports, spreadsheets, and other office documents, evaluate whether Pages, Numbers, and Keynote will be suitable. If not, you may need to add Microsoft Office apps such as Word and Excel to the iPads.

Understanding Your Options for Managing iPads

This section briefly considers two different ways of managing your school's iPads: manually, using Apple Configurator, or using third-party mobile device management (MDM) apps.

Managing iPads Manually

Your first option is to manage the iPads manually—choosing settings directly on the devices by working manually with them, as you would with your own personal iPad. This hands-on approach is straightforward and can be effective if you have only a few iPads to manage. If you have to deal with a full classroom's worth of iPads, though, you'll likely need to use an automated means of management.

Chapter 3 covers essential iPad skills for administrators and teachers, including how to manage iPads manually. For example, you can apply restrictions to prevent an iPad's user from taking undesirable actions, such as installing apps or deleting apps (see Figure 1-1).

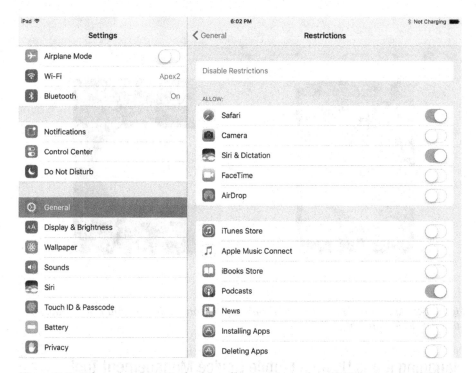

Figure 1-1. When managing iPads manually, you can apply restrictions to prevent the user from taking actions you don't want

Managing iPads Using Apple Configurator

Your second option is to manage the iPads using Apple Configurator, an app that Apple provides for configuring iPads, other iOS devices, and Apple TV. Apple Configurator runs only on Macs, so you need a Mac to be able to use it. Apple Configurator works only with devices connected directly to the Mac via USB, whereas many MDM tools can work via Wi-Fi as well. But if you can work with these limitations, Apple Configurator is a powerful tool for setting up, configuring, and managing iPads for a school or organization.

Chapter 4 explains how to manage iPads with Apple Configurator. Figure 1-2 shows Apple Configurator displaying information about iPads connected to a Mac.

Figure 1-2. *Apple Configurator is a Mac-only tool for configuring and managing iPads, other iOS devices, and Apple TV*

Managing iPads Using a Mobile Device Management Tool

Your third option is to manage the iPads using a mobile device management (MDM) tool from a third party. You can choose from a wide range of MDM solutions—unless your school already has an MDM tool for managing other clients, in which case you may be able to add the iPads using that tool. MDM tools vary in their capabilities, such as managing different types of clients. But most MDM tools that work with iOS devices can tap into all the management features that Apple has built into iOS, which means most of the MDM tools you'll need to consider for managing your iPads have similar capabilities for managing iPads.

Chapter 6 covers how to manage iPads with MDM tools. Figure 1-3 shows TabPilot, one of the MDM tools discussed in Chapter 6.

Figure 1-3. *TabPilot is a third-party MDM tool that you can use to manage iPads*

Planning to Train Yourself and Your Colleagues

While evaluating the iPad as an educational tool, you'll likely develop your own iPad skills to the point where you need only minimal or self-directed training to use an iPad as a teaching tool. But given how important it is for teachers to be not only proficient but also confident with iPads in class, you should plan full training on iPad use for all your colleagues who will use iPads for teaching. Some staff, especially those who have already used iPads, will likely get up to speed with only short sessions of formal training, but others may need multiple sessions of individual training to develop the skills and confidence required.

■ **Note**   Chapter 3 provides in-depth coverage of the iPad skills you and your colleagues will need to know. Chapter 8 covers running a class with the Classroom app.

To make your training as effective as possible, get feedback from the teachers you train, both at the end of the training session and after they have been teaching with the iPad for a few weeks or months. If you will be training many teachers, you'll likely benefit from creating a feedback questionnaire and logging the responses you get. If you know you'll be training only a few teachers, less formal feedback may be all you need to identify any areas of the training that need strengthening, other topics from which teachers will benefit, and any included information that's confusing or unnecessary.

■ **Tip** Aim to develop an ongoing process of review and improvement for your iPad deployment, training, and teaching. You'll need to involve teachers, support staff, students, and in some cases students' parents in the process.

Checking Your School's Wireless Network Infrastructure and Bandwidth

Next, you need to make sure that your school's network infrastructure will be able to handle the additional load the iPads will impose on it. You also need to make sure that the network and the Internet connection have enough bandwidth for the traffic the iPads will cause.

SHOULD YOU BOOST EXISTING NETWORK CAPACITY OR ADD A SEPARATE NETWORK FOR IPADS?

If you find that your school's Wi-Fi network won't be adequate to handle the extra traffic from the iPads you're planning to add, you may need to decide between boosting the capacity of the existing network and adding a separate network to handle only the iPads.

Which approach makes more sense for you will depend on the school's existing network and the capacity you need to add to bring the network up to scratch. But if you find yourself evaluating this issue, don't dismiss out of hand the possibility of adding a separate Wi-Fi network for the iPads. Rather, look into any benefits that a separate, iPad-only network can offer you, such as being able to give the iPads different access rules to school resources and the Internet. If your existing network's management tools can identify the iPads and implement filtering for them, that would be an argument in favor of beefing up the existing network rather than adding a network.

Determining Whether Your Wireless Network Infrastructure Is Adequate

You will need to determine whether your school's wireless network infrastructure is adequate to handle the additional load that the iPads will generate. You will need to check four main things:

Verifying the Signal Strength

Check that there is strong Wi-Fi signal everywhere that students and teachers will use the iPads in the school. For example, you may need to check the following areas:

- *Classrooms*: Make sure each classroom has a strong Wi-Fi signal.

- *Other teaching areas*: Verify signal strength in other teaching areas, such as labs, where students and teachers will be using iPads.

- *Teacher office and lounge*: Make sure teachers will have an adequate Wi-Fi signal where they prepare their lessons.

- *Common areas*: For a one-to-one deployment, check the signal in other areas where students will use their iPads. For example, the student lounge and cafeteria will likely need good connectivity.

Although an iPad *can* transfer data over a weak connection, you'll get better results if the signal is strong, especially when many iPads are sharing the same wireless access point. You may have to add wireless access points, repeaters, or antennae to boost the signal.

■ **Tip** If your school's budget permits, overspecify the wireless network—make the network more powerful than you currently need—so that you can expand your deployment of iPads and other devices easily in the future. Spending money on extra wireless access points and other infrastructure up front will generally save you money in the long term by reducing performance problems that you'd need to troubleshoot.

Checking for Wireless Dead Spots

While checking signal strength, make sure there are no dead spots—places where there is no wireless signal at all. Murphy's Law guarantees that if there any dead spots, students (or teachers) will find they need to use the iPads there. You may need to add wireless access points to eliminate dead spots.

■ **Tip** Add to your school's intranet site a page where students can report low signal or dead spots to the network administrators.

Checking the Network Bandwidth

Use a traffic analyzer to measure network bandwidth and see if you need to increase it to handle the number of iPads you're expecting the school to use. To increase bandwidth, you may need to add access points or upgrade switches and cabling.

SHARED IPAD MAY CAUSE LARGE TRAFFIC SPIKES

If you will use the Shared iPad feature to allocate iPads to the students in classes, you'll need to plan to handle large spikes in Wi-Fi network traffic. These spikes will typically occur at the start of a lesson, when students log in to the iPads and the iPads automatically pull their files and settings across the network.

Shared iPad attempts to reduce the amount of traffic by, wherever possible, allocating each iPad to a student whose files are currently stored on that iPad. But even with this smart allocation, Shared iPad can cause a large amount of network traffic, so you should budget for plenty of capacity.

Checking the Capacity for Devices to Connect

Make sure your wireless access points have enough capacity for all the iPads and other devices that may connect at once. You may need to add wireless access points in order to get enough iPads (and other devices) connected to the network at the speeds you require.

■ **Caution**   Take the advertised capacity of enterprise-grade wireless access points with a pinch of salt. In real-world use, you're likely to find that an access point with an advertised capacity of 100+ clients can handle only 50 or so clients effectively. Similarly, an access point that claims to be able to handle 200 or more clients may not perform well with more than, say, 75 active clients. Test the performance of your access points both when you install them and when your iPad deployment is up and running.

Determining Whether Your Internet Bandwidth Is Adequate

You'll also need to determine whether your school's Internet bandwidth is adequate for the increased traffic that the iPads will produce. As you'd expect, bandwidth adequacy will depend partly on the speed of the Internet connection and how much of the bandwidth the school is using already—if the connection is already maxed out, you can be sure that adding the iPad to the demand will make matters worse.

The effect of the iPads will also depend on how the students and teachers are using them and what measures you can take to mitigate the amount of traffic the iPads generate. For example, students may need to stream videos from YouTube to assist with their schoolwork. If each student in a class will need to watch the same video, having a caching server can greatly reduce the amount of Internet bandwidth needed. But if each student will need to watch their own choice of videos, a caching server won't help much because each video will need to be streamed across the Internet connection.

The nearby sidebar suggests some measures you can take to reduce the Internet bandwidth the iPads require.

WAYS TO REDUCE THE INTERNET BANDWIDTH THE IPADS REQUIRE

Depending on your network, its configuration, and how your school will use its iPads, you may be able to take some of the following measures to reduce the amount of Internet bandwidth the iPads consume:

- *Spread the iPad lessons around the timetable*: If the timetable permits, schedule the iPad lessons that are likely to cause heavy Internet traffic so that they occur at different times rather than overlap. This move works better in a class or classroom deployment than a one-to-one deployment.

- *Keep files on your intranet rather than on the Internet*: Where possible, have students and teachers store files on the school's intranet rather than on the Internet so the files can be downloaded and shared quickly without burdening the Internet connection.

- *Restrict access to websites*: iOS includes restrictions that enable you to limit the websites an iPad can access. You can choose between permitting only specific sites, blocking specific sites, and blocking sites that meet certain criteria (such as sites that identify themselves as having adult content). See Chapter 3 for details.

- *Use a caching server*: If multiple students will need to access the same content on the Internet, a caching server on your network can greatly reduce the bandwidth required. Once one client has requested the content, and the server has downloaded the content and saved it to its cache, the server can provide the content to other clients from the cache rather than having to download it again.

- *Control updates centrally*: Assuming you manage the iPads centrally, you can schedule iOS and app updates to happen at night, when your school's network is (or should be) less busy.

- *Prevent or limit cloud backup*: The iPad can be configured to back up data automatically to Apple's iCloud service. Automatic backup can be a great way for users to avoid losing files if the iPad gets lost, stolen, or broken, but it can impose heavy demands on your school's Internet connection. To avoid this problem, you can disallow the use of iCloud through policy (restrictions you apply). Disallowing iCloud may be easier in a class or classroom deployment than in a one-to-one deployment, because in a one-to-one deployment students will typically need to back up their iPads to iCloud or another online destination for security.

Summary

This chapter discussed in general terms how to plan your deployment of iPads in the classroom. It covered the capabilities of iPads and how they stack up against laptops and desktops for use in schools. You're now equipped to decide between a one-to-one deployment of iPads—issuing an iPad to each student in a class or year—and a deployment based on classrooms or classes. You know about the benefits that turning iPads into supervised iPads brings, and you're in a position to choose among managing iPads manually, managing them using Apple Configurator, and managing them using a third-party MDM tool. You also know you need to determine whether your school has robust enough infrastructure and sufficient bandwidth to handle the iPads or whether you will need to improve the infrastructure or increase the bandwidth.

In the next chapter, I'll discuss how to choose the best iPads for your school and how to select suitable accessories for the iPads.

CHAPTER 2

■ ■ ■

Choosing iPads and Accessories

In this chapter, we'll consider how to choose the right iPads for your school's needs and how to select suitable accessories to enable you, your students, and your colleagues to make the most of the iPads.

We'll start by going over the salient features of the current iPad models, from the device size and screen size through the amount of storage to the processor and the amount of RAM each iPad contains. We'll then look at how to choose chargers, cases, screen protectors, and mounts and stands (if you'll need them). Finally, we'll discuss your options for adding hardware keyboards to iPads, consider where you will store the iPads, and evaluate whether to add the Apple Pencil stylus to any iPad Pro models you get.

Reviewing the iPad Models

Since releasing the first iPad in April 2010, Apple has released a wide variety of iPad models. As of Fall 2017, there are three main sizes of iPad:

- *Small*: iPad mini
- *Medium*: iPad and smaller iPad Pro
- *Large*: Full-size iPad Pro

© Guy Hart-Davis 2017
G. Hart-Davis, *Deploying iPads in the Classroom*,
https://doi.org/10.1007/978-1-4842-2928-6_2

Figure 2-1 shows the relative sizes of the iPad models.

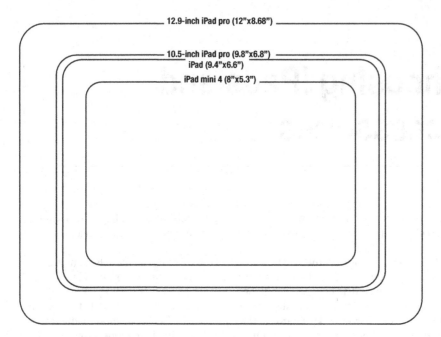

Figure 2-1. *Relative sizes of iPad models*

Device Size, Screen Size, and Resolution

The most obvious differences among the three sizes of iPad models is the physical size of the devices and the screens they contain. As is normal for tablet computers, the screen dominates the front of the iPad and largely controls the size of the device, with a relatively slim bezel (the rim around the screen) taking up the rest of the front.

Table 2-1 shows the dimensions, screen sizes, screen resolutions, and weights of the current iPad models.

Table 2-1. *iPad Dimensions, Screen Sizes, Screen Resolutions, and Weights*

iPad Model	Height	Width	Depth	Screen Size	Resolution	Weight
iPad Pro 12.9-inch Wi-Fi	12 in (305.7 mm)	8.68 in (220.6 mm)	0.27 in (6.9 mm)	12.9 in	2732 × 2048	1.49 lb (677 g)
iPad Pro 12.9-inch Wi-Fi + Cellular	12 in (305.7 mm)	8.68 in (220.6 mm)	0.27 in (6.9 mm)	12.9 in	2732 × 2048	1.53 lb (692 g)
iPad Pro 10.5-inch Wi-Fi	9.8 in (250.6 mm)	6.8 in (174.1 mm)	0.24 in (6.1 mm)	10.5 in	2048 × 1536	1.03 lb (469 g)
iPad Pro 10.5-inch Wi-Fi + Cellular	9.8 in (250.6 mm)	6.8 in (174.1 mm)	0.24 in (6.1 mm)	10.5 in	2048 × 1536	1.05 lb (477 g)
iPad Wi-Fi	9.4 in (240 mm)	6.6 in (169.5 mm)	0.29 in (7.7 mm)	9.7 in	2048 × 1536	1.03 lb (469 g)
iPad Wi-Fi + Cellular	9.4 in (240 mm)	6.6 in (169.5 mm)	0.29 in (7.7 mm)	9.7 in	2048 × 1536	1.05 lb (477 g)
iPad mini 4 Wi-Fi	8 in (203.2 mm)	5.3 in (134.8 mm)	0.24 in (6.1 mm)	7.9 in	2048 × 1536	0.65 lb (299 g)
iPad mini 4 Wi-Fi + Cellular	8 in (203.2 mm)	5.3 in (134.8 mm)	0.24 in (6.1 mm)	7.9 in	2048 × 1536	0.67 lb (304 g)

25

Amount of Storage

iPads come with different amounts of internal storage. As of this writing, the storage on current models ranges from 32 GB to 256 GB; see Table 2-2 for details. Older iPad models have had other capacities, such as 16 GB and 64 GB.

Table 2-2. *iPad Models and Their Storage Amounts*

iPad Model	32 GB	64 GB	128 GB	256 GB	512 GB
iPad Pro 12.9-inch Wi-Fi	✗	✓	✗	✓	✓
iPad Pro 12-9-inch Wi-Fi + Cellular	✗	✓	✗	✓	✓
iPad Pro 10.5-inch Wi-Fi	✗	✓	✗	✓	✓
iPad Pro 10.5-inch Wi-Fi + Cellular	✗	✓	✗	✓	✓
iPad Wi-Fi	✓	✗	✓	✗	✗
iPad Wi-Fi + Cellular	✓	✗	✓	✗	✗
iPad mini 4 Wi-Fi	✗	✗	✓	✗	✗
iPad mini 4 Wi-Fi + Cellular	✗	✗	✓	✗	✗

WHY DOES A 32 GB IPAD HAVE ONLY 27.5 GB AVAILABLE?

When deciding how much storage you need on the iPads, bear in mind that the actual amount of storage available on an iPad is substantially less than the advertised number. For example, a 32 GB iPad normally has around 27.5 GB of free space. Part of the difference is the iPad's operating system, which consumes a couple of gigabytes and which you can't sensibly do without, and the apps that come with the operating system, which Apple makes difficult to remove.

The other reason for the difference is that, like most manufacturers of computers and devices, Apple uses decimal (base 10) numbers rather than binary (base 2) numbers for measuring storage capacity. In *decimal*, a gigabyte has 1,000,000,000 bytes of storage—1000 × 1000 × 1000. But in binary, a gigabyte has 1,073,741,824 bytes—1024 × 1024 × 1024—or 7.4% more; technically, this is a *gibibyte*, or 1 GiB, but few people use that term. So when Apple describes an iPad as having 32 GB of storage, that means it has 32,000,000,000 bytes, which translates to 29.8 GB in binary. Add the operating system, and the available space drops to 27.5 GB.

■ **Note**   The storage on an iPad is fixed and can't be increased. iPads also don't include SD card slots or other expansion slots for adding storage, so it's important to assess realisitically how much storage your iPads will need. Given that app sizes tend to increase rather than decrease, it's wise to allow extra space over and above current needs.

As you'd likely expect, the more storage an iPad model has, the more it costs. So unless you need a lot of storage on the iPads, you'll probably do best to buy the lower-capacity models of the type of iPad your school needs.

Apple designed the iPad models to handle both consumer use and business use rather than having different models of iPad for different uses. Both consumers and businesses may require large storage capacity, though for different reasons; for example, a consumer may want to store many song and movie files on their iPad, whereas a businessperson may want to carry documentation, large presentations, or demonstration videos.

How much storage your school's iPads will need will vary depending on how you will use the iPads. Here are three examples:

- If you will keep the iPads in the classroom, where different students use the iPads for different classes, you'll normally do best to keep all data files on the network, where you can back them up easily, rather than on the iPads themselves. As a result, you likely can get away with small amounts of storage on the iPads: even if the students shoot or edit videos on the iPads during lessons, 32 GB should be plenty of storage.

- If each student will have an iPad to take home as a quasi-personal device, they will likely need to store more files on them. For such iPads, 128 GB is normally a better choice.

- If staff members will have dedicated iPads as teaching devices, you'll probably want to allow plenty of storage. If these iPads are iPad Pro models, consider going for 256 GB; otherwise, go for 128 GB. Even on the iPad Pro, 512 GB is usually overkill unless the users will be shooting large amounts of video and editing it on the iPads.

Video is the item that's likely to consume the most space on iPads used in the classroom. If your students will shoot and edit videos during lessons, but not store the videos on the iPads from one lesson to the next, 32 GB may be enough. But if your students will shoot and edit video on the iPads over the long term, you will likely want to get higher-capacity iPads—especially if the students are working with high-resolution video. Table 2-3 shows the resolutions and capabilities of the iPad models' rear camera, the one you'll normally use for shooting photos and videos. Table 2-4 shows the resolutions and capabilities of the front camera, which is designed for selfies and video calling.

Table 2-3. *Rear Camera Resolutions and Capabilities of iPad Models*

iPad Model	Resolution	Aperture	Live Photos	Maximum Video Resolution	Video Zoom	Video Focus
iPad Pro 12.9-inch	12 megapixels	f/1.8	Yes	4K HD (3840 × 2160)	3X	Continuous autofocus
iPad Pro 10.5-inch	12 megapixels	f/1.8	Yes	4K HD (3840 × 2160)	3X	Continuous autofocus
iPad	8 megapixels	f/2.4	Yes	1080p HD	3X	Tap to focus
iPad mini 4	8 megapixels	f/2.4	No	1080p HD	3X	Tap to focus

Table 2-4. *Front Camera Resolutions and Capabilities of iPad Models*

iPad Model	Retina Flash	Resolution	Aperture	Maximum Video Resolution	Video Zoom	Video Focus
iPad Pro 12.9-inch	Yes	7 megapixels	f/2.2	720p HD	No	Tap to focus
iPad Pro 10.5-inch	Yes	7 megapixels	f/2.2	720p HD	No	Tap to focus
iPad	Yes	1.2 megapixels	f/2.2	720p HD	No	Tap to focus
iPad mini 4	No	1.2 megapixels Front Camera	f/2.2	720p HD	No	Tap to focus

■ **Note** A *live* photo is a photo embedded in a three-second video clip that gives the context of the photo.

Table 2-5 shows how much space the different video resolutions take up. All the figures are approximate, because they depend on the subject matter and how well the iPad can compress the footage. Unless you need 4K resolution on an iPad Pro or space is already painfully low, it's usually best to shoot at 1080p HD and 60 fps on the rear camera. You can then reduce the resolution if necessary when editing it.

Table 2-5. *Amount of Space Required to Store Video Video of Different Resolutions*

Resolution	Frames per Second	Space Required per Minute
4K	N/A	350 MB
1080p HD	60 fps	175 MB
1080p HD	30 fps	130 MB
720p HD	30 fps	60 MB

RAM

The iPad models contain different amounts of RAM, as listed in Table 2-6. Each iPad has a fixed amount of RAM; the RAM is not upgradeable, even if you have the skills of a repair technician. Apple doesn't promote the amount of RAM as a feature, instead taking the position that each iPad has the amount of RAM it needs, and that RAM is something that the user doesn't need to worry about.

Table 2-6. *Amount of RAM on iPad Models*

iPad Model	RAM
iPad Pro 12.9-inch	4 GB
iPad Pro 10.5-inch	4 GB
iPad Air 2	2 GB
iPad mini 4	2 GB

As with most computers, having more RAM enables an iPad to process more information at once, so it typically improves performance.

Processor

The iPad models use the A series of processors developed by Apple. Recent iPad models include motion coprocessors from Apple's M series as well. The motion coprocessor collects data from the iPad's accelerometers, compasses, and gyroscopes and processes the data.

As with the RAM, each iPad model comes with a specific processor; you don't get to choose among different processor options for a particular iPad model. Table 2-7 has the details. Even so, it's worth keeping the processor in mind when selecting iPad models. Apple gives these performance comparisons:

- The 12.9-inch iPad Pro and 10.5-inch iPad Pro have a processor 2.5 times faster than the A8 processor in the iPad mini. Graphics performance in the iPad Pro models is 4.3 times faster than in the iPad mini.

- The iPad model's A9 processor is 1.6 times faster than the A8 in the iPad mini, and graphics performance is 1.8 times faster.

Table 2-7. *Processors and Coprocessors on iPad Models*

iPad Model	Processor	Motion Coprocessor
iPad Pro 12.9-inch	A10X Fusion	Embedded M10
iPad Pro 10.5-inch	A10X Fusion	Embedded M10
iPad	A9	Embedded M9
iPad mini 4	A8	M8

Touch ID

All current iPad models all have Touch ID, which uses a fingerprint sensor built into the Home button as a means of authentication. Some older iPad models, such as the recently discontinued iPad mini 2, don't have Touch ID.

Touch ID is a great feature for anyone who uses the same iPad regularly: it unlocks the iPad more quickly and with less effort than typing a passcode. You can register up to five fingerprints (or thumbprints), which enables you to use Touch ID even if some of your fingertips get rough or abraded. In a school situation, you can have multiple people register a fingerprint each—for example, if you want several teachers or technicians to be able to unlock the iPads. Touch ID normally works well no matter the orientation in which the fingerprint is applied to the Home button, so you don't have to hold the iPad in a particular orientation.

For iPads kept in classrooms and used by many students, Touch ID is less useful: you can't register more than five fingerprints per iPad, so students will need to use passcodes to unlock the iPads.

Suggestions for Choosing the Right iPads for Your School

Now that you know the salient features of the three sizes of iPads available, you should be in a position to determine which models will best suit your school. Your choice will naturally depend on your school, your students, and how you plan to use the iPads. But here are general suggestions for consideration:

- *Younger students*: If your students are young and have smaller hands, the iPad mini may be a better choice for handheld use than the iPad or iPad Pro.

- *Teenage or older students*: The iPad model is usually the best choice for general use. If you need more power, go for the 10.5-inch iPad Pro.

- *Staff members*: The iPad model is usually the best choice for general use for staff members too. If staff members will need a more powerful tablet, go for one of the iPad Pro models. The 12.9-inch iPad Pro is great for any staff member who needs more screen space to work on documents or monitor what students are doing, but it's large enough to be awkward to carry around, especially if you add a protective case.

Normally, each iPad that will be used as a handheld device will need a case, and preferably a rugged one. If the iPads will be fixed in place, each will need a mount or stand. I talk more about mounts and stands later in this chapter.

Choosing Chargers for Your iPads

Each iPad comes with a charger that connects to the iPad via the same USB cable used for connecting the iPad to a computer for management and synchronization. All current and recent iPad models use the Lightning connector, which is a small reversible connector capable of transferring both power and data. Older iPad models used a larger connector called the Dock connector, which Apple originally introduced with the first iPod models.

The iPad's own charger is almost always the fastest and most consistent way to charge an iPad, so it should be your default choice for charging. These are the three main alternatives:

- *Third-party charger*: Many third-party manufacturers make chargers that can charge an iPad—or several iPads. Unless you lose an iPad's own charger, or the charger stops working, the main reason for getting a third-party charger is to charge multiple iPads (or other devices) at the same time. You may also want to get a second charger for an iPad you use in two locations, such as at work and at home.

- *USB port on computer*: You can charge an iPad from the USB port on a computer. Charging from a USB port typically takes much longer than using the iPad's own charger, so normally you'll want to do this only in a pinch.

- *Charging cabinet or cart*: For iPads that you'll keep in your classroom, another means of charging is a secure storage cabinet that provides charging or syncing capabilities; for iPads that need to move from classroom to classroom, you can get a cart instead. See the section "Choosing Storage Locations for iPads," later in this chapter, for suggestions.

CRITERIA FOR CHOOSING CHARGERS FOR IPADS

Here are three recommendations for choosing chargers for iPads:

- *Make sure the charger provides enough power*. Many multi-device chargers are designed to power smaller devices, such as smartphones, rather than tablets with large batteries. The standard Apple power supply for the iPad is the Apple 12W USB Power Adapter, and it takes several hours to charge an iPad fully. So you might consider 12W as the baseline per port for charging iPads at a reasonable speed.

- *Make sure the charger is certified by Apple*. To verify that the charger is both safe to use and compatible with the iPad, get a model that's certified by Apple. Certified models tend to be more expensive than uncertified ones, but an uncertified charger has the potential to damage the iPad or cause other electrical problems, so it may prove a false economy.

- *Upgrade your charging of the 12.9-inch iPad Pro*. The 12.9-inch iPad Pro comes with a Apple 12W USB Power Adapter, which takes four or five hours for a full charge. If you need to charge this iPad model more quickly, go to the Apple Store (online or offline) and get the Apple 29W USB-C Power Adapter ($49.00) with Apple's USB-C to Lightning Cable ($19.00 for 1 meter—usually sufficient—or $29.00 for 2 meters). The Apple 29W USB-C Power Adapter is essentially the MacBook's power adapter, and you'll find it listed under MacBook Accessories, but it works for the iPad Pro as well. (The cable is listed under iPad Accessories.) This combination charges the 12.9-inch iPad Pro in two to three hours.

Choosing and Using Cases

Apple's focus on making its handheld devices thin, light, and beautiful means that they're all too easy to drop and even easier to damage. As a result, most people who buy an iPad, an iPhone, or an iPod touch choose to protect their device with a case, even though doing so makes the device less thin, less light, and usually less beautiful.

Normally, you'll want to get cases for your school's iPads unless you're using another means of protection, such as mounts or stands (see the next section, "Choosing and Using iPad Mounts and Stands"). Students are often insouciant with sleek and expensive technology, especially when it belongs to someone else, but each iPad represents a capital investment for your school—an investment you'll presumably want to protect.

You can choose from a bewildering variety of cases, depending on which models your iPads are, what kinds of cases you need, and how much you're prepared to pay for them. The following sections introduce you to the four main categories of cases that are likely to prove useful for school iPads:

- Rugged cases

- Smart covers

- Flip cases or folio cases

- Keyboard cases

WHAT KINDS OF CASES DO YOUR IPADS NEED?

The kinds of cases you need will likely depend on how your school will use the iPads. For example, consider the following:

- *iPads kept in the classroom*: iPads that live indoors and are used as handheld devices (as opposed to being fixed on stands or mounts) will need cases that provide protection against drops, knocks, and student exuberance.

- *iPads used in and outside the school*: iPads that venture beyond the classroom will need heavy-duty cases, preferably ones that provide water resistance as well as drop protection.

- *iPads issued to students*: If the school issues an iPad to each student in a class, you may be better off to let each student choose a suitable case, either freely or from a pool of available approved cases. Letting the student choose the case increases the chance that the student will be able to recognize the iPad and perhaps even treat it more carefully.

Depending on your situation, you'll likely have to consider other factors as well when choosing cases. For example, for iPads you keep in the classroom and store in a security cabinet or cart (see the section "Choosing Storage Locations for iPads," later in this chapter), you'll also need to make sure that the cased iPads fit in the storage slots.

Evaluating Rugged Cases

Call me overly cautious, but I've yet to see a case that's too rugged for an iPad that will be used as a handheld device in a school or out in the wide world. Even a minor drop can do severe damage to an iPad, and repairs to iPads are expensive and disruptive. Fortunately, case manufacturers have produced a wide range of rugged cases for the various iPad models.

Here are three examples of rugged cases for iPads:

- *OtterBox Defender*: One of the heaviest-duty cases around, the OtterBox Defender transforms a sleek iPad into a rugged tablet somewhat reminiscent of those used by delivery drivers and supermarket stock-checkers. The OtterBox Defender (prices start from $89.99, available at www.otterbox.com or at major online stores) offers what OtterBox calls Certified Drop+ Protection, for which you may want to watch the video rather than try the experiment yourself. The main part of the case has a rigid internal frame with a rubberized outer covering and a built-in screen protector. There's also a hard-shell back that unclips to form a stand that can hold the iPad at a shallow angle or a steeper angle, either in portrait orientation or landscape orientation.

- *Griffin Survivor All-Terrain*: The Survivor All-Terrain series from Griffin Technology (www.griffintechnology.com) is a sturdy two-layer case with sealed ports to keep out dust and water. A built-in screen protector shields the screen from scratches, and a kickstand props up the iPad at either a steep angle or a low angle in landscape orientation. The Survivor All-Terrain series starts at around $50.

- *Gumdrop DropTech*: The DropTech case series from Gumdrop (www.gumdropcases.com), has a rigid internal frame, an outer silicone skin, and a built-in screen protector that is replaceable. The DropTech iPad Air 2 Case ($59.95) is certified compliant with the MIL-STD-810G military specification test, which means that it has protected the tablet against 26 drops from a four-foot height. Gumdrop sells cases singly or in 10-packs.

Evaluating Smart Covers

A *smart cover* is a lightweight cover for the iPad's screen that connects magnetically to the side and front of the iPad but leaves the back uncovered. Opening the smart cover automatically wakes the iPad, and closing it puts the iPad to sleep. The smart cover folds in several ways to make a stand that props the iPad up at angles suitable for typing on the onscreen keyboard (a shallow angle) or for watching videos (a steeper angle).

Smart covers are popular because they protect the screen while the iPad is not in use and increase the iPad's bulk by only a little. But because it provides no protection to the iPad's back when the screen is covered, and no protection to the screen when the screen isn't covered, it doesn't offer enough protection for most classroom use.

Apple made the original Smart Covers, but various third-party smart covers are also available, generally at lower prices than Apple's—sometimes much lower. Because there's substantial variation in quality among third-party smart covers, it's a good idea to examine them in a physical store before buying.

■ **Note**   You can also get *smart cases* for iPads. As you'd guess, these are cases that wake the iPad on opening and put it to sleep on closing.

Evaluating Folio Cases

Folio cases can be a good choice for iPads that need only a moderate amount of protection. They're not usually sufficient for the rough-and-tumble life of iPads shared in the classroom, but they may be adequate for iPads issued as personal devices to students who can be trusted to take care of them.

There are many kinds of folio cases, but the basic idea is a case that encloses the iPad and has a cover that closes over the top. The cover may include magnets and may make the case act as a smart case, automatically waking the iPad on opening and putting it to sleep on closing. The cover folds back when the iPad is in use, and may do double-duty as a stand.

Evaluating Keyboard Cases

If your iPads will be used for creating documents or otherwise entering substantial amounts of text, you may want to consider keyboard cases for them. A *keyboard case* can turn an iPad into a sort of touchscreen laptop, enabling a user who can touch-type to enter text far more quickly than by using the on-screen keyboard.

You can find a wide variety of different types of keyboard cases. Here are three examples to use as a starting point in your research:

- *Zagg Rugged Book and Slim Book series*: The Rugged Book series and Slim Book series from Zagg Inc. (www.zagg.com) consist of protective cases for the iPad and a detachable Bluetooth keyboard. The two-part design enables you to use the iPad separately from the keyboard (which Zagg calls Case Mode) or in three positions with the keyboard: laptop style (Keyboard Mode), with the keyboard as a stand (Video Mode), or with the keyboard folded flat beneath the iPad (Book Mode).

- *Brydge series*: Brydge (www.brydgekeyboards.com) makes a series of keyboards for iPads and for Microsoft Surface Pro. Of the models designed for iPad, the Brydge 9.7 ($129.99) fits the iPad (and older models, such as the iPad Air 2, iPad Air, and 9.7-inch iPad Pro); the Brydge 10.5 ($139.99) fits the 10.5-inch iPad Pro; the Brydge 12.9 ($149.99) fits the 12.9-inch iPad Pro; and the Brydge 7.9 ($99.99) fits the iPad mini 4.

- *Logitech CREATE*: The CREATE series of keyboard cases from Logitech (www.logitech.com) includes models for the older 9.7-inch iPad Pro ($129.99) and the 12.9-inch iPad Pro ($149.99); as of this writing, there is no CREATE keyboard for the 10.5-inch iPad Pro.

Choosing Screen Protectors

The touchscreen is one of the most vulnerable parts of the iPad—and one of the most expensive parts to replace. You can protect it to some extent with a screen protector. As you've seen earlier in this chapter, some iPad cases include built-in screen protectors. If you'll be using such cases, you're all set for screen protectors; if not, you can apply a separate screen protector.

DECIDING WHETHER YOUR IPADS NEED SCREEN PROTECTORS

Some pundits recommend against using screen protectors, saying that the iPad's Gorilla Glass screen is tough enough to resist most scratches and that heavier-duty screen protectors can make the touchscreen harder to use. But in a high-impact environment such as a school, iPads usually need as much protection as you can give them.

For iPad Pro models that will be used with the Apple Pencil, you may want to either skip the screen protector or apply an ultra-thin tempered glass one. It's a good idea to test different types of screen protectors to see which work best with the Apple Pencil.

You can choose among three main types of screen protectors:

- *Plastic screen protectors*: Plastic screen protectors are usually the least expensive, but can still be effective. You'll find a wide variety of plastic screen protectors on online stores. The thickness of the plastic varies, as does the feel of the surface and the responsiveness of the touchscreen through it.

- *Tempered glass screen protectors*: Tempered glass screen protectors are typically more expensive than plastic screen protectors, but they can provide better protection and give the iPad's screen a better feel. Different thicknesses are available, but generally thinness is a selling point. You can find a wide variety of these too on online stores.

- *Liquid treatments*: Instead of applying a solid sheet of plastic or tempered glass, you can apply a liquid coating that, once it's dried, resists grease, dirt, and scratches. Examples include Liquid Armor from Dynaflo (around $19.99 at online stores).

You'll likely want to try several types and thicknesses of screen protectors to find out which work best for you and your school. Apart from the protection and the feel that the screen protectors deliver, you'll likely want to consider how easy they are to apply.

Application is easy in principle:

- Clean the screen with a microfiber cloth (which most screen protectors include).

- Peel the protective plastic off the first side of the screen protector.

- Apply the screen protector to the screen, aligning its edges to the edges of the iPad's screen.

- Smooth out any bubbles using either a provided tool, a credit card, or another straight edge (such as a ruler).

- Peel the protective plastic off the second side of the screen protector.

As usual, the devil is in the details. Unless you get the screen absolutely clean, bits of lint or dust may be trapped under the screen protector. Unless you get the screen protector straight, it won't fit properly. And with most plastic screen protectors or tempered glass screen protectors, it's easy to get bubbles under the film that are difficult to remove. So it's a good idea to buy plenty of extra screen protectors to practice with. And if you find applying screen protectors difficult, see whether any of your students are already skilled at applying screen protectors—or if they want to develop the skill.

Choosing and Using iPad Mounts and Stands

If your iPads will remain in one place—whether that place is the classroom or elsewhere—you might want to use mounts or stands to secure and protect the tablets. The right mount or stand can ensure the iPad doesn't stray from where it's supposed to be, that it doesn't get dashed against the floor or other unforgiving objects, and that it stays connected to power.

■ **Note**   Many laptop and desktop computers have a built-in Kensington Security Slot, an anti-theft feature that enables you to secure the computer using a Kensington security cable that locks into the slot. As of this writing, no iPad model has a built-in Kensington Slot, nor is there an equivalent security device. So, to secure an iPad, you need to put it in a mount, frame, or enclosure that has a locking mechanism or Kensington Slot.

You can choose from a wide variety of stands and mounts, some designed specifically for the iPad family and others for tablets in general. The following subsections review the main categories of stands and mounts.

SUGGESTIONS FOR CHOOSING MOUNTS AND STANDS FOR SCHOOL USE

Many mounts and stands are designed for home use rather than business use. These vary widely in price, materials, and construction, but—generally speaking—many are lightweight and do little more than prop up the iPad at one or more convenient angles. Such mounts and stands are designed to be easy to move around as needed, so you can use them on the kitchen table, on your desk, in the den, or wherever. The iPad may simply be placed in the mount or stand rather than secured in it.

Such mounts and stands are fine for home use, but for school use, you'll typically want mounts or stands that fix—and preferably lock—the iPad in place and that themselves are fixed (and perhaps locked) to large or immovable objects, preferably in a way that's hard to undo. You'll want the mounts and stands to be sturdy enough to withstand robust handling themselves; you may also want them to protect the iPads from damage.

This means you'll be looking for mounts and stands designed and built for commercial and industrial uses rather than home use. Such mounts and stands tend to be considerably more expensive than ones designed for home use, but the extra utility they deliver should more than offset the extra cost.

Desk Mounts

A *desk mount* enables you to fix an iPad firmly to a school desk, table, or other flat surface. You can choose from a wide variety of desk mounts, including these two:

- *Kensington SecureBack Enclosure and Stand for 9.7-inch iPad Models*: This enclosure and stand, made by hardware security specialist Kensington (http://www.kensington.com), locks the iPad firmly in a jacket that connects securely to a stand that provides 360° rotation. The enclosure and stand together cost $159.99.

- *POS Lock Belt and X Lock System*: The POS Lock Belt series from Proper (www.studioproper.com) enables you to connect an iPad, iPad Pro, or iPad mini securely to a variety of stands and mounts. The POS Lock Belt—*POS* is the abbreviation for point of sale, not a term of abuse—connects to the iPad and tightens with Allen bolts. The POS Lock Belt then connects to a stand or mount, such as the POS Swivel Stand, via the X-shaped cutout.

VESA Mounts

You can find various VESA mounts that work with iPads, enabling you to mount the iPad on stands, monitor arms, or other devices that have standard VESA fittings. (See the nearby sidebar "What Is VESA, and What Is a VESA Mount?" for more information on VESA mounts.) VESA mounts can be great if you already have stands, monitor arms, or other devices on which you want to mount the iPads. They're also useful if you need to ensure you have a standard mounting mechanism rather than a custom mounting mechanism.

Some VESA mounts are specifically designed for individual iPad models; others work with a range of tablets and similar devices. For school use, it's worth evaluating both, but in most cases, mounts designed for the iPad models you're using will normally work best. You'll normally want to get lockable iPad mounts. Many of these require you to put the iPad in a particular enclosure or case.

Here are two examples of VESA mounts for iPads:

- *Full Metal Jacket 3.0 series and Evolve iPad series:* The Full Metal Jacket 3.0 series and the Evolve iPad series, both from ArmorActive (www.armoractive.com), consist of secure iPad enclosures with 75 mm and 100 mm VESA mounting holes. Each series includes enclosures for 9.7-inch iPad models (such as the iPad, the older iPad Air and iPad Air 2, and the older 9.7-inch iPad Pro).

- *Kensington SecureBack Rugged Enclosure*: The SecureBack Rugged Enclosure from Kensington (www.kensington.com, $69.99) provides an easy way to secure an iPad to a 75 mm VESA mount.

WHAT IS VESA, AND WHAT IS A VESA MOUNT?

VESA is the acronym for Video Electronics Standards Association, a technical standards organization that has developed and promoted a wide variety of computer display standards since its establishment in 1989. Many of the VESA-developed standards, such as the VESA Local Bus video bus and the VESA Advanced Feature Connector (VAFC) connector for video cards, have been swamped by the tides of technology, but the VESA mount is still extremely widely used.

The VESA mount, formally known as either the Flat Display Mounting Interface (FDMI) or VESA Mounting Interface Standard (MIS), has four screw holes on either a square or X-shaped mount. VESA mounts use different hole spacings and screw sizes for different sizes and weights of displays.

- *VESA 75*: 75 mm × 7 5mm, with M4 screws, for up to 17.5 lbs

- *VESA 100*: 100 mm × 100 mm, with M4 screws, for up to 30.8 lbs

- *VESA 200*: 200 mm × 200 mm, with M6 screws, for up to 110 lbs

- *VESA 200*: 200 mm × 200 mm or larger, with M8 screws, for up to 250 lbs

Most VESA mounts for iPads and other tablets have 75 mm VESA holes, 100 mm VESA holes, or both.

Wall Mounts

Wall mounts enable you to secure iPads to walls and other flat surfaces. You can choose between fixed mounts and ones that fold out or slide out, enabling you to reposition the iPad.

Here are two examples of wall mounts:

- *Slimline 10 Wall Mounted Secure Tablet Enclosure*: This enclosure enables you to mount an iPad or other tablet securely on the wall, either simply to display information or to let users interact with the device. The Slimline 10 Wall Mounted Secure Tablet Enclosure is from imageHOLDERS Ltd. (`www.imageholders.com`); prices start at $299.99.

- *FlexStand Series iPad Wall Mount with Adjustable Arm*: This mount, available from Displays2go (`www.displays2go.com`), enables you to lock an iPad securely in the mount and position it using the adjustable arm. The FlexStand costs around $150.

Other Mounts and Stands

Apart from desk mounts and stands, VESA mounts, and wall mounts, you can find various other types of mounts and stands for iPads. The following list introduces three types of mounts and stands you may need to round out your students' iPad activities:

- *Floor*: A *floor* stand can be great for using an iPad for activities such as music, art, or delivering presentations. Most floor stands are mobile rather than fixed, making them relatively easy to knock over, so normally you'd want to use them only for staff members or your more responsible students.

- *Tripod mounts*: If your students will use the iPads for shooting photos or videos, you may want to get *tripod* mounts. Most tripod mounts are designed for home use rather than industrial use, so they simply hold the iPad, usually using tension clips, rather than locking the iPad into place. If your iPads wear cases, look for tripod mounts that fit over the cases; that way, the iPads will have a decent amount of protection.

■ **Tip** Tripod mounts can work as an alternative to floor stands. Even if the tripod looks a bit odd in the context, it has the advantage that it's much harder to knock over than a typical floor stand.

- *Car mounts*: You can find various types of car mounts for iPads, such as mounts that attach an iPad to the front seat headrest. Most of these mounts are aimed at the consumer market, but they can come in useful for school trips as well.

Choosing Hardware Keyboards Where Needed

The iPad's operating system includes a selection of on-screen keyboards. In many apps, the default on-screen keyboard appears automatically when you activate a text field, so you can start typing without having to summon the keyboard manually. You can also display and hide the on-screen keyboard manually as needed. When the keyboard is displayed, you can switch among different available modes, such as letters mode, numbers mode, and symbols mode.

Typing on the screen works pretty well for casual typing in the classroom. But if you or your students need to enter serious amounts of text on the iPad, you'll probably want to connect hardware keyboards, especially if your students can type well.

You can add hardware keyboards by using three means of connection:

- Bluetooth

- USB

- Smart Keyboard for iPad Pro

The following subsections explain these means of connection and how to choose among them.

Pros and Cons of Bluetooth Keyboards for iPads

Bluetooth is normally the most convenient way to connect keyboards to iPads in general. You have three main options for Bluetooth keyboards:

- *General-purpose Bluetooth keyboards*: Many general-purpose Bluetooth keyboards are compatible with iOS—so if you have any Bluetooth keyboards, it's worth trying them. Once you have compatible Bluetooth keyboards, you can move them from one iPad to another fairly quickly.

- *Bluetooth keyboards designed for iPads in general*: You can find many Bluetooth keyboards designed for use with iPads or iPhones. Such keyboards have dedicated keys or key combinations for actions such as displaying the Home screen and changing the audio volume. These keyboards tend to be a little more expensive than general-purpose Bluetooth keyboards, but if the extra functionality they offer is helpful (and it usually is), the extra expense is easy to justify.

- *Bluetooth keyboards designed for specific iPad models*: Your third choice is Bluetooth keyboards designed to fit specific iPad models. These keyboards are often built into iPad covers or cases. Prices range widely, but normally this is the most expensive type of Bluetooth keyboard. Keyboards built into covers or cases can be a good solution for any iPad that you plan to use mostly (or frequently) as a laptop.

The first time you connect a Bluetooth keyboard to an iPad, you put the keyboard into pairing mode, and then usually you enter a pairing code: the iPad displays the code, and you must type it on the keyboard to confirm the pairing. Once you've done this, you can connect and disconnect the keyboard quickly from the iPad by working on the Bluetooth screen in the Settings app. See the section "Connecting and Using Bluetooth Devices" in Chapter 3 for detailed instructions.

■ **Caution**   Some Bluetooth keyboards don't require a pairing code when pairing the device. This makes pairing quicker and works well for consumers who use a single Bluetooth keyboard at a time. But if you're setting up multiple Bluetooth keyboards, you'll need to double-check which keyboard you're pairing with which iPad. Unless you keep both the keyboards and the iPads carefully labeled, things can become confusing.

Bluetooth keyboards have two main disadvantages in the classroom:

- *Powering the keyboards*: Most Bluetooth keyboards are designed to run on battery power to avoid having supposedly unsightly cables in the way. This is fine, but you'll need to keep the keyboards recharged. That means plugging them in to a power source—usually via a USB cable—every few days, depending on how much usage they get.

- *Identifying which keyboard is linked to which iPad*: Unless you label your Bluetooth keyboards and iPads clearly, and keep a log of which keyboard you've connected to which iPad, you may find it hard to keep straight which keyboard belongs with which iPad. How hard this will be depends on your classroom setup. For example, if you have the iPads mounted in stands, and the keyboards secured near them, you may find it easy to keep the keyboard and iPad pairs straight. But if the iPads and keyboards are free to move and you need to put them away at the end of the lesson, the day, or the week, you'll need clear labels to keep each pair together.

Pros and Cons of USB Keyboards for iPads

It's possible to connect some USB keyboards to the iPad by using a Lightning-to-USB connector plugged into the iPad's Lightning port. The keyboard must be compatible with iOS and must not draw too much power. If you connect a keyboard that won't work, the iPad displays a dialog telling you that there's a problem—so if you have a Lightning-to-USB connector, you can quickly determine which (if any) of your USB keyboards will work.

Connecting a keyboard via USB can be convenient in a pinch, especially if the iPad is yours and the keyboard is one that you find comfortable. A bonus point is that the keyboard draws power from the iPad, so you don't need to worry about powering the keyboard separately. But USB isn't normally a great solution for classroom use because the Lightning-to-USB connector is easy to damage or break, even if the iPad is secured in a mount or a stand.

Pros and Cons of Smart Keyboards for iPad Pro Models

For an iPad that has Apple's Smart Connector, such as the iPad Pro, you can connect a keyboard that uses this connector. Apple's own keyboards with the Smart Connector are called Smart Keyboard; other companies make Smart Connector-equipped keyboards with different names. These keyboards are relatively expensive, and most are designed fit a particular iPad model, so (for example) a Smart Keyboard for a 10.5-inch iPad Pro won't fit a 12.9-inch iPad Pro.

SHOULD YOU GET SMART KEYBOARDS?

Smart Keyboards can be great for the iPad, because they give a convenient way to enter text quickly. But you'll likely find that Smart Keyboards are too expensive and too easily damaged for use by students. Another problem is that most Smart Keyboards provide only a small amount of protection for the iPad, although some companies do make heavier-duty Smart Keyboards.

So you may want to get Smart Keyboards only for iPads that are dedicated to teachers—or perhaps only for your own dedicated iPad.

Choosing Storage Locations for iPads

If your iPads will remain at school, or in the classroom, you'll need to choose a suitable storage location for them if they're not secured in stands or mounts. Because the iPad is designed to be a portable device, it's all too easy for someone to remove an iPad from the classroom undetected.

Here are suggestions for storing iPads securely in the classroom or school:

- *Closet*: If the classroom has a lockable closet, placing the iPads in it at the end of the lesson or end of the school day may be adequate. If the closet includes power outlets, you can plug in power adapters to charge the iPads. If you need to charge many iPads, you'll probably want to have an electrician outfit the closet with extra power outlets.

- *iPad cart or tablet cart*: You can find a wide variety of carts designed to secure iPads or other tablets (or laptops such as Chromebooks), charge them, and convey them safely from one classroom to another.

- *iPad charging and syncing cabinet*: If the iPads will remain in the same classroom, consider a charging and syncing cabinet rather than a cart. You can find both cabinets designed specifically for iPads and cabinets designed to hold tablets and small laptops. One example is the Charge & Sync Cabinet for iPad Air, iPad and iPad mini from Kensington (www.kensington.com), which provides storage for 10 iPads. You can stack two or three Charge & Sync Cabinets on top of each other.

43

■ **Note**　Another possibility for preventing an iPad from wandering is to use a protective case, such as the SecureBack M series from Kensington, that lets you attach a standard Kensington locking cable. This can be an effective solution for uses where you need the iPad to be freely movable over the short distance that the cable permits, but it still exposes the iPad to the risk of being damaged by being knocked over.

Evaluating Apple Pencil for iPad Pro

If you decide to buy iPad Pro models for staff or students, you'll also need to decide whether to get the Apple Pencil to use with them. The Apple Pencil is a stylus that's custom designed for the iPad Pro model; it doesn't work with non-Pro iPad models or with other devices, such as the iPhone. So if you don't have iPad Pro models, you don't need to worry about the Apple Pencil.

The Apple Pencil enables you to interact with the iPad's touchscreen much more precisely than your finger does. The Apple Pencil detects how hard you're pressing with the point, enabling you to draw lines of different weights by varying the pressure. The Apple Pencil also calculates the degree of tilt you're using, and adds more shading when it detects that you're tilting the stylus further. These features work only with apps that are designed to support the Apple Pencil, but by now, a good number of such apps are available.

The Apple Pencil is good for drawing and painting apps, but it's also good for taking notes in handwriting and for adding sketches to notes in apps such as the built-in Notes app. You can also use the Apple Pencil to draw on attachments in the Mail app—for example, to mark up a document or a contract with changes—or to add signatures to PDF files.

In the classroom, the Apple Pencil has some obvious disadvantages:

- *Cost*: The Apple Pencil costs $99.

- *Vulnerability*: The Apple Pencil is easy to break and even easier to lose. The iPad Pro models themselves don't have a silo or holder for the Apple Pencil, but some iPad Pro cases do have a silo or holder.

- *Power*: The Apple Pencil requires charging, either from the iPad or from a Lightning adapter. Charging is simple enough, but it's another task you have to ensure gets performed if you plan to have your students use the Apple Pencil with iPad Pros. A full charge delivers up to 12 hours of use, but you can also get 30 minutes of use by charging the Apple Pencil for 15 seconds from the iPad Pro.

Armed with this information, you should be able to decide quickly whether you, your colleagues, and your students will benefit from having the Apple Pencil with the iPad Pro or whether Apple Pencil will prove a strain on your resources and your patience.

Summary

In this chapter, you've learned how to choose the right iPads for your school's needs, how to protect the iPads with cases, screen protectors, or mounts and stands, and how to accessorize the iPads with keyboards and the Apple Pencil. You've also evaluated your options for storing the iPads if you'll keep them in the school rather than issue them to students.

In the next chapter, you'll learn essential iPad skills for administrators and teachers.

CHAPTER 3

■ ■ ■

Essential iPad Skills for Administrators and Teachers

In this chapter, you learn essential skills for using an iPad as an administrator or as a teacher. We'll start with the basics, since there's little worse than missing some vital piece of information that people assume is obvious. We'll cover how to set up an iPad, perform basic power operations, navigate the interface, connect to Wi-Fi networks, and so on. Once you know those moves, we'll look at how to configure an iPad's essential settings manually: Notifications, Do Not Disturb, Restrictions, and Accessibility. Toward the end of the chapter, I'll cover connecting keyboards to the iPad, updating the operating system, installing, removing, and organizing apps, and managing both local storage and iCloud storage.

Unless you've never touched an iPad before, chances are that you already know some—or perhaps most—of the material that this chapter covers. But even if you're expert with the iPad, have a quick look through the chapter to dig out any nuggets of extra information that will benefit you.

Setting Up an iPad

If you're unboxing new iPads, or if you power on a used iPad and find it displays the Hello screen because it's been erased, you'll need to go through the setup routine, which includes specifying the country or region, connecting the iPad to a Wi-Fi network, and implementing security measures. The following list tells you what you need to do on the various setup screens:

- *Hello screen*: Press the Home button to get started. On older versions of iOS, you swipe a slider across to get started. The prompt tells you—in multiple languages—whether to press the Home button or to swipe.

© Guy Hart-Davis 2017
G. Hart-Davis, *Deploying iPads in the Classroom*,
https://doi.org/10.1007/978-1-4842-2928-6_3

- *Select Your Country or Region screen*: Tap the country or region whose format settings you want the iPad to use. Normally, this will be the country or region where you're physically located—for example, if you're in the U.S.A., you'd normally want to tap the United States item. The country or region sets for format for items such as time (for example, 12:34 PM), date (as in Saturday, November 4, 2017), and currency (such as $4567.89).

■ **Note**   On a cellular iPad, you can also tap the Use Cellular Connection button on the Choose a Wi-Fi Network screen to start setting up the iPad via the cellular network rather than via Wi-Fi. This capability is occasionally useful, but in general, Wi-Fi is easier.

- *Choose a Wi-Fi Network screen*: On this screen, tap the button for the Wi-Fi network you want to connect the iPad to. If the network has a password, the Enter Password dialog opens, and you can type the password and tap the Join button.

■ **Note**   If the Wi-Fi network you want the iPad to join doesn't appear on the Choose a Wi-Fi Network screen, but you believe the network is within range of the iPad, the network probably hides its name (more formally, the SSID, which stands for *service set identifier*) as a security measure. To connect to the network, tap the Choose Another Network button. The Other Network dialog box opens. Type the network's name (the SSID) in the Name field, tap the Security button to open the Security dialog, tap the appropriate button (such as WPA2 or WPA2 Enterprise), and then tap the Other Network button to return to the Other Network dialog box. Type the password in the Password field, and then tap the Join button.

- *Location Services screen*: Tap the Enable Location Services button if you want to allow the Location Services feature to determine the iPad's location by using data from crowd-source Wi-Fi hotspots, nearby Bluetooth devices, and (for a cellular iPad) GPS and cell tower locations. Tap the Disable Location Services button if you don't want the iPad to use Location Services.

■ **Caution**   Disabling Location Services prevents you from using Apple's Find My iPad service to locate the iPad if it goes missing. Unless you secure the iPad physically, being able to locate it via Find My iPad is normally helpful.

- *Touch ID screen*: From this screen, you can start registering a fingerprint for unlocking the iPad without typing a passcode or password. If you're setting up the iPad for yourself, you'll likely want to set up Touch ID. Tap the Continue button, and then follow the prompts to register a fingerprint or a thumbprint. If not, tap the Set Up Touch ID Later button instead to skip ahead to the Create a Passcode screen.

- *Create a Passcode screen*: On this screen, choose and type a six-digit passcode that you will use to unlock the iPad. If you didn't set up Touch ID, this passcode is your regular way of unlocking the iPad, but even if you did set up Touch ID, you'll need to enter the passcode sometimes, such as after restarting the iPad or after not using the iPad for a couple of days. If you prefer to use a shorter passcode, longer passcode, or an alphanumeric passcode (or password, if you like), tap the Passcode Options button and see the nearby sidebar titled "Setting a Custom Passcode."

■ **Note**   If you try to set a passcode that contains an obvious sequence, such as 111111 or 123456, the iPad displays the Are You Sure You Want to Use This Code? dialog (see Figure 3-1). Tap the Change button if you want to change the code to something more challenging, or tap the Use Code button if you're determined to use this code.

Are You Sure You Want to Use This Code?

This code is commonly used and can be easily guessed.

Use Code

Choose New Code

Figure 3-1. *The iPad displays the Are You Sure You Want to Use This Code? dialog if you try to set an easy-to-guess passcode (such as 987654) or a very short one. Tap the Use Code button or the Choose New Code button, as appropriate*

SETTING A CUSTOM PASSCODE

By default, the iPad uses a numeric passcode consisting of six digits—long enough for reasonable protection against passcode cracking, but short enough to be easy to remember and to type when you unlock the iPad. But if you want, you can set a numeric code of a different length or an alphanumeric code instead. On the Create a Passcode screen, tap the Passcode Options button to display the pop-up menu, tap the appropriate button (see the following list), and then follow the prompts:

- *Custom Alphanumeric Code*: Tap this button to create an alphanumeric code or password. You can make this code as short as a single character if you override the iPad's warning that the code can be easily guessed.

- *Custom Numeric Code*: Tap this button to create a numeric code of a length that you choose. Normally, you'd create a custom numeric code so that you can use more numbers and get greater protection against the password being cracked, but you can also create a shorter numeric password if you so choose. If the code is very short, you must override the iPad's warning that the code can be easily guessed.

- *4-Digit Numeric Code*: Tap this button to create a numeric passcode that's only four digits long. This is the passcode length that older versions of iOS used by default. Four digits aren't really enough to provide effective security for an iPad that contains sensitive personal information, but if your iPads don't contain personal information and can't access any sensitive data, you may feel that a four-digit passcode gives adequate protection.

- *Apps & Data screen*: On this screen (see Figure 3-2), you specify the method you will use to complete setup of the iPad. You have four choices:

  - *Restore from iCloud Backup*: This option enables you to restore data to the iPad from a backup on Apple's iCloud service. You can use this option both to restore data that you've backed up from this particular iPad and to restore data from another iPad, iPhone, or iPod touch.

  - *Restore from iTunes Backup*: This option enables you to restore data to the iPad from a backup created on a Mac or PC using iTunes. As with the iCloud backup, this backup can be one from this particular iPad or from another iPad, iPhone, or iPod touch.

■ **Note** An iTunes backup is much more complete than an iCloud backup—so if you have the choice between the two, the iTunes backup is the better choice. But normally the iPad will have been backed up to either iCloud or iTunes, not to both.

- *Set Up as New iPad*: This option lets you set up the iPad from scratch.

- *Move Data from Android*: This option enables you to transfer data, such as your Google account and your photos, from an Android phone or tablet. You need to install Apple's Move to iOS app on the Android device. This option is handy for consumers switching platforms.

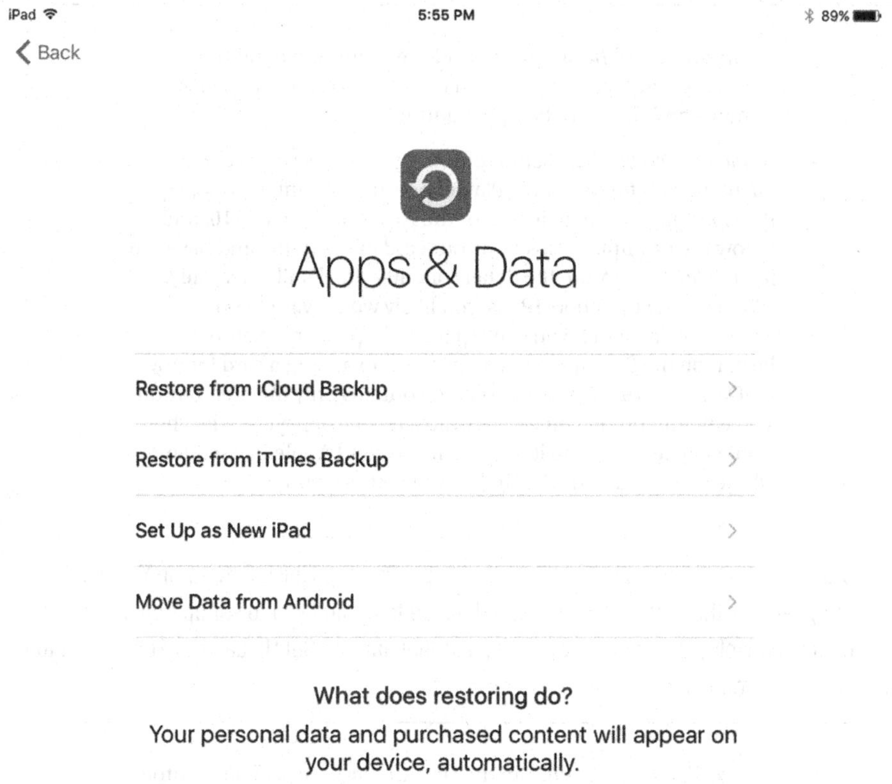

Apps & Data

Restore from iCloud Backup	>
Restore from iTunes Backup	>
Set Up as New iPad	>
Move Data from Android	>

What does restoring do?

Your personal data and purchased content will appear on
your device, automatically.

Figure 3-2. *On the Apps & Data screen, choose whether to set up the iPad from scratch or to restore data from an iCloud backup or an iTunes backup. You can also transfer some data from an Android phone or tablet*

After you tap the Set Up as New iPad button, follow through this sequence of screens to complete setup:

- *Apple ID screen*: On this screen, type your Apple ID and the corresponding password, and then tap the Next button.

■ **Note**   On the Apple ID screen, you can tap the Don't Have an Apple ID or Forgot It? button to either get a new Apple ID or retrieve the details for an Apple ID you've forgotten. You can also tap the Use Different Apple IDs for iCloud and iTunes button to set up the iPad to use a different account for iCloud than for iTunes. On the iCloud screen that appears, enter the details of the Apple ID you want to use for iCloud, and tap the Next button. Then, on the iTunes screen that appears next, enter the details of the Apple ID to use for iTunes, and tap the Next button again.

- *Terms and Conditions screen*: Read the terms and conditions— or tap the Send by E-mail button to send a copy to yourself via e-mail—and then tap the Agree button.

- *Apple Pay screens*: The setup routine encourages you to add a payment card for the Apple Pay service. If you want to do so, tap the Continue button in iOS 11 or the Next button in iOS 10, and follow the prompts to position your card in the frame and have the iPad's camera capture the details or enter the details manually. When setting up school iPads, you likely won't want to set up Apple Pay. In iOS 11, you can tap the Set Up Later in Settings button on the first Apple Pay screen to skip adding a card for now. In iOS 10, the first Apple Pay screen contains only the Next button, so—whether or not you want to add a means of payment for the Apple Pay service—tap it to reach the second Apple Pay screen, where you can tap the Set Up Later in Settings button.

■ **Note**   If you don't add a payment card to Apple Pay, the Finish Setting Up Your iPad button appears in the Setting app with a red badge to remind you to set up Apple Pay. Tap this button to display the Apple Pay screen, and then tap the Set Up Later in Settings button to dismiss this reminder.

- *iCloud Keychain screen*: Tap the Use iCloud Security code button to display the iCloud Security Code screen, and then type your iCloud security code to enable the iPad to use the passwords you've stored in iCloud Keychain. If you don't want to set up iCloud Keychain, tap the Don't Restore Passwords button instead, and then tap the Continue button in the Don't Restore Passwords? dialog that opens.

▪ **Note** iCloud Keychain is a feature for storing passwords and other sensitive information securely in your iCloud account so that you can use that information on all the devices and computers that log into your iCloud account.

- *Siri screen*: If you want to set up the Siri voice assistant feature now, tap the Turn On Siri button and follow the prompts to teach Siri to recognize your voice. If you don't want to use Siri, tap the Turn On Siri Later button instead.

- *Diagnostics screen*: Tap the Send to Apple button if you're prepared to let the iPad send diagnostic information to Apple automatically. Otherwise, tap the Don't Send button.

- *App Analytics screen*: Tap the Share with App Developers button if you want to let apps send activity and crash data to Apple for Apple to share with the apps' developers. Otherwise, tap the Don't Share button.

- *Welcome to iPad screen*: Tap the Get Started button to display the Home screen and start using the iPad.

Startup, Sleep and Wake, Shutdown, and Restart

Here's how to perform essential power operations on the iPad:

- *Start up the iPad*: Press and hold the Sleep/Wake button on the right side of the top of the iPad for a few seconds. Release the button when the Apple logo appears on the screen. When the lock screen appears, press the Home button to unlock it using Touch ID; if the iPad prompts you to enter your passcode, do so.

- *Put the iPad to sleep*: Press the Sleep/Wake button. The iPad also normally puts itself to sleep after several minutes of inactivity.

- *Wake the iPad from sleep*: Press the Home button or the Sleep/Wake button.

- *Shut down the iPad*: Press and hold the Sleep/Wake button for several seconds until the "slide to power off" slider appears on the screen (see Figure 3-3). Drag the slider to the right. The iPad shuts down.

Figure 3-3. *To shut down the iPad, press and hold the Sleep/Wake button until the "slide to power off" slider appears, and then drag the slider to the right*

- *Restart the iPad*: There's no separate command for restarting the iPad, so normally you would shut down the iPad and then start it. If the iPad stops responding to the touchscreen, you can perform a hard restart by holding down the Sleep/Wake button and the Home button simultaneously until the iPad restarts and the Apple logo appears on the screen.

Navigating the Interface

This section makes sure you know the essentials of navigating the iPad's interface: how to unlock the iPad, navigate the Home screen pages, and use Notification Center, Control Center, and Today View. You'll see how to launch apps, switch among apps, and close apps when necessary, how to search the iPad and beyond using Spotlight Search, and how to use the iPad's multitasking features.

Unlocking the iPad

After starting up, the iPad displays the lock screen. You need to unlock the iPad using Touch ID or the passcode before you can use most of the iPad's features. To unlock the iPad using Touch ID, press the Home button with a finger you registered for Touch ID. If Touch ID doesn't work, or if you haven't registered a finger, pressing the Home button displays a keypad on screen. Type your passcode on the keypad to unlock the iPad.

■ **Note**   From the lock screen, you can access four apps and features without unlocking the iPad. Swipe down from the top of the screen to open Cover Sheet in iOS 11 or Notification Center in iOS 10, a screen that shows notifications. Swipe left to access the Camera app. Swipe right to access Today View, which provides current information (see the section "Using Today View," later in this chapter, for more information). Swipe up from the bottom of the screen to access Control Center, which provides quick access to essential controls (see the section "Using Control Center," also later in this chapter, for more information).

Navigating the Home Screen Pages

After you unlock the iPad at first, the Home screen appears. The Home screen enables you to see some status information about the iPad and to launch apps.

The Home screen is a little different in iOS 11 and iOS 10. Figure 3-4 shows the iOS 11 Home screen with labels on a Wi-Fi-only iPad. Figure 3-5 shows the iOS 10 Home screen on a cellular-and–Wi-Fi iPad.

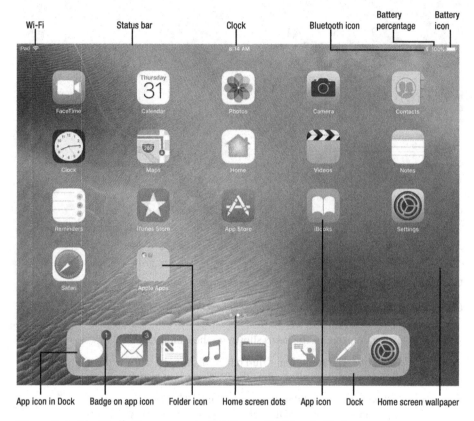

Figure 3-4. The iPad's Home screen in iOS 11 on a Wi-Fi–only iPad

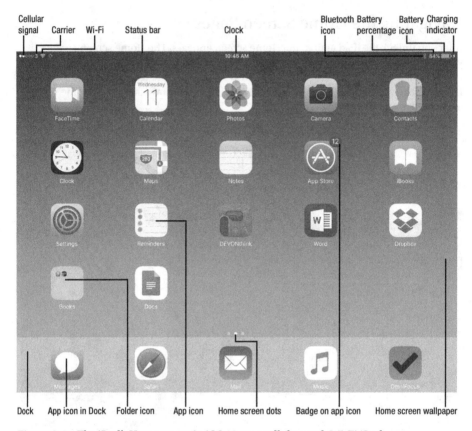

Figure 3-5. The iPad's Home screen in iOS 10 on a cellular-and-Wi-Fi iPad

The following list explains the items shown on the Home screen:

- *Status bar*: The status bar, a thin bar across the top of the screen, shows various icons indicating the iPad's current status.

- *Cellular signal*: [Cellular iPad models only] The five dots show the approximate strength of the cellular signal—the more white dots, the stronger the signal.

- *Carrier*: [Cellular iPad models only] The carrier name (in the example, 3) appears to the right of the cellular signal icon.

- *Wi-Fi*: The Wi-Fi symbol shows the approximate strength of the Wi-Fi network connection, if there is one.

- *Clock*: The clock shows the time.

- *Bluetooth icon*: The Bluetooth icon appears when the Bluetooth communications capability is enabled. Bluetooth provides a means of connecting devices such as keyboards, headsets, and assistive devices.

- *Battery percentage*: The readout shows the battery's charge percentage, such as 83%. You can disable the battery readout by choosing Settings ➤ Battery from the Home screen and then setting the Battery Percentage switch to Off.

- *Battery icon*: The battery icon shows the battery's approximate charge status graphically. The icon appears green when the battery is charging and white when it's not charging.

- *Charging indicator*: The charging indicator, a lightning symbol, appears when the iPad is connected to power and the battery is charging.

- *Home screen wallpaper*: The wallpaper is a graphic that provides the backdrop for the Home screen. Each Home screen page shows the same wallpaper.

- *App icons*: The app icons enable you to launch apps that aren't running or switch to apps that are running.

- *Badges*: A *badge* is a red circle or rounded rectangle that appears on the upper-right corner of an app icon to indicate that there are new items, such as app updates or new e-mail messages.

- *Home screen dots*: These dots, between the main part of the Home screen and the Dock, show which of the Home screen pages is currently being displayed. The leftmost dot represents Today View, which you'll meet in the section "Using Today View," a little later in this chapter. The second dot represents the first of the Home screen pages that show apps and folders. The third dot and subsequent dots represent other Home screen pages that contain apps and folders. You can create other Home screen pages as needed to organize the Home screen. You can swipe left or right on a Home screen page to display another page. You can also tap the dots, but doing so is a precise movement, and they're easy to miss.

- *Dock*: The Dock is the area at the bottom of the screen that contains a handful of app icons. The Dock stays in place as you swipe among the Home screen pages that contain apps and folders, giving you quick access to your most-used apps. In iOS 10, the Dock appears only on the Home screen, but in iOS 11, you can display the Dock from other screens as well by performing a short swipe up from the bottom of the screen.

- *Folder icons*: You can create folders that contain multiple app icons. Folders are useful for grouping related apps (such as music apps or productivity apps) or simply for reducing clutter (such as a folder for apps you seldom use).

When the Home screen isn't displayed, you can press the Home button once to display the Home screen page you last used. Press the Home button again to display the first Home screen page that shows apps and folders.

■ **Tip** You can change the number of Home screen pages displayed. See the section "Installing and Removing Apps and Customizing the Home Screen Pages," later in this chapter, for details.

Using Cover Sheet and Notification Center

iOS includes a feature that displays an overview of the notifications waiting for your attention. In iOS 11, this feature is called Cover Sheet, whereas in iOS 10 and earlier iOS versions it's called Notification Center. Apart from the name, there are small differences, but Cover Sheet and Notification Center largely work the same way.

You can open Cover Sheet or Notification Center by swiping down from the top of the Home screen, the lock screen, or many app screens (some apps block opening Cover Sheet or Notification Center). Figure 3-6 shows Cover Sheet in iOS 11.

■ **Tip** You can also open Cover Sheet or Notification Center by swiping left in Today View.

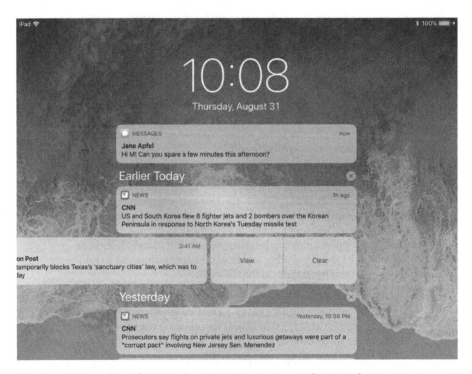

Figure 3-6. *Cover Sheet (in iOS 11) and Notification Center (in iOS 10) give you an overview of the notifications awaiting your attention. You can swipe a notification to the left to display the View button and the Clear button*

You can take the following actions in Notification Center:

- *Clear a category of notifications*: Tap the X button to the right of a category such as Earlier Today or Yesterday.

- *Clear a notification*: Swipe the notification to the left, and then tap the Clear button that appears.

- *View a notification in the app that raised it*: Tap the notification. You can also swipe the notification left and then tap the View button, but this method has no advantage over simply tapping the notification.

- *Search your notifications*: In Notification Center, tap the Search field at the top of the screen, and then type your search term. As of this writing, Cover Sheet doesn't provide search functionality.

- *Display Today View*: Swipe right on Cover Sheet or Notification Center to display Today View.

Using Control Center

Control Center is a feature that provides quick access to some of the most important controls. Control Center is substantially different in iOS 11 than in iOS 10, so I'll cover the two iOS versions separately.

Using Control Center in iOS 11

In iOS 11, Control Center consists of a single group of controls that appear on the right side of the screen when you swipe up from the bottom of the screen. When you swipe up, the Dock appears first; when you swipe further, Control Center appears, together with a thumbnail for each app that's running. Figure 3-7 shows Control Center in iOS 11 with labels.

■ **Note**   Swiping up from the bottom of the lock screen displays only Control Center, not the Dock nor the app thumbnails.

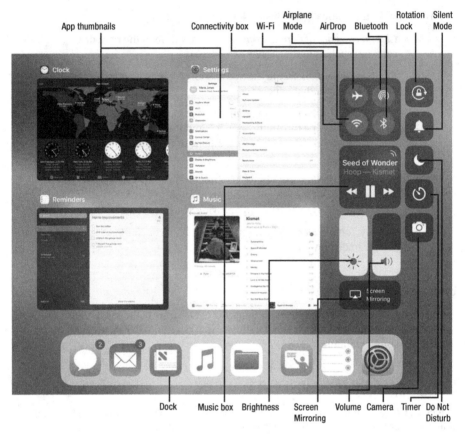

Figure 3-7. *In iOS 11, Control Center consists of a single group of controls on the right side of the screen*

The following list explains the controls in Control Center in iOS 11:

- *Airplane Mode*: Tap this button to enable or disable Airplane Mode. Enabling Airplane Mode disables Wi-Fi, Bluetooth, and (on cellular iPad models) cellular connectivity.

- *Wi-Fi*: Tap this button to enable or disable Wi-Fi.

- *AirDrop*: Tap this button to change the status of AirDrop, the feature for quickly transferring files wirelessly between computers and devices. In the dialog that opens, tap the Receiving Off button, the Contacts Only button, or the Everyone button, as needed.

■ **Note**   On a cellular-and–Wi-Fi iPad, the Cellular Data icon appears in place of the AirDrop icon. To reach the AirDrop icon, press and hold the Connectivity box until it expands.

- *Bluetooth*: Tap this button to enable or disable Bluetooth.

- *Rotation Lock*: Tap this button to enable or disable Rotation Lock, which prevents the iPad's screen from rotating to match the device's orientation.

- *Silent Mode*: Tap this button to turn on Silent Mode, muting sound; tap again to turn off Silent Mode.

- *Do Not Disturb*: Tap this button to enable or disable the Do Not Disturb feature, which helps you minimize interruptions.

- *Timer*: Tap this button to display the Timer feature in the Clock app.

- *Camera*: Tap this button to go directly to the Camera app.

- *Brightness*: Drag this slider up to decrease the screen's brightness or down to increase it.

- *Volume*: Drag this slider up to increase the volume or down to decrease it. You may find the physical Volume Up button and Volume Down button on the right side of the iPad easier for quick use.

- *Screen Mirroring*: Tap this button to display the Screen Mirroring dialog, and then tap the Apple TV on which you want to mirror the iPad's screen.

To reach some other features, you need to tap and hold some of the controls that appear at first:

- *Connectivity box*: Tap and hold this box to expand it, showing further controls on a cellular iPad (see the left screen in Figure 3-8):

  - *AirDrop*: On a cellular-and–Wi-Fi iPad, the AirDrop icon appears in the expanded Connectivity box.

  - *Personal Hotspot*: Tap this icon to enable or disable Personal Hotspot, the feature that enables you to share your iPad's cellular Internet connection with other devices and computers.

Figure 3-8. *Tap and hold the Connectivity box to display extra controls on a cellular-and-Wi-Fi iPad (left). On any iPad, tap and hold the Music box to display extra controls (center), or tap and hold the Brightness slider to display the Night Shift icon (right)*

- *Music box*: Tap and hold this box to expand it, showing extra controls (see the center screen in Figure 3-8):

  - *CD artwork*: Tap this button or the current item's details to jump to the Now Playing screen in the Music app.

  - *Current item*: Tap the details to jump to the Now Playing screen in the Music app.

  - *AirPlay*: Tap the icon to the right of the song name to open the AirPlay dialog. You can then tap the device to which you want to play audio. The device list shows the iPad at the top of the list, followed by the AirPlay-capable devices on the network to which the iPad is connected.

  - *Playhead*: Drag the white dot along the timeline to move quickly through the audio.

- *Previous*: Tap this button once to go to the beginning of the current song. Tap again to go to the beginning of the previous song. Tap and hold the button to "scrub" backward through the song.

- *Pause*: Tap this button to pause playback. Tap the Play button (which replaces the Pause button) to restart playback.

- *Next*: Tap this button to go to the beginning of the next song. Tap and hold the button to scrub forward through the song.

- *Brightness*: Tap and hold the Brightness slider until it expands to display the Night Shift button (see the right screen in Figure 3-8). You can then tap the Night Shift button to toggle the Night Shift feature on or off. Night Shift automatically reduces the amount of blue light the iPad's screen outputs in the evening, because blue light may make it hard for users to sleep.

■ **Note**   Tap and hold the Timer button to display a pop-up bar of frequently used timings and a Start button that you can use to set a timer quickly. Tap and hold the Camera button to display the Camera dialog, which contains the Take Selfie button, the Record Video button, the Record Slo-Mo button, and the Take Photo button for quick photos and recording. Tap and hold the Volume slider to display a larger version of the slider, which gives you finer control.

If you've expanded one of the controls, tap outside it or press the Home button to return to Control Center. You can then tap blank space on the screen or press the Home button again to display the Home screen, or tap an app's thumbnail to display that app.

Using Control Center in iOS 10

In iOS 10, Control Center consists of two panels called *cards*: the iPad Controls card and the Now Playing card. You can swipe left or right to move from one card to the other.

Swipe up from the bottom of the screen to open Control Center. Normally, the iPad Controls card appears at first (see Figure 3-9); if the Now Playing card appears instead, swipe right on it to display the iPad Controls card.

Airplane Mode Wi-Fi Bluetooth Do Not Disturb Sound Orientation Lock Brightness

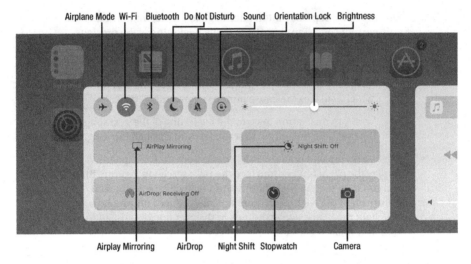

Airplay Mirroring   AirDrop   Night Shift Stopwatch   Camera

Figure 3-9. *In iOS 10, the iPad Controls card in Control Center gives you instant access to features such as Airplane Mode, Wi-Fi, AirPlay Mirroring, Night Shift, and AirDrop*

The following list explains the controls on the iPad Controls card:

- *Airplane Mode*: Tap this button to enable or disable Airplane Mode. Enabling Airplane Mode disables Wi-Fi, Bluetooth, and (on cellular iPad models) cellular connectivity.

- *Wi-Fi*: Tap this button to enable or disable Wi-Fi.

- *Bluetooth*: Tap this button to enable or disable Bluetooth.

- *Do Not Disturb*: Tap this button to enable or disable the Do Not Disturb feature, which helps you minimize interruptions.

- *Sound*: Tap this button to mute sound or to enable it.

- *Orientation Lock*: Tap this button to enable or disable Orientation Lock, which prevents the iPad's screen from rotating to match the device's orientation.

- *Brightness*: Drag this slider left to decrease the screen's brightness or right to increase it.

- *AirPlay Mirroring*: Tap this button to display the AirPlay dialog, and then tap the Apple TV or other AirPlay device on which you want to mirror the iPad's screen.

- *AirDrop*: Tap this button to change the status of AirDrop, the feature for quickly transferring files wirelessly between computers and devices. In the dialog that opens, tap the Receiving Off button, the Contacts Only button, or the Everyone button, as needed.

- *Night Shift*: Tap this button to toggle the Night Shift feature on or off. Night Shift automatically reduces the amount of blue light the iPad's screen outputs in the evening, because blue light may make it hard for users to sleep.

- *Stopwatch*: Tap this button to display the Stopwatch feature in the Clock app.

- *Camera*: Tap this button to go directly to the Camera app.

The Now Playing card (see Figure 3-10) contains controls for managing the playback of music and other audio:

- *CD artwork*: Tap this button or the current item's details to jump to the Now Playing screen in the Music app.

- *Current item*: Tap the details to jump to the Now Playing screen in the Music app.

- *Device list*: Tap the device on which you want to play audio. The device list shows the iPad at the top of the list, followed by the AirPlay-capable devices on the network to which the iPad is connected.

- *Current device*: The check mark indicates the device through which the iPad is playing audio.

- *Playhead*: Drag the white dot along the timeline to move quickly through the audio.

- *Previous*: Tap this button once to go to the beginning of the current song. Tap again to go to the beginning of the previous song. Tap and hold the button to "scrub" backward through the song.

- *Volume*: Drag this slider to set the volume. You may find the physical Volume Up button and Volume Down button on the right side of the iPad easier for quick use.

- *Pause*: Tap this button to pause playback. Tap the Play button (which replaces the Pause button) to restart playback.

- *Next*: Tap this button to go to the beginning of the next song. Tap and hold the button to scrub forward through the song.

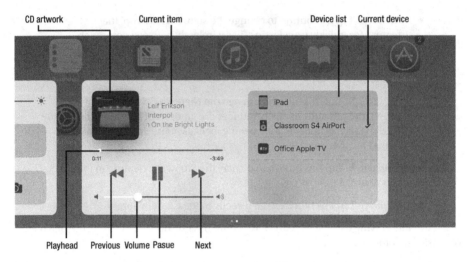

Figure 3-10. *In iOS 10, the Now Playing card in Control Center enables you to control audio playback, including selecting the output device*

When you finish using Control Center, you can close it in either of these two ways:

- *Tap the screen above Control Center*: This is usually the easiest way to close Control Center.

- *Swipe Control Center down*: Tap the top of the current card and swipe it down to the bottom of the screen.

Using Today View

Today View presents an overview of current information, such as the weather, calendar appointments and reminders, and news. You can edit the selection of items in Today View.

■ **Note** In iOS 11, Today View has a single column, whereas in iOS 10, Today View has two columns. Apart from this difference, the feature works almost the same on the two iOS versions.

To open Today View, swipe right from either the first Home screen page that contains apps or from the lock screen. The Today View screen appears (see Figure 3-11, which shows iOS 11). You can then take the following actions:

- *Expand a widget*: Tap the Show More button on a widget to expand the widget, showing more information. For example, tap the Show More button on the News widget to display more news headlines.

- *Go to an app*: Tap the app's widget. For example, tap the Calendar widget to display the Calendar app. You can also tap an app's icon in the Siri App Suggestions box. If the iPad is locked, you'll need to unlock it using Touch ID or your passcode.

Figure 3-11. *Today View gives you an overview of current information, including your calendar events and your reminders*

- *Mark a reminder as complete*: Tap the reminder's selection circle to mark the reminder as complete.

- *Search for information*: Tap in the Search box at the top of the screen and type your search term.

- *Change the items on the Today View screen*: Tap the Edit button near the bottom of the screen. The Add Widgets screen appears (see Figure 3-12), which enables you to add widgets (tap the green + button to the left of a widget), remove widgets (tap the red minus button to the left of a widget, and then tap the Remove button to its right), and change the order of widgets (drag a widget by the three-line handle). Tap the Done button when you finish editing Today View.

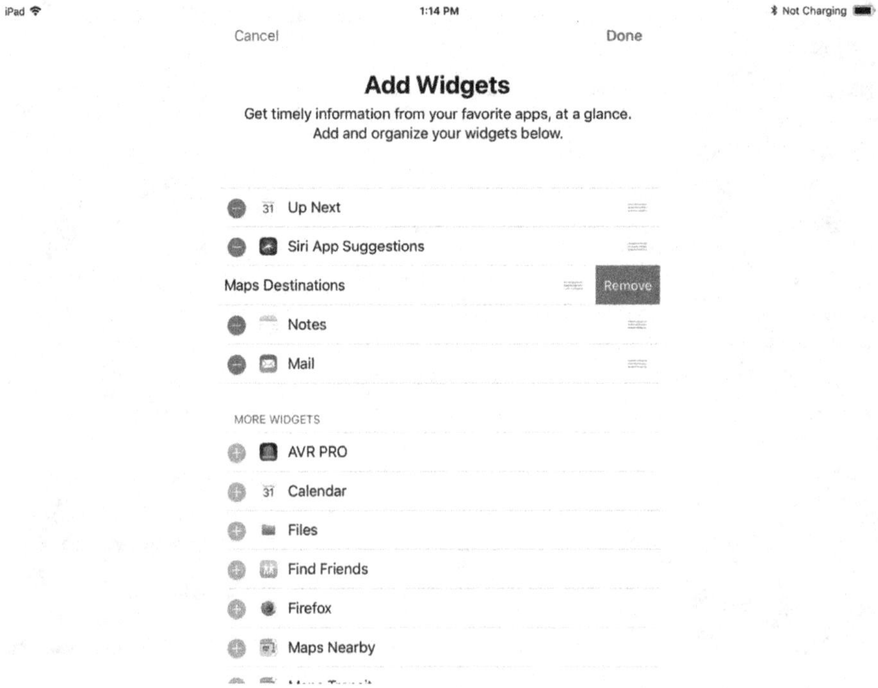

Figure 3-12. *Use the Add Widgets screen to add or remove widgets in Today View and change the order of the widgets displayed*

To return from Today View to the Home screen or the lock screen, swipe left. If the iPad is unlocked, you can also press the Home button.

Launching Apps

Launching an app is straightforward:

1. Press the Home button to display the Home screen. The iPad displays whichever Home screen page you last used; if this isn't the first Home screen page that contains apps, you can press the Home button again to display the first page.

2. If the app's icon doesn't appear on the Home screen page you're currently viewing, swipe left or right until you reach the right Home screen page.

3. Tap the app's icon.

Switching Among Running Apps

The iPad enables you to switch quickly among running apps by swiping, using the App Switcher, or using the Home screen. Swiping and using the Home screen work in the same way on iOS 11 and iOS 10, but the App Switcher is substantially different in iOS 11 than in earlier iOS versions.

Swiping Between Apps

To swipe between apps, swipe left or right with four or five fingers to display the next app in that direction. This works only if multitasking gestures are enabled on the iPad; see the nearby sidebar "Enabling and Using Multitasking Gestures" for instructions on enabling them.

ENABLING AND USING MULTITASKING GESTURES

To enable multitasking gestures, press the Home button, tap the Settings icon, tap the General button, and then tap the Multitasking button. On the Multitasking screen, set the Gestures switch to On.

Once you've done that, you can use these three multitasking gestures:

- *Display the Home screen:* Pinch inward with four or five fingers.

- *Swipe between apps:* Swipe left or right with four or five fingers.

- *Display the App Switcher:* Swipe up with four or five fingers.

Using the App Switcher in iOS 11

Here's how to use the App Switcher in iOS 11:

1. Swipe up from the bottom of the screen or double-click the Home button. The Dock, Control Center, and the App Switcher appear (see Figure 3-13).

Figure 3-13. *In iOS 11, the Dock, Control Center, and App Switcher appear together. Tap the thumbnail for the app you want to display*

2. If necessary, swipe right to display other app thumbnails.

3. Tap the thumbnail for the app you want to display.

Using the App Switcher in iOS 10

Here's how you use the App Switcher in iOS 10:

1. Swipe up from the bottom of the screen with four or five fingers, or double-click the Home button. The App Switcher screen appears, showing the Home screen and the running apps as large thumbnails on a carousel (see Figure 3-14). The Home screen appears on the right, with the app you were just using immediately to its left, and your previous apps to the left of that app.

Figure 3-14. *In iOS 10, the App Switcher appears as a carousel of large thumbnails, with the Home screen on the right*

2. If necessary, swipe right until you can see the thumbnail for the app you want to switch to.

3. Tap the app's thumbnail. The app appears, and you can resume work in it.

Switching Apps via the Home Screen

To switch apps via the Home screen, use the same technique as when launching the app: press the Home button to display the Home screen, navigate to the Home screen page that contains the app's icon, and then tap the app's icon.

Closing an App

On the iPad, you don't normally need to close apps—you can just leave them running until you need them again. iOS manages memory efficiently, automatically reclaiming memory from apps that you haven't used for a while so that there's enough memory for the apps you're currently using and for other apps that you launch.

However, if an app stops responding, or if you actively want to close it for another reason, you can easily do so. Follow these steps:

1. Display the App Switcher by swiping up from the bottom of the screen, using one finger in iOS 11 or four or five fingers in iOS 10, or by double-clicking the Home button.

2. Swipe right until you can see the thumbnail for the app you want to close.

3. Swipe the app up off the App Switcher carousel.

Searching with Search

The iPad's Search feature enables you to locate information either on the iPad itself or on the Internet. You can customize Search to narrow down the results it delivers.

■ **Note**   In iOS 11, the search feature's name is Search, whereas in iOS 10 and earlier versions, the search feature's name is Spotlight Search.

To display the Search field, press the Home button to display the Home screen, and then draw your finger a short way down the screen, either on open space or on an icon. The Search field appears (see Figure 3-15), together with the Siri App Suggestions box (by default) and the keyboard.

Figure 3-15. *Draw your finger a short way down the Home screen to display the Search field*

Start typing your search term or terms. Results appear you type (see Figure 3-16), and you can scroll down if necessary to see more. You can tap a result to display that item in an app that can open it, or you can tap the Search Web button, the Search App Store button, or the Search Maps button at the bottom of the screen to search in another location. Tap the Cancel button if you decide to cancel the search instead.

Figure 3-16. *Type your search term or terms, and then tap the search result you want to view*

Controlling Where Search Searches in iOS 11

To control where Search searches in iOS 11, choose Settings ➤ Siri & Search and choose settings on the Siri & Search screen (see Figure 3-17). The following list explains your choices:

- *Suggestions in Search*: Set this switch to Off if you don't want the Siri App Suggestions box to appear under the Search field.

- *Suggestions in Look Up*: Set this switch to Off if you don't want the Siri Knowledge box to appear when you use the Look Up feature (where you tap and hold a word and then tap the Look Up button on a command bar to display information about the word).

- *Apps list*: Tap the app you want to affect, and then set the Search & Siri Suggestions switch on the resulting screen to On if you want the app to appear in search results or to Off if you don't want it to appear.

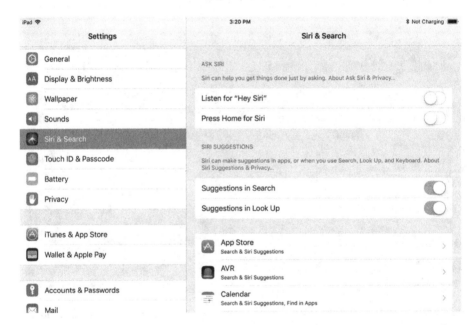

Figure 3-17. *In iOS 11, set the Suggestions in Search switch and the Suggestions in Look Up switch to On or Off, as needed. Then tap the button for each app you want to affect and set the Search and Siri Suggestions switch on the resulting screen to On or Off, as needed*

Controlling Where Spotlight Search Searches in iOS 10

To control where Spotlight Search searches in iOS 10, choose Settings ➤ General ➤ Spotlight Search and choose settings on the Spotlight Search screen. The following list explains your choices:

- *Siri Suggestions*: Set this switch to Off if you don't want the Siri Suggestions box to appear under the Spotlight Search field.

- *Spotlight Suggestions*: Set the Suggestions in Search switch to On if you want to see Spotlight's suggestions when you search; for example, the Suggested Website item in Figure 3-17 is a Spotlight suggestion. Set the Suggestions in Lookup switch to On if you want to see Spotlight suggestions when you give the Look Up command to look up a selected word.

- *Search Results*: In this box, set the switch to Off for each app for which you don't want to see Spotlight results.

Multitasking

The iPad enables you to display two apps on screen at the same time, which Apple calls *multitasking*. Most recent iPad models offer three types of multitasking:

- *Slide Over*: Slide Over works differently in iOS 11 from iOS 10:

  - *iOS 11*: With an app displayed (not the Home screen), swipe up from the bottom of the screen to display the Dock. Tap and hold the icon for the app you want to open in Slide Over view and then drag upward. When the icon expands (see the Messages panel in Figure 3-18), release it, and it moves to the right side of the screen in Slide Over view (see Figure 3-19). The window is floating, and you can drag it by the top handle (the short horizontal gray bar) to the left side of the screen if you want.

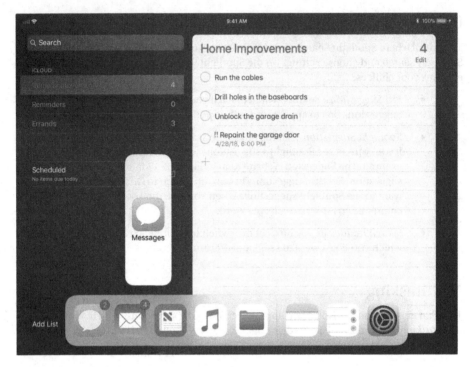

Figure 3-18. In iOS 11, swipe up to display the Dock, and then tap and hold the icon for the app you want to open and drag it upward. When the icon expands, like the Messages icon here, lift your finger

Figure 3-19. *The app you dragged appears in Slide Over view on the right side of the screen*

- *iOS 10*: Swipe left from the right side of the screen to open the app you were using previously. Figure 3-20 shows an example with the Word app in the main part of the screen, dimmed because it's not active, and the Notes app displayed on the right side. To display a different app, swipe down on the gray handle at the top of the right pane, and then tap the appropriate app in the list of apps that appears.

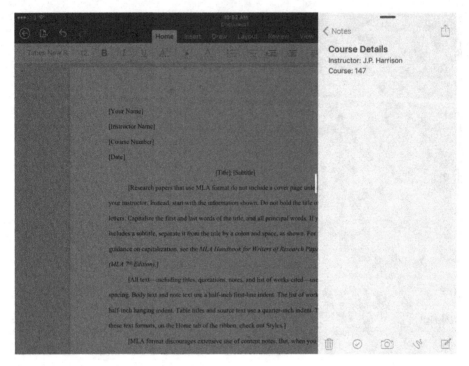

Figure 3-20. *Swipe left from the right side of the screen to display your previous app in Slide Over view. You can then change the app by swiping down the handle at the top and then tapping the app you want*

■ **Note**   The key difference between Slide Over and Split View is that Slide Over is designed to enable you to work quickly with another app (such as your previous app), whereas Split View enables you to work in two apps at the same time.

- *Split View*: After opening the apps you want in Slide Over, you can switch them to Split view, dividing the screen between them. In iOS 11, drag the top handle (the short horizontal gray bar) down a short way, and the Slide Over app switches to Split view. You can then drag the handle on the vertical bar, dividing the apps to adjust the amount of space each app has. In iOS 10, simply drag the handle on the vertical bar dividing the apps left to the middle of the screen. Both apps become active, and you can work in either app by tapping in it (see Figure 3-21). Drag the handle all the way to the left or to the right when you want to return to a single app.

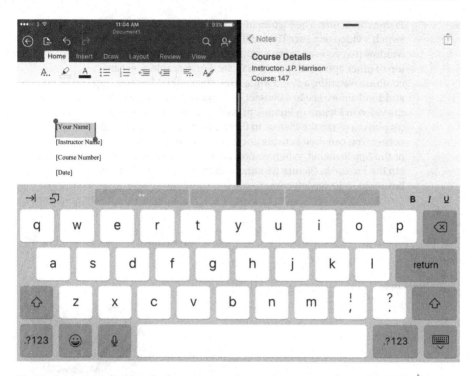

Figure 3-21. *In Split View, both apps are active, and you can work in either of them by tapping the app you want to work in*

■ **Note**   Split View is available only with some apps. Apps such as Settings don't support Split View.

■ **Tip**   Safari has a couple of shortcuts to Split View, enabling you to view two web pages side by side. Open Safari from the Home screen as usual. On the touchscreen, tap and hold the Tabs button to display the pop-up menu, and then tap Open Split View to open a new Safari window side by side with the existing window. On a hardware keyboard, press Cmd-N to open a new window in Split View. When you want to leave Split View, tap and hold the Tabs button, and then tap Merge All Tabs on the pop-up menu.

- *Picture in Picture*: The Picture in Picture view enables you to switch a video or a FaceTime call from full screen to a small window that you can move around the screen and that stays on top of other apps you open or activate. For example, you can continue watching a video while you activate the Messages app and send a message to a contact (see Figure 3-22). To switch the video to Picture in Picture, press the Home button while it's playing or tap the Picture in Picture button in its lower-right corner. You can then activate another app from the Home screen or the App Switcher. When you're ready to return to the video, tap the Picture in Picture window, and then tap the Full Screen button in its lower-left corner.

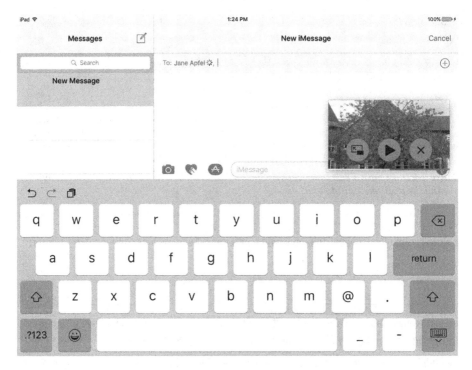

Figure 3-22. *The Picture in Picture view enables you to shrink down a video or a FaceTime call to a small window that stays on top of other apps and that you can move around the screen as needed*

■ **Note** Depending on the tasks you or your students are trying to perform, multitasking can be highly useful. When you're creating content, the on-screen keyboard takes up about half the screen, greatly reducing the amount you can see of each app—often enough to make multitasking less efficient than switching back and forth between full-screen apps. But if you're using a hardware keyboard instead of the on-screen keyboard, you can see enough of each app to make multitasking effective.

Connecting to Wi-Fi Networks

Normally, you'll configure a connection to a Wi-Fi network during setup, unless you're setting up a cellular-capable iPad and choose to use the cellular connection instead. You can configure other Wi-Fi networks afterward either directly on the iPad or by using profiles, as discussed in Chapter 4.

Setting Up Another Wi-Fi Network Manually

To set up a Wi-Fi network manually, you work on the Wi-Fi screen in the Settings app. You can connect either to a network that broadcasts its network name or to one that doesn't. The following subsections explain how to connect to each type of network in turn.

UNDERSTANDING SSIDS AND OPEN AND CLOSED WI-FI NETWORKS

Each Wi-Fi network has a name that identifies it. The name is formally known as a *service set identifier*, abbreviated to SSID. The name can be up to 32 characters or 32 bytes long. The characters can include upper- and lowercase letters (including spaces), numbers, and symbols (such as underscores or periods). An SSID is case sensitive, so School_AP1 is different from SCHOOL_AP1.

Most wireless access points come with default names that identify the device's manufacturer or the company that supplies it. If you're setting up the Wi-Fi network, you'll do best to give each wireless access point a name that makes sense for your school or institution so that staff and students can instantly tell whether a particular Wi-Fi network is part of the school or not. Unless your school's buildings are surrounded by open space, it's likely that some Wi-Fi networks from neighboring buildings will reach into your school's buildings. (Similarly, neighboring buildings will be able to see any of your school's wireless networks that reach beyond its grounds.)

A Wi-Fi network can be either open or closed. An *open* Wi-Fi network is one that broadcasts its SSID for all to see; any Wi-Fi–capable device within range will detect the network and can attempt to connect to it. By contrast, a *closed* Wi-Fi network doesn't broadcast its SSID, and anyone trying to connect a device to it must type in the correct SSID on the device.

At first sight, preventing a network from broadcasting its SSID appears a reasonable security measure. But because Wi-Fi scanning apps and devices can detect the SSID of even a closed network, closing a network works only to deter casual access. Anyone with a scanning app (which you can get for free) or device can learn the SSID in seconds and can then try to connect to the network. In most cases, it's best to create open Wi-Fi networks and implement effective security rather than create closed networks.

If you get to choose the SSIDs for your network, you need to balance several conflicting factors:

- *Readability and clarity.* Normally, you'll want to make the names readable (rather than gobbledygook) and their meanings clear. This way you'll be able to tell your colleagues and students clearly which networks they're supposed to be using.

- *Uniqueness in their context.* Each SSID should be unique so that users and devices can tell which network they're trying to connect to. Some devices assume that an SSID uniquely identifies a network. This assumption enables a malefactor to set up a malicious Wi-Fi hotspot that uses the same name and password as a genuine hotspot nearby, causing devices to connect to the malicious hotspot instead of the genuine one. (The malicious hotspot can capture information from the devices that connect to it.)

- *Security.* The Wi-Fi router uses the SSID, together with the security method you choose, to encrypt the information it transmits. So, technically it's better to choose a longer and more complex name than a short name.

Displaying the Wi-Fi Screen in the Settings App

1. To get started, choose Settings ➤ Wi-Fi from the Home screen to the Wi-Fi screen. Figure 3-23 shows the Wi-Fi screen without a connection yet established.

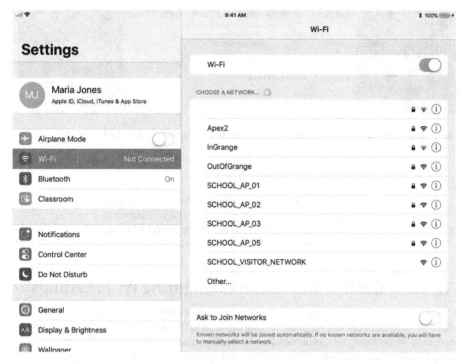

Figure 3-23. *From the Wi-Fi screen in the Settings app, you can connect the iPad to a Wi-Fi network manually*

Connecting to an Open Wi-Fi Network

If the Wi-Fi network to which you want to connect the iPad is open (broadcasting its SSID), follow these steps to connect:

1. In the Choose a Network box on the Wi-Fi screen, tap the button for the appropriate Wi-Fi network. The Enter Password dialog opens (see Figure 3-24).

■ **Note**　If the Wi-Fi network has no security set, the iPad connects to the network without prompting you for the password.

Figure 3-24. *In the Enter Password dialog, type the password for the Wi-Fi network and tap the Join button*

2. Type the password in the Password field.

3. Tap the Join button. The iPad connects to the Wi-Fi network, and the network's name appears both on the Wi-Fi button in the left column and on a button at the top of the Wi-Fi screen, under the button that contains the Wi-Fi switch.

Checking the IP Address and Configuring Wi-Fi Settings

If the Wi-Fi network uses Dynamic Host Configuration Protocol (DHCP) to allocate IP addresses and network settings, connecting the iPad to the network as explained in the preceding section may be all you need to do. But if you need to check the IP address, subnet mask, router address, or DNS server addresses, tap the Information (i) button at the right end of the Wi-Fi network's button to display the Information screen. This screen is different in iOS 11 and iOS 11. The following sections explain the iOS versions separately.

Checking the IP Address and Configuring Wi-Fi Settings on iOS 11

In iOS 11, the IP address information appears in the IPv4 Address box on the Information screen (see Figure 3-25). The IP Address button shows the IP address, such as 10.0.0.26; the Subnet Mask button shows the subnet mask, such as 255.255.255.0; and the Router button shows the address of the router used for the connection, such as 10.0.0.1. You can copy any of these details by tapping and holding the appropriate button and then tapping the Copy button that appears.

84

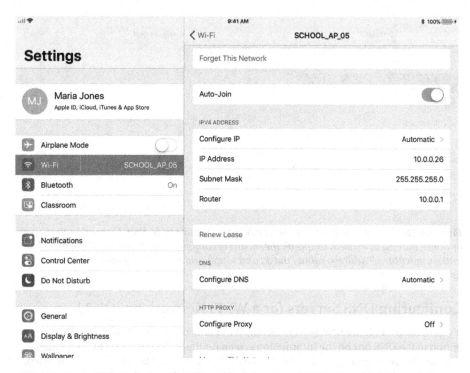

Figure 3-25. *In iOS 11, look at the IPv4 Address box on a Wi-Fi network's Information screen to see the IP address, subnet mask, and router details*

■ **Note** On iOS 11, set the Auto-Join switch near the top of the Information screen for a Wi-Fi network to On if you want the iPad to join this network automatically in the future.

---

iOS 11 normally configures Wi-Fi connections to get the IP address and connection information automatically from a DHCP server. Getting these details automatically is usually the best choice, but if you need to configure the IP details manually or set the iPad to use the BootP protocol instead, tap the Configure IP button on the Information screen and work on the Configure IPv4 screen (see Figure 3-26). For example, tap the Manual button to display the Manual IP box, and then type in the IP address, the subnet mask, and the router address.

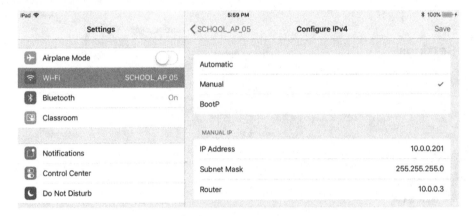

Figure 3-26. *On the Configure IPv4 screen, tap the Automatic button, Manual button, or BootP button, as needed, to specify the means of configuration. If you tap the Manual button, enter the IP address, subnet mask, and router address in the Manual IP box that appears*

Configuring DNS Servers for a Wi-Fi Network on iOS 11

If you need to configure DNS servers for this Wi-Fi network, tap the Configure DNS button in the DNS box on the Information screen for the Wi-Fi network. On the Configure DNS screen (see Figure 3-27), tap the Automatic button or the Manual button, as needed. If you tap the Manual button, use the controls in the DNS Servers box to set up the list of DNS servers:

- *Remove a DNS server*: Tap the red minus button to the left of the server, and then tap the Delete button that appears to the right of the server.

- *Add a DNS server*: Tap the Add Server button, and then type its IP address or its hostname.

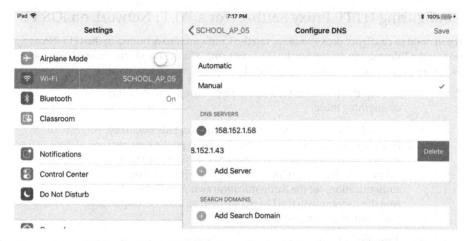

Figure 3-27. *On the Configure DNS screen in iOS 11, tap the Automatic button or the Manual button, as needed. If you tap the Manual button, configure the DNS servers in the DNS Servers box and configure any search domains needed in the Search Domains box*

If necessary, tap the Add Search Domain button to add a *search domain*—a domain name that you supply to enable iOS to convert host names to fully qualified domain names. For example, if you add the search domain notionalacademy.com to the iPad's settings, the iPad's user can access the staff.notionalacademy.com address by entering only staff, with the iPad adding the search domain automatically after the unqualified name (staff) fails to return a result.

■ **Note**   You can enter multiple search domains, separating one from another with commas. iOS uses the search domains in the order in which you enter them, so put the most important search domain first.

Tap the Save button when you finish setting up the manual configuration on the Configure DNS screen.

Configuring HTTP Proxy Settings for a Wi-Fi Network on iOS 11

If you need to configure proxy settings, tap the Configure Proxy button in the HTTP Proxy box on the Information screen for the Wi-Fi network. On the Configure Proxy screen (see Figure 3-28), tap the appropriate button and choose the settings needed:

- *Off*: Tap this button to turn off HTTP proxying. You don't need to do anything more.

- *Manual*: Tap this button to enter the proxy details manually. Fields appear for you to enter the details. Type the hostname or IP address of the proxy server in the Server field, and then type the port (such as 80) in the Port field. If the proxy server requires authentication, set the Authentication switch to On and then type the username in the Username field and the corresponding password in the Password field.

- *Auto*: Tap this button to use automatic proxy configuration via a Proxy Auto-Configuration file (PAC file for short). In the URL field, type the address at which the iPad will find the PAC file.

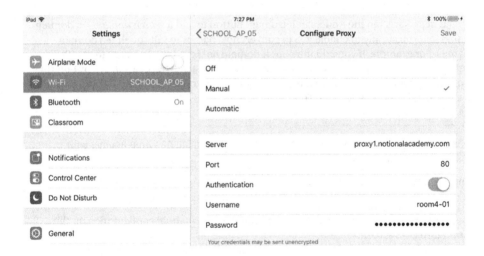

Figure 3-28. *On the Configure Proxy screen in iOS 11, tap the Off button, the Manual button, or the Automatic button, as needed. If you tap the Manual button, enter the server, port, and authentication (if necessary). If you tap the Automatic button, enter the URL for the Proxy Auto-Configuration file*

Checking the IP Address and Configuring Wi-Fi Settings on iOS 10

On iOS 10, the Information screen for a Wi-Fi network has three tabs: the DHCP tab, BootP tab, and Static tab. Normally, the DHCP tab (see Figure 3-29) appears first.

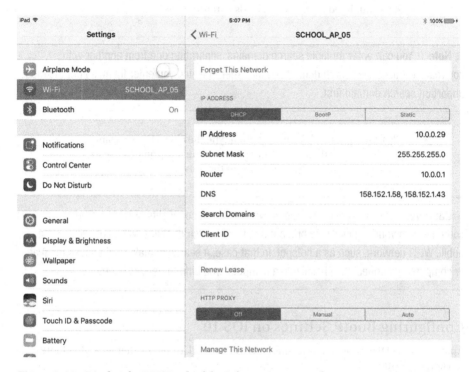

Figure 3-29. *Display the DHCP tab of the Information screen for a Wi-Fi network when you want to check the IP address, subnet mask, router address, or DNS server addresses*

On the DHCP tab, you can't change the IP address, subnet mask, or router, because this information is set automatically. However, you can change the DNS server addresses, and you can add search domains and a client ID if necessary. Here's what you need to know:

- *DNS*: Tap this field to make it editable, and then edit the existing information or delete it and type new information, as needed. Normally, you'll want to provide the addresses of two DNS servers, the primary DNS server and the secondary DNS server, separating the two with a comma. You can enter the DNS server addresses either as IP addresses (as in the example) or as hostnames.

89

- *Search Domains*: A search domain is a domain name that you supply to enable iOS to convert host names to fully qualified domain names. For example, if you add the search domain notionalacademy.com to the iPad's settings, the iPad's user can access the staff.notionalacademy.com address by entering only staff, with the iPad adding the search domain automatically after the unqualified name (staff) fails to return a result.

■ **Note**   You can enter multiple search domains, separating one from another with commas. iOS uses the search domains in the order in which you enter them, so put the most important search domain first.

- *Client ID*: Tap this button, and then type the client ID you want to assign to the iPad. The client ID is a name that you can use to make each iPad easier to identify on the network.

■ **Caution**   Search domains can be convenient when connecting iPads (or other computers) to your school's network, but don't use search domains when connecting to a public Wi-Fi network, such as a hotspot. In that case, a search domain might cause the iPad or computer to connect accidentally to a computer you didn't intend to access.

Configuring BootP Settings on iOS 10

Apart from the DHCP tab, the screen for a Wi-Fi network has two other tabs: the BootP tab and the Static tab.

BootP is short for Bootstrap Protocol, a protocol for assigning IP addresses automatically to network devices. BootP can perform a similar role to DHCP, which is newer, but BootP can also direct a client to load an operating system image across the network from a server, which DHCP can't. BootP can communicate with a device only while that device is starting, whereas DHCP can communicate with a device both during startup and after it.

■ **Note**   You can't use BootP to load an operating system image on an iPad or other iOS device across the network.

If your Wi-Fi network uses BootP to provide IP addresses, tap the BootP tab on the information screen for the network to view the IP address, subnet mask, router address, and DNS server addresses. Figure 3-30 shows the BootP tab of the information screen.

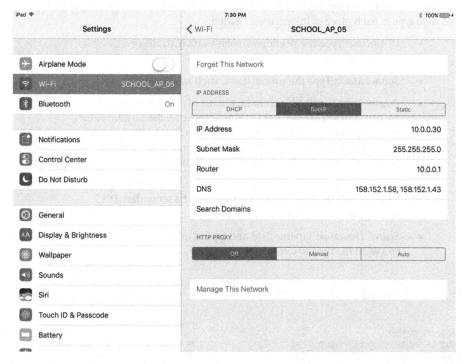

Figure 3-30. *On the BootP tab Wi-Fi networks:IP Address and configuration, iOS 10: of the information screen for a Wi-Fi network, you can see the IP address, subnet mask, router address, and DNS server addresses. You can edit the DNS server addresses if necessary; you can also add search domains*

You can make two changes on the BootP tab:

- *DNS*: Tap this field to make it editable, and then edit the existing addresses or type new addresses, as necessary. Put the address or hostname of the primary DNS server first, followed by a comma and the address or hostname of the secondary DNS server.

- *Search Domains*: Tap this field and type in any search domains you want the iPad to use.

Configuring Static IP Settings on iOS 10

Instead of having an iPad get its IP address and network settings from a DHCP server or a BootP server, you can set the iPad to use a static IP address and network settings. To do so, tap the Static tab on the information screen to display its contents (see Figure 3-31), and then type in each piece of information needed:

- *IP Address*: Type the IP address, such as 10.0.0.101 or 192.168.1.200.

- *Subnet Mask*: Type the subnet mask, such as 255.255.255.0.

- *Router*: Type the IP address or hostname of the router, such as 10.0.0.1 or wireless1.notionalacademy.com; the hostname can be only partially qualified if you include the appropriate search domain in the Search Domains field, but usually it's better to include the fully qualified address in the Router field.

- *DNS*: Type the IP address or hostname of the primary DNS server, followed by the IP address or hostname of the secondary DNS server, separating them with a comma.

- *Search Domains*: Tap this field and type in any search domains you want the iPad to use.

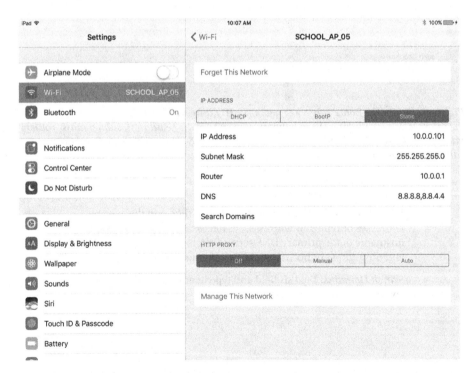

Figure 3-31. *On the Static tab of the information screen for a Wi-Fi network, you can set a static IP address and other network parameters by typing in the details*

Configuring HTTP Proxy Settings on iOS 10

From the information screen for a Wi-Fi network, you can also configure HTTP proxy settings for the iPad. You can either specify the proxy settings manually or enter a URL from which the iPad can automatically pick up proxy settings.

In the HTTP Proxy section of the information screen, tap the appropriate tab button and enter such information as is needed:

- *Off*: Tap this tab button to turn off HTTP proxying. As you'd imagine, you don't need to enter any information.

- *Manual*: Tap this tab button to use manual proxy setup. In the Server field (see Figure 3-32), type the hostname or IP address of the proxy server, and then type the port (such as 80) in the Port field. If the proxy server requires authentication, set the Authentication switch to On and then type the username in the Username field and the corresponding password in the Password field.

Figure 3-32. *To specify proxy settings manually, tap the Manual tab button in the HTTP Proxy section of the information screen for the appropriate Wi-Fi network, and then type in the information needed*

- *Auto*: Tap this tab button to use automatic proxy configuration via a Proxy Auto-Configuration file (PAC file for short). In the URL field (see Figure 3-33), type the address at which the iPad will find the PAC file.

Figure 3-33. *To set the iPad to use automatic proxy configuration, tap the Auto tab button in the HTTP Proxy section of the information screen, and then enter the URL at which to find the PAC file*

SETTING PROXY EXCEPTIONS FOR THE IPAD

For some network configurations, you may need to set *proxy exceptions*—addresses for which the iPad shouldn't use the proxy server.

The iPad's interface doesn't give you a way to create proxy exceptions, so you need to set the iPad to use Auto proxy configuration and point it to a PAC file that contains the exceptions along with the other proxy settings.

Connecting and Using Bluetooth Devices

The iPad includes full Bluetooth functionality, enabling you to connect a wide range of Bluetooth devices. For example, you can connect a Bluetooth keyboard to input data, a Bluetooth speaker or headset to output data, or a Bluetooth assistive device to provide enhanced accessibility for the iPad.

The first time you connect a Bluetooth device, you must pair it with the iPad. After you've paired the device, you can connect it quickly.

Pairing a Bluetooth Device

Follow these general steps to set up a Bluetooth device:

1. Turn on the Bluetooth device and put it in pairing mode. How you do this depends on the device, but it often involves either pressing a dedicated key or a sustained press (such as 10 seconds) on the master control key.

2. From the Home screen, choose Settings ➤ Bluetooth to display the Bluetooth screen.

3. Make sure the Bluetooth switch is set to On. The iPad scans for Bluetooth devices, and the Devices list shows those it has found (see Figure 3-34). This example uses a Bluetooth speaker.

Figure 3-34. *On the Bluetooth screen in Settings, set the Bluetooth switch to On, and then tap the device in the Other Devices list*

4. In the Other Devices list, tap the button for the device. The iPad attempts to connect to the device.

■ **Note**   If the Bluetooth Pairing Request dialog opens, prompting you to type a pairing code on a device such as a keyboard or another computer, type the code to confirm the pairing request.

---

5. When the iPad has connected to the device, the device appears on a button in the My Devices list with a status Connected (see Figure 3-35). You can then start using the device.

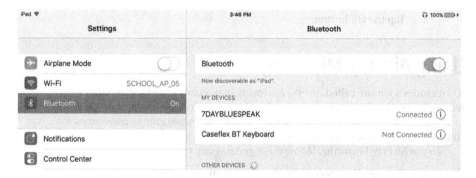

Figure 3-35. *Once connected, the device appears in the My Devices list on the Bluetooth screen*

Disconnecting and Reconnecting a Bluetooth Device

When you finish using a Bluetooth device, tap the Info (i) icon on the device's button in the My Devices list on the Bluetooth screen to display the Info screen for the device (see Figure 3-36). You can then tap the Disconnect button to disconnect the device.

Figure 3-36. *Tap the Disconnect button on the Info screen for a Bluetooth device to disconnect the device*

When you need to reconnect the device, make sure the device is powered on, and then tap its button in the My Devices list on the Bluetooth screen.

Forgetting a Bluetooth Device

When you no longer need to use a particular Bluetooth device with an iPad, tell the iPad to forget the device. To do so, follow these steps:

1. Tap the Info (i) icon on the device's button in the My Devices list on the Bluetooth screen to display the Info screen for the device.

2. Tap the Forget This Device button. The Forget dialog opens.

3. Tap the OK button.

Using AirPlay Mirroring

iOS includes a feature called AirPlay Mirroring that enables you to show what's happening on the iPad's screen on another device, such as the monitor or TV connected to an Apple TV device. AirPlay Mirroring is a popular feature among consumers for sharing content, but it can be great for classroom usage as well.

To use AirPlay Mirroring, follow these general steps:

1. Connect the Apple TV to the TV or monitor via HDMI.

2. Power on the Apple TV and the TV or monitor.

3. On the iPad, open the content you want to display. For example, open a document that you want to share with others.

4.   On the iPad, swipe up from the bottom of the screen to open
     Control Center. In iOS 10, if the Now Playing card appears
     rather than the iPad Controls card, swipe the card right to
     display the iPad Controls card.

5.   Tap the Screen Mirroring button or the AirPlay Mirroring
     button:

     •   *iOS 11*: Tap the Screen Mirroring button to display the Screen
         Mirroring dialog (shown on the left in Figure 3-37).

     •   *iOS 10*: Tap the AirPlay Mirroring button to display the
         AirPlay dialog (shown on the right in Figure 3-37).

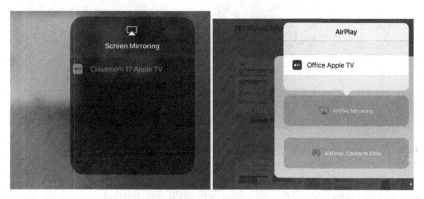

Figure 3-37.   *To mirror the iPad's screen, open Control Center. In iOS 11, tap the Screen
Mirroring button to open the Screen Mirroring dialog (left); in iOS 10, tap the AirPlay
Mirroring button on the iPad Controls card to open the AirPlay dialog (right). Then tap the
Apple TV you want to use*

6.   Tap the button for the Apple TV you want to use. The iPad's
     screen appears on the TV or monitor connected to the
     Apple TV.

When you're ready to stop mirroring the screen's contents, open Control Center,
open the Screen Mirroring dialog or the AirPlay dialog again, and then tap the Stop
Mirroring button in iOS 11 or the Turn Off AirPlay Mirroring button in iOS 10.

Transferring Files Using AirDrop

iOS and macOS include a feature called AirDrop that lets you transfer files easily between
iOS devices and Macs. AirDrop is widely viewed as a consumer-oriented feature, but it also
works well in the classroom when you need to share files with specific iPads (or their users).

Making an iOS Device or a Mac Discoverable in AirDrop

To receive files via AirDrop, you must make the iPad (or other iOS device) or the Mac discoverable in AirDrop:

- *iOS 11*: Open Control Center, tap the AirDrop button (see the left screen in Figure 3-38), and then tap the Everyone button in the AirDrop dialog that opens (see the right screen in Figure 3-38).

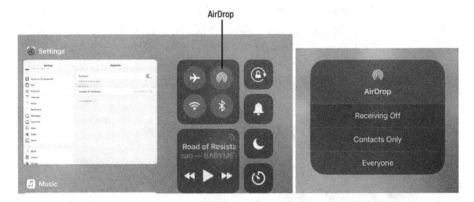

Figure 3-38. *In iOS 11, to make an iPad discoverable in AirDrop, tap the AirDrop button, and then tap Everyone in the AirDrop dialog*

- *iOS 10*: Open Control Center, swipe right to display the iPad Controls card, tap the AirDrop button, and then tap Everyone in the dialog that opens (see Figure 3-39). If you want to restrict the iPad to receiving files from contacts listed in the Contacts app, tap Contacts Only instead.

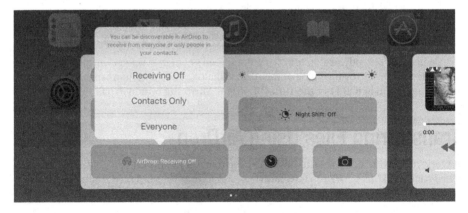

Figure 3-39. *To make an iPad discoverable in AirDrop, tap the AirDrop button on the iPad Controls card in Control Center, and then tap Everyone in the dialog that opens*

- *Mac*: Open a Finder window, or a new tab in an existing Finder window, and then click the AirDrop icon in the Favorites list in the sidebar. Open the "Allow me to be discovered by" pop-up menu, and then click Everyone or Contacts Only, as needed.

Sending and Receiving Files from an iOS Device Using AirDrop

To send a file from an iOS device using AirDrop, follow these steps:

1. Open the file you want to send. This example uses a note in the Notes app.

2. Tap the Share button, the button that shows a rectangular outline with an arrow pointing up through the top side. The Share sheet opens (see Figure 3-40).

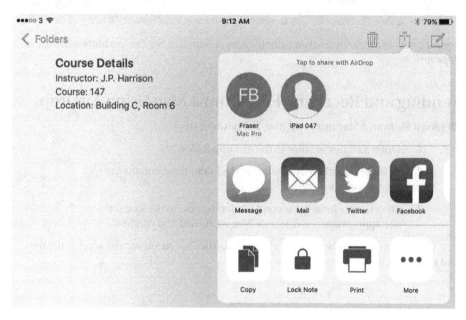

Figure 3-40. *To send a file via AirDrop, open the Share sheet and tap the icon for the destination iOS device or Mac*

3. In the "Tap to share with AirDrop" area, tap the iOS device or Mac you want to send the file to.

4. If the user of the iOS device or Mac accepts the file, AirDrop transfers it. The readout Sent then appears on the recipient's icon in the Tap to share with AirDrop area.

5. If necessary, tap another icon to send the same file to another iPad or Mac. Otherwise, tap outside the Share sheet.

When someone sends you a file, the AirDrop dialog opens (see Figure 3-41), telling you the sender's name and the item type. Tap the Accept or Decline button, as appropriate. If you accept the file, the iPad opens it in the default app for that file type (assuming there is a default app).

Figure 3-41. *In the AirDrop dialog, tap the Accept button or the Decline button, as appropriate*

Sending and Receiving Files from a Mac Using AirDrop

To send a file from a Mac using AirDrop, follow these steps:

1. Open a Finder window to the AirDrop folder.

2. Open another Finder window to the folder that contains the file you want to send.

3. Drag the file from the second Finder window to the icon for the appropriate iOS device or Mac in the AirDrop window.

When someone sends you a file via AirDrop, the Mac automatically accepts the file and stores it in the Downloads folder.

Configuring Notifications

The iPad can notify its user about many different types of events, such as incoming messages, fresh news stories, and reminders. You can control which apps can raise notifications and the style of notifications they can raise. You'll likely want to configure the Notifications settings to make sure your students aren't distracted by a barrage of irrelevant notifications.

1. To configure Notifications settings, first display the Notifications screen (see Figure 3-42) by choosing Settings ➤ Notifications from the Home screen.

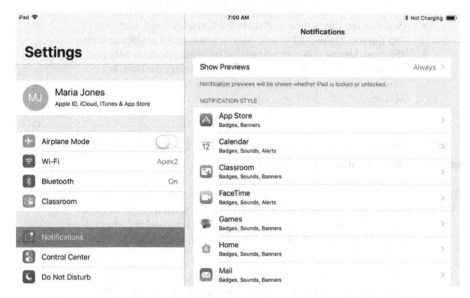

Figure 3-42. *From the Notifications screen, you can control which apps can raise notifications and which types of notifications they can raise. On iOS 11, you can choose whether to show previews of notifications*

In iOS 11, the Show Previews button appears at the top of the Notifications screen, enabling you to choose an overall setting for previews of notifications; you can then choose a different preview setting for individual apps as needed. (iOS 10 doesn't have this setting.) Tap the Show Previews button to display the Show Previews screen, and then tap the appropriate button:

- *Always*: Tap this button to show previews whether the iPad is locked or not.

- *When Unlocked*: Tap this button to show previews when the iPad is unlocked but not when it's locked.

- *Never*: Tap this button to not show previews at all.

Next, tap the button for the app whose notifications you want to configure. The screen for the app appears, such as the Messages screen (see Figure 3-43) for the Messages app. The contents of these screens vary depending on the app's features and capabilities, but the principles are the same; there are also some small differences between iOS 11 and iOS 10. These are the settings you can normally configure:

- *Allow Notifications*: Set this switch to Off if you want to prevent the app from raising notifications. All the other controls on the app's screen disappear when you do this, so you can skip the rest of the list.

- *Show in Notification Center*: [iOS 10 only] Set this switch to On to have this app's notifications appear in Notification Center.

- *Sounds*: Tap this button to display the Sounds screen, and then tap the sound the iPad should play to announce a notification for this app. Setting different sounds for different apps can help you identify important notifications aurally on your own iPad. For classroom use, you'll often want to choose None on the Sounds screen.

■ **Note** Some apps have a Sounds switch rather than a Sounds button. Set the Sounds switch to Off if you want to suppress sounds.

- *Badge App Icon*: Set this switch to On if you want the app's icon to display a badge (the red circle or rounded rectangle) showing the number of new notifications. Set this switch to Off if you want to remove this potential distraction.

- *Show on Cover Sheet*: [iOS 11 only] Set this switch to On if you want the app's notifications to be included on Cover Sheet, the screen that shows a list of notifications.

- *Show in History*: [iOS 11 only] Set this switch to On if you want the app's notifications to be included in History, the list of older notifications.

- *Show as Banners*: [iOS 11 only] Set this switch to On if you want to use either persistent banners or temporary banners (see the nearby sidebar, "Understanding the Different Alert Types," for an explanation of these banners). Then tap the Temporary icon or the Persistent icon to specify the banner type.

- *Show on Lock Screen*: [iOS 10 only] Set this switch to On if you want the app's notifications to appear on the lock screen.

- *Alert Style When Unlocked*: [iOS 10 only] In this area, choose the type of notification for the app: None, Banners, or Alerts. See the nearby sidebar, "Understanding the Different Alert Types," for an explanation of banners and alerts.

UNDERSTANDING THE DIFFERENT ALERT TYPES

iOS offers two different types of alerts, but iOS 11 uses different names for the types than iOS 10 uses. These are the two alert types:

- *Persistent banner (iOS 11), Alert (iOS 10)*: This is a panel that appears at the top of the screen and remains there until you dismiss it.

- *Temporary banner (iOS 11), Banner (iOS 10)*: This is a panel that appears at the top of the screen for a few seconds and then disappears automatically.

Normally, you'll want to use persistent banners (iOS 11) or alerts (iOS 10) only for notifications that are vital for the user see in real time.

- *Options box*: In this box, tap each button and choose settings as appropriate. The contents of this box vary depending on the app. For example, the Messages Options box contains the Show Previews button, which lets you control whether message previews appear (the settings are Always, When Unlocked, and Off), and the Repeat Alerts button, which lets you control how many times an alert reappears—at two-minute intervals—before iOS automatically suppresses it if the user doesn't.

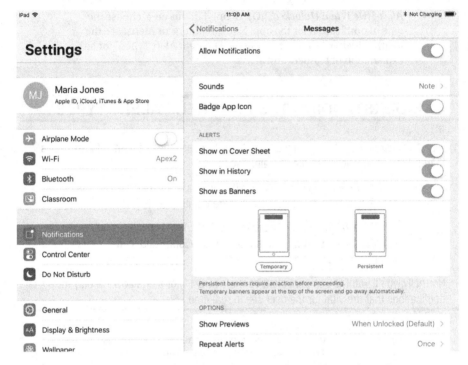

Figure 3-43. *Use the controls on an app's screen to configure that app's notifications. This screen shows iOS 11*

Configuring Do Not Disturb

The Do Not Disturb feature enables you to specify times when incoming calls and messages are silenced. You can run Do Not Disturb on a schedule, which is good for day-to-day use, but you can also enable the feature manually any time you need it.

To configure Do Not Disturb, choose Settings ➤ Do Not Disturb from the Home screen. You can then configure the following settings on the Do Not Disturb screen (see Figure 3-44):

- *Manual*: Set this switch to On to enable Do Not Disturb. Normally, it's easiest to tap the Do Not Disturb icon on the iPad Controls card in Control Center.

- *Scheduled*: To run Do Not Disturb on a schedule, set this switch to On. Tap the From/To button to display the Quiet Hours dialog. Tap the From button and set the time dials to the appropriate hour and minute for the starting time, then tap the To button and set the time dials for the ending time.

- *Allow Calls From*: To specify who (if anyone) can call when Do Not Disturb is on, tap this button to display the Allow Calls From screen, and then tap the appropriate button: Everyone, No One, All Contacts, or a particular group of contacts (such as Colleagues).

- *Repeated Calls*: Set this switch to On if you want a second FaceTime call from the same person within three minutes to ring through. Normally, you'll want to set this switch to Off. This setting is more useful on the iPhone, where you're more likely to receive important calls when Do Not Disturb is on.

- *Silence*: In this box, tap the Always button if you want Do Not Disturb to be enforced whether the iPad is locked or not. Tap the "Only while iPad is locked" button if you'll allow interruptions when Do Not Disturb is on but the iPad is unlocked (and presumably in use).

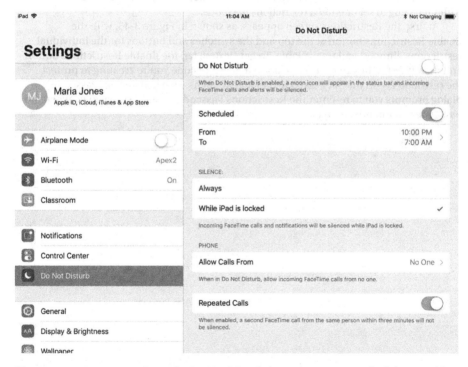

Figure 3-44. *You can configure the Do Not Disturb feature to run on a schedule or enable it manually as needed*

Setting Restrictions on What Users Can Do

iOS provides an extensive range of settings for restricting actions a user can take with an iPad. For example, you can prevent a user from using the camera, or allow use of the camera but disable FaceTime. You can prevent the user from installing or deleting apps or making in-app purchases, and you can lock down privacy settings. You create a Restrictions Passcode to prevent unauthorized changes to the restrictions.

To make the most of your school's deployment of iPads, you'll almost certainly want to understand the options available to you and—most likely—implement at least some of them.

Displaying the Restrictions Screen and Setting a Restrictions Passcode

To display the Restrictions screen, choose Settings ➤ General ➤ Restrictions from the Home screen. Until you enable restrictions, you can access the Restrictions screen without having to set or enter a restrictions passcode.

At first, the Restrictions screen appears, as shown in Figure 3-45, with the Enable Restrictions button at the top and the switches and buttons for the individual restrictions dimmed and unavailable. To get started, tap the Enable Restrictions button and then type the Restrictions Passcode—a new passcode you're creating to protect the restrictions—in the Set Passcode dialog that opens. As usual, the Set Passcode dialog prompts you to re-enter the Restrictions Passcode to make sure you've typed the passcode you intended to type.

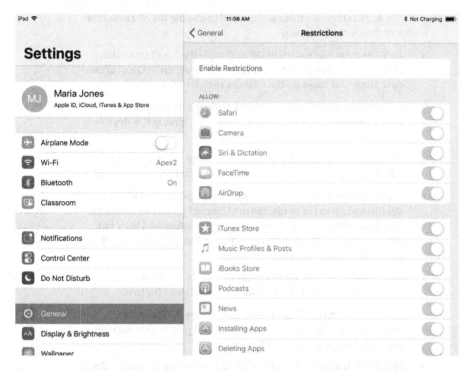

Figure 3-45. *On the Restrictions screen in the Settings app, tap the Enable Restrictions button, and then create your Restrictions Passcode in the Set Passcode dialog that opens*

Understanding and Applying Restrictions

Once you've set your Restrictions Passcode, the Restrictions screen appears again, now with all the switches and buttons enabled. You can then set the following restrictions in the Allow section at the top of the Restrictions screen:

- *Safari*: Set this switch to Off if you want to prevent the user from using Safari—for example, if you want to prevent the user from browsing the web or intend for the user to browse with a different browser.

- *Camera*: Set this switch to Off to prevent the user from using the Camera feature, either for taking photos and videos or for FaceTime and similar apps.

■ **Note**   Setting the Camera switch on the Restrictions screen to Off sets the FaceTime switch to Off—but it doesn't do so immediately, as of this writing—it only makes the change after you leave the Restrictions screen.

- *Siri & Dictation*: Set this switch to Off to disable the Siri assistant and the Dictation feature.

- *FaceTime*: Set this switch to Off to disable the FaceTime video-chat and audio-chat feature. If you set this switch to On to allow FaceTime, you must set the Camera switch to On as well.

- *AirDrop*: Set this switch to Off to disable the AirDrop feature, which provides an easy way to transfer files among iOS devices and Macs.

- *iTunes Store*: Set this switch to Off to disable the iTunes Store app, which sells music, movies, TV shows, and other media content.

- *Music Profiles & Posts (iOS 11), Apple Music Connect (iOS 10)*: Set this switch to Off to disable the Connect feature in the Music app. Connect is a feature intended to help artists and their fans connect with each other, but as of this writing, Apple appears to be phasing out Connect.

- *iBooks Store*: Set this switch to Off to disable the iBooks Store app, which sells e-books (and provides some e-books for free).

- *Podcasts*: Set this switch to Off to disable the Podcasts app, which lets the user stream, download, and play audio and video podcasts on a wide variety of topics.

- *News*: Set this switch to Off to disable the News app, which allows the user to read news stories from a range of sources.

- *Installing Apps*: Set this switch to Off to prevent the user from installing apps from the App Store. Setting this switch to Off hides the App Store app in the iPad's interface.

- *Deleting Apps*: Set this switch to Off to prevent the user from deleting apps from the iPad.

- *In-App Purchases*: Set this switch to Off to prevent the user from making purchases within apps.

In the Allowed Content section of the Restrictions screen, you can set switches to On or Off to enable or disable the following apps and features:

- *Ratings For*: Tap this button to display the Ratings For screen, and then tap the country or region whose ratings you want to use—for example, United States, Canada, or United Kingdom.

- *Music, Podcasts & News*: Tap this button to display the Music, Podcasts & News screen, and then set the Explicit switch to On or Off, as needed.

- *Movies*: Tap this button to display the Movies screen. In the Allow Movies Rated box, tap the button for the highest-rated movies you'll allow.

■ **Note**   The choices on the Movies screen and the TV Shows screen vary depending on the Ratings For setting you choose. For example, if you choose United States on the Ratings For screen, the choices on the Movies screen are Don't Allow Movies, G, PG, PG-13, R, NC-17, and Allow All Movies.

- *TV Shows*: Tap this button to display the TV Shows screen. In the Allow TV Shows Rated box, tap the button for the highest-rated TV shows you'll permit the user to watch.

- *Books*: Tap this button to display the Books screen, and then set the Explicit Sexual Content switch to Off if needed.

- *Apps*: Tap this button to display the Apps screen. In the Allow Apps Rated box, tap the button for the oldest-ranked apps you'll permit. Your choices are Don't Allow Apps, 4+, 9+, 12+, 17+, and Allow All Apps.

- *Siri*: Tap this button to display the Siri screen, and then set the two switches in the Allow box as needed. Set the Explicit Language switch to Off if you want to block any content in which iOS can detect explicit language. Set the Web Search Content switch to Off if you want to block Siri from searching Wikipedia, Bing, and Twitter.

- *Websites*: Tap this button to display the Websites screen (see Figure 3-46). In the Allowed Websites box at the top, tap the appropriate button: All Websites, Limit Adult Content, or Specific Websites Only. If you choose Specific Websites Only, the Only Allow These Websites list appears, providing a list of suggested websites and an Add a Website button. To add a website, tap the Add a Website button, enter the website's name and URL on the Add a Website screen (see Figure 3-47), and then tap the Websites button to return to the Websites screen.

■ **Note**   To view the URL for one of the suggested websites, tap its button in the Only Allow These Websites box. On the screen that appears, you can edit the website's name (in the Title field) and the URL as needed. For example, you might choose to change the Apple – Start website to point to Apple's Support area rather than to Apple's Start page. To remove one of the suggested websites, tap the Edit button in the upper-right corner of the screen, tap the red minus icon to the left of the website's name, and then tap the Delete button that appears to the right of the website's name. Tap the Done button (which replaces the Edit button in the upper-right corner) when you finish making your changes.

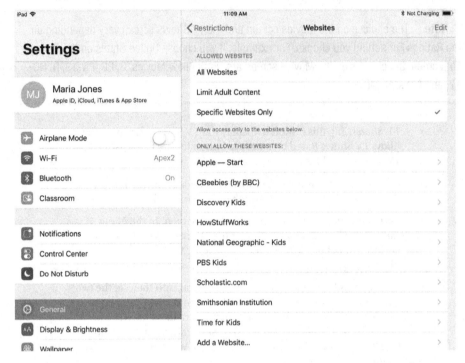

Figure 3-46. *On the Websites screen in the Settings app, you can choose among allowing the user to visit all websites, limiting sites that claim to host adult content, and restricting the user to only an approved list of websites*

Figure 3-47. *On the Add a Website screen, enter in the Title field the name you want Safari to display for the website. Type or paste the website's address in the URL field*

- *Password Settings*: Tap this button to display the Password
  Settings screen (see Figure 3-48). In the Purchases and In-App
  Purchases box, tap the Always Require button for extra security or
  the Require After 15 Minutes button if you prefer the convenience
  of being able to purchase multiple apps in a 15-minute time
  window without having to re-enter your password. In the Free
  Downloads box, set the Require Password switch to On or Off, as
  needed.

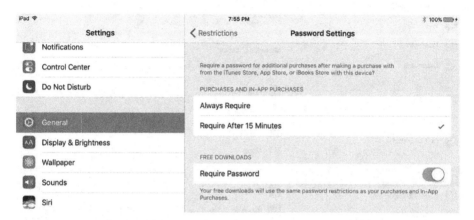

Figure 3-48. *On the Password Settings screen, choose whether to always require a password for purchases or only after 15 minutes, and whether to require a password for free downloads*

In the Privacy section of the Restrictions screen, tap the Location Services button to display the Location Services screen (see Figure 3-49). Here, you can control the following settings:

- *Allow Changes/Don't Allow Changes*: Tap the appropriate button
  to control whether the user can change Location Services settings.

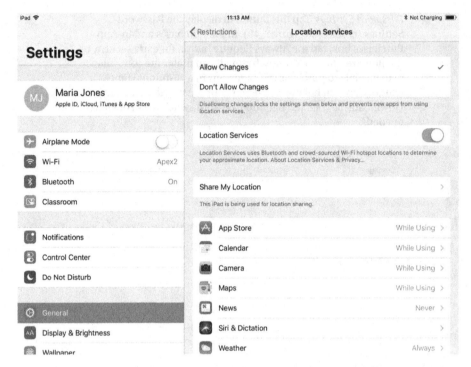

Figure 3-49. *On the Location Services screen, first tap the Allow Changes button or the Don't Allow Changes button to control whether the user can change settings for Location Services. Then set the Location Services switch and the permissions for the individual features as needed*

- *Location Services*: Set this switch to On or Off, as appropriate.

- *Share My Location*: Tap this button to display the Share My Location screen (see Figure 3-50). Set the Share My Location switch to On if you want the iPad's user to be able to share his or her location with contacts in the Messages app and the Find My Friends app, or to Off if you don't want the location to be available. If you set the Share My Location switch to On, tap the From button and make sure the right device is selected on the Share Location From screen. Normally, you'll want to select This Device here, but you can also select another iOS device—such as an iPhone—instead.

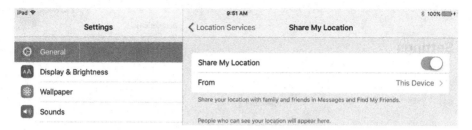

Figure 3-50. *On the Share My Location screen, set the Share My Location switch to On or Off, as needed. If you set it to On, tap the From button and then select the appropriate device on the Share Location From screen*

■ **Note**   The Share My Location switch on the Share My Location screen affects only whether iOS makes the user's location available for sharing in the Messages app and the Find My Friends app. It doesn't affect whether the Find My iPad feature in iCloud can track the iPad's location.

- *Apps and features*: Review the list of apps and features that have been granted permission to use Location Services, such as App Store, Calendar, and Camera in the example. If any app or feature appears there that you don't want to permit, tap its button to display the screen for the app or feature, and then tap the Never button instead of the When Using button.

Once you've made these changes, go back from the Location Services screen to the Restrictions screen and work your way through the buttons belong the Location Services button in the Privacy box: Contacts, Calendars, Reminders, Photos, and so on (see Figure 3-51).

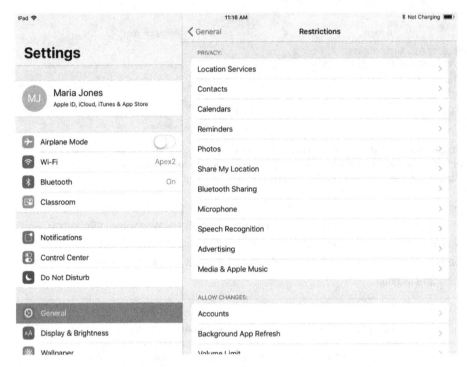

Figure 3-51. *In the Privacy box, further down the Restrictions screen in the Settings app, choose settings for Location Services and then for individual apps and features, such as Contacts, Calendars, and Reminders*

For each app or feature, tap the button to display the screen for the app or feature. For example, Figure 3-52 shows the Photos screen, which enables you to control access to the Photos app. On these screens, you can make the following changes:

- *Allow Changes/Don't Allow Changes*: Tap to select the appropriate button.

- *Apps that have requested permission to use the app or feature*: In this list, set the switch for each app to On or Off, as needed.

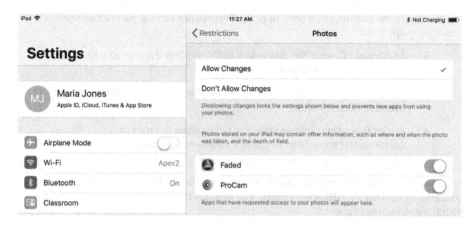

Figure 3-52. *On the Restrictions screens for apps and features, such as the Photos screen shown here, select the Allow Changes button or the Don't Allow Changes button, as needed. Then go to the list of apps and set each switch to On or Off, as needed*

In the Allow Changes section of the Restrictions screen, you can set the following restrictions:

- *Accounts*: Tap this button to display the Accounts screen, and then tap the Allow Changes button or the Don't Allow Changes button, as needed.

- *Background App Refresh*: Tap this button to display the Background App Refresh screen, and then tap the Allow Changes button or the Don't Allow Changes button, as needed.

- *Volume Limit*: Tap this button to display the Volume Limit screen, and then tap the Allow Changes button or the Don't Allow Changes button, as needed.

■ **Tip**   In many classroom situations, you'll want to enforce a volume limit lower than the iPad's maximum volume. To do so, choose Settings ➤ Music ➤ Volume Limit to display the Volume Limit screen, and then drag the Max Volume slider to set the maximum volume. Then choose Settings ➤ General ➤ Restrictions to display the Restrictions screen, tap the Volume Limit button to display the Volume Limit screen in Restrictions, and select the Don't Allow Changes button there.

- *TV Provider*: Tap this button to display the TV Provider screen, and then tap the Allow Changes button or the Don't Allow Changes button, as needed.

115

Finally, in the Game Center section of the Restrictions screen, you can set the following restrictions:

- *Multiplayer Games*: Set this switch to On to allow the user to take part in multiplayer games.

- *Adding Friends*: Set this switch to On to allow the user to add friends in Game Center.

- *Screen Recording*: Set this switch to On to allow the user to create screen recordings in Game Center—for example, to share gameplay achievements with others.

The restrictions take effect as soon as you leave the Restrictions screen—for example, by moving to a different category of settings in the Settings app or by switching to another app.

Choosing Accessibility Settings

iOS includes an impressive suite of accessibility settings designed to make the iPad, iPhone, and iPod touch easier to use for people who suffer from problems with vision, hearing, interaction and touch, or learning. Chances are, some of your students will benefit from some of the accessibility settings—which means you'll have to know about all the accessibility settings so that you can apply the ones the students need.

Displaying the Accessibility Screen

To display the Accessibility screen, choose Settings ➤ General ➤ Accessibility from the Home screen. Figure 3-53 shows the upper part of the Accessibility screen, which contains the Vision category and the Interaction category.

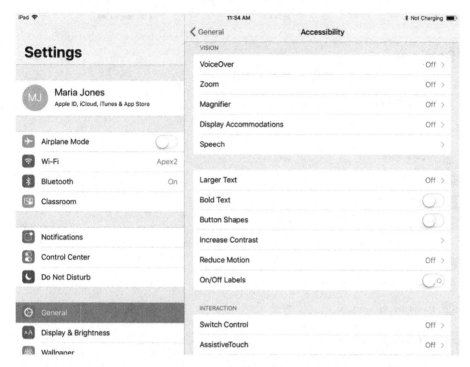

Figure 3-53. *The upper part of the Accessibility screen contains the Vision category and the Interaction category*

Configuring the VoiceOver Feature

The VoiceOver feature lets you have iOS speak the names of items on the screen, enabling those with vision problems to navigate the interface. With VoiceOver enabled, iOS's basic behavior changes: instead of tapping an item to activate it, you tap the item to select it, which makes VoiceOver place the cursor (a black line) around the item and announce the item's name. You then double-tap the selected item to activate it. To scroll with VoiceOver activated, you swipe with three fingers.

To enable VoiceOver, tap the VoiceOver button in the Vision box on the Accessibility screen. Then, on the VoiceOver screen (see Figure 3-54), set the VoiceOver switch at the top to On. If a confirmation dialog opens, tap the OK button to select it, and then double-tap the OK button to activate it. Then tap and double-tap the VoiceOver Practice button to display the VoiceOver Practice screen, where you can practice VoiceOver gestures until you get the hang of them. Tap and then double-tap the Done button when you finish.

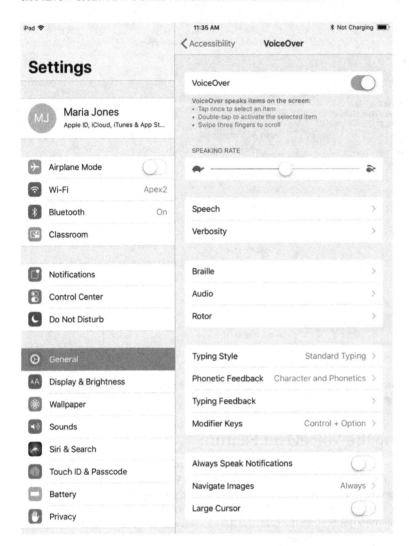

Figure 3-54. *You can configure the VoiceOver feature to speak the names of items on the screen, enabling someone with vision problems to use the iPad's interface*

■ **Tip**   If you're exploring the VoiceOver settings rather than configuring them for actual use, don't set the VoiceOver switch to On yet. Instead, explore the settings using regular iOS gestures and without having VoiceOver announce every item you touch.

Apart from the VoiceOver switch and the VoiceOver Practice button, these are the settings you can configure for VoiceOver:

- *Speaking Rate*: Drag this slider to set the rate at which VoiceOver speaks its announcements.

- *Speech*: On iOS 11, tap this button to display the Speech screen. Here, you can tap the Voice button and choose the voice for VoiceOver to use; a few voices are preinstalled, but you can download plenty of others. You can tap the Pronunciations button to display the Pronunciations screen, which lets you set up custom pronunciations—or substitutions—of individual words and terms. You can drag the Pitch slider to change the pitch of the voice. And you can set the Use Pitch Change switch to On if you want VoiceOver to change the pitch of its voice when reading a list of items, using a higher pitch for the first item and a lower pitch for the last item as an aural clue; set this switch to Off if you prefer to have VoiceOver use a constant pitch.

■ **Note**   In iOS 10, the Use Pitch Change switch is on the VoiceOver screen, not on the Speech screen.

- *Verbosity*: Tap this button to display the Verbosity screen, where you can choose which items you want VoiceOver to speak. For example, you can set the Speak Hints switch to On or Off, as needed; hints are often helpful at first, but you'll likely want to turn them off after a while. Set the Emoji Suffix switch to On if you want VoiceOver to add the word "emoji" after an emoji character it reads as text.

- *Braille*: Tap this button to display the Braille screen (see Figure 3-55), where you can configure settings for using a Braille display with the iPad.

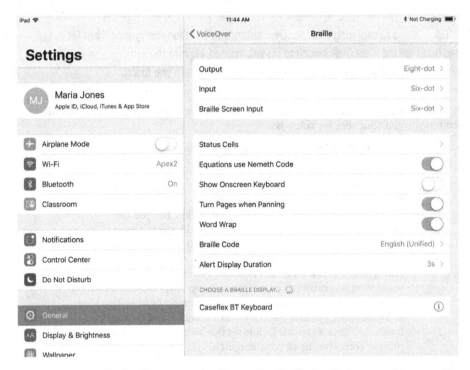

Figure 3-55. *Use the Braille screen to configure a Braille display for input and output with the iPad*

- *Audio*: Tap this button to display the Audio screen. Here, you can set the Use Sound Effects switch to On or Off, as needed, to control whether the iPad plays sound effects as usual; you may want to switch off sound effects to avoid them making VoiceOver hard to hear. You can also set the Audio Ducking switch to On or Off to control whether the iPad *ducks* (reduces the volume of) any audio playing when VoiceOver speaks. Usually, ducking is helpful.

- *Rotor*: Tap this button to display the Rotor screen, which you use to configure the Rotor, a quick-access control for settings you want to be able to access with a gesture when VoiceOver is turned on. You display the Rotor (see Figure 3-56) by placing two fingers on the screen and rotating them clockwise or counterclockwise; VoiceOver announces the name of the item the Rotor is pointing to, and the item's name appears above the dial. The Rotor screen in Settings (see Figure 3-57) enables you to choose which items appear on the Rotor and drag them into the order in which you want them to appear.

Figure 3-56. *With VoiceOver enabled, you can display the Rotor by placing two fingers on the screen and rotating them in either direction. The readout above the dial shows the item the Rotor is pointing to*

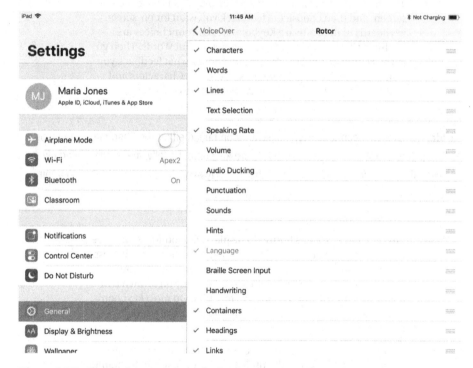

Figure 3-57. *Use the Rotor screen in the Settings app to configure the Rotor to display the items you need. Use the handles at the right end of the buttons to drag the items into your preferred order*

- *Typing Style*: Tap this button to display the Typing Style screen, and then tap the Standard Typing button, the Touch Typing button, or the Direct Touch Typing button to specify the typing style. With the Touch Typing setting, you type a character by pressing its key as usual, except that VoiceOver puts a black selection outline around the key when you tap it. With the Direct Touch Typing setting, you tap the key to select it, and then double-tap the key to type the character.

- *Phonetic Feedback*: Tap this button to display the Phonetic Feedback screen, and then tap the Off button, the Character and Phonetics button, or the Phonetics Only button. For example, when you select the F key with the Character and Phonetics setting, VoiceOver announces "F, Foxtrot"; with the Phonetics Only setting, VoiceOver announces "Foxtrot" without the letter.

- *Typing Feedback*: Tap this button to display the Typing Feedback screen, and then choose the feedback you want for on-screen keyboards in the Software Keyboards box. Your choices are Nothing, Characters, Words, or Characters and Words. Then go to the Hardware Keyboards box and choose what feedback you want—again, Nothing, Characters, Words, or Characters and Words—for hardware keyboards you attach to the iPad.

■ **Note**   A user who can touch-type typically won't need either the Characters setting or the Characters and Words setting for a hardware keyboard. Usually, the Words setting gives the best balance between confirming that the user's typing is accurate and allowing a fair rate of progress.

- *Modifier Keys*: Tap this button to display the Modifier Keys screen, and then tap the button for the modifier keys the user will press on a hardware keyboard to activate VoiceOver key commands. The choice is between using the Caps Lock key on its own and using the Control and Option keys together. On most keyboards, the Alt key has the same effect as the Option key on a Mac keyboard.

- *Always Speak Notifications*: Set this switch to On if you want VoiceOver to announce all notifications. Doing so can be helpful but may prove overkill.

- *Navigate Images*: Tap this button to display the Navigate Images screen, and then tap the Always button, the With Descriptions button, or the Never button to control whether and how VoiceOver announces images. The Always setting makes VoiceOver announce every image, whereas the With Descriptions button makes VoiceOver announce only those images that have an alternative text description.

- *Large Cursor*: Set this switch to on to have the cursor (the selection outline) appear as a thick black line instead of a thin black line.

- *Double-tap Timeout*: Tap this button to display the Double-tap Timeout screen, and then tap the + and – buttons as needed to adjust the timeout. This is the length of time you have to tap twice for VoiceOver to register a double-tap. Increase the timeout if your double-taps aren't registering, or decrease the timeout if VoiceOver is reading two single taps as a double-tap.

Configuring the Zoom Feature

The Zoom feature enables you to magnify either the entire screen or a part of it so that you can see items more clearly. You can configure various zoom settings, including setting the maximum zoom level and choosing whether to display the Zoom Controller tool that provides quick access to zoom commands.

To get started, display the Zoom screen (see Figure 3-58) by tapping the Zoom button in the Vision box on the Accessibility screen in Settings. You can then configure the following settings:

- *Zoom*: Set this switch to On to enable the Zoom feature. When you do this, the whole screen zooms in if you have set the Zoom Region setting to Full Screen Zoom. If you have set the Zoom Region setting to Window Zoom, the Lens appears. The Lens is the rounded rectangle you see in the lower-left corner of Figure 3-58. You move the Lens either by dragging it by its frame or the handle (the jellybean-shaped button at the bottom), or by using the Zoom Controller, which you'll meet in a moment.

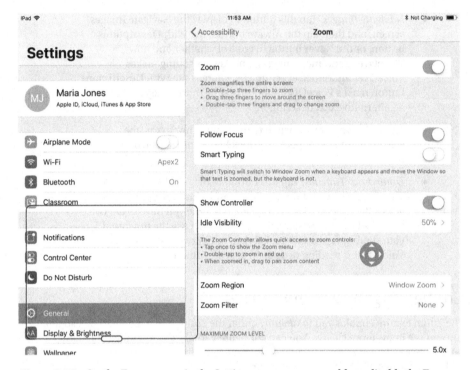

Figure 3-58. *On the Zoom screen in the Settings app, you can enable or disable the Zoom feature and configure its settings. In this example, the Lens appears in the lower-left corner of the screen, and the Zoom Controller appears on the right side*

- *Follow Focus*: Set this switch to On if you want the Lens to automatically follow the text you type so you can see what's happening.

- *Smart Typing*: Set this switch to On to make the Zoom feature switch automatically to Window Zoom when the keyboard appears on screen. The Zoom feature positions the Lens so that the active text is zoomed rather than the keyboard being zoomed.

- *Show Controller*: Set this switch to On to display the Zoom Controller, the gray circle containing a white dot and four arrow buttons pointing up, down, left, and right. With the Zoom Controller displayed, you tap it and then drag the white dot in the direction you want to pan the zoom, as if the dot were a joystick. You can reposition the Zoom Controller by tapping and holding it until it expands and then dragging it.

- *Idle Visibility*: Tap this button to display the Idle Visibility screen, and then drag the slider left or right to make the Zoom Controller more or less see-through when you're not using it. The Zoom Controller darkens when you're using it.

- *Zoom Region*: Tap this button to display the Zoom Region screen, and then tap the Full Screen Zoom button or the Window Zoom button to specify which type of zoom you want to use.

- *Zoom Filter*: If you want to apply a color filter to the zoomed area, tap this button to display the Zoom Filter screen, and then tap the filter you want: Inverted, Grayscale, Grayscale Inverted, or Low Light.

- *Maximum Zoom Level*: Drag this slider to set the maximum zoom level you want to use.

Using Zoom Shortcuts

Once you've configured the settings you want for the Zoom feature, you can simply leave Zoom turned on and pan either the entire screen or the Lens by swiping with three fingers. But you may also benefit from these three moves:

- *Toggle zoom on or off*: Double-tap with three fingers anywhere on the screen.

- *Change the zoom level*: Double-tap with three fingers in the zoomed area and, on the second tap, draw your fingers up the screen to zoom in or down the screen to zoom out.

- *Display the Zoom dialog*: Tap the Zoom Controller or triple-tap the screen with three fingers to display the Zoom dialog (see Figure 3-59), which contains commands for zooming in or out, switching between Full Screen Zoom and Window Zoom, resizing the Lens, choosing a Zoom Filter, and showing or hiding the Zoom Controller. You can also drag the slider at the bottom of the Zoom dialog to adjust the zoom level.

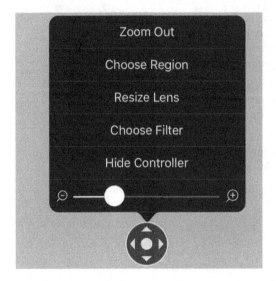

Figure 3-59. *Tap the Zoom Controller or triple-tap the screen to display the Zoom dialog, which contains commands for configuring the zoom quickly*

Configuring the Magnifier Feature

The Magnifier feature lets you use the iPad's rear camera to magnify things you want to see better. To turn Magnifier on, tap the Magnifier button in the Vision box on the Accessibility screen, and then set the Magnifier switch on the Magnifier screen (see Figure 3-60) to On. On the Magnifier screen, you can also set the Auto-Brightness switch to On if you want Magnifier to adjust the brightness and contrast to suit the ambient light conditions the iPad detects.

Figure 3-60. *On the Magnifier screen, set the Magnifier switch to On if you want to use the iPad's camera to magnify objects*

Once you've enabled Magnifier, you can invoke it at any point by triple-clicking the Home button and then tapping the Magnifier button in the Accessibility Shortcuts dialog (see Figure 3-61).

Figure 3-61. *You can enable and disable Magnifier quickly by triple-clicking the Home button and then tapping the Magnifier button in the Accessibility Shortcuts dialog*

Configuring Display Accommodations

The display accommodations in iOS enable you to change the screen's colors to make them easier to view. You can invert the screen's colors, apply color filters designed to help different types of color blindness, and reduce the screen's white point to make bright colors appear less intense.

To get started, tap the Display Accommodations button in the Vision box on the Accessibility screen. The Display Accommodations screen appears (see Figure 3-62), where you can choose the following three settings:

- *Invert Colors*: In iOS 11, tap this button to display the Invert Colors screen. Here, you can set the Smart Invert switch to On to invert each color—changing white to black, the blue selection highlight to rusty orange, and the green switch color to lazy magenta—for all objects except images, other media, and some apps that use dark color styles. Alternatively, you can set the Classic Invert switch to On to invert all the colors on the screen, not sparing images, media, or dark-themed apps.

■ **Note**   Inverting the colors can make the screen easier to view in certain lighting conditions. You may also find that some students simply like the inverted effect, which is reminiscent of early versions of Android before Google beefed up its graphical design department.

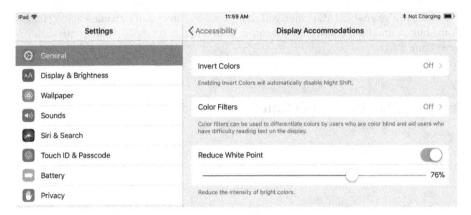

Figure 3-62. *On the Display Accommodations screen in Accessibility settings, you can invert the screen colors, apply color filters for color blindness, and reduce the white point*

■ **Note**   In iOS 10, the Invert Colors switch appears on the Display Accommodations screen. This switch has the same effect as the Classic Invert switch in iOS 11. iOS 10 doesn't have the Smart Invert feature.

- *Color Filters*: Tap this button to display the Color Filters screen (see Figure 3-63). Set the Color Filters switch to On, and then tap the filter you want to apply: Grayscale, Red/Green Filter, Green/Red Filter, Blue/Yellow Filter, or Color Tint. For any color filter except Grayscale, drag the Intensity slider left or right to adjust the intensity. For the Color Tint filter, drag the Hue slider left or right to tweak the hue.

■ **Tip**   Swipe left once or twice on the colored pencils at the top of the Color Filters screen to display other color samples to help you judge the effect of the color filter you've applied.

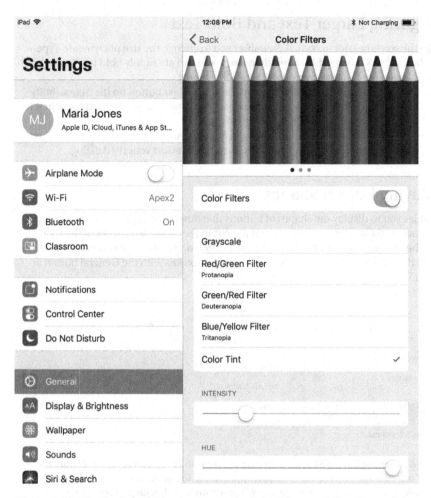

Figure 3-63. *On the Color Filters screen, set the Color Filters switch to On, and then select the appropriate filter—such as Grayscale or Red/Green Filter—in the main box. Adjust the Intensity slider and Hue slider if they appear for that filter*

- *Reduce White Point*: Set this switch to On if you want to reduce the intensity of bright colors. Then drag the slider left or right to adjust the intensity.

Configuring Larger Text and Bold Text

To make the screen easier to read, iOS enables you to change the size of Dynamic Type—type with size that's changeable rather than fixed. You can also apply bold text throughout the operating system; doing so requires the iPad to restart.

To change the size of Dynamic Type, tap the Larger Text button on the Accessibility screen. On the Larger Text screen that appears, set the Larger Accessibility Sizes switch to On, and then drag the slider to adjust the size of the type.

To turn on bold text, set the Bold Text switch on the Accessibility screen to On, then tap the Continue button in the Applying this setting will restart your iPad dialog.

Displaying Button Shapes

iOS enables you to display the shapes of buttons that otherwise appear only as text and arrows, such as the navigation buttons that appear in the upper-left corner of the right pane in the Settings app. Set the Button Shapes switch on the Accessibility screen to On if you want the buttons to appear as shaded shapes, as you see with the General button at the top of Figure 3-64.

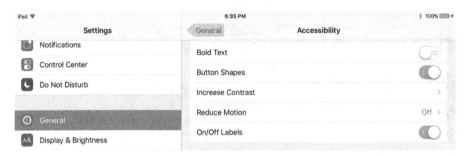

Figure 3-64. *Set the Button Shapes switch on the Accesibility screen to On to display the shapes of text buttons, such as the General button at the top of the screen here. Set the On/Off Labels switch to On to display I and O labels on switches for greater clarity*

Increasing Contrast and Reducing Motion

To make the iPad's screen easier to read, you can increase the contrast. Tap the Increase Contrast button on the Accessibility screen to display the Increase Contrast screen, and then set the Reduce Transparency switch and the Darken Colors switch to On.

Displaying On/Off Labels on Switches

The switches in iOS are generally easy to understand—green for On, and white for Off. But you can display On/Off labels to make the switches even clearer. To do so, set the On/Off Labels switch on the Accessibility screen to On. Each switch then shows I when it's on and O when it's off, as you see on the switches in Figure 3-64.

Choosing Interaction Settings for Accessibility

The Interaction section of the Accessibility screen (see Figure 3-65) enables you to configure the Switch Control feature, the AssistiveTouch feature, the Touch Accommodations feature, keyboard settings, the Shake to Undo feature, how to route audio calls, and how the Home button responds to clicks and presses.

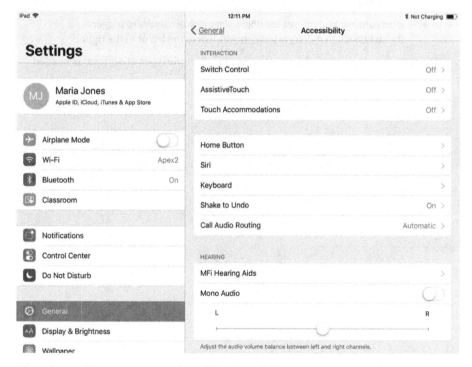

Figure 3-65. The Interaction section of the Accessibility screen gives you access to interaction features, including Switch Control, Assistive Touch, Touch Accommodations, and Shake to Undo

Configuring the Switch Control Feature

The Switch Control feature enables you to use a switch to control the iPad. This feature is designed to help users with physical impairments or motor-skills impairments to use iPads. Switch Control works by the iPad highlighting each available option on screen in turn so that the user can use the switch to select the right option when it's highlighted. iOS enables you to create *recipes*—sequences of actions similar to macros—for controlling switches.

For Switch Control, you can use three types of devices:

- *External switch*: You connect a physical switch device to the iPad, either via Bluetooth or via the Lightning port. This switch device can have either a single switch or multiple switches.

- *iPad screen*: You can tap anywhere on the iPad's screen to trigger the switch.

- *iPad camera*: You can set the iPad's screen-side camera to trigger the switch when it detects head movement to the left or to the right.

You can use a single type of device or combine multiple types of devices, as needed.

Getting Started by Displaying the Switch Control Screen

To get started with Switch Control, tap the Switch Control button in the Interaction box on the Accessibility screen to display the Switch Control screen (see Figure 3-66).

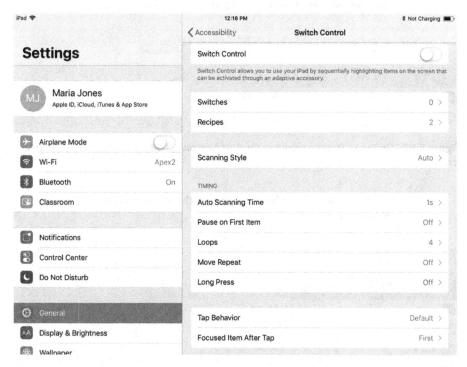

Figure 3-66. *On the Switch Control screen, first tap the Switches button and add the switch you will use for controlling the iPad. You can then choose settings for the switch's behavior and set the Switch Control switch to On*

Specifying Which Switch Type to Use

To specify which switch type to use, follow these steps:

1. Tap the Switches button on the Switch Control screen to display the Switches screen (see Figure 3-67).

Figure 3-67. *On the Switches screen, tap the Add New Switch button to display the Source screen*

2. Tap the Add New Switch button to display the Source screen (see Figure 3-68).

Figure 3-68. *On the Source screen, specify the switch source by tapping the External button, the Screen button, or the Camera button*

3. Tap the appropriate button:

    a. *External*: Tap this button to use an external switch device. The External screen appears. Activate your external switch device, and then follow the prompts on screen to associate it with the iPad. Tap the button for the switch you want to configure, and the Actions screen appears. Continue with step 4 of the main list.

■ **Note** Some iOS-compatible switch devices tap into Apple's auto-configuration feature for switches, which enables iOS to detect the switch device and the number of switches it offers. For other devices, visit the manufacturer's website and consult the latest instructions for setting up the switch if the on-screen prompts aren't easy to follow.

    b.   *Screen*: Tap this button to use the iPad's screen as the switch. The Screen screen appears. Tap this button to display the Actions screen, and then continue from step 4 of the main list.

    c.   *Camera*: Tap this button to use the iPad's screenside camera as the switch. The Camera screen appears (see Figure 3-69). Tap the Left Head Movement button or the Right Head Movement button to display the Actions screen, and then continue from step 4 of the main list.

Figure 3-69. *On the Camera screen for setting up Switch Control, tap the Left Head Movement button or the Right Head Movement button, as needed*

    4.   On the Actions screen (see Figure 3-70), tap the button for the switch action you want, either in the Scanner box or the System box. For example, tap the Select Item button in the Scanner box to use this switch to select the current item in the scanner. The Switches screen then appears again.

■ **Tip** To make Switch Control work correctly, you'll need to assign a switch to the Select Item action.

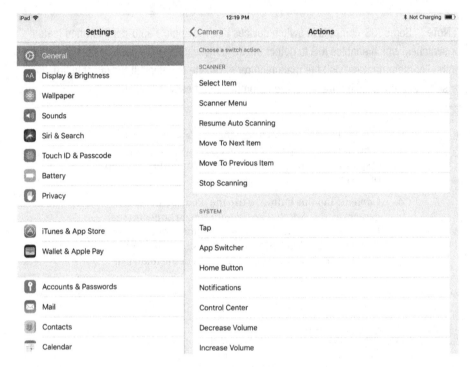

Figure 3-70. *On the Actions screen, tap the button for the switch action you want to assign to the switch you're configuring*

> 5. Repeat steps 2–4 to add other switches as needed. For example, if you're using the iPad's camera as the switch, and you added the Left Head Movement switch, you might add the Right Head Movement switch next.

Creating and Setting Up Recipes for Switch Control

After setting up the switches you'll use and the switch actions the switches represent, tap the Recipes button to display the Recipes screen (see Figure 3-71). Here, you can edit the list of existing recipes, create new recipes as needed, and choose a recipe to launch automatically when Switch Control starts. Here's what you need to know:

- *Edit the list of recipes*: Tap the Edit button in the upper-right corner of the screen to switch to Edit mode. You can then rearrange the list of recipes by dragging a recipe up or down by the handle at the right end of its button, or delete a recipe by tapping the red minus icon to its left and then tapping the Delete button that appears to its right. Tap the Done button in the upper-right corner of the screen when you finish editing.

Figure 3-71. *On the Recipes screen for Switch Control, you can edit the existing recipes, create new recipes, and set up a launch recipe*

- *Edit an existing recipe*: Tap the recipe's button to display the screen for the recipe. This screen bears the recipe's name. Figure 3-72 shows the Tap Middle of Screen screen. Here, you can edit the recipe's name in the Name box or change the switches used for the recipe. You can also configure a timeout if needed: set the Timeout switch to On, and then use the + and – buttons to specify the number of seconds.

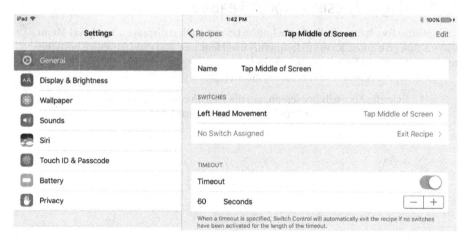

Figure 3-72. *On the screen for a Switch Control recipe, you can edit the recipe's name, change the switches used for the recipe, and configure the timeout*

137

- *Create a new recipe*: Tap the Create New Recipe button to display
  the New Recipe screen (see Figure 3-73). Type the name for the
  recipe in the Name box, tap the first button in the Switches box,
  and choose the appropriate switch action for that switch on the
  resulting screen.

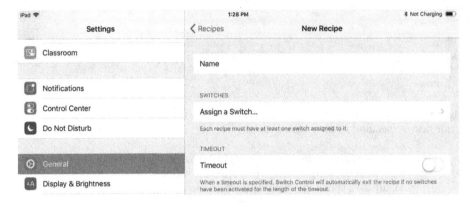

Figure 3-73. *On the New Recipe screen, type the name for the recipe, assign the switches and their actions, and configure any timeout needed*

Configuring the AssistiveTouch Feature

The AssistiveTouch feature displays a button on screen that displays a Top Level Menu
of icons that give quick access to frequently used features. You can customize both the
numbers of icons and the icons themselves.

To configure AssistiveTouch, follow these steps:

1. On the Accessibility screen, tap the AssistiveTouch button to
   display the AssistiveTouch screen (see Figure 3-74).

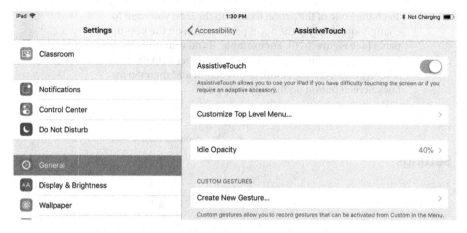

Figure 3-74. *On the AssistiveTouchscreen, set the AssistiveTouch switch to On to enable the feature, and then tap the Customize Top Level Menu button to display the Customize Top Level Menu screen*

2. Set the AssistiveTouch switch to On. The AssistiveTouch icon, a gray square with rounded corners and a lighter gray circle in the middle, appears on the screen.

3. Tap the Customize Top Level Menu button to display the Customize Top Level Menu screen (see Figure 3-75).

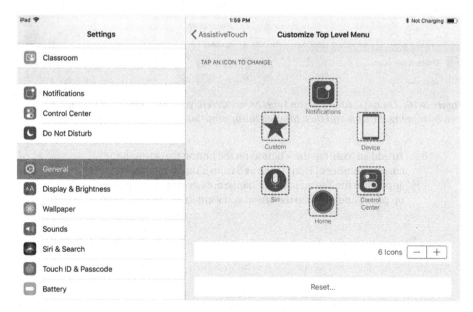

Figure 3-75. *From the Customize Top Level Menu screen, you can change the actions for the current icons, add or remove icons, or reset the icons to their default actions*

4. To change one of the action icons, tap the icon you want to change, and then tap the appropriate action on the pop-up panel (see Figure 3-76). For example, if you want the topmost icon (by default, the Notifications icon) to perform the Lock Screen action, tap the Notifications action and then tap the Lock Screen button on the pop-up panel.

Figure 3-76. *On the Customize Top Level Menu screen, you can change the action for an icon by tapping the icon and then tapping the appropriate action on the pop-up panel*

5. To add an icon, tap the + button on the button that gives the current number of icons (such as *6 icons*). Tap the + icon that appears in the Tap an Icon to Change area to display the pop-up panel, and then tap the action you want to assign to the icon.

6. To remove an icon, tap the – button on the button that gives the current number of icons. iOS removes the last icon added, or the last of the default icons if you haven't added any. You may need to change the actions of one of the remaining icons if iOS removes a different icon than you wanted to remove.

7. If you need to reset the icons to their default action, tap the Reset button.

8. When you finish customizing the Top Level Menu, tap the AssistiveTouch button to return to the AssistiveTouch screen.

■ **Note**   If you want to create a custom gesture and assign it to AssistiveTouch, tap the Create New Gesture button on the AssistiveTouch screen, and then use the controls on the New Gesture screen to create the gesture. Creating the gesture works in the same way as for Switch Control, discussed in the earlier section "Configuring the Switch Control Feature."

Once you've enabled AssistiveTouch, you can tap the AssistiveTouch icon to display the Top Level Menu (see the left screen in Figure 3-77). From here, you can tap an icon to display either that item (for example, tap the Home icon to display the Home screen) or another AssistiveTouch menu, such as the Device menu shown on the right in Figure 3-77.

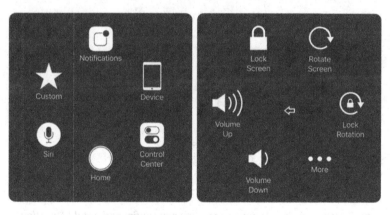

Figure 3-77. *Tap the AssistiveTouch icon to display the Top Level Menu (left). You can then tap an icon either to display the corresponding item (such as Notifications) or another AssistiveTouch menu, such as the Device menu (right)*

Configuring the Touch Accommodations Feature

The Touch Accommodations feature enables you to control how the iPad's screen responds to touches. You'll want to configure Touch Accommodations for a user who finds that the iPad registers unintended touches, repeat touches, or moving touch that miss their target.

Tap the Touch Accommodations button on the Accessibility screen to display the Touch Accommodations screen (see Figure 3-78). You can then configure the following settings:

- *Touch Accommodations*: Set this switch to On to enable Touch Accommodations, and then tap the OK button in the confirmation dialog that opens.

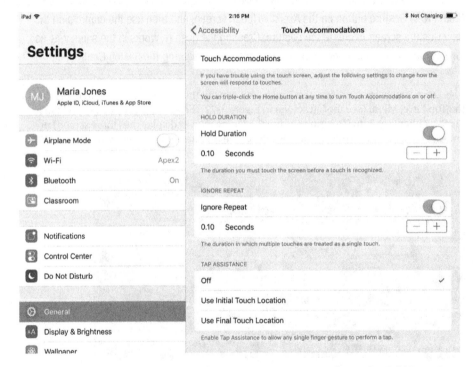

Figure 3-78. *On the Touch Accommodations screen, you can configure the Hold Duration feature, the Ignore Repeat feature, and the Tap Assistance feature*

- *Hold Duration*: Set this switch to On to make the iPad wait for a short time before registering a touch. This is useful if the iPad is detecting unintended touches. On the Seconds button that appears below the Hold Duration button, tap the + or – button to adjust the hold duration as needed.

- *Ignore Repeat*: Set this switch to On to make the iPad wait for a short time before registering a repeat touch. This is useful if the iPad is detecting double-taps when the user intends only a single tap. On the Seconds button that appears below the Ignore Repeat button, tap the + or – button to adjust the time as needed.

- *Tap Assistance*: In this box, tap the Use Initial Touch Location button if you want the iPad to use the strike point of a sliding touch as the location for the tap. Tap the Use Final Touch Location button if you want the iPad to use the liftoff point of a sliding touch as the location for the tap. Tap the Off button if you don't need Tap Assistance.

■ **Tip**   After enabling Touch Accommodations, you can turn them on or off quickly by triple-clicking the Home button. If you have only Touch Accommodations set up on the Accessibility Shortcut, the triple-click toggles Touch Accommodations. If you have multiple items set up on the Accessibility Shortcut, the Accessibility Shortcut dialog opens; tap the Touch Accommodations button in the dialog to toggle Touch Accommodations.

Configuring Home Button Presses for Accessibility

You can configure several Accessibility settings to make the Home button work the way you (or the iPad's user) prefer. To access these settings, tap the Home Button button in the Interaction section of the Accessibility screen, and then work on the Home Button screen (see Figure 3-79).

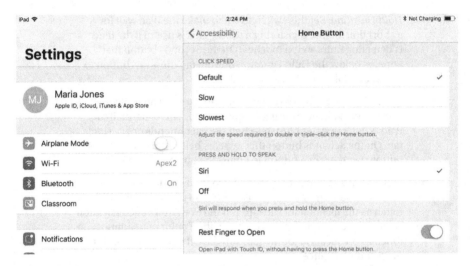

Figure 3-79. *On the Home Button screen in iOS 11, you can configure the click speed, the Press and Hold to Speak action, and whether you can unlock the iPad by resting your finger on the Home button without clicking*

On the Home Button screen, you can configure the following three settings:

- *Click Speed*: In this box, set the click speed by tapping the Default button, the Slow button, or the Slowest button. Generally, you'll want to change from the default speed only for users who find it hard to click the Home button fast enough.

- *Press and Hold to Open*: In this box, tap the Siri button if you want iOS to activate Siri when the Home button is pressed and held. Tap the Off button if you want to turn this feature off—for example, for a user who keeps invoking Siri unintentionally.

- *Rest Finger to Open*: Set this switch to On if you want the iPad to unlock when the user rests her finger on the Home button without clicking it.

Configuring Siri Settings for Accessibility in iOS 11

In iOS 11, you can configure two Accessibility settings for Siri. To access these settings, tap the Siri button in the Interaction section of the Accessibility screen, and then work on the Siri screen (see Figure 3-80). Here, you can configure these settings:

- *Type to Siri*: Set this switch to On if you want to be able to type queries into Siri rather than speak them.

- *Voice Feedback*: In this box, tap the Always On button if you want Siri to provide voice feedback even when Mute is turned on. Tap the Hands Free button if you want Siri to provide voice feedback only when you're using "Hey Siri" or a Bluetooth device or headphones.

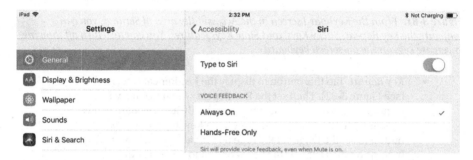

Figure 3-80. *On the Siri screen in iOS 11, you can enable the Type to Siri feature and choose when Siri gives voice feedback*

Configuring Keyboard Settings for Accessibility

iOS offers several accessibility settings for hardware keyboards you connect to the iPad. You can adjust the rate at which keys repeat when held down, enable the Sticky Keys feature for setting a modifier key so you don't have to keep holding it down for a keyboard shortcut, and enable the Slow Keys feature to adjust the length of time between when you press a key and the iPad registers the keypress. You can also choose whether to display lowercase letters on the on-screen keyboard or keep it uppercase all the time.

To configure keyboard settings, tap the Keyboard button on the Accessibility screen. On the Keyboard screen that appears (see Figure 3-81), you can then configure the following settings:

- *Show Lowercase Keys*: Set this switch to Off (it's On by default) to make keyboards that normally switch between lowercase letters and uppercase letters display uppercase letters all the time.

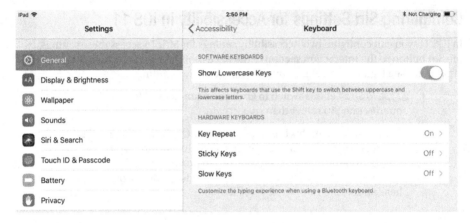

Figure 3-81. *From the Keyboard screen in the Accessibility area of Settings, you can configure the Key Repeat, Sticky Keys, and Slow Keys features. You can also turn off showing lowercase keys on the on-screen keyboard*

- *Key Repeat*: Tap this button to display the Key Repeat screen (see Figure 3-82). Then set the Key Repeat switch to On if you want to slow down the repeat rate for a hardware keyboard you've attached. Tap the + and – buttons on the Key Repeat Interval button to set the length of the repeat interval. Tap the + and – buttons on the Delay Until Repeat button to adjust the delay before repetition begins.

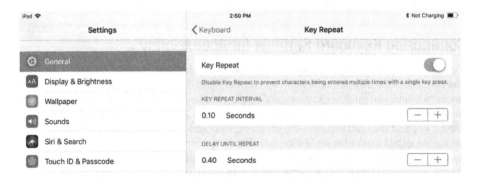

Figure 3-82. *On the Key Repeat screen, you can enable the Key Repeat feature and adjust the repeat interval and the delay until repeating begins*

- *Sticky Keys*: Tap this button to display the Sticky Keys screen (see Figure 3-83). Set the Sticky Keys switch to On if you want to enable the Sticky Keys feature, which enables you to press a modifier key (such as Shift) and have it stay down until you press another key (such as A) instead of having to hold down Shift while you press the other key (Shift-A, in the example). Set the Toggle With Shift Key switch to On if you want to be able to toggle Sticky Keys on or off by pressing the Shift key five times in sequence.

■ **Note**   The Toggle With Shift Key feature is often useful for conventional use, but it can conflict with games that require the Shift key to be pressed repeatedly or held down to control movement, violence, or other aspects of gameplay.

- *Sound*: Set this switch to On if you want Sticky Keys to play a sound when a modifier key is *set* (stuck on). The sound can be helpful when the user is getting the hang of Sticky Keys, but it may prove irksome for experienced users.

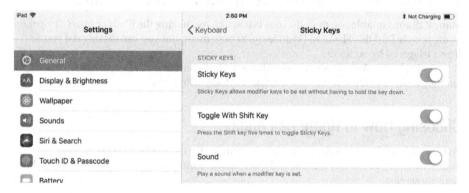

Figure 3-83. *On the Sticky Keys screen, you can enable or disable Sticky Keys, choose whether to use the Shift key to toggle Sticky Keys, and control whether iOS plays a sound when a modifier key is set*

- *Slow Keys*: Tap this button to display the Slow Keys screen (see Figure 3-84). Here, you can set the Slow Keys switch to On to enable the feature, and then tap the + and – buttons on the lower button to set the length of time between a key being pressed and iOS registering the keypress.

Figure 3-84. *On the Slow Keys screen, you can enable or disable the Slow Keys feature. If you enable it, you can adjust the time between a key being pressed and the keypress being registered*

Enabling and Disabling the Shake to Undo Feature

Many iOS apps enable you to undo your last action by shaking the iPad (or other device). Many people find this Shake to Undo feature convenient, but you can disable it if you find it gets triggered by accident.

To disable Shake to Undo, tap the Shake to Undo button on the Accessibility screen. On the Shake to Undo screen, set the Shake to Undo switch to Off.

Choosing How to Route Call Audio

To control how the iPad routes audio in FaceTime calls, tap the Call Audio Routing button on the Accessibility screen, and then tap the appropriate button on the Call Audio Routing screen:

- *Automatic*: Tap this button to send the audio to the default device. Normally, that device is the speaker unless you've connected a headset or Bluetooth headset, in which case that headset receives the audio.

- *Bluetooth Headset*: Tap this button to send the audio to the Bluetooth headset always.

- *Speaker*: Tap this button to send the audio to the speaker always, even if a Bluetooth headset is connected.

Configuring Hearing Settings for Accessibility

In the Hearing box on the Accessibility screen, you can configure the following settings:

- *Hearing Devices*: Tap this button to display the Hearing Device screen, and then tap the button for the hearing device you want to set up. Use this feature for setting up hearing devices that meet the Made for iPad Hearing Aids standard. For regular Bluetooth hearing aids, use regular Bluetooth setup, as explained in the earlier section "Connecting and Using Bluetooth Devices."

- *Mono Audio*: Set this switch to On to make the iPad play mono audio instead of stereo audio.

- *Sound Balance*: Drag this slider along the L–R axis to set the sound balance between left and right.

Choosing Media Settings for Accessibility

The Media box on the Accessibility screen allows you to configure subtitles, captioning, and audio descriptions:

- *Subtitles & Captioning*: Tap this button to display the Subtitles & Captioning screen. Here, you can set the Closed Captions & SDH switch to On to enable closed captioning or subtitles for the deaf and hard-of-hearing. You can also tap the Style button to display the Style screen, which enables you to configure a suitable subtitle style. For example, you can tap the Large Text button to have subtitles appear in large text, or tap the Create New Style button and create a custom style of subtitles.

- *Audio Descriptions*: Tap this button to display the Audio Descriptions screen, and then set the Prefer Audio Descriptions switch to On if you want the iPad to automatically play audio descriptions when they're available.

Enabling Guided Access

The Guided Access feature enables you to set the iPad to run a single app, so that the user can explore that app without distractions. You can lock the iPad into this app with a passcode, set time limits for the user to use the app, and control whether the Accessibility Shortcut functions while Guided Access is on.

To set up Guided Access, follow these steps:

1. Tap the Guided Access button on the Accessibility screen to display the Guided Access screen (see Figure 3-85).

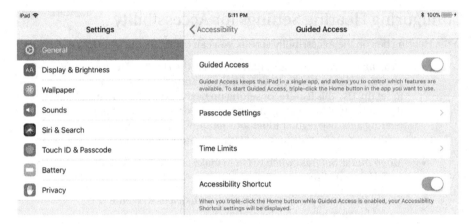

Figure 3-85. *The Guided Access feature enables you to restrict the iPad's user to a single app and choose which features are available for use*

2. Set the Guided Access switch to On. The Passcode Settings button, the Time Limits button, and the Accessibility Shortcuts switch appear.

3. Tap the Passcode Settings button to display the Passcode Settings screen (see Figure 3-86).

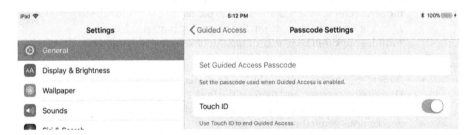

Figure 3-86. *On the Passcode Settings screen for Guided Access, tap the Set Guided Access Passcode button and set the passcode in the Set Passcode dialog. Then set the Touch ID switch to On or Off, as needed*

4. Tap the Set Guided Access Passcode button. The Set Passcode dialog opens.

5. Type a six-digit passcode for use with Guided Access. You'll want to keep this passcode strictly to yourself unless you want your students to be able to override Guided Access.

6. Type the passcode again when the Set Passcode dialog prompts you to do so. The Passcode Settings screen appears again.

7. Set the Touch ID switch to On if you want to be able to use Touch ID to end the Guided Access session. This move is often helpful.

8. Tap the Guided Access button to display the Guided Access screen again.

9. Tap the Time Limits button to display the Time Limits screen (see Figure 3-87).

Figure 3-87. *On the Time Limits screen, choose which sound to play and whether to have the remaining time spoken aloud to warn the user that time is running out*

10. Tap the Sound button to display the Sound screen, and then tap the sound you want the iPad to play to warn the user that time is running short.

11. Set the Speak switch to On if you want the iPad to announce the remaining time aloud.

12. Tap the Guided Access button to display the Guided Access screen again.

13. Set the Accessibility Shortcut switch to On if you want triple-clicking the Home button to display the Accessibility Shortcut dialog while Guided Access is on.

Once you've configured Guided Access, you can run a Guided Access session like this:

1. Open the app you want the user to work with. This example uses the Photos app.

2. If necessary, set up the app the way you want it to be for the user. In this example, I set up the app by opening a photo for editing.

3. Triple-click the Home button. If you have only Guided Access set up to use the Accessibility Shortcut, Guided Access starts—go to the next step. If you have multiple accessibility features set to use the Accessibility Shortcut, the Accessibility Shortcuts dialog opens (see Figure 3-88).

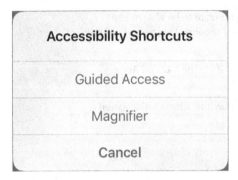

Figure 3-88. *In the Accessibility Shortcuts dialog, tap the Guided Access button to display the setup screen for Guided Access*

4. Tap the Guided Access button. The Guided Access setup screen appears, showing the app at a reduced size, with the controls for customizing the Guided Access session below it (see Figure 3-89).

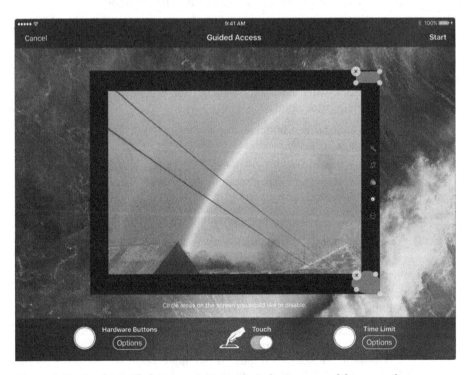

Figure 3-89. *On the Guided Access setup screen, circle any areas of the screen that you want to disable, such as the control buttons in this example*

5. Optionally, circle any areas of the screen that you want to disable. For example, you may want to disable some of the control buttons to limit the actions that students can take.

6. Tap the Options button under the Hardware Buttons heading to display the Hardware Buttons pop-up panel (see Figure 3-90), and then set the Sleep/Wake Button switch, Volume Buttons switch, Motion switch, and Keyboards switch to On or off, as needed.

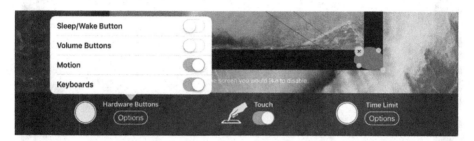

Figure 3-90. *Tap the Options button under the Hardware Buttons heading to display the Hardware Buttons pop-up panel, and then set each switch to On or Off, as needed for the Guided Access session*

7. Set the Touch switch to Off if you don't want the user to be able to interact with the touchscreen. In most cases, you'll want to leave this switch set to On.

8. If you want to set a time limit for the Guided Access session, tap the Options button under the Time Limit heading to display the Time Limit pop-up panel (see Figure 3-91). Set the Time Limit switch to On, and then use the hours dial and the min dial to set the length of time.

Figure 3-91. *To set a time limit for the Guided Access session, tap the Options button under the Time Limit heading, set the Time Limit switch to On, and then turn the dials to set the length of time*

9.   Tap the Start button in the upper-right corner of the screen. The Guided Access Started readout appears briefly on the screen, together with the time limit if you set one (see Figure 3-92).

Figure 3-92. *The Guided Access Started readout confirms that the Guided Access session has started. Any disabled areas appear grayed out, as you see in the upper-right and lower-right corners here*

You can now hand the iPad to the user and let them work with the app.

If you set a time limit for the Guided Access session, the Time Expired Message appears when the time runs out (see Figure 3-93). You can then triple-click to display the Enter Passcode dialog, in which you type the passcode to turn off Guided Access.

Figure 3-93. *The Time Expired message appears when the Guided Access session reaches its time limit*

If you didn't set a time limit for the Guided Access session, triple-click the Home button at any point to display the Enter Passcode dialog, and then enter the passcode. Alternatively, if you enabled Touch ID for ending the Guided Access session, use Touch ID instead.

Configuring the Accessibility Shortcut

You've already met the Accessibility Shortcut, triggered by triple-clicking the Home button, several times in this chapter. You can assign either a single action or multiple actions to the Accessibility Shortcut. If you assign a single action, triple-clicking the Home button performs that action; if you assign multiple actions, triple-clicking the Home button displays the Accessibility Shortcuts dialog, in which you then tap the button for the action you want to take this time.

iOS automatically adds some actions to the Accessibility Shortcut if you set up Accessibility features such as Magnifier and Guided Access. To control which other actions appear, tap the Accessibility Shortcut button at the bottom of the Accessibility screen. On the Accessibility Shortcut screen (see Figure 3-94), tap the button for each action you want to have appear, placing a check mark on the button.

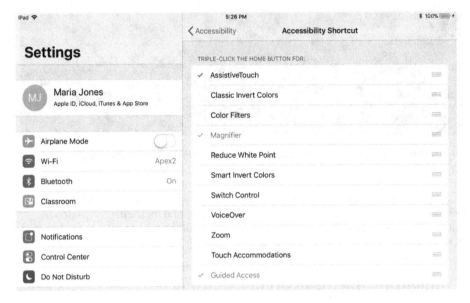

Figure 3-94. *Use the Accessibility Shortcut screen in the Settings app to control which actions appear in the Accessibility Shortcut dialog, which you display by triple-clicking the Home button*

Configuring Keyboards for the iPad

As you know, the iPad comes with a variety of on-screen keyboards that pop up automatically when you need to enter text—for example, when you select a text field or when you start a new note in the Notes app. By default, the on-screen keyboard uses the layouts for the region you specified when setting up the iPad, but you can apply different layouts as needed.

You can also connect a hardware keyboard to the iPad. Once you've done so, you can choose your preferred layout for it.

■ **Note**   See the section "Choosing Hardware Keyboards Where Needed" in Chapter 2 for details on the different types of keyboards you can connect to an iPad.

For both the on-screen keyboard and any hardware keyboard you use, you can set up text replacements (which work in a similar way to the AutoCorrect feature in the Microsoft Office apps) and configure assistive typing features such as automatic capitalization, Caps Lock, and the split keyboard.

Choosing the Layout for the On-screen Keyboard

You can configure the on-screen keyboard by changing its layout. To do so, follow these steps:

1. From the Home screen, choose Settings ➤ General ➤ Keyboard to display the first Keyboards screen (see Figure 3-95).

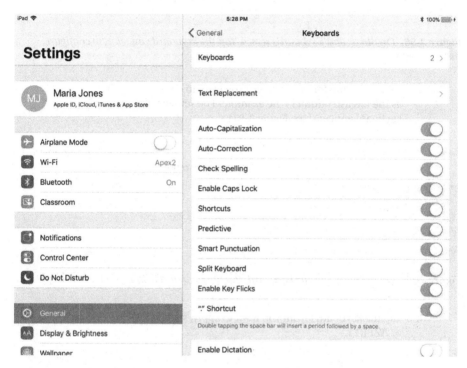

Figure 3-95. *From the first Keyboards screen in the Settings app, you can configure keyboards, set up text replacements, and choose which assistive typing options to use*

2. Tap the Keyboards button to display the second Keyboards screen (see Figure 3-96).

Figure 3-96. *On the second Keyboards screen, tap the keyboard you want to configure,* such as English

3. Tap the button for the keyboard you want to configure, such as the English button in the example. The screen for that keyboard appears (see Figure 3-97).

Figure 3-97. *On the screen for the keyboard, tap the keyboard layout you want to apply*

4. Tap the keyboard layout you want to apply, such as QWERTY or AZERTY.

Connecting and Configuring a Hardware Keyboard

If you're going to use a hardware keyboard with the iPad, connect it now. You can then configure the keyboard's layout as needed.

As you may remember from Chapter 2, you can use three main types of hardware keyboards with the iPad: Bluetooth keyboards, USB keyboards, and Smart Keyboards. I'll deal with each type in turn.

Connecting a Bluetooth Keyboard

To connect a Bluetooth keyboard to the iPad, you need to pair it using the same technique as for other Bluetooth devices. Follow these steps:

1. From the Home screen, choose Settings ➤ Bluetooth to display the Bluetooth screen.

2. Make sure the Bluetooth switch is set to On. The iPad scans for Bluetooth devices, and the Devices list shows those it has found.

■ **Note** Until you pair a Bluetooth device, the Bluetooth screen shows only the Devices list. Once you pair a device, that device appears in the My Devices list, and other devices (ones you haven't paired) appear in the Other Devices list.

---

3. Put the Bluetooth keyboard into pairing mode. How you do this depends on the keyboard, but most of them have either a dedicated switch or a key combination. A few seconds after you do this, the keyboard should appear in the Devices list.

4. Tap the keyboard's button in the Devices list. For most keyboards, the Bluetooth Pairing Request dialog opens (see Figure 3-98) .

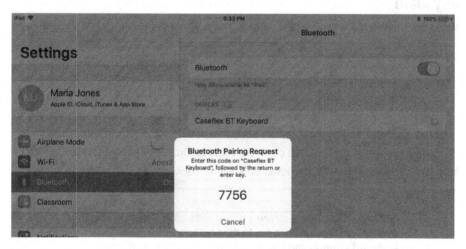

Figure 3-98. *To pair a Bluetooth keyboard, tap its button in the Devices list. Type the code shown in the Bluetooth Pairing Request dialog and press the Return key*

159

5. Type the code shown in the Bluetooth Pairing Request dialog
    on the keyboard and then press the Return key. The iPad
    establishes the pairing with the keyboard, and the keyboard
    appears in the My Devices list, marked as Connected
    (see Figure 3-99).

Figure 3-99. *The My Devices list on the Bluetooth screen shows devices you've paired with
your iPad, together with their status, such as Connected or Not Connected. You can tap the
blue Information (i) button to display information for a device*

You can now start using the keyboard to type text and give commands.

Disconnecting, Reconnecting, and Forgetting a Bluetooth Keyboard

When you finish using a Bluetooth keyboard, disconnect it from your iPad. You can do
this in two ways:

- *Keyboard*. Turn off the keyboard's power. The iPad then
  disconnects the keyboard after a few seconds.

■ **Note**   To avoid running out of battery power, many Bluetooth keyboards switch off
after a few minutes of inactivity. You can wake some keyboards by pressing a key. On other
keyboards, you need to switch the power off and then back on.

- *iPad*. From the Home screen, choose Settings ➤ Bluetooth to
  display the Bluetooth screen. In the My Devices list, go to the
  keyboard's button and tap the Information (i) icon to display
  the control screen for the keyboard. Figure 3-100 shows an
  example of this screen. Then tap the Disconnect button. The iPad
  disconnects the keyboard.

Figure 3-100. *On the iPad, tap the Disconnect button on the control screen for a Bluetooth keyboard to disconnect that keyboard*

To reconnect a keyboard, turn it back on. Normally, this is enough to cause the iPad to reestablish the connection. If not, choose Settings ➤ Bluetooth from the Home screen to display the Bluetooth screen, and then tap the keyboard's button in the My Devices list. When the button's readout changes from Not Connected to Connected, you can start using the keyboard again.

To forget a keyboard, use the same technique as for any other Bluetooth device. From the Home screen, choose Settings ➤ Bluetooth to display the Bluetooth screen. In the My Devices list, go to the keyboard's button and tap the Information (i) icon to display the control screen for the keyboard. Tap the Forget This Device button, and then tap the OK button in the Forget dialog that opens (see Figure 3-101).

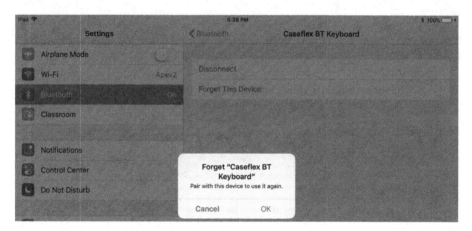

Figure 3-101. *To forget a Bluetooth keyboard, tap the Forget This Device button on the control screen for the keyboard, and then tap the OK button in the Forget dialog*

Creating Text Replacements and Configuring Assistive Text Features

On the Keyboards screen in the Settings app, you can create text replacements and configure assistive text features.

Text replacements are strings of text that you want iOS to replace automatically. For example, you could create a text replacement that replaces the shortcut *thissch* with your school's full name. After creating the replacement, you could type the shortcut to enter the full name quickly.

To create a text replacement, follow these steps:

1. On the first Keyboards screen, tap the Text Replacement button to display the first Text Replacement screen (see Figure 3-102). This screen may contain Apple's example shortcut omw, which expands to the phrase On my way!

Figure 3-102. *The first Text Replacement screen shows any existing text replacements. Tap the + button in the upper-right corner to start creating a new text replacement*

2. Tap the + button in the upper-right corner of the first Text Replacement screen to display the second Text Replacement screen (see Figure 3-103).

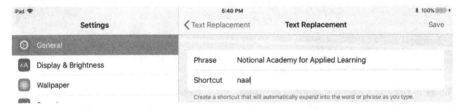

Figure 3-103. *On the second Text Replacement screen, type the phrase and the shortcut, and then tap the Save button*

3. In the Phrase box, type the replacement text.

■ **Tip**   The Shortcut field on the second Text Replacement screen is marked "Optional" because you can create a phrase without a shortcut. Doing so adds the phrase to the dictionary, exempting the phrase from spell checking, but doesn't create a shortcut for it.

---

4.   In the Shortcut box, type the shortcut for the replacement. Normally, you'll want to keep the shortcut short so you can type it easily. Avoid using a real word for the shortcut so that you don't trigger the replacement unintentionally.

5.   Tap the Save button. The first Text Replacement screen appears again, now with the new text replacement on it.

To configure assistive text features, set the switches on the first Keyboards screen to On or Off, as needed. The following list explains the features:

- *Auto-Capitalization*: Set this switch to On to have iOS capitalize the first letter of a new sentence or paragraph.

- *Auto-Correction*: Set this switch to On to have iOS automatically correct items in its database of frequent typos, such as correcting teh to the.

- *Check Spelling*: Set this switch to On to enable spell checking.

- *Enable Caps Lock*: Set this switch to On to enable the Caps Lock feature, which you trigger by double-tapping the Shift key.

- *Shortcuts*: Set this switch to On to enable text replacements.

- *Predictive*: Set this switch to On to enable predictive text. The predictive text suggestions appear on the Suggestions bar above the keyboard.

- *Smart Punctuation*: [iOS 11 only] Set this switch to On to enable smart punctuation, which inserts typographical characters for plain typed characters—for example, substituting smart quotes ("") for straight quotes ("").

- *Split Keyboard*: Set this switch to On to enable the command for splitting the keyboard into left and right sections. The split keyboard can be good for thumb typing.

- *Enable Key Flicks*: (iOS 11 only.) Set this switch to On to enable flicking down on a key on the on-screen keyboard to type the character shown in gray above the main character. For example, you can flick downward on Q to type 1, flick downward on W to type 2, and so on.

- *"." Shortcut*: Set this switch to On to have iOS type a period (.) when you type two spaces in quick succession at the end of a word.

Enabling Dictation

iOS's Dictation feature enables you to dictate text into your iPad with fair speed and impressive accuracy. Dictation can be a great way of entering text quickly, but in most cases it's best used by individuals or small groups; if you have a full classroom of students trying to dictate text simultaneously, chances are the noise will rapidly reach cocktail-party levels, and voice recognition will become difficult.

■ **Caution**   iOS implements dictation by recording your input and sending it to Apple's voice-recognition servers, which process the audio and return the corresponding text. For most consumers and many businesses, this is simply a practical arrangement that doesn't raise privacy concerns. But if your school has tight privacy policies, you might need to check that using dictation on iOS conforms to them.

To enable Dictation, set the Enable Dictation switch at the bottom of the first Keyboards screen to On, and then tap the Enable Dictation button in the Enable Dictation? dialog (see Figure 3-104).

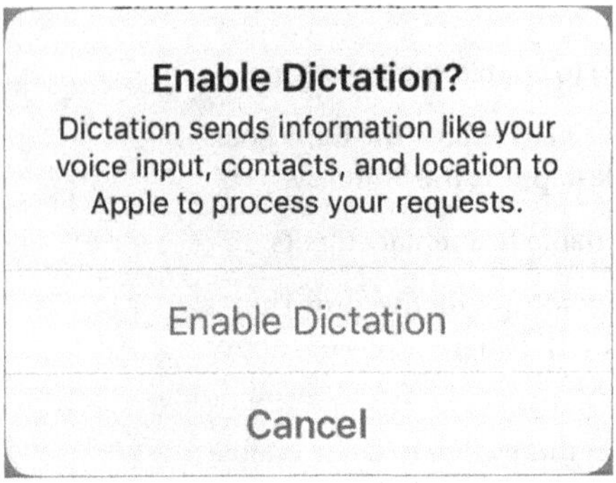

Enable Dictation?

Dictation sends information like your voice input, contacts, and location to Apple to process your requests.

Enable Dictation

Cancel

Figure 3-104. Tap the Enable Dictation button in the Enable Dictation? dialog to enable dictation

Once you've enabled Dictation, you can use it by tapping the microphone button that appears to the left of the spacebar on the keyboard.

Updating the Operating System

Apple frequently issues updates to iOS to resolve security issues, improve performance, and add new features. To keep your iPads running well, it's usually a good idea to apply iOS updates soon after Apple releases them. This section shows you how to update iOS directly on the iPad.

■ **Caution**   Software updates sometimes cause incompatibilities and unexpected problems. Rather than applying each update the moment it becomes available, you may prefer to wait a few days to see if other users report problems with the update. If problems occur, wait for an update to the update; if not, install the update.

Updating the Operating System Manually

The most straightforward way to update the operating system on an iPad is by working manually. When an update is available, a red badge appears on the Settings app icon on the Home screen. The badge normally shows the number 1, unless there are multiple updates.

Here's how to update the operating system manually:

1. From the Home screen, choose Settings ➤ General ➤ Software Update to display the Software Update screen (see Figure 3-105). iOS checks automatically for an update, even if it's already established that one is available, because there may now be a newer update. If an update is available, the update's details appear; if not, you'll see a readout saying that the software is up to date.

Figure 3-105. *The Software Update screen in the Settings app displays any available software update for the iPad's operating system. Tap the Install Now button to start installing the update*

■ **Note**   You can tap the Learn More button on the Software Update screen to display the About This Update dialog box, which shows fuller details of the fixes and improvements the update contains. When you finish looking through the details, tap the Done button to close the About This Update dialog box.

2. If an update is available, but hasn't yet been downloaded, tap the Download and Install button. Otherwise, if there's an update that has been downloaded, tap the Install Now button. Either way, the Enter Passcode dialog opens, demanding your login passcode.

3. Type the passcode. The Terms and Conditions dialog opens.

4. Read the terms and conditions, or tap the Send by E-mail button and enter the e-mail address to which you want to have them sent so you can add them to your files.

5. Tap the Agree button. A smaller Terms and Conditions dialog then opens.

6. Tap the Agree button in this dialog as well. The download or the update then starts.

Installing and Removing Apps and Customizing the Home Screen Pages

Each iPad comes with a suite of built-in apps, such as the Safari app for browsing the Web, the Mail app for communicating via e-mail, and the Camera app for taking photos and videos. You can install other apps manually from the App Store—and remove any apps you find aren't useful—either by working on the iPad itself or by managing the iPad from iTunes.

■ **Note** You can also install and remove apps via policy. For example, if you order customized iPads from the Apple Store or via Apple School Manager, the iPads will come with the apps and settings you specify.

You can customize the Home screen pages by rearranging the icons on them, creating folders, and arranging the icons into folders.

Installing an App Directly on the iPad

Installing an app from the App Store is straightforward. Tap the App Store icon on the Home screen to launch the App Store app, and then browse or search to find the app you want to install. For example, to find a calculator app for the iPad, tap the Search button at the bottom of the screen, and then type a search term (such as *calculator*). Figure 3-106 shows the information screen for a calculator app called The Calculator.

■ **Note**   If the App Store icon doesn't appear on the Home screen or when you search for it, the iPad has restrictions applied to it. If you manage this iPad directly, choose Settings ➤ General ➤ Restrictions from the Home screen, enter your Restrictions Passcode when prompted, and then set the Installing Apps switch and the Deleting Apps switch to On. Go back to the Home screen, and the App Store icon will be present.

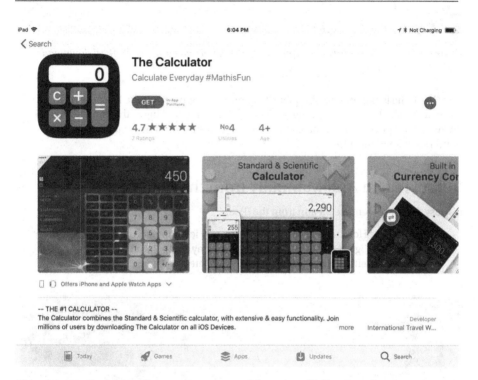

Figure 3-106. *In the App Store app, tap an app's button to display the information screen for the app. You can then tap the Get button (for a free app) or the price button (for a paid app) to start the installation*

If you want to install the app, tap the Get button (for a free app) or the price button (for a paid app), and then tap the Install button that replaces the Get button or the price button. Sign in if the App Store prompts you to do so. The iPad then downloads the app and installs it. While the app is downloading and installing, the Loading icon appears on the Home screen (see Figure 3-107).

Figure 3-107. *The Loading icon appears on the Home screen while the iPad downloads and installs the app*

When the installation is complete, the app's icon appears on the Home screen, and you can launch the app by tapping the icon. If you're still looking at the app's information dialog in the App Store app, you can tap the Open button (which replaces the Install button) to launch the app.

Removing an App Manually from the iPad

It's easy to quickly remove an app from the iPad:

1. On the Home screen, tap and hold an app icon until the icons start to jiggle. A gray circle containing a gray X appears at the upper-left corner of each app you can delete (see Figure 3-108).

Figure 3-108. *To remove an app, tap and hold its icon on the Home screen until the icons start to jiggle, and then tap the X button on the icon*

2. Tap the X button. The Delete dialog for the app opens (see Figure 3-109), warning you that deleting the app will delete its data as well.

Figure 3-109. *Tap the Delete button in the Delete dialog to delete the app and its data*

3. Tap the Delete button. iOS deletes the app and its data, and the app's icon disappears from the Home screen.

4. Press the Home button. The icons stop jiggling.

Customizing the Home Screen Pages Manually

You can customize the Home screen pages by rearranging the icons either on the pages themselves or by placing the icons in folders you create.

iOS 11 makes customizing the Home screen a little easier than it is in iOS 10—and in iOS 11, you can also customize the Dock (which iOS 10 doesn't have).

In iOS 10, you must first open the appropriate Home screen page for customization by tapping and holding an icon on that page. It doesn't matter which icon you tap and hold, but usually it's easiest to tap and hold an icon that you want to move or that you want to put in a folder. When the icons start jiggling, and an X button appears on the upper-left corner of the icon for each app you can remove, the page is open for customization. You can use this method in iOS 11 as well—and you need to use it for moves such as creating a folder and giving the folder a name—but iOS 11 also lets you simply tap and hold an icon until it expands momentarily, indicating that it's movable and that you can drag it.

After these preliminaries, you can take the following actions:

- *Move an icon*: Drag the icon to where you want it. The other icons move out of the way as needed. Figure 3-110 shows a Home screen page open for editing and an icon being dragged in iOS 10. To move the icon to a different Home screen page, drag to the left or right edge of the screen, wait until the previous page or next page appears, and then continue dragging to the desired position.

Figure 3-110. *After tapping and holding an icon to open the Home screen page for editing, you can drag an icon to where you want it*

- *Create a folder*: Drag the icon for an app you want to include in the folder onto the icon for another app you want to include. iOS creates the folder, puts the app icons in it, and suggests a name (see Figure 3-111, which also shows iOS 10). You can tap the X button to the right of the name to delete the suggestion, or simply edit it as needed. When you're ready to close the folder, tap outside it.

Figure 3-111. *iOS creates a folder when you drop one icon on top of another. You can edit the folder name as needed*

■ **Tip**   Each folder can contain multiple pages. To move to the next page, drag an icon within the folder to the right edge of the folder area.

■ **Note**   In iOS 11, you can create a folder by dragging one app's icon onto another without opening the Home screen page for customization. When you do this, though, iOS gives the folder a default name and doesn't give you the option of changing it until you open the Home screen page for customization.

- *Add an app to a folder*: Drag the app's icon to the folder and drop it there.

- *Remove an app from a folder*: Tap the folder to open it, and then drag the app out of the folder.

Installing and Removing Apps Using iTunes

If you've used iTunes to set up an iPad, you can use iTunes to manage the apps on the iPad as well. iTunes enables you to browse the App Store easily, buy and download apps, and install them on iOS devices.

Browsing and Buying Apps Using iTunes

To browse and buy apps using iTunes, follow these steps:

1. Open iTunes as usual.

2. Click the Store button on the Navigation bar at the top of the window to display the Store screen.

3. Click the pop-up menu on the right, and then click App Store to display the App Store section of the Store.

4. Click the iPad tab button at the top of the screen to display iPad apps rather than iPhone apps (see Figure 3-112).

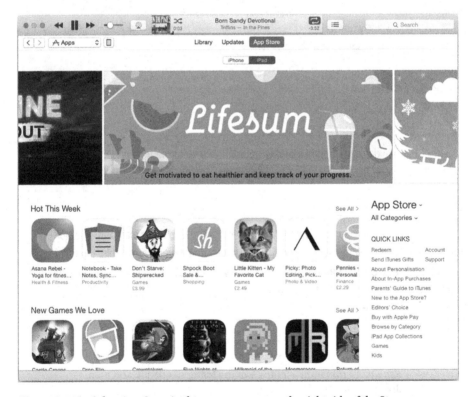

Figure 3-112. *Select App Store in the pop-up menu on the right side of the Store screen, and then click the iPad tab at the top of the screen to display iPad apps. You can then browse apps by using the lists or categories, or by searching*

You can then locate the apps you want in any of the following three ways:

- *Browse by lists*: The App Store includes many lists, such as Get Productive, Great with Apple Pencil, and New Games We Love.

- *Browse by categories*: Click the Categories pop-up menu (which appears as All Categories in Figure 3-112), and then click the appropriate category, such as Education, Productivity, or Utilities.

- *Search by name or keyword*: Tap the Search box in the upper-right corner of the iTunes window, click the Store tab button instead of the In Library tab button, and then type your search terms.

When you locate the right app, click the Get button (for a free app—see Figure 3-113) or the price button (for a paid app). Sign in to the Store if iTunes prompts you to do so. iTunes then downloads the app to the computer.

Figure 3-113. *Click the Get button (for a free app) or the price button (for a paid app) to download an app from the App Store to the computer*

Browsing Your Library of Apps

When you want to see all the apps you've purchased or downloaded for free from the App Store, click the Library tab button in the Navigation bar at the top of the iTunes window. The Library screen appears, showing the available apps (see Figure 3-114). The Sidebar shows the Library category and the Devices category, in which any iPad appears that is connected to the computer.

Figure 3-114. *Display the Library screen when you want to see all the apps you've purchased or downloaded for free from the App Store. The Update flash indicates an app for which an update is available*

From the Library screen, you can take the following actions:

- *View details for an app*: Right-click (or Ctrl-click on the Mac) the app's icon and then click Get Info on the shortcut menu. In the dialog that opens, look at the Details tab to see the app's name, the developer, and the version. Look at the File tab to see the app's size, its kind (such as iPhone/iPod touch/iPad app), the iCloud account that purchased the app and the purchase date, and the location and filename of the app file. Click the OK button when you finish examining the details.

- *Open a Finder window to the folder containing an app*: Right-click (or Ctrl-click on the Mac) the app's icon and then click Show in Finder on the shortcut menu.

- *Display an app's page in the App Store*: Right-click (or Ctrl-click on the Mac) the app's icon and then click Show in iTunes Store on the shortcut menu.

- *Update an app*: If an Update flash appears across the upper-right corner of the app's icon, you can update the app by right-clicking (or Ctrl-clicking on the Mac) the app's icon and then clicking Update App on the shortcut menu.

■ **Tip**   Instead of updating apps individually, you may prefer to update all apps at once by working on the Updates tab. See the next section for details.

- *Delete an app*: Right-click (or Ctrl-click on the Mac) the app's icon, click Delete From Library on the shortcut menu, and then click the Delete App button in the confirmation dialog that opens.

- *Install an app*: Drag the app from the Library screen to the iPad in the sidebar.

Updating Apps in Your Library

The Updates screen enables you to see which apps have updates available. You can click the Update All Apps button to update all the apps in a single operation. Alternatively, you can update a single app by right-clicking (or Ctrl-clicking on the Mac) its icon and then clicking Update App on the shortcut menu.

Installing and Removing Apps Using iTunes

You can quickly install apps on the iPad and remove apps from it by using iTunes. Follow these steps:

1.   Connect the iPad to the Mac or PC.

■ **Note**   You can connect the iPad either directly, via USB, or via Wi-Fi (if you have enabled Wi-Fi sync). USB is usually the fastest and easiest means for syncing an iPad.

---

2.   Click the iPad button on the Navigation bar at the top of the iTunes window. The screens for managing the iPad appear.

3.   In the Settings section of the sidebar, click the Apps item. The Apps screen appears (see Figure 3-115).

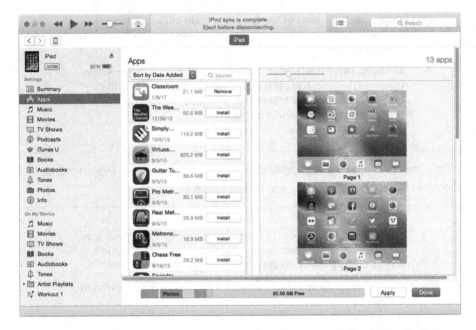

Figure 3-115. *On the Apps screen, you can install and remove apps by clicking the buttons in the Apps list or by dragging apps to and from the Home screen pages in the Home Screens list*

4. Click the Sort pop-up menu under the Apps heading and then click the Show Only iPad Apps item instead of the Show All Apps item at the bottom of the pop-up menu.

To locate the apps you need, you can sort or search the list of apps. To sort the apps, click the Sort pop-up menu under the Apps heading and then click the sort type you want:

- *Sort by Name*: Sorts the apps in alphabetical order.

- *Sort by Kind*: Sorts the apps into three kinds: Universal (apps designed to run on all iOS devices), iPad (apps designed to run only on the iPad), and iPhone (apps designed to run on the iPhone ad iPod touch).

■ **Note**   Selecting the Show Only iPad Apps item on the Sort pop-up menu makes the Apps list display Universal apps and iPad apps. Normally, selecting Show Only iPad Apps is more helpful than sorting by Kind.

- *Sort by Category*: Sorts the apps into App Store categories such as Books, Business, Education, Entertainment, and Finance.

- *Sort by Date Added*: Sorts the apps into reverse date order, so the apps added most recently appear at the top of the list. Sort by Date Added is useful for quickly locating apps you've just downloaded.

- *Sort by Size*: Sorts the apps into descending order by size. Sort by Size is useful for locating space hogs.

You can also search by clicking the Search field and typing part of an app's name, a keyword in a description, or a category name.

Once you've located the apps you're interested in, you can set apps to be installed or removed:

- *Set an app to be installed*: Click the Install button for the app. The Will Install button replaces the Install button. The app's icon appears on one of the Home screen pages in the Home Screens list on the right side of the iTunes window.

■ **Tip**   When you click the Install button, iTunes places the app's icon in a default position on a Home screen page—usually after the last existing app icon. If you want to move the app's icon to a different position, double-click the Home screen page to open that page for editing. You can then drag the icons around. Click outside the open page when you're ready to close it.

- *Set an app to be removed*: Click the Remove button for the app. The Will Remove button replaces the Remove button, and the app's icon disappears from the Home screen page it was on.

■ **Tip**   You can also drag an app's icon from the Apps list to a particular spot on the Home screen page of your choice. You may find this an easier way to control icon placement than clicking the Install button and then dragging the icon after iTunes places it.

When you're ready to commit the changes you've made, click the Apply button. iTunes syncs the iPad's apps, installing those you've marked for installation, removing those you've marked for removal, and making other changes you've marked (such as rearranging app icons).

Customizing the Home Screen Pages

From the Apps screen, you can customize the Home screen pages in the following ways:

- *Add a Home screen page*: Click the + button at the right end of the Home Screens bar. A new page appears at the bottom of the list; you may need to scroll down to see it.

- *Rearrange the Home screen pages*: Click the Home screen page you want to move, and then drag it up or down the list. When rearranging pages, you may find it helpful to zoom the Home screen pages out by dragging the slider at the top of the Home Screens list to the left.

- *Remove a Home screen page*: You can't directly remove a Home screen page, but iTunes automatically removes any page that contains no icons when you apply the changes.

- *Remove an app*: Double-click the Home screen page that contains the app's icon. The Home screen page opens for editing. Move the pointer over the icon for the app you want to remove, and then click the X button that appears on the upper-left corner of the app's icon.

- *Create a folder*: Double-click the Home screen page that contains the first two apps you want to put into the folder. The page opens for editing. Drag one app's icon onto the other app's icon and drop it there. iTunes creates a folder, to which it gives a suggested name based on the categories of the apps. Edit the name as needed—or type another name—and press the Return key or the Enter key to apply it. Click outside the page when you finish editing it.

- *Put an app in a folder*: Double-click the Home screen page that contains the app and the folder. The page opens for editing. Drag the app's icon to the folder and drop it there.

Managing Local Storage and iCloud Storage

Each iPad has built-in storage for storing apps and files. When you connect the iPad to an iCloud account, the iPad can also store data in iCloud. For example, iCloud-enabled apps (such as Pages and Numbers) can store documents in iCloud so that you can access them from any iOS device, from Macs, and from most computers. You can also choose which other items—such as photos, videos, and backups—to save from an iPad to iCloud.

These features work differently in iOS 11 than in iOS 10, so I'll cover them in separate sections.

Managing Local Storage and iCloud Storage on iOS 11

This section explains how to manage local storage and iCloud storage on iOS 11. First, we'll get an overview of the iPad's storage situation and how you can manage it and clear space when needed. After that, we'll explore how you manage iCloud storage and how you buy more storage if you need it.

Assessing the iPad's Storage Situation and Managing Local Storage

To get an overview of the iPad's storage situation, display the Home screen and then choose Settings ➤ General ➤ iPad Storage. On the iPad Storage screen (see Figure 3-116), start by looking at the iPad histogram at the top to see how much space has been used and which items—photos, apps, media, books, mail, and other—are using it. The headline figure, such as 13.5 GB of 32 GB Used, gives you an idea of the overall picture.

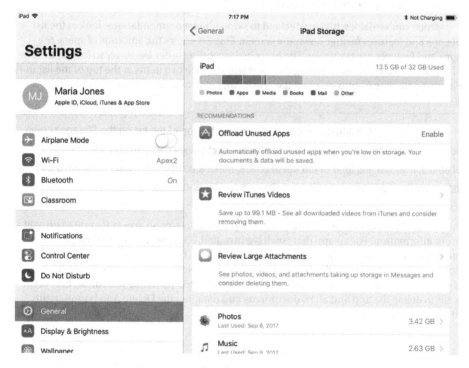

Figure 3-116. *Look at the iPad Storage screen in the Settings app to get an overview of how much of the iPad's local storage is currently in use and how much is still available*

Next, look at the Recommendations box, which shows suggestions for ways you can reclaim storage. The recommendations depend on your iPad and its contents, but here are three examples:

- *Offload Unused Apps*: Tap the Enable button to turn on the Offload Unused Apps feature, which—when storage is low—automatically deletes you haven't used for a long time. The iPad retains the documents and data for the apps, and you can download the apps again from the App Store when you need to use them again.

- *Review iTunes Videos*: Tap this button to see a list of videos you've downloaded from iTunes and that you can delete to recover space.

- *Review Large Attachments*: Tap this button to see a list of large attachments that are taking up space in the Messages app. If you no longer need these attachments, you can delete them to recover the space they're occupying.

Once you've dealt with—or decided to skip—the recommendations, look at the list of apps and features further down the screen. This list shows the amounts of space the apps and features are taking up. The list is in descending order by usage, so look at the top of the list to see what's consuming the most storage. The two items at the top of the list in Figure 3-116—the Photos app and the Music App—are frequent offenders.

■ **Note**   The Photos app often appears at or near the top of the list on the Storage screen, because photos take up a large amount of space and videos can take up a huge amount of space. If your iPads tend to run out of space, make a point of reviewing the photos and videos on the iPads and removing any that are no longer needed.

From the iPad Storage screen, you can tap the button for an app or feature to display more information. For an app that you have installed, iOS displays an Info screen that includes the Offload App button for offloading the app (removing the app but keeping its documents and data) and the Delete App button for deleting the app (see Figure 3-117). If you tap the Delete App button, iOS displays the Delete App dialog to confirm that you want to delete the app and all its documents and data; tap the Delete App button in the dialog if you want to proceed.

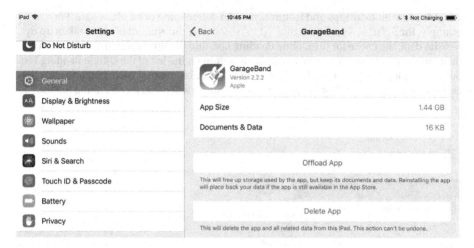

Figure 3-117. *On the Info screen for an app in iOS 11, you can tap the Delete App button to delete the app together with its documents and data, freeing up the storage they're consuming, or tap the Offload App button to delete the app but keep its documents and data on the iPad*

For a built-in app or a feature that you can't remove, iOS displays a screen showing the name of the app or feature and more information about the space it's consuming. For example, if you tap the Videos button on the iPad Storage screen, you'll see the Videos screen (see Figure 3-118), which shows a Documents & Data readout showing the space that videos are taking up. There's an Edit button that you can tap to switch to Edit Mode, but for this app, Edit Mode doesn't actually let you make any changes.

Figure 3-118. *The information screen for a built-in app or feature shows its name and details of the items that are taking up space on the iPad*

For some built-in apps and features, you can delete some or all of the data. For example, the Safari screen (see Figure 3-119) shows you the amount of space taken up by website data, the cache for the Offline Reading List, and the browsing History. You can then tap the Edit button to reveal a red minus button on the left of the Offline Reading List button; tapping this red minus button reveals a Delete button that you can tap to clear the cache for the offline Reading List. Tap the Done button when you finish editing the list.

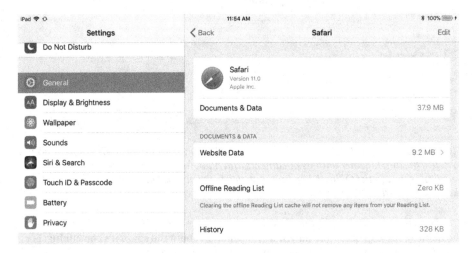

Figure 3-119. *On the Safari screen, you can tap the Edit button to reveal controls for deleting the Offline Reading List cache*

Managing iCloud Storage and Buying More If Necessary

A standard iCloud account includes 5 GB of storage for free, which is enough for light use, especially if the iPad doesn't need to store many photos and videos. To stay within the iCloud storage allowance, you can monitor the amount of space that items are taking up, and delete items no longer needed on the iPad. If necessary, you can change the storage plan for the iCloud account.

To manage storage, first display the iCloud screen by choosing Settings ➤ Apple ID ➤ iCloud. The Storage readout at the top of the iCloud screen (see Figure 3-120) shows the amount of space occupied and the amount that's free.

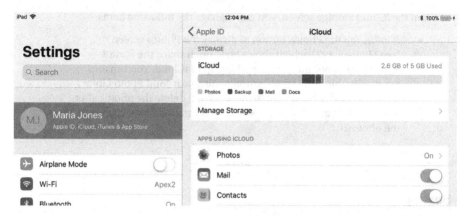

Figure 3-120. *To monitor the amount of iCloud storage used and available, display the iCloud screen in Settings and look at the Storage readout*

Tap the Manage Storage button in the Storage box to display the iCloud Storage screen (see Figure 3-121).

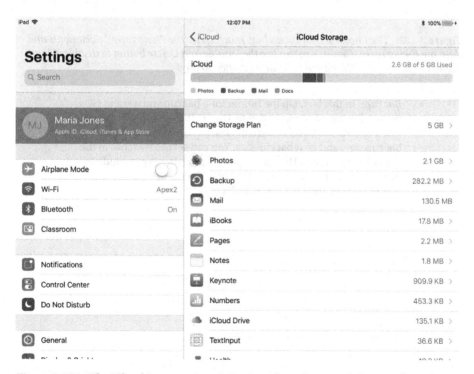

Figure 3-121. *The iCloud Storage screen in Settings shows how much items such as photos, backups, documents and data, and mail are taking up in the iCloud account*

From the iCloud Storage screen, you can manage the following items:

- *Photos*: Tap the Photos button to display the Photos screen
  (see Figure 3-122), which shows how much space the Photos
  app's documents and data are taking up in iCloud. You can also
  tap the Disable and Delete button to disable iCloud Photo Library
  on this iCloud account and to make iCloud delete the photos after
  30 days. (This grace period is so that you can download copies of
  the photos.)

Figure 3-122. The Photos screen shows how much space the Photos apps' documents and data are taking up in iCloud. You can tap the Disable and Delete button to disable iCloud Photo Library and set the photos to be deleted after 30 days

- *Backups*: In this box, tap the button for a backup you want to view
  more information about or delete. On the Info screen that appears
  (see Figure 3-123), you can see the last backup date, current
  backup size, and next backup size. You can set the switches in the
  Choose Data to Back Up box to specify which items to include in
  the backup and which to exclude. If you decide this backup is no
  longer needed, tap the Delete Backup button to delete it.

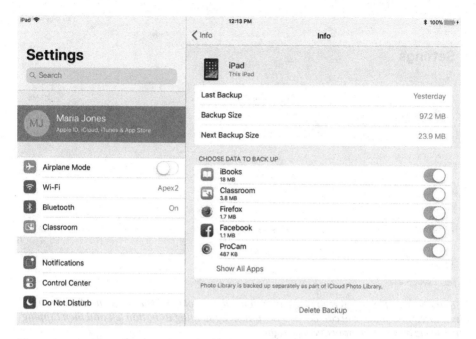

Figure 3-123. *The Info screen for a backup shows the last backup date, current backup size, and next backup size. You can set switches in the Choose Data to Back Up box to specify which items to include in backups. Tap the Delete Backup button to delete the backup*

- *List of apps storing data in iCloud*: In this box, tap the button for an app to display its Info screen. Figure 3-124 shows the Info screen for the Pages app. Here, you can see the documents the app has stored on iCloud, which enables you to delete any that are no longer needed or that are taking up too much space. To delete one or more documents, swipe the item's button left, and then tap the Delete button that appears to the right of the button. Alternatively, tap the Delete Documents & Data button to delete all the documents and data.

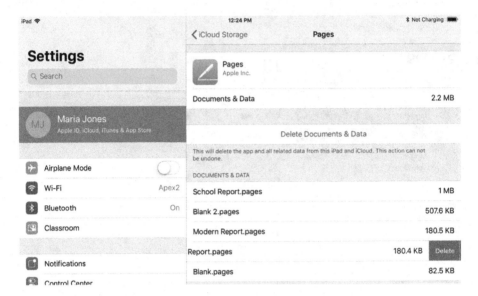

Figure 3-124. *The Info screen for an app shows details of the documents and data the app has stored in iCloud. You can delete a document by swiping its button left and then tapping the Delete button that appears to its right*

If you need to increase the storage available for this iCloud account, tap the Change Storage Plan button. In the Upgrade iCloud Storage dialog (see Figure 3-125), tap the button for the new plan, and then tap the Buy button.

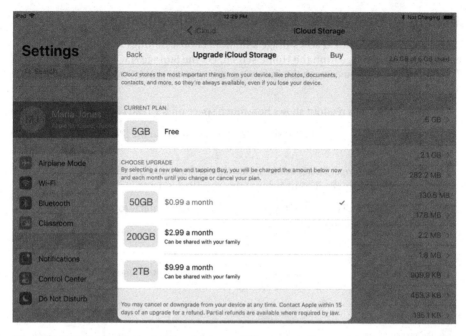

Figure 3-125. *In the Upgrade iCloud Storage dialog, tap the button for the plan you want to change to, and then tap the Buy button*

■ **Note**   Despite its name, the Upgrade iCloud Storage dialog lets you *reduce* your iCloud storage if you have more than the minimum. Tap the Downgrade Options button to access these options.

Managing Local Storage and iCloud Storage on iOS 10

This section explains how to manage local storage and iCloud storage on iOS 10. I'll start by giving an overview of the iPad's storage situation, move along to managing the built-in storage, and then cover managing iCloud storage and buying more if you need it.

Getting an Overview of the iPad's Storage Situation

To get an overview of the iPad's storage situation, choose Settings ➤ General ➤ Storage & iCloud Usage from the Home screen. On the Storage & iCloud Usage screen (see Figure 3-126), you can see the following information in the Storage box and in the iCloud box:

- *Used*: This readout shows how much space on the iPad is in use.

- *Available*: This readout shows how much space on the iPad is available.

- *Total Storage*: This readout shows the total amount of space available in the iCloud account that this iPad is using.

- *Available*: This readout shows how much of the total iCloud storage is available.

Figure 3-126. *Look at the Storage & iCloud Usage screen in the Settings app to get an overview of how much storage is currently in use and how much is available on the iPad itself and in the associated iCloud account*

Managing the iPad's Built-In Storage

To see what's taking up space in the iPad's built-in storage, and to free up space if necessary, tap the Manage Storage button in the Storage box on the Storage & iCloud Usage screen. The Storage screen appears (see Figure 3-127), showing the following information:

- *Used*: This readout shows the amount of storage used—the same figure that appears on the Storage & iCloud Usage screen.

- *Available*: This readout shows the amount of storage available— also the same figure that appears on the Storage & iCloud Usage screen.

- *Apps and features*: This list shows the amounts of space that apps and features are taking up on the iPad. The list is in descending order by usage, so look at the top of the list to see what's consuming the most storage.

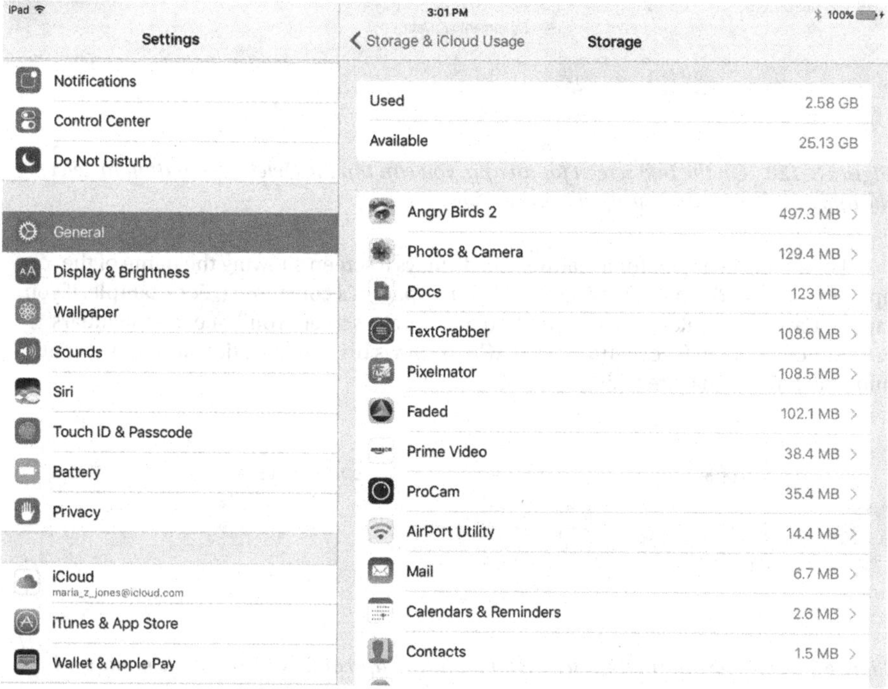

iPad 🤖	3:01 PM	⚹ 100% 💶 ⨁
Settings	❮ Storage & iCloud Usage	**Storage**

🔲 Notifications	Used	2.58 GB
🔲 Control Center	Available	25.13 GB
🌙 Do Not Disturb		
⚙️ General	🐦 Angry Birds 2	497.3 MB ❯
	🌼 Photos & Camera	129.4 MB ❯
🅰️🅰️ Display & Brightness	📄 Docs	123 MB ❯
🌸 Wallpaper	📇 TextGrabber	108.6 MB ❯
🔊 Sounds	🖼️ Pixelmator	108.5 MB ❯
🌊 Siri	◉ Faded	102.1 MB ❯
🔒 Touch ID & Passcode	▬ Prime Video	38.4 MB ❯
📷 Battery	⭕ ProCam	35.4 MB ❯
🖐️ Privacy	📶 AirPort Utility	14.4 MB ❯
☁️ iCloud	✉️ Mail	6.7 MB ❯
maria_z_jones@icloud.com	📅 Calendars & Reminders	2.6 MB ❯
🅐 iTunes & App Store	👤 Contacts	1.5 MB ❯
🔳 Wallet & Apple Pay		

Figure 3-127. *Look at the list in the lower box on the Storage screen to see which apps and features are taking up the most space on an iPad*

■ **Note** The Photos & Camera feature often appears at or near the top of the list on the Storage screen, because photos take up a large amount of space and videos can take up a huge amount of space. If your iPads tend to run out of space, make a point of reviewing the photos and videos on the iPads and removing any that are no longer needed. Look also at podcasts—they too can take up a lot of space.

From the Storage screen, you can tap the button for an app or feature to display more information. For an app that you have installed, iOS displays an Info screen that includes a Delete App button for deleting the app (see Figure 3-128). iOS displays the Delete App dialog to confirm that you want to delete the app and all its documents and data; tap the Delete App button in the dialog if you want to proceed.

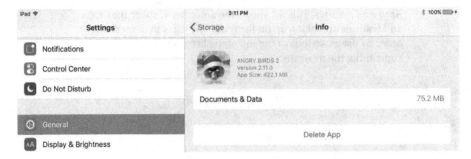

Figure 3-128. *On the Info screen for an app, you can tap the Delete App button to delete the app and free up the storage it's consuming*

For a built-in app or for a feature, iOS displays a screen showing the name of the app or feature and more information about the space it's consuming. For example, if you tap the Calendars & Reminders button on the Storage screen, you'll see the Calendars & Reminders screen (see Figure 3-129), which shows brief information about the events and attachments that are taking up space.

iPad 🕱	3:17 PM	🔋 100% 💷 ⨍
Settings	❮ Storage **Calendars & Reminders**	
⚙ General	CALENDARS & REMINDERS	2.6 MB
AA Display & Brightness	Events	2.6 MB
❀ Wallpaper	Attachments	Zero KB

Figure 3-129. *The information screen for a built-in app or feature shows its name and details of the items that are taking up space on the iPad*

For some built-in apps and features, you can delete some or all of the data. For example, the Safari screen (see Figure 3-130) shows you the amount of space taken up by website data, the cache for the offline Reading List, and the browsing History. You can tap the Edit button to reveal a graphical Delete button on the left of the Offline Reading List button; tapping this graphical Delete button reveals a textual Delete button that you can tap to clear the cache for the offline Reading List. Tap the Done button when you finish editing the list.

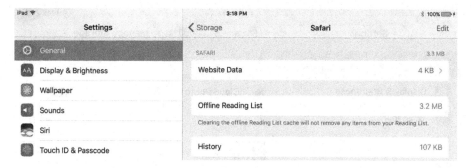

Figure 3-130. *On the Safari screen, you can tap the Edit button to reveal controls for deleting the offline Reading List cache*

Managing iCloud Storage and Buying More If Necessary

A standard iCloud account includes 5 GB of storage for free, which is enough for light use, especially if the iPad doesn't need to store many photos and videos. To stay within the iCloud storage allowance, you can monitor the amount of space that items are taking up, and delete items no longer needed on the iPad. If necessary, you can change the storage plan for the iCloud account.

You can manage iCloud storage either from the Storage & iCloud Usage screen, which you met earlier in this section, or from the Storage screen in iCloud Settings (choose Settings ➤ iCloud ➤ Storage). On the Storage & iCloud Usage screen, tap the Manage Storage button in the iCloud box; on the Storage screen, tap the Manage Storage button in the Storage box. Either way, the Manage Storage screen for managing iCloud store appears (see Figure 3-131).

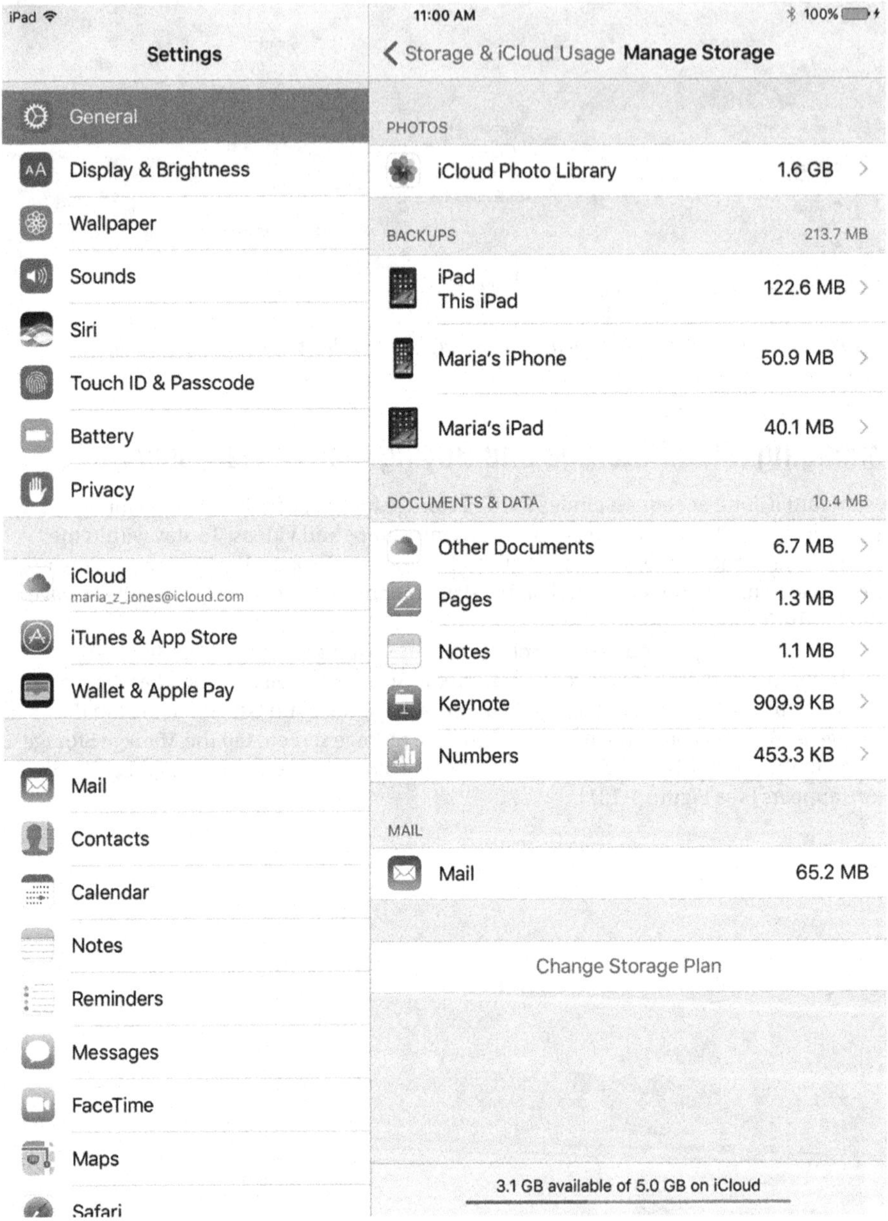

iPad 🛜	11:00 AM	🔋 100% 🔋 ⚡
Settings	‹ Storage & iCloud Usage **Manage Storage**	

⚙️ General	PHOTOS			
🅰️ Display & Brightness	🌸 iCloud Photo Library	1.6 GB	>
⚅ Wallpaper	BACKUPS		213.7 MB	
🔊 Sounds	📱 iPad This iPad	122.6 MB	>
Siri			
👆 Touch ID & Passcode	📱 Maria's iPhone	50.9 MB	>
🔋 Battery	📱 Maria's iPad	40.1 MB	>
✋ Privacy	DOCUMENTS & DATA		10.4 MB	
	☁️ Other Documents	6.7 MB	>
☁️ iCloud maria_z_jones@icloud.com	✏️ Pages	1.3 MB	>
Ⓐ iTunes & App Store	Notes	1.1 MB	>
💳 Wallet & Apple Pay	Keynote	909.9 KB	>
	📊 Numbers	453.3 KB	>
✉️ Mail			
👤 Contacts	MAIL		
📅 Calendar	✉️ Mail	65.2 MB	
Notes			
Reminders	Change Storage Plan		
💬 Messages			
📹 FaceTime			
🗺️ Maps	3.1 GB available of 5.0 GB on iCloud		
Safari			

Figure 3-131. *The Manage Storage screen in Settings shows how much items such as photos, backups, documents and data, and mail are taking up in the iCloud account*

From the Manage Storage screen, you can manage the following items:

- *Photos*: Tap the iCloud Photo Library button to display the Info screen (see Figure 3-132), which shows how many photos and videos this iCloud account is storing in iCloud. You can tap the "manage your photo library in the Photos app" link to jump to the Photos app, where you can delete photos or (better) videos to free up space. You can also tap the Disable and Delete button to disable iCloud Photo Library on this iCloud account and to make iCloud delete the photos after 30 days. (This grace period is so that you can download copies of the photos.)

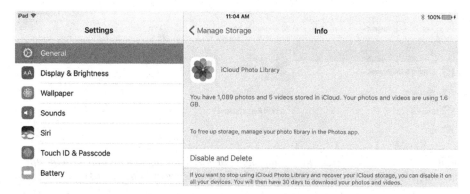

Figure 3-132. *The Info screen for iCloud Photo Library shows how many photos and videos this account has stored in iCloud. You can tap the Disable and Delete button to disable iCloud Photo Library and set the photos to be deleted after 30 days*

- *Backups*: In this box, tap the button for a backup you want to view more information about or delete. On the Info screen that appears (see Figure 3-133), you can see the last backup date and the backup size. If you decide this backup is no longer needed, tap the Delete Backup button to delete it.

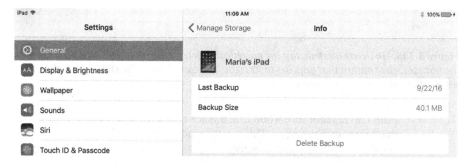

Figure 3-133. *The Info screen for a backup shows the last backup date and the backup size. You can tap the Delete Backup button to delete the backup*

- *Documents & Data*: In this box, tap the button for an app to display its Info screen. Figure 3-134 shows the Info screen for the Pages app. Here, you can see the documents the app has stored on iCloud, which enables you to delete any that are no longer needed or taking up too much space. To delete one or more documents, tap the Edit button to enable editing mode (see Figure 3-135). You can then tap the graphical Delete button to the left of an item to display the textual Delete button that you tap to delete the item. Alternatively, tap the Delete All button to delete all the documents and data.

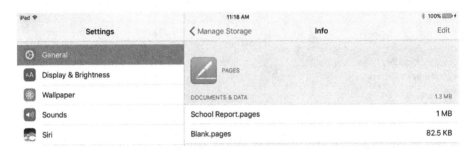

Figure 3-134. *The Info screen for an app shows details of the documents and data the app has stored in iCloud. Tap the Edit button if you need to delete any documents or data*

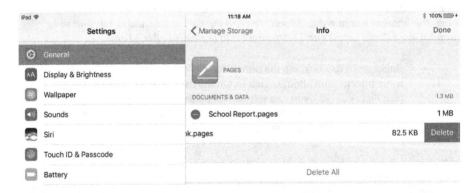

Figure 3-135. *To delete an item, tap the graphical Delete button to its left, and then tap the textual Delete button that appears to its right. You can also tap the Delete All button to delete all the documents and data*

- *Mail*: This readout shows how much space e-mail messages and attachments are taking up. This is just a readout—you can't tap the button to display an Info screen.

If you need to increase the storage available for this iCloud account, tap the Change Storage Plan button. In the Upgrade iCloud Storage dialog (see Figure 3-136), tap the button for the new plan, and then tap the Buy button.

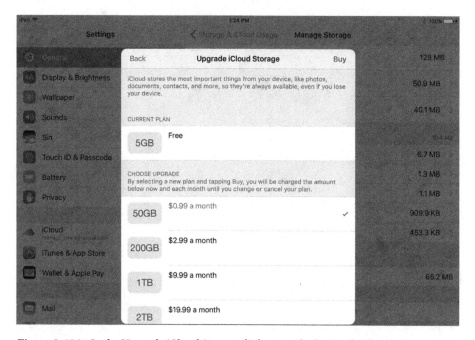

Figure 3-136. *In the Upgrade iCloud Storage dialog, tap the button for the plan you want to change to, and then tap the Buy button*

■ **Note**   Despite its name, the Upgrade iCloud Storage dialog lets you *reduce* your iCloud storage if you have more than the minimum. Tap the Downgrade Options button to access these options.

Summary

In this chapter, you've learned essential skills for using an iPad as an administrator or as a teacher. You know how to set up an iPad from scratch and connect it to Wi-Fi networks and Bluetooth devices, how to navigate the interface and restart the iPad, and how to configure the settings that are usually most important in the classroom. You also know how to connect keyboards, update the operating system, install and organize apps, and manage storage both on the iPad itself and on the iCloud account it connects to.

CHAPTER 4

■ ■ ■

Managing iPads with Apple Configurator

In this chapter, we'll look at how to use the Apple Configurator app to configure iPads automatically. We'll start with a quick overview of what you can do with the app. We'll get the app downloaded, installed, and configured on your Mac, and then work through the actions it enables you to take. These actions include connecting and updating iPads, organizing and sorting them, backing them up, and restoring them. You'll see how to prepare the iPads for deployment, build configuration profiles and apply them to iPads, and create templates called *blueprints* and apply them to iPads.

As explained in Chapter 1, Apple Configurator is only one of your options for configuring iPads automatically. You would normally use Apple Configurator only if your school doesn't have a Mobile Device Management (MDM) solution that can manage iPads and other iOS devices. If your school does have an iPad-capable MDM system, you would normally use that to configure the iPads.

Understanding What You Can Do with Apple Configurator

Apple Configurator is an Apple-developed app for configuring iOS devices—the iPad, iPhone, iPod touch, and Apple TV—connected to a Mac via a USB cable. As of this writing, the current version of Apple Configurator is version 2, and that's what the screens in this chapter show. Apple Configurator enables you to configure iOS devices—here, we'll assume they're iPads—in eight main ways:

- *Install apps and documents*: You can install apps and documents directly onto a connected iPad.

- *Configure iPads directly*: You can perform some minor configuration directly via Apple Configurator, such as changing the iPad's name, modifying its wallpaper, or customizing the Home screen layout.

- *Update iPads*: You can update iOS and apps to the latest versions.

© Guy Hart-Davis 2017
G. Hart-Davis, *Deploying iPads in the Classroom*,
https://doi.org/10.1007/978-1-4842-2928-6_4

- *Backup and restore iPads*: You can back up an iPad and restore an iPad from backup—either a backup you've made from the iPad itself or the backup of a configuration that you want to clone onto the iPad. You can also restore an iPad to factory settings.

- *Create and apply configuration profiles*: A configuration profile is a file that can contain any of a very wide range of settings for a device. You can apply either a single profile or multiple profiles to an iPad. For example, you might apply one profile that configures networking settings (such as Wi-Fi, VPN, and proxy server) for your school and another that sets up specific accounts for e-mail, contacts, calendars, and so on. By adding these two profiles to your school's iPads, you can perform a large amount of the configuration automatically.

- *Create and apply blueprints*: A blueprint is a template that can contain configuration profiles, apps, or both. You can build blueprints in Apple Configurator and apply them to the appropriate iPads. For example, you might create a blueprint for student iPads that contains the two profiles mentioned in the previous bullet plus the apps that every student will need.

- *Make a device a supervised device*: Out of the box, an iPad is normally an unsupervised device, because the iPad's owner is free to change its configuration. By contrast, a *supervised* device is one over which you retain administrative control. Supervising a device gives you tight control over which changes (if any) a user can make to the device. Assuming your school buys the iPads that you're deploying, you'll likely want to supervise the iPads. Table 4-1 explains the settings that are available only for supervised iPads and that you apply through MDM. Some of the settings that you can include in configuration profiles are also limited to supervised devices; you'll learn about these in the section "Working with Configuration Profiles," later in this chapter.

- *Prepare devices for deployment*: You can use the Prepare Assistant feature in Apple Configurator to quickly set up a large number of iPads for deployment to students or staff.

Table 4-1. *Settings Available Only for Supervised iPads*

Setting	Turn Off This Setting to
Allow screen observation by Classroom	Prevent teachers from observing the screen using the Classroom app.
Allow iMessage	Hide the Messages app on a Wi-Fi–only iPad. On a cellular iPad, prevent Messages from using the iMessage service, restricting Messages to using SMS and MMS.
Allow Apple Music	Prevent the user from using Apple Music.
Allow Radio	Prevent the user from using the Radio feature in Apple Music.
Allow user-generated content in Siri	Prevent Siri from including user-generated content in search results. This is content users have created themselves.
Enable Siri profanity filter	Detect and avoid profanity in the search results Siri returns.
Allow iBooks Store	Prevent the user from accessing the iBooks Store.
Allow installing apps using App Store	Prevent the user from installing apps from the App Store.
Allow automatic app downloads	Prevent the App Store app from downloading apps automatically.
Allow removing apps	Prevent the user from removing apps.
Allow Erase All Content and Settings	Prevent the user from erasing the iPad and resetting it to factory default settings.
Allow manual installation of configuration files	Prevent the user from installing configuration profiles manually.
Allow account modification	Prevent the user from changing their username, password, or other account settings, and from creating new accounts.
Allow Bluetooth modification	Prevent the user from modifying Bluetooth settings.
Allow cellular data settings modification	Prevent the user from modifying settings that control how apps use cellular data.
Allow modifying device name	Prevent the user from changing the iPad's name (on the Settings ➤ General ➤ About screen).
Allow Find My Friends settings modification	Prevent the user from changing Find My Friends settings.
Allow passcode modification	Prevent the user from changing the passcode.
Allow the modification of Touch ID fingerprints	Prevent the user from adding or removing Touch ID fingerprints.
Allow modifying restrictions	Prevent the user from changing Restrictions settings.

(continued)

199

Table 4-1. (*continued*)

Setting	Turn Off This Setting to
Allow modifying Wallpaper	Prevent the user from changing the lock screen wallpaper and the Home screen wallpaper.
Allow pairing to computers for content sync	Prevent the user from pairing the iPad with a computer other than the Mac used to apply supervision to the iPad.
Allow modifying sending diagnostic usage data to Apple	Prevent the user from changing the settings for sending diagnostic usage data.
Allow predictive keyboard	Hide the predictive keyboard.
Allow keyboard shortcuts	Disable keyboard shortcuts.
Allow auto correction	Disable the auto-correction feature, which suggests corrections for apparently misspelled words.
Allow spell check	Disable the spell checker.
Allow Define	Prevent the user from using the Define feature to look up a word's definition.
Allow News	Prevent the user from downloading content in the News app.
Allow Podcasts	Prevent the user from downloading podcasts.
Allow Game Center	Hide the Game Center app.
Restrict app usage	Enable yourself to place any app other than Settings into either an approved list or a disapproved list.
Allow AirDrop	Prevent users from using AirDrop with managed apps. You must turn off the "Allow documents from managed sources in unmanaged destinations" setting to make the Allow AirDrop setting work.
Single App Mode	Remove the restriction limiting the user to a single app that you selected.
Accessibility settings	Enable specific accessibility settings when the iPad is in Single App Mode.

SHOULD YOU USE APPLE CONFIGURATOR, MDM, OR BOTH?

Depending on your school's size and organization, you may find that Apple Configurator on its own provides enough configuration and management capabilities for your iPads. But if Apple Configurator doesn't meet all your needs, you can turn to a Mobile Device Management (MDM) solution. MDM solutions typically offer greater control of the devices you enroll in them, especially after you deploy the devices. For example, whereas Apple Configurator requires each device to be connected via

USB to the Mac you're using (you can connect multiple devices at once), most MDM solutions can configure devices "over the air" via a Wi-Fi or cellular connection. MDM solutions also typically let you distribute custom apps to enrolled devices, monitor the apps installed on them, and lock or even erase the devices remotely.

Various MDM solutions are available; we'll look at some options in Chapter 6. If you decide to use an MDM solution, you can either use Apple Configurator along with it or use the MDM solution on its own.

Getting Apple Configurator

In this section, we'll download the Apple Configurator app from the App Store, install it on your Mac, and configure it to suit your needs.

■ **Note** Apple Configurator requires a Mac running macOS 10.12.2 or later as of this writing. There is no version of Apple Configurator for Windows.

Downloading and Installing Apple Configurator

To download and install Apple Configurator, follow these steps:

1. On your Mac, open the App Store app from the Dock or from Launchpad.

2. Click the Search box in the upper-right corner of the window, and then type *apple configurator*. A list of search results appears.

3. Click the appropriate search result, such as Apple Configurator 2. The information screen for the app appears.

4. Click the Get button. The Get button changes to an Install button (or, depending on how you look at it, the Install button replaces the Get button).

5. Click the Install button. Your Mac downloads Apple Configurator and installs it.

■ **Note** If an alert dialog box opens saying "The required framework 'MobileDevice' is out of date. Please update iTunes," click the OK button, and then update iTunes to the latest version.

Setting Up Apple Configurator and Meeting the Interface

After installing Apple Configurator, launch the app from Launchpad; if the App Store app is still open and showing the information screen for Apple Configurator, you can click the Open button on that screen to launch the app instead.

The first time you run Apple Configurator, the License Agreement dialog opens. Click the Accept button if you want to proceed. The Welcome screen then appears. Here, you can click the Take a Quick Tour button to launch the Quick Tour feature, which walks you through the main features of Apple Configurator, or click the Get Started button to get down to business.

Once you click the Get Started button, you'll see the Apple Configurator main window showing the device browser (see Figure 4-1). The Connect Devices icon and message appear in the main pane until you connect one or more devices that Apple Configurator can manage.

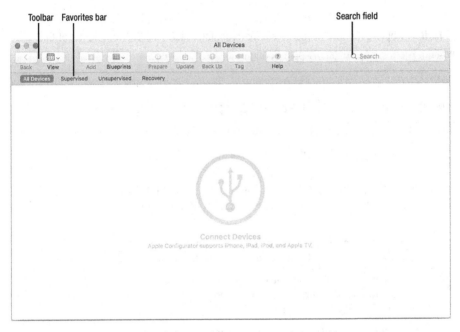

Figure 4-1. *The device browser displays the Connect Devices icon and message until you connect iPads or other iOS devices that Apple Configurator can manage*

Apple Configurator uses multiple windows to enable you to work with different types of devices, profiles, and othe objects:

- *Main window*: This window normally appears automatically when you launch Apple Configurator. The main window displays the device browser at first, showing all connected devices; if there are no connected devices, the Connect Devices message appears. You can click the Blueprints button to switch the main window to display the blueprint browser for working with blueprints.

■ **Tip** You can open multiple instances of the main window to work with different objects at the same time. To open a new window, choose File ➤ New Window or press Cmd-Opt-N.

- *Profile window*: This window appears when you give the File ➤ New Profile command (or press the Cmd-N keyboard shortcut) to start creating a new configuration profile.

- *Activity window*: This window shows the progress of any current operations, such as restoring an iPad. The window opens automatically when there's something you need to see, but you can also pop it open at any time by choosing Window ➤ Activity from the menu bar. To close the Activity window, click the Close button, the red button at the left end of the window's title bar.

- *VPP Assignments window*: This window displays details on apps you've acquired via Apple's Volume Purchase Program (VPP). You can open this window by choosing Window ➤ VPP Assignments from the menu bar. If the command is unavailable, the window isn't relevant for what you're working with. Again, click the red Close button at the left end of the window's title bar to close the window.

Configuring Apple Configurator to Suit Your Needs

Like most apps, Apple Configurator offers various preferences that you can configure to make the app work your way. As usual for Mac apps, you access the preferences through the Preferences window, which you can open by choosing Apple Configurator ➤ Preferences from the menu bar or pressing the Cmd-, (Cmd and comma) keyboard shortcut.

■ **Note** In the following subsections, we'll look at the General preferences, Organizations preferences, Servers preferences, and Tags preferences. You'll meet the final category of preferences, Backup preferences, later in the chapter in the section "Managing Your Backups."

Choosing General Preferences

The General preference pane for Apple Configurator (see Figure 4-2) enables you to control settings for sounds, reset warning dialogs, and choose whether to display the device browser when you launch the app. These are the preferences you can set:

- *Play sound on completion*: If you want Apple Configurator to play a sound when it completes a task, open this pop-up menu and click the sound you want.

- *Play sound on warning*: If you want Apple Configurator to play a sound as a warning when something goes wrong, open this pop-up menu and click the sound to play.

- *Reset all warning dialogs*: Click this button if you want to reset all the warning dialogs to their defaults. These are dialogs that open automatically to warn you when a problem has occurred; you can tell Apple Configurator not to display them again. Resetting the warning dialogs to their defaults means that you'll receive each warning again. There's no confirmation when you click this button.

- *Always show device window on launch*: Select this check box if you want Apple Configurator to display the device browser (the main window) each time you launch the app. This is usually helpful. Deselect this check box if you prefer to open the device browser manually when you need it.

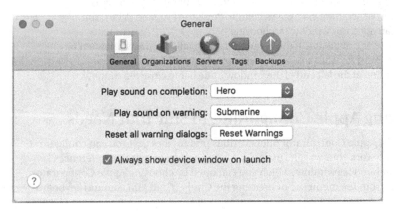

Figure 4-2. *In the General preference pane, you can control whether Apple Configurator plays sounds for warnings and for task completion and whether the app displays the device browser when you launch it. You can also reset all warning dialogs.*

Setting Up Your Organizations in the Organizations Preferences Pane

In the Organizations preferences pane (shown in Figure 4-3 with two organizations added), you can set up the organizations that you'll use to supervise the iPads. An *organization* is a named item that contains the contact information and supervision identity for a supervised device. For example, you might set up an organization to represent an entire small school. In a larger school, you might set up multiple organizations for different departments or locations.

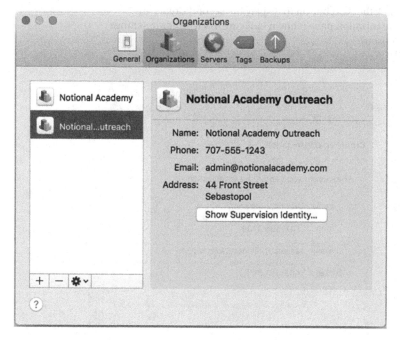

Figure 4-3. *Work in the Organizations pane in the Preferences window to set up the organizations for supervising your school's iPads*

You can add one or more organizations manually or import each organization from an existing file. When adding an organization manually, you can choose between generating a new supervision identity and choosing an existing supervision identity.

Adding an Organization

To start adding an organization, follow these steps:

1. In the Apple Configurator Preferences window, click the Organizations button on the toolbar.

2. Click the Add (+) button below the lower-left corner of the Organizations box in the Organizations pane. The first Create an Organization pane appears, giving a brief explanation of what an organization is.

3. Click the Next button to display the second Create an Organization pane (shown in Figure 4-4 with some settings chosen).

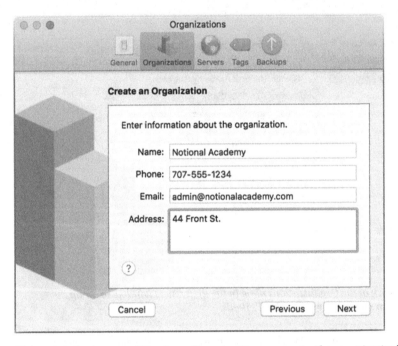

Figure 4-4. *In the second Create an Organization pane, enter the organization's name and details, and then click the Next button*

4. Type the name in the Name box. This field is required.

5. Optionally, type the phone number in the Phone box.

6. Optionally, type the e-mail address in the Email box.

7. Optionally, type the address in the Address box.

8. Click the Next button to display the third Create an Organization pane (see Figure 4-5), where you choose between generating a new supervision identity and selecting an existing supervision identity. A *supervision identity* is a digital identifier used for supervising the organization.

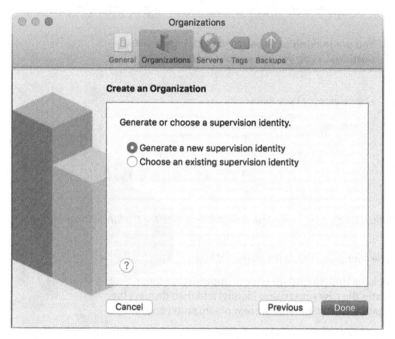

Figure 4-5. *In the third Create an Organization pane, choose between creating a new supervision identity or using an existing supervision identity*

9. Select the "Generate a new supervision identity" option button if you don't have a supervision identity to use, or the "Choose an existing supervision identity" option button if you do have one. This list assumes you've selected the "Generate a new supervision identity" option button; a little later in this section, we'll look at what happens when you select the "Choose an existing supervision identity" option button.

10. Click the Done button. The dialog shown in Figure 4-6
appears, alerting you that you're making changes to the
Certificate Trust Settings on the Mac and demanding your
password.

Figure 4-6. In this dialog, type your password and then click the Update Settings button

11. Type your password in the Password box.

12. Click the Update Settings button. Apple Configurator
creates the new supervision identity and then displays the
Organizations pane with the new organization added.

When you select the "Choose an existing supervision identity" option button in the third Create an Organization pane, the Next button replaces the Done button. To complete the process of choosing an existing supervision identity, you need to specify the digital certificate to use to encrypt the supervision identity. Follow these steps:

1. Click the Next button. The fourth Create an Organization pane appears (see Figure 4-7).

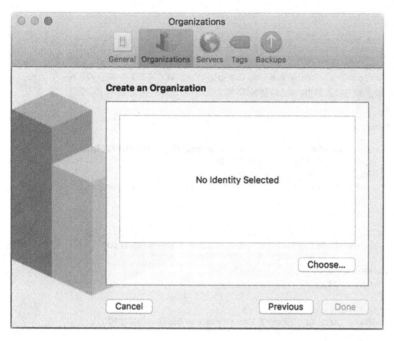

Figure 4-7. *Click the Choose button in the fourth Create an Organization pane*

2. Click the Choose button to display the "Choose a supervising identity for the organization" pane (see Figure 4-8).

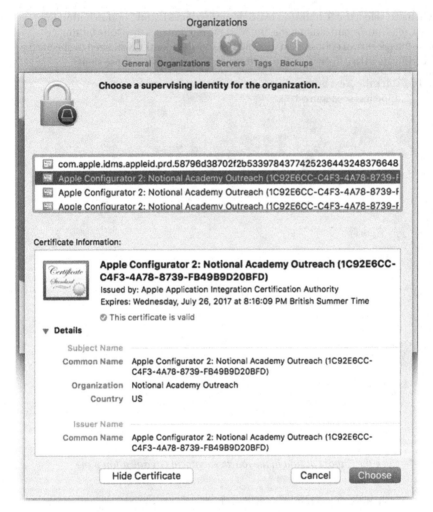

Figure 4-8. In the "Choose a supervising identity for the organization" pane, click the certificate you want to use as the supervising identity. You can click the Show Certificate button or the Hide Certificate button to toggle the display of the certificate's details.

3. Click the certificate you want to use. If the certificate's details don't appear at first, click the Show Certificate button to display them.

4. Click the Choose button. The certificate appears in the Create an Organization pane.

5. Click the Done button. Apple Configurator adds the new supervision identity to the organization and then displays the Organizations pane with the new organization added.

Importing and Exporting Organizations

If you already have an organization set up, you can import it into the Organizations pane without having to go through the steps of setting it up. To import an organization, follow these steps:

1. If you don't already have the Organizations pane displayed, click the Organizations button on the toolbar in the Apple Configurator Preferences window.

2. Click the Action pop-up menu (the gear icon with the downward caret to its right) below the Organizations list, and then click the Import Organization item. The Select Organization to Import dialog opens.

3. Navigate to the folder that contains the organization file, and then click the file.

■ **Note** Apple Configurator stores organizations in files with the `.organization` file extension.

---

4. Click the Import button. Apple Configurator imports the organization.

Similarly, after setting up an organization, you can export it for backup or for use elsewhere. To export an organization, follow these steps:

1. Click the organization in the Organizations list box in the Organizations pane.

2. Click the Action pop-up menu, and then click the Export Organization item. The "Choose a password for the organization" dialog opens. This password is used to secure the organization.

3. Type a password in the Password box, and then type it again in the Verify box.

4. Click the Set Password button. A Save sheet opens.

5. Apple Configurator displays a default name for the exported organization in the Save As box. This default name is based on the name of the organization you picked for exporting. You can edit this default name for the organization as needed.

6. In the Tags box, apply any tags needed. For example, you might apply a tag that identifies the location for the organization.

7. Specify the location where you want to save the exported file by using the Where pop-up menu or by clicking the button to the right of the Save As box and browsing to the appropriate folder.

8. Click the Save button. Apple Configurator exports the organization file.

You can also export a supervision identity. You might export a supervision identity for backup or so that you can use it elsewhere. To export a supervision identity, follow these steps:

1. In the Organizations list box in the Organizations pane, click the organization with the supervision identity you want to export.

2. Click the Action pop-up menu, and then click the Export Supervision Identity item. A Save sheet opens.

3. Apple Configurator displays a default name for the exported supervision identity in the Save As box. This default name is based on the name of the supervision identity you picked for exporting. You can edit this default name for the supervision identity as needed.

4. In the Tags box, apply any tags needed.

5. Specify the location by using the Where pop-up menu or by clicking the button to the right of the Save As box and browsing to the appropriate folder.

6. Click the Format pop-up menu, and then click the format you want to use. Your choice is between Encrypted PKCS12 (.p12) and Unencrypted DER (.crt and .key, for Automator and cfgutil). Choose the Encrypted PKCS12 (.p12) item for a supervision identity you'll use interactively with Apple Configurator itself. Choose the Unencrypted DER (.crt and .key, for Automator and cfgutil) item for a supervision identity you'll use with Apple's Automator app or with the cfgutil command-line utility.

7. Click the Save button. The Choose a password to encrypt the identity dialog opens (see Figure 4-9).

Figure 4-9. *In the "Choose a password to encrypt the identity" dialog, either type a password or click the Password Assistant icon (the key icon) and use the Password Assistant dialog to select a password*

8. Type a password for encrypting the identity in the Password box and the Verify box, looking at the Password Strength meter to make sure the password is strong. Alternatively, click the Password Assistant icon (the key icon) to display the Password Assistant dialog, and then use its controls to select a password.

9. Click the OK button. Apple Configurator saves the supervision identity to the file.

Setting Up Your MDM Servers in the Servers Preferences Pane

If you're going to use Apple Configurator to enroll your school's iPads in an MDM solution, you can use the Servers preferences pane to specify which servers to use. Some MDM solutions enable you to use Apple Configurator to enroll the iPads like this. With other MDM solutions, you use other means of enrolling the iPads, such as navigating to an enrollment URL in a web browser (such as Safari) or installing a custom enrollment app on the iPad.

If you'll use Apple Configurator to enroll the iPads in MDM, display the Servers preferences pane by clicking the Servers button on the toolbar in the Apple Configurator Preferences window. At first, the Servers preferences pane usually appears with no servers configured, as shown in Figure 4-10.

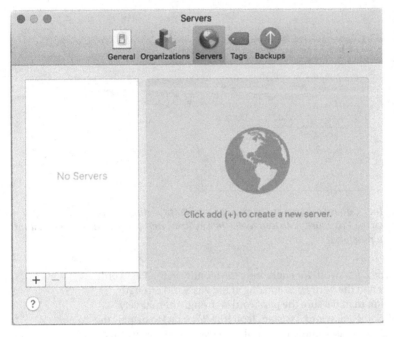

Figure 4-10. *Use the Server preferences pane for Apple Configurator to specify your MDM servers and their URLs*

To add a server, follow these steps:

1. Click the Add (+) button. The first Define an MDM Server pane appears, explaining what MDM servers are.

2. Click the Next button. The second Define an MDM Server pane appears (see Figure 4-11).

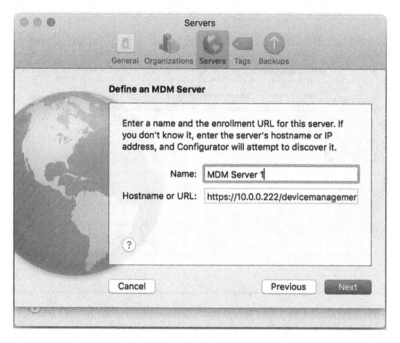

Figure 4-11. *In the second Define an MDM Server pane, type the server's name and the enrollment URL*

3. In the Name box, type a descriptive name for the MDM server. This name is to help you and your colleagues identify the server clearly.

4. In the Hostname or URL box, type or paste the server's hostname or the enrollment URL—the web address at which the devices can enroll in the MDM. You would get the hostname or enrollment URL from the MDM vendor.

5. Click the Next button. Apple Configurator verifies the server's enrollment URL and fetches the server's *trust anchor certificates*, certificates used to specify which certificates to trust as a basis for the MDM. The third Define an MDM Server pane then appears (see Figure 4-12), enabling you to choose which trust anchor certificates to add.

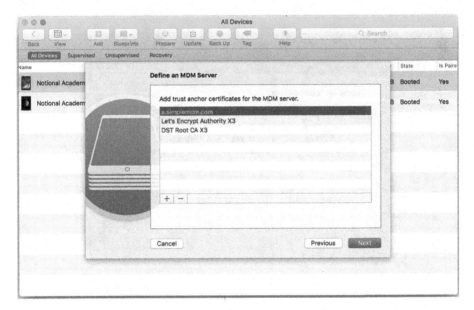

Figure 4-12. *In the third Define an MDM Server pane, choose which of the server's trust anchor certificates to add*

6. If necessary, remove a trust anchor certificate by clicking it and then clicking the Remove (–) button, or add a trust anchor certificate by clicking the Add (+) button, selecting the certificate file in the dialog that opens, and then clicking the Open button.

7. Click the Next button. The MDM server appears in the Servers pane. You can subsequently use it for enrolling iPads in the MDM solution.

Setting Up Your Tags for Tagging iOS Devices

Apple Configurator enables you to apply tags to iPads and other iOS devices so that you can identify them more easily. Apple Configurator comes with predefined color tags, much like those you can use in the Finder in macOS, but you can rename the predefined tags and create other tags as needed. For example, you might create tags for different groups, such as Teachers, Support Staff, and Students, tags for departments, such as Science, or tags for particular classes.

To work with tags, click the Tags button on the toolbar of the Preferences window. The Tags preferences pane appears (see Figure 4-13). You can then take the following actions:

- *Rename an existing tag*: Double-click the tag to select its existing name, and then type the new name. Press the Return key or click elsewhere when you finish.

- *Create a new tag*: Click the Add (+) button on the left below the list of tags. Apple Configurator adds a new tag with the default name Untitled tag, selecting the name so that you can type over it. Press the Return key or click elsewhere after typing the name.

- *Delete an existing tag*: Click the tag and then click the Remove (-) button on the left below the list of tags.

- *Change the color for a tag*: Click the tag, click the Change Color button to display the Colors window (see Figure 4-14), and then click the color you want. Click the buttons on the toolbar to switch among the Color Wheel, Color Sliders, Color Palettes, Image Palettes, and Pencils tabs of the Colors window.

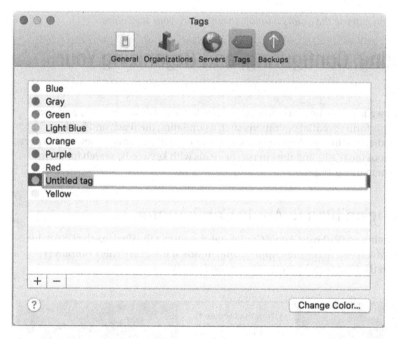

Figure 4-13. In the Tags preferences pane, edit the predefined tags as needed, and create any other tags you'll use to identify your school's iPads and other iOS devices

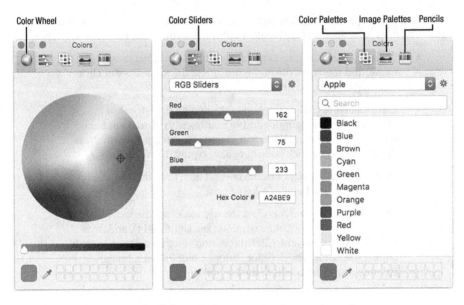

Figure 4-14. *You can use the Colors window to customize your tag colors*

Connecting, Configuring, and Organizing Your iPads

In this section, we'll look at how to connect iPads to Apple Configurator, view and sort the iPads, and perform essential operations such as updating the iPads and backing them up. We'll then go through how to choose advanced settings, how to view and export information about the iPads, and how to tag the iPads with keywords, search for them, and organize them into groups.

Connecting an iPad to Apple Configurator

To get started using an iPad with Apple Configurator, connect the iPad via the USB cable to the Mac on which you're running Apple Configurator. If the Trust This Computer? dialog opens on the iPad (see Figure 4-15), tap the Trust button.

Figure 4-15. *Tap the Trust button in the Trust This Computer? dialog the first time you connect an iPad to the Mac on which you're running Apple Configurator*

■ **Tip**   You can either plug the USB cable directly into a USB port on the Mac or into a USB hub that's plugged into the Mac. Using a powered hub enables you to connect multiple iPads at once, which is usually faster and more convenient than working on one device at a time. For best results, use a powered hub that bears the MFi logo, meaning that it has passed Apple's MFi licensing program. (MFi stands for Made for iPhone/iPod/iPad.)

Once you've set the iPad to trust the Mac, the iPad appears in the device browser in Apple Configurator. You can then click the iPad to select it. Once the iPad is selected (see Figure 4-16), the command buttons on the toolbar become available.

Figure 4-16. *Select the iPad in the device browser in Apple Configurator to enable the command buttons on the toolbar. This screen shows the device browser in Collection view, which displays a thumbnail for each iPad. The red badge at the upper-right corner of the iPad indicates that an update is available.*

Viewing and Sorting the Connected iPads

You can view the iPads you've connected to Apple Configurator as either a collection or as a list, and you can sort the iPads in a variety of different ways.

Collection view shows a large thumbnail for each iPad, whereas List view shows a list of iPads with various columns of details, such as the operating system version, iPad model, and iPad capacity; you can customize this list to show the details you want to see. List view is good for seeing many iPads at once and getting an overview of their configuration.

You can switch views in any of these three ways:

- *Toolbar*: Open the View pop-up menu and click the Collection item or the List item.

- *Menu bar*: Open the View menu and click the As Collection item or the As List item.

- *Keyboard*: Press Cmd-1 for Collection view or Cmd-2 for List view.

In List view (see Figure 4-17), you can choose which columns of data to display and the order in which to display them. To change the columns displayed, Ctrl-click or right-click one of the currently displayed column headings. On the pop-up menu that appears, click to place a check mark next to a column you want to display or to remove the check mark from a column you want to remove. Table 4-2 explains the columns.

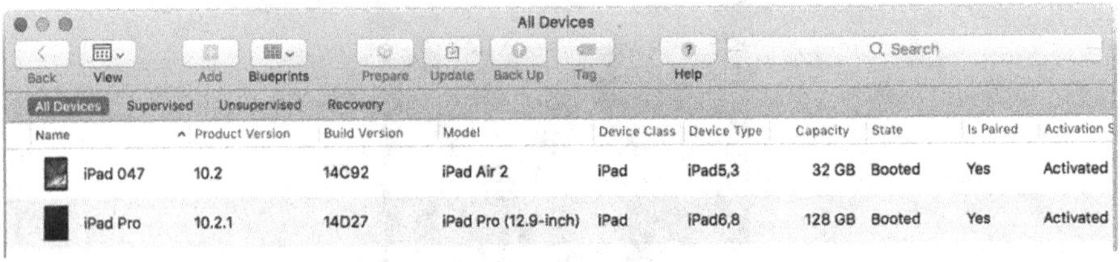

Figure 4-17. *In List view, you can customize the columns displayed. Click a column heading to sort the list by that column.*

Table 4-2. *Columns in List View in Apple Configurator*

Column	What It Shows
Accepts Supervision	Yes if the iPad accepts supervision, No if it doesn't.
Activation State	Activated if the iPad has been activated, Not Activated if it hasn't been activated.
Battery	The battery's charge percentage, such as 94%.
Build Version	The iPad's internal build version number, such as 14D27.
Capacity	The iPad's nominal storage capacity, such as 32 GB or 128 GB.
Charging	Yes if the iPad is currently charging, No if it isn't charging.
Device Class	iPad for an iPad, iPhone for an iPhone, and so on.
Device Type	The iPad's model number, such as iPad5,3 or iPad6,8.
ECID	The iPad's Exclusive Chip ID (ECID), a hexadecimal number (such as 0x1D504238F3AC26) used to identify the iPad uniquely to Apple's servers.

(continued)

Table 4-2. *(continued)*

Column	What It Shows
Encrypts Backups	Yes if the iPad is set to encrypt its backups, No if it isn't.
iCloud Backups	Yes if the iPad is set to back up data to an iCloud account, No if it isn't.
Is Paired	Yes if the iPad is paired with a Mac or PC, No if it isn't.
Is Supervised	Yes if the iPad is set up as a supervised device, No if it isn't.
Model	The descriptive name of the iPad model, such as `iPad Air 2` or `iPad Pro (12.9-inch)`.
Organization Department	The iPad's organization department, if set; otherwise, blank.
Organization E-mail	The iPad's organization e-mail, if set; otherwise, blank.
Organization Name	The iPad's organization name, if set; otherwise, blank.
Organization Phone	The iPad's organization phone number, if set; otherwise, blank.
Passcode Locked	Yes if the iPad is currently locked with a passcode, No if it's unlocked.
Port	The port to which the iPad is connected.
Product Version	The iOS version the iPad is running, such as `10.3.3`.
Serial Number	The iPad's serial number, a hexadecimal number.
State	The iPad's current state, such as `Booted` if it's running.
Station	The station at which the iPad is located.
UDID	The iPad's Unique Device ID (UDID), a long hexadecimal number that identifies the iPad uniquely.
Updates	If any updates are available, the number appears, such as 1. If no updates are available, the readout is blank.

■ **Tip**   You can adjust the width of a column by dragging its right border, but you can't make a column narrower than its column heading. You can change the order of the columns by clicking a column heading and dragging it left or right along the heading bar.

In List view, you can sort the iPads quickly by clicking the column heading you want to sort by. The right side of the column heading displays a caret (∧) to indicate an ascending sort or a downward caret (∨) to indicate a descending sort. You can click the same column heading again to reverse the sort order.

In either Collection view or List view, you can sort the iPads either by choosing View ➤ Sort By from the menu bar or View ➤ Sort By from the toolbar and then clicking the appropriate item on the Sort By submenu. In either view, the Sort By submenu shows the columns you've displayed in List view, so if you want to sort by a column that doesn't appear on the Sort By submenu, go into List view and add that column.

Updating an iPad's Software

Apple Configurator enables you to update iOS and the apps on one or more iPads easily. This feature is very convenient, but because Apple Configurator may need to download multiple versions of iOS and apps, the update may take one or more hours, depending on the speed of your Internet connection. While the updates are running, you can't perform other tasks in the device browser, so you may want to run the updates overnight or when you're about to leave the office for a while.

To update the iPads, follow these steps:

1. Connect the iPads to the Mac or to a USB hub connected to the Mac.

2. Launch Apple Configurator if it's not already running. The iPads appear in the device browser.

3. Select each iPad you want to update.

4. Give the Update command. You can do this by clicking the Update button on the toolbar, by choosing Actions ➤ Update from the menu bar, or by Ctrl-clicking or right-clicking in the selection and then clicking the Update item on the shortcut menu. Apple Configurator checks for available updates and displays the Update dialog (see Figure 4-18).

Figure 4-18. *In the Update dialog, open the pop-up menu and choose the "Latest iOS only" item, "Apps only" item, or "Latest iOS and Apps" item, and then click the Update button*

5. Open the pop-up menu and choose the "Latest iOS only" item, "Apps only" item, or "Latest iOS and App" item, as needed. Depending on which updates are available, you may have no choice here.

6. Click the Update button. Apple Configurator downloads the updates if it hasn't already done so. The License Agreement dialog then opens.

7. Read the license information, and click the Accept button if you want to proceed. Apple Configurator downloads the latest updates and applies them to the iPad.

■ **Note**   You may need to enter the iPad's passcode one or more times during the update process.

Changing an iPad's Name, Wallpaper, or Home Screen

Apple Configurator enables you to rename an iPad, change its wallpaper, and change its Home screen. You can make these changes either directly or by using a blueprint. This section shows you how to change them directly. The section "Modifying a Device's Information via a Blueprint," later in this chapter, explains how to make the changes via a blueprint.

BUILDING NAMES FOR YOUR IPADS

To work effectively with your school's iPads, you'll need to be able to identify them easily, both by looking at the iPads in the flesh (as it were) and by using management tools.

To create device names, Apple Configurator lets you use a static value, any of four variables in your device, and either or both of two pieces of current information. As the static value, you might want to use your school's name or the department's name. You can not only assign a name to an iPad but also display a name—the same name or a different one—on the lock screen.

These are the four variables you can use in names:

- *Number.* This variable enters a number (such as 1) that Apple Configurator automatically increments for each device (1, 2, 3, and so on).

- *Serial Number.* This variable enters the iPad's serial number (which is unique).

- *Type.* This variable enters the device type, such as iPad for an iPad.

- *Capacity.* This variable enters the device's capacity, such as 32 GB or 128 GB.

These are the two pieces of information you can use in names:

- *Port.* This enters the device's current port.

- *Station.* This enters the device's current station.

By combining the static value, one or more variables, and one or more pieces of information, you can assign each iPad a unique name that clearly identifies it.

Changing the Names of iPads

To change the names of one or more iPads, follow these steps in Apple Configurator:

1. In the device browser, select the iPad or iPads you want to rename.

2. Choose Actions ➤ Modify ➤ Device Name from the menu bar, or Ctrl-click or right-click in the selection and choose Modify ➤ Device Name from the shortcut menu. The Rename device dialog opens. Figure 4-19 shows the Rename device dialog with some settings chosen and the Add (+) pop-up menu open.

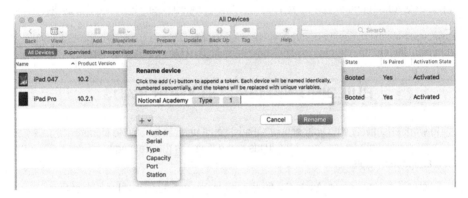

Figure 4-19. *The Add (+) pop-up menu in the Rename device dialog allows you to add variables and current information as well as static text to device names.*

3. In the text box, type any static text that you want to have at the beginning of the name, such as the school name or department name.

4. Click the Add (+) button to open the pop-up menu. This pop-up menu contains fields of information you can add to the name; Apple Configurator calls these fields *tokens*.

5. Click the item you want to add to the name: Number, Serial, Type, Capacity, Port, or Station. A blue button containing the item appears.

6. Add other text or items as needed. You can drag an item's button to a different position if necessary.

7. Click the Rename button. Apple Configurator applies the names to the iPads.

Changing the Wallpaper

To change the wallpaper on one or more iPads, follow these steps in Apple Configurator:

1. In the device browser, select the iPad or iPads you want to affect.

2. Choose Actions ➤ Modify ➤ Wallpapers from the menu bar, or Ctrl-click or right-click in the selection and choose Modify ➤ Wallpapers from the shortcut menu. The Change the Wallpaper dialog opens. Figure 4-20 shows the Change the Wallpaper dialog with one wallpaper chosen.

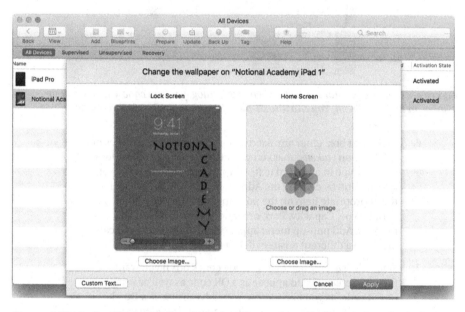

Figure 4-20. *In the Change Wallpaper dialog, choose the wallpaper pictures for the lock screen and Home screen. You can also apply custom text to the lock screen.*

3. Click the Choose Image button under the Lock Screen thumbnail to open the "Select wallpaper image" dialog, click the image file, and then click the Select button. Alternatively, drag in an image from a Finder window or the Desktop.

4. Click the Choose Image button under the Home Screen thumbnail to open the "Select wallpaper image" dialog, click the image file, and then click the Select button. Here, too, you can drag in an image from a Finder window or the Desktop.

5.   If you want to display custom text on the lock screen, click the
      Custom Text button. The Customize lock screen text dialog
      opens (see Figure 4-21).

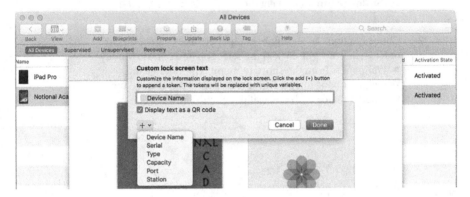

Figure 4-21. In the "Customize lock screen text" dialog, you can choose which text to display on the lock screen. You can also display the text as a QR code if you want.

6.   In the text box, enter any fixed text, variable text, and pieces of
      information (*tokens*) that you want to have appear on the lock
      screen. Type in any fixed text. Add variable text and pieces of
      information by clicking the Add (+) button and then clicking
      the appropriate item on the pop-up menu: Device Name,
      Serial, Type, Capacity, Port, or Station. Each item you add
      from the Add pop-up menu appears as a button, and you can
      drag it to a different position if necessary.

7.   Select the Display text as a QR code check box if you want
      the lock screen text to appear as a QR code as well as text.
      (A QR code, as you likely know from advertising, is a Quick
      Response code that consists of information encoded as a two-
      dimensional barcode that you can scan with a device.)

8.   Click the Done button. The text (and QR code, if you chose it)
      appears on the Lock Screen thumbnail.

9.   Click the Apply button. The "Change the wallpaper" dialog
      closes, and Apple Configurator applies your choices of
      wallpaper and lock screen text to the selected iPads.

Customizing the Home Screen Layout

Apple Configurator enables you to customize the Home screen layout for iOS devices.
You might want to customize the Home screen panels to make sure that students are all
looking at the same layout and can follow your instructions easily.

To customize the Home screen layout on one or more iPads, follow these steps in Apple Configurator:

1. In the device browser, select the iPad or iPads you want to affect.

2. Choose Actions ➤ Modify ➤ Home Screen Layout from the menu bar, or Ctrl-click or right-click in the selection and choose Modify ➤ Home Screen Layout from the shortcut menu. The "Modify the home screen layout" dialog opens (see Figure 4-22), showing the first three Home screen panels. In the example, the third Home screen panel is empty.

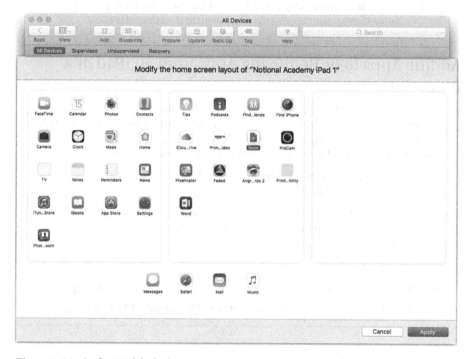

Figure 4-22. *In the Modify the home screen layout dialog, drag the icons to the positions in which you want them to appear on the iPads panels.*

3. Drag the icons to the positions where you want them to appear.

■ **Note**   In the "Modify the home screen layout" dialog, you can take most of the same actions as when you're customizing the Home screen layout interactively either on the iPad itself or in iTunes. Drag one app icon onto another app icon to create a folder. Double-click a folder to display it so that you can rename it or adjust its contents. Click the X button in the upper-left corner to return from the folder to the main part of the dialog. Drag an icon from the rightmost Home screen panel further to the right to add a new Home screen panel panels.

4. When you finish making your changes, click the Apply button. Apple Configurator applies the new layout to the selected iPads.

Adding Apps to or Removing Apps from an iPad or a Blueprint

You can add apps to an iPad by working in the device browser. You use the same technique for adding apps to a *blueprint* (a template containing profiles and apps that you can apply quickly to a device), so I'll cover both together here.

To add apps to an iPad directly or to a blueprint, follow these steps:

1. Select the iPad in the device browser or the blueprint in the blueprint browser.

2. Click the Add button on the toolbar, and then click Apps on the pop-up menu. A dialog opens for adding apps (see Figure 4-23).

■ **Note**   If the Sign In button appears in the dialog for adding apps, click the button and sign in to the account on which you've purchased the apps (or gotten them for free).

Figure 4-23. In this dialog, select the iPad item in the pop-up menu in the upper-left corner, choose the apps to add to the blueprint, and then click the Add button

---

■ **Note**   If you need to install apps stored on your Mac (such as iPad apps that your school has developed) instead of from the App Store, click the Choose from my Mac button. In the dialog that opens, navigate to the folder that contains the apps, select the apps, and then click the Add button.

---

3. If you want to restrict the list to iPad apps, open the pop-up menu in the upper-left corner of the dialog and click the iPad item. Your other choices here are All (which makes the dialog show all available iOS apps) and iPhone/iPod touch (which makes the dialog show apps designed for those devices).

4. If necessary, click the Icons button or the List button in the upper middle area of the dialog to switch the display to Icon view or to List view.

5. To locate apps by name, click in the Search box and type the first part of the name.

6. In the main part of the dialog, select the apps you want to add. As usual, click the first, and then either Shift-click to select the apps in between that first one and the next one you click, or Cmd-click to add individual apps to the selection.

7. Click the Add button to add the apps to the iPad or the blueprint. Apple Configurator displays a progress dialog as it updates the iPad or the blueprint.

To remove one or more apps from an iPad or a blueprint, follow these steps:

1. Ctrl-click or right-click the iPad in the device browser or the blueprint in the blueprint browser and choose Remove ➤ Apps from the shortcut menu.

2. Alternatively, select the profile and choose Actions ➤ Remove ➤ Apps from the menu bar.

3. In the dialog that opens, select the apps, and then click the Remove Apps button.

Backing Up, Restoring, and Cloning iPads

Apple Configurator provides tools for backing up iPads and restoring them. You can use these tools either to back up and restore a single iPad or to clone an iPad that you've configured the way you want it onto multiple iPads.

Backing Up an iPad to the Mac Running Apple Configurator

To back up an iPad, follow these steps:

1. Connect the iPad to the Mac on which you're running Apple Configurator.

2. Select the iPad in the device browser.

3. Click the Back Up button on the toolbar. Alternatively, choose Actions ➤ Back Up from the menu bar, or Ctrl-click or right-click in the selection and then click Back Up on the shortcut menu. Apple Configurator backs up the iPad, displaying the Backing up dialog showing its progress as it does so (see Figure 4-24).

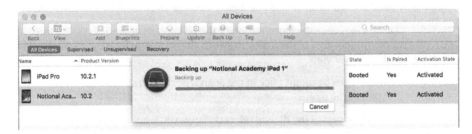

Figure 4-24. The Backing up dialog shows the progress of the current backup

Restoring an iPad from a Backup

Restoring an iPad with Apple Configurator has two purposes:

- *Restore the iPad to its previous state*: If you've previously backed up this iPad, you can restore that backup to return the iPad to the state it was in at the time of the backup.

- *Clone an iPad with your preferred configuration*: You can restore a backup from an iPad that you've configured the way you want your iPads to be.

To restore an iPad from a backup, follow these steps:

1. Connect the iPad to the Mac on which you're running Apple Configurator.

2. Select the iPad in the device browser.

3. Choose Actions ➤ Restore from Backup from the menu bar, or Ctrl-click or right-click in the selection and then click Restore from Backup on the shortcut menu. The Restore from this backup dialog opens (see Figure 4-25).

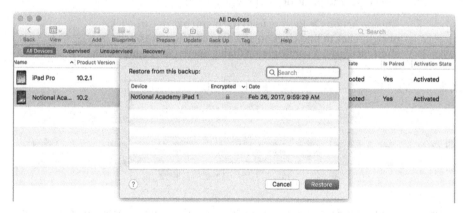

Figure 4-25. *In the "Restore from this backup" dialog, select the backup you want to restore to the iPad*

4. Locate and click the backup you want to restore to the iPad. You can click one of the column headings—Device, Encrypted, or Date—to sort by that column. The right side of the column heading displays a caret (^) to indicate an ascending sort or a downward caret (∨) to indicate a descending sort. Click the column heading again to reverse the sort order.

5. Click the Restore button. If the backup is encrypted, the Enter password used for this backup dialog opens; if not, the restore operation starts.

6. Type the password in the password box.

7. Click the Restore Backup button. Apple Configurator restores the backup to the iPad.

■ **Note**   If a dialog opens saying that "Configurator could not perform the requested action because the iPad has already been prepared," click the Erase button if you want to erase the iPad. Click the Stop button otherwise.

Restoring an iPad to Factory Default Settings

Using Apple Configurator, you can quickly restore an iPad to factory default settings. This move is useful when you need to erase an iPad's current configuration, such as when you need to repurpose the iPad or when its configuration has become corrupted.

To restore an iPad to factory default settings, follow these steps:

1. Connect the iPad to the Mac on which you're running Apple Configurator.

2. Select the iPad in the device browser.

3. Choose Actions ➤ Restore from the menu bar, or Ctrl-click or right-click in the selection and then click Restore on the shortcut menu. A confirmation dialog opens (see Figure 4-26).

Figure 4-26. *In the confirmation dialog, double-check that you've chosen the right iPad to restore to factory default settings. Then click the Restore button.*

4. Verify that you've selected the right iPad.

5. Click the Restore button. Apple Configurator restores the iPad to factory default settings.

Managing Your Backups

Apple Configurator stores backups in the ~/Library/Application Support/MobileSync/ Backups folder, where the tilde (~) represents your Home folder. Each backup is stored in a folder with a 40-character hexadecimal name that Apple Configurator generates automatically. This folder contains 256 folders numbered with sequential hexadecimal names (00, 0a, 0b, and so on through ff), three preference list files (Info.plist, Manifest.plist, and Status.plist), and a manifest database file (Manifest.db). Each backup can be from several hundred megabytes to many gigabytes in size, depending on what the iPad contains.

To get an overview of your backups and to delete any backups you no longer need, choose Apple Configurator ➤ Preferences to open the Preferences window, and then click the Backups button on the toolbar to display the Backups pane. The Backups pane (see Figure 4-27) contains a list of backups that you can sort by clicking the Device, Encrypted, or Date column heading. As usual, click the current column heading again to reverse the sort direction. To locate a specific backup quickly, you can click in the Search box and type a search term.

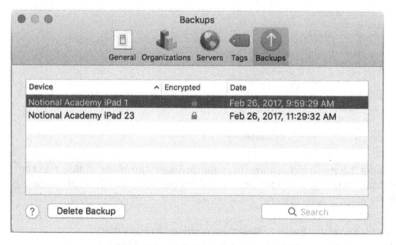

Figure 4-27. *The Backups pane in Apple Configurator's Preferences enables you to sort your backups, search for specific backups, and delete backups you no longer need*

To delete a backup, select it and click the Delete Backup button. In the confirmation dialog that opens, click the Delete button.

Choosing Advanced Settings for an iPad or a Blueprint

Apart from the items discussed so far in this section, Apple Configurator enables you to add any of a handful of advanced settings to either an iPad itself or to a blueprint. You'll find the commands for these advanced settings on the Actions ➤ Advanced submenu on the menu bar and on the Advanced submenu on the shortcut menu.

These are the commands for the advanced settings:

- *Save Unlock Token*: Give this command to add an unlock token (a digital file) that will unlock a supervised iPad whose user has forgotten the passcode for unlocking the device.

- *Clear Passcode*: Give this command to clear the iPad's passcode.

- *Clear Restrictions Passcode*: Give this command to clear the restrictions passcode on a supervised iPad.

- *Start Single App Mode*: Give this command to start setting up the iPad to run Single App Mode, which restricts the iPad to a single app. In the dialog that opens, click the app you want the iPad to run. Next, click the Options button to display the "Choose which features to enable in Single App Mode" dialog (see Figure 4-28), select and clear the check boxes as appropriate, and then click the Apply button. Back in the dialog for choosing the app, click the Select App button.

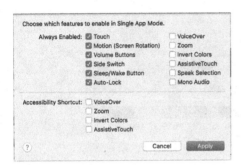

Figure 4-28. *In the "Choose which features to enable in Single App Mode" dialog, select or clear the check boxes to specify which features should be available while the iPad is running Single App Mode.*

- *Enable Encrypted Backups*: Give this command to allow the iPad to create encrypted backups. Type the password to use for encryption, and then click the Set Password button.

■ **Note** To disable encrypted backups, select an iPad or a blueprint for which you've enabled encrypted backups, and then choose Actions ➤ Advanced ➤ Disable Encrypted Backups from the menu bar or Advanced ➤ Disable Encrypted Backups from the shortcut menu. When prompted, type the encryption password, and then click the Clear Password button.

- *Revive Device*: Give this command to try to revive an iPad that is stuck in recovery mode or that has been only partially configured.

- *Erase All Content and Settings*: Give this command to start erasing all the content and settings on the iPad. There's no confirmation on this command, so be sure to choose the right iPad first.

Viewing Information About Your iPads

List view in the device browser enables you to get an overview of the configuration details for multiple iPads quickly. But when you want to zero in on the details of one particular iPad, you can use the Quick Look pane or the Info pane instead.

To view details in the Quick Look pane (see Figure 4-29), select the iPad and give the Quick Look command in one of these ways:

- *Keyboard*: Press the spacebar or the Cmd-Y keyboard shortcut.

- *Menu bar*: Choose File ➤ Quick Look.

- *Shortcut menu*: Ctrl-click or right-click the iPad and then click the Quick Look item.

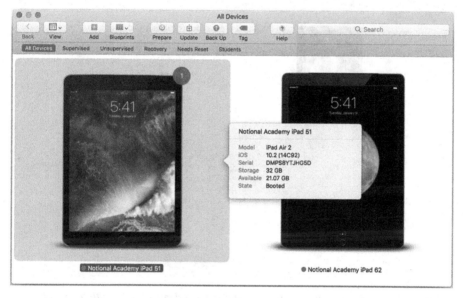

Figure 4-29. *Open the Quick Look pane when you want to view a brief summary of the information for a device*

When you're ready to close the Quick Look pane, click elsewhere or press the spacebar again.

To see full details about the selected iPad, display the Info pane by giving the Get Info command in one of these ways:

- *Keyboard*: Press Ctrl-I.

- *Menu bar*: Choose File ➤ Get Info.

- *Shortcut menu*: Ctrl-click or right-click the iPad and then click the Get Info item.

The Info pane contains a wealth of information broken down into four categories: Info, Apps, Profiles, and Console. These categories appear in the sidebar on the left of the window, and you can navigate among them as usual by clicking the category you want to view.

The Info category (see Figure 4-30) shows the iPad's name at the top and the following three sections of information about the iPad:

- *About*: This section contains details on the device model (such as iPad Air 2), capacity (such as 32 GB), state (such as Booted), battery charge state (such as 100%), and any tags you've applied to the device.

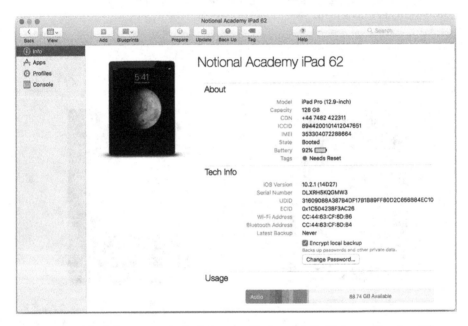

Figure 4-30. *The Info category in the Info pane displays detailed information about the iPad including technical information and the amount of space used*

■ **Note**   For a cellular iPad, the CDN, the ICCID, and IMEI also appear in the About section of the Info category. The CDN is the phone number for cellular service. The ICCID is the Integrated Circuit Card ID, the SIM card's unique identifier. The IMEI is the International Mobile Equipment Identity number, the cellular iPad's unique identifier.

- *Tech Info*: This section shows the iOS version (such as 10.2 (14C92)) with an Update button if an update is available, the serial number, UDID, and ECID, the MAC addresses for the Wi-Fi adapter and the Bluetooth adapter, and the latest backup date. You can select or clear the "Encrypt local backup" check box to control whether the backup is encrypted, and click the Change Password button to display the dialog for changing the password to use for the encryption.

- *Usage*: This section displays a histogram showing how much of the iPad's storage is in use and by which items. For example, a blue section at the left end shows the amount of space taken up by audio files (such as music).

The Apps category on the Info page displays the third-party apps installed on the iPad (see Figure 4-31). You can display the apps either as a collection or as a list by clicking the View button on the toolbar and then clicking the Collection item or the List item on the pop-up menu, by choosing View ➤ As Collection or View ➤ As List from the menu bar, or by pressing Cmd-1 for Collection view or Cmd-2 for List view. Normally, List view is the more helpful view, because you can see details such as each app's version, seller, genre, and kind, and you can sort by any column by clicking its heading. To change the columns displayed, Ctrl-click or right-click a column heading, and then click the appropriate item on the shortcut menu to add a check mark (displaying the column), or remove the existing check mark (removing the column from display).

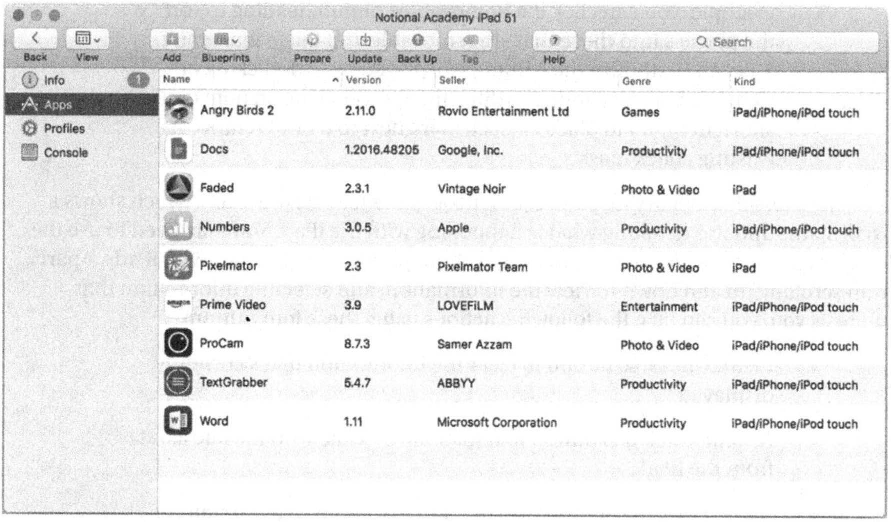

Figure 4-31. Use the Apps category in the Info pane to see which apps are installed on the iPad. List view enables you to see the apps' version, seller, genre, and kind; you can sort by any column by clicking its heading.

■ **Note**   To remove an app from the iPad, select the app, press the Delete key, and then click the Remove button in the confirmation dialog that opens.

The Profiles category displays the profiles installed on the iPad. You can take three main actions here:

- *Add a profile*: If the iPad contains no profile yet, click the Add Profiles button, select the profile in the dialog that opens, and then click the Add button. If the iPad does contain one or more profiles, the Add Profiles button doesn't appear, but you can add other profiles by dragging them in from a Finder window or from the desktop.

- *Remove a profile*: Click the profile, press the Delete key or choose Edit ➤ Delete from the menu bar, and then click the Remove button in the confirmation dialog.

- *View the profiles as a collection or a list*: Click the View button on the toolbar, and then click the Collection item or the List item on the pop-up menu. Usually, List view is more helpful, because you can sort the profiles quickly by clicking the column headings. For example, you can click the Removable column heading to sort the profiles into those that are removable and those that aren't. You can customize the columns displayed by Ctrl-clicking or right-clicking a column heading and then clicking an item on the shortcut menu to place a check mark next to it or to remove its existing check mark.

The Console category displays the Console pane (see Figure 4-32), which shows a list of status updates detailing what is happening with the iPad. You may need to use the information in the Console pane to troubleshoot problems that occur with iPads. Apart from scrolling up and down to view the information, and selecting information that interests you, you can take the following actions using these four button:

- *Clear*: Click this button to clear the information that's currently displayed.

- *Reload*: Click this button to reload the console with the latest data from the iPad.

- *Mark*: Click this button to insert a row of equal signs containing the current date and time (such as ======== Apr 1, 2017, 10:46:12 AM ========) to provide a point that you can easily identify.

- *Save Selection*: Click this button to save the text you've selected to a log file. In the dialog that opens, enter the filename, choose the location, and then click the Save button.

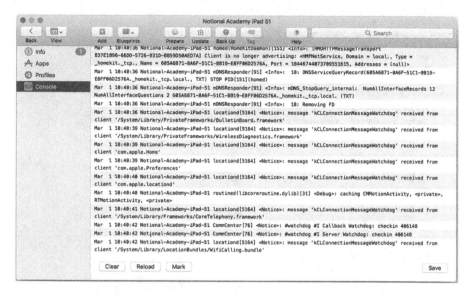

Figure 4-32. The Console category shows detailed status updates for the iPad

When you finish working in the Info pane, click the Back (<) button at the left end of the toolbar to return to the device browser.

Exporting Information About Your iPads

Apple Configurator enables you to export information about your devices to a file. You can choose among three file formats:

- *Device ID file*: This is a file that you would normally upload to the iOS developer portal for troubleshooting.

- *CSV file*: A CSV (comma-separated values) file is good for adding to a spreadsheet or database that you use to track your hardware and software.

- *Property List file*: This is a file in the format that Apple uses for storing configuration information for apps and other objects.

To export information from Apple Configurator, follow these steps:

1. In the device browser, select the iPad or iPads with the information you want to export.

2. Choose Actions ➤ Export ➤ Info from the menu bar, or Ctrl-click or right-click in the selection and choose Export ➤ Info from the shortcut menu. A dialog opens (see Figure 4-33).

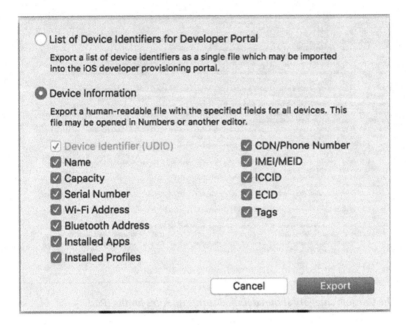

Figure 4-33. In this dialog, select the List of Device Identifiers for Developer Portal option button or the Device Information option button, as needed. If you select the Device Information option button, choose which fields of data to export.

3. Select the List of Device Identifiers for Developer Portal option button if you want to create a device IDs file. Select the Device Information option button if you want to create a CSV file.

4. If you select the Device Information button, select or clear the check boxes below it to specify which fields of information to include: Name, Capacity, Serial Number, Wi-Fi Address, Bluetooth Address, Installed Apps, Installed Profiles, CDN/Phone Number, IMEI/MEID, ICCID, ECID, and Tags.

5. Click the Export button. The dialog closes, and a Save sheet opens.

6. Type the filename in the Save As box.

7. Enter any tags in the Tags box to help identify the information you're exporting.

8. Specify the location by using the Where pop-up menu or by clicking the button to the right of the Save As box and browsing to the appropriate folder.

9. If you selected the Device Information button in step 3, open the Format pop-up menu and choose the CSV item or the Property List item, as appropriate.

10. Click the Save button. Apple Configurator saves the file.

Exporting Documents from an iPad

Apple Configurator lets you export any documents that the iPad's apps have stored in iCloud folders. To export documents, follow these steps:

1. In the device browser, select the iPad or iPads with the information you want to export.

2. Choose Actions ➤ Export ➤ Documents from the menu bar, or Ctrl-click or right-click in the selection and choose Export ➤ Documents from the shortcut menu. A dialog opens (see Figure 4-34) showing a folder for each app that contains documents you can export.

Figure 4-34. *In this dialog, select the folder for each app with documents you want to export*

3. Select the icon for each app with documents you want to export. As usual, after selecting one icon, you can Shift-click to select a range of icons or Cmd-click to add individual icons to the selection.

■ **Note**   You can also open an app's folder in the dialog and then select individual documents for export.

---

   4.   Click the Choose button. A Save sheet opens to let you select
        the destination folder.

   5.   Click the appropriate folder, and then click the Export button.
        Apple Configurator exports the documents.

Organizing Your iPads in Apple Configurator

To manage your iPads efficiently, you'll normally want to organize them into different administrative groups. For example, you may want to treat iPads issued to staff differently from iPads issued to students, or you may want to be able to isolate the iPads that belong to each department or to each class.

Understanding the Four Default Groups

Apple Configurator provides the following four default groups that you can access by clicking the buttons on the Favorites bar below the toolbar, or by choosing View ➤ All Devices, View ➤ Favorites ➤ Supervised, View ➤ Favorites ➤ Unsupervised, or View ➤ Favorites ➤ Recovery from the menu bar:

   •   *All devices*: This group contains all the iOS devices you've
       connected to your Mac.

   •   *Supervised*: This group contains all the connected iOS devices
       that are supervised.

   •   *Unsupervised*: This group contains all the connected iOS devices
       that are not supervised.

   •   *Recovery*: This group contains all the connected iOS devices that
       are currently in recovery mode.

Organizing Devices with Tags

Once you've customized Apple Configurator's default tags (see the section "Setting Up Your Tags for Tagging iOS Devices," earlier in this chapter), you can organize your iPads by applying tags to them.

   To apply a tag, select the iPads to which you want to apply it, click the Tags button on the toolbar, and then click the appropriate tag or tags on the Assign tags pop-up menu. If the tag you want to apply doesn't appear in the top part of the Assign tags pop-up menu, click the Show All button at the bottom of the pop-up menu to display the hidden tags. When you finish applying tags, press the Return key or click outside the pop-up menu.

■ **Note**   You can remove a tag by opening the Assign tags pop-up menu, selecting the tag
(or placing the insertion point after it), and then pressing the Delete key.

After you apply tags to the iPads, you can search by using tags. Click in the Search
field in the upper-right corner of the Apple Configurator window, start typing the tag
name, and then click the appropriate item in the Tags section of the Search pop-up menu
(see Figure 4-35). The tag appears in the Search field as a button, and you can perform the
search.

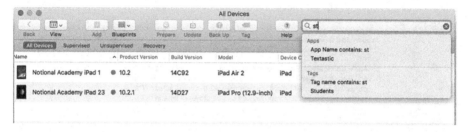

Figure 4-35.   *To search using a tag, start typing the tag name in the Search box, and then
click the tag in the Tags section of the Search pop-up menu. You can see tags here to the left
of the Product Version column.*

You can save a search by clicking the Save button at the right end of the Favorites
bar, typing a name for the saved search in the "Specify the name of your favorites group"
dialog, and then clicking the Save button. The saved search appears on the Favorites bar,
where you can click it to perform that search instantly.

■ **Note**   To remove a saved search from the Favorites bar, click the button for the saved
search, drag it into the device window, and drop it there. The button vanishes in a puff of
smoke.

Preparing iPads for Deployment

Apple Configurator includes a Prepare Assistant feature that helps you prepare iPads and
other iOS devices for deployment. You can prepare an iPad either manually or by pointing
it at an MDM solution for automated enrollment. While setting up the preparation
process, you can choose whether to supervise the iPad or not.

Here, we'll look first at the process of preparing iPads manually, and then move on
to pointing an iPad at an MDM solution. The steps for preparing an iPad manually are
standard, but those for using an MDM solution vary depending on the MDM.

Preparing iPads Manually

To prepare iPads manually, follow these steps:

1. In the device browser, select the iPad or iPads you want to prepare.

2. Click the Prepare button on the toolbar. You can also choose Actions ➤ Prepare from the menu bar or Ctrl-click or right-click the selection and then click the Prepare item on the shortcut menu. The Prepare iOS Devices pane appears (see Figure 4-36).

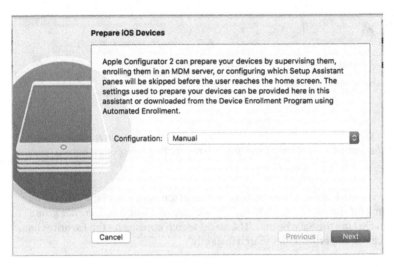

Prepare iOS Devices

Apple Configurator 2 can prepare your devices by supervising them, enrolling them in an MDM server, or configuring which Setup Assistant panes will be skipped before the user reaches the home screen. The settings used to prepare your devices can be provided here in this assistant or downloaded from the Device Enrollment Program using Automated Enrollment.

Configuration: Manual

Cancel   Previous   Next

Figure 4-36. In the Prepare iOS Devices pane, choose the Manual item in the Configuration pop-up menu

3. Open the Configuration pop-up menu and click the Manual item.

4. Click the Next button. The Enroll in MDM Server pane appears (see Figure 4-37).

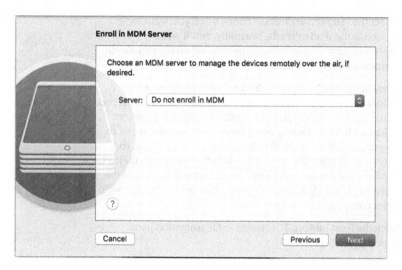

Figure 4-37. *In the Enroll in MDM Server pane, open the pop-up menu and choose the "Do not enroll in MDM" item*

5. Open the Server pop-up menu and click the "Do not enroll in MDM" item.

6. Click the Next button. The Supervise Devices pane appears (see Figure 4-38).

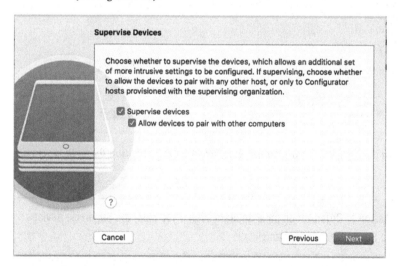

Figure 4-38. *In the Supervise Devices pane, choose whether to supervise the iPads you're preparing. If you supervise the iPads, you can control whether they can pair with other computers.*

7. Select the "Supervise devices" check box if you want to supervise the iPad or iPads. Normally, you'll want to supervise them in a school setting so that you have in-depth management capabilities.

8. If you select the "Supervise devices" check box, select the "Allow devices to pair with other computers" check box if you want to allow users to pair the iPads with other computers or just with Apple Configurator hosts. For example, if you're preparing iPads to issue to students for individual use, you may want to allow the students to pair the iPads with their PCs or Macs. But if you're preparing iPads that will remain in the classroom, you likely won't want them to be able to pair with other computers.

9. Click the Next button. The Assign to Organization pane appears (see Figure 4-39).

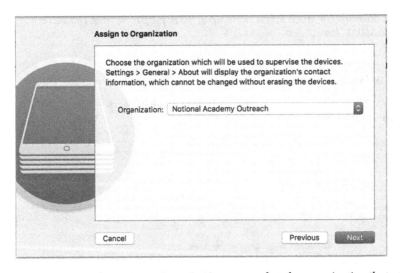

Figure 4-39. In the Assign to Organization pane, select the organization that will supervise the iPads.

■ **Note** The Assign to Organization pane appears even if you clear the Supervise devices check box in the Supervise Devices pane.

---

10. Open the Organization pop-up menu and click the organization that will supervise the iPads. If you have multiple supervisory organizations, make sure you pick the right one, because you'll need to erase the iPads to change the organization. If you cleared the "Supervise devices" check box in the Supervise Devices pane in step 7, select the None item in the Organization pop-up menu.

▪ **Note** The Organization pop-up menu in the Assign to Organization pane shows the list of organizations you've added to the Organizations preferences pane. If you need to add another organization at this point, open the Organization pop-up menu, click the New organization item, and the follow through the screens for adding the details.

11. Click the Next button. The Configure iOS Setup Assistant pane appears. Setup Assistant is the iOS feature that walks you through setting up the iPad; this pane enables you to choose which steps of Setup Assistant to include. Figure 4-40 shows the Configure iOS Setup Assistant pane with the Show Only Some Steps item selected in the Setup Assistant pop-up menu.

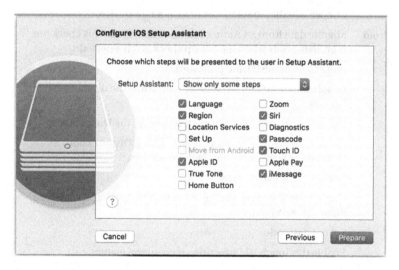

Figure 4-40. In the Configure iOS Setup Assistant pane, choose whether the iPad should display all setup steps, some setup steps, or no setup steps at all

12. Open the Setup Assistant pop-up menu and click the appropriate item: "Show all steps," "Show only some steps," or "Don't show any of these steps." Selecting the "Show all" steps item selects all the check boxes and makes them dimmed and unavailable; selecting the "Show only some steps" item enables most of the check boxes; and selecting the "Don't show any of these steps" item clears all the check boxes and makes them dimmed and unavailable.

13. If you select the "Show only some steps" item, select the check boxes for the setup steps you want users to see, and clear all the other check boxes. Table 4-3 briefly explains the choices.

Table 4-3. *Setup Assistant Steps*

Step	Enables the User To
Language	Choose the interface language, such as English (United States). If you clear this check box, the iPad uses the same language as the Mac you're using to configure it.
Region	Choose the country or region, such as United States. If you clear this check box, the iPad uses the same region as the Mac you're using to configure it.
Location Services	Enable or disable location services.
Set Up	Choose whether to set up the iPad as a new device.
Move from Android	Migrate data from an Android device to the iPad. This check box is available only when the Set Up check box is selected.
Apple ID	Enter their Apple ID and password.
True Tone	Enable the feature for dynamically adjusting the display's white balance.
Home Button	Choose an Accessibility Shortcut setting for the Home button.
Zoom	Change the Display Zoom setting. In iPads, Display Zoom is available only on the larger iPad Pro models.
Siri	Enable the Siri voice assistant.
Diagnostics	Choose whether to send diagnostic data to Apple and share app data with developers.
Passcode	Set the passcode.
Touch ID	Enable the Touch ID fingerprint-recognition feature.
Apple Pay	Enable the Apple Pay payment service.
iMessage	Set up an account in the iMessage service.

14. Click the Prepare button. Apple Configurator begins applying the configuration to the iPad or iPads.

■ **Note** If, when you click the Prepare button, Apple Configurator displays an alert saying it cannot perform the requested action because the iPad has already been prepared, either click the Erase button or click the Stop button and start again with a different iPad, one that hasn't been prepared.

Preparing iPads for Automated Enrollment in an MDM Solution

To prepare iPads for use with an MDM solution, follow these steps in Apple Configurator:

1. Select the iPad or iPads you want to prepare.

2. Click the Prepare button on the toolbar. You can also choose Actions ➤ Prepare from the menu bar or Ctrl-click or right-click the selection and then click the Prepare item on the shortcut menu. The Prepare iOS Devices pane appears.

3. Open the Configuration pop-up and click the Manual item. The alternative is the Automated Enrollment item, which you would normally need to use if you're using Apple's DEP program.

4. Click the Next button. The Enroll in MDM Server pane appears.

5. Open the Server pop-up menu and then click the appropriate server, such as one that you added earlier in the Servers preferences pane.

■ **Note** If you haven't yet added the server, click the New Server item on the Server pop-up menu. Click the Next button to display the first Define an MDM Server pane. Enter the name for the server in the Name box and the server's hostname or URL in the Hostname or URL box. Click the Next button. Apple Configurator fetches the trust anchor certificates from the server and then displays the next Define an MDM Server pane, which shows a list of the trust anchor certificates. Edit the list as needed by removing certificates or by adding them, and then click the Next button. The Supervise Devices pane then appears.

---

6. Click the Next button. The Supervise Devices pane appears.

7. Select the Supervise devices check box if you want to supervise the iPad or iPads. Normally, you'll want to supervise them in a school setting.

8. If you select the Supervise devices check box, select the "Allow devices to pair with other computers" check box if you want to allow users to pair the iPads with other computers other than Apple Configurator hosts registered to the supervising organization.

■ **Caution** Depending on the MDM solution you're using, the steps after this point may be different.

---

9. Click the Next button. The Assign to Organization pane appears.

10. Open the Organization pop-up menu and click the appropriate organization.

11. Click the Next button. The Configure iOS Setup Assistant pane appears.

12. Open the Setup Assistant pop-up menu and click the appropriate item: "Show all steps," "Show only some steps," or "Don't show any of these steps." Selecting the "Show all steps" item selects all the check boxes and makes them dimmed and unavailable; selecting the "Show only some steps" item enables most of the check boxes; and selecting the "Don't show any of these steps" item clears all the check boxes and makes them dimmed and unavailable.

13. If you select the "Show only some steps" item, select the check boxes for the setup steps you want users to see, and clear all the other check boxes. See Table 4-3, earlier in this chapter, for details on the steps.

14. Click the Prepare button. Apple Configurator begins applying the configuration to the iPad or iPads.

■ **Tip** To see how progress is going, choose Window ➤ Activity and look at the information in the Activity window.

Working with Configuration Profiles

Apple Configurator enables you to create configuration profiles to configure iOS automatically. A *configuration profile* is an XML file that contains predefined settings and authentication credentials, such as digital certificates. The settings and credentials are contained in *payloads* that you define. For example, you can add a restrictions payload to implement restrictions to what the user can do, add a Wi-Fi payload to load the settings for one or more Wi-Fi networks onto the iPad, or add a Certificates payload to install digital certificates on the iPad.

You can apply various security measures to a profile:

- *Encryption and signing*: You can encrypt and sign a configuration profile to make it work with only a specific iOS device.

- *Locking*: You can lock a profile to a device with a password. Removing the profile then requires the password—or erasing the device entirely and reinstalling iOS.

- *Account fixing*: You can lock an account to a device by configuring the account via a profile. For example, you can use a profile to configure an Exchange ActiveSync account on an iPad. Once you've done that, the account is fixed on the iPad unless you remove the profile.

CREATING SEPARATE PROFILES FOR CONSTANT SETTINGS AND CHANGING SETTINGS

As you'll see in this section, a profile can contain a huge number of settings—everything from General settings, such as whether the profile can be removed from the device, to Web Clips settings, which create shortcuts on the Home screen to specific web pages. By working your way through the different categories in the sidebar in Apple Configurator, you can add payloads for each category that you need the profile to contain.

It's easy enough to put all the settings for an iPad into a single profile, but you may find it more efficient in the long run to create multiple profiles that you can apply singly or in groups, as needed. Usually, it's best to create a separate profile (or multiple profiles) for settings that largely remain constant and another profile (or multiple profiles) for settings that change frequently. You can then update the profiles for settings that change frequently without needing to change the profiles for settings that remain constant.

Settings categories that remain constant typically include Restrictions, Domains, Global HTTP Proxy, Passcode, Wi-Fi, and the various account types—Calendar, Subscribed Calendars, Contacts, Exchange ActiveSync, Google Account, LDAP, Mail, and macOS Server Account. Settings categories that typically change more often include Web Clips, Certificates, and VPN. Some categories, such as AirPrint and AirPlay, may fall into either settings group—or both.

Starting a New Profile and Configuring the General Settings

To get started creating a new profile in Apple Configurator, choose File ➤ New Profile from the menu bar or press Cmd-N. A new window opens for working on the profile. At first, the window is called Untitled – Edited.

■ **Tip** When Apple Configurator is running, you can also start a new profile by Ctrl-clicking or right-clicking the Apple Configurator icon on the Dock and then clicking New Profile on the shortcut menu.

Figure 4-41 shows the profile window. As you can see, the window has two panes. The left pane is the sidebar, which contains the list of categories of settings. The right pane, the main pane, contains the settings for the currently selected category.

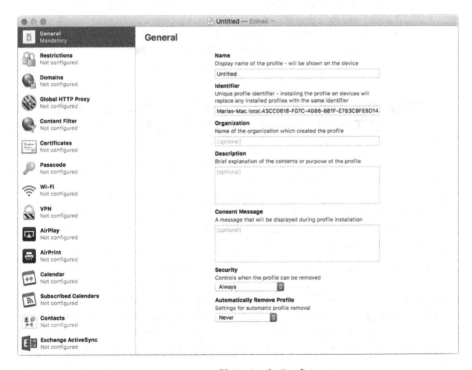

Figure 4-41. *Starting to create a new profile in Apple Configurator*

Normally, it's a good idea to save the profile immediately, and to keep saving it as you create your payloads. Apple Configurator complains if you haven't added a payload to the profile, but you can override this protest. Follow these steps to save the profile:

1. Press Cmd-S or choose File ➤ Save from the menu bar. A Save sheet opens.

2. Type the profile name in the Save As box. Apple Configurator suggests the name in the Name box.

3. In the Tags box, apply any tags needed. For example, if you have tags for different departments, apply the appropriate department tag.

4. Specify the location by using the Where pop-up menu or by clicking the button to the right of the Save As box and browsing to the appropriate folder.

5. Click the Save button. Apple Configurator displays a dialog warning you that the profile contains no payloads and can't be installed on devices (see Figure 4-42).

Figure 4-42. *If Apple Configurator warns you that the profile contains no payloads, click the Save Anyway button*

6. Click the Save Anyway button. Apple Configurator saves the profile, and the name appears at the top of the profile window. You can then configure the payloads for the profile.

These are the settings you can configure in the General category:

- *Name*: Type the name that you want the iOS device (we'll assume it's an iPad) to display to identify the profile. For example, for the standard iPad profile for a student at Notional Academy, you might use a name such as Notional Academy iPad profile for student.

- *Identifier*: Type the name to identify the profile on the iPad. Apple Configurator suggests a default name based on the name of your Mac, but you may prefer to use something more descriptive. For example, instead of an identifier such as macserver1.8D0328D6-0416-4C61-B3B8-216DEC8AEB46, you might use a descriptive name such as macserver1.students.general.

- *Organization*: Type the name of your organization—for example, Notional Academy. This is an optional field, but normally it's helpful to fill it in.

- *Description*: Type a short description of what the profile is for and what it does. The Description field too is an optional field, but including it is usually a good idea.

- *Consent Message*: Type any message you want the iPad to display to the user as a prompt during the installation of the profile. For example, you might enter a message telling the user that they must install the profile in order to be able to connect the iPad to the school's Wi-Fi network and to the Internet.

- *Security*: In this pop-up menu, choose whether and (if so) when the user can remove the profile from the iPad. Your choices are Always, With Authorization, and Never. If you're keeping the iPads under your control, you'll normally choose either With Authorization or Never here.

- *Automatically Remove Profile*: In this pop-up menu, choose whether and (if so) when you want the profile to be removed automatically from the iPad. Your choices are Never, On date, and After interval. The Never setting gives you the tightest control, whereas the On date setting and the After interval setting enable you to apply a profile that lasts only until a specific date or for a specific interval.

Moving Along to the Next Payload

Once you finish configuring settings for the General category, go to the sidebar and click the next category you want to configure. If the category is one you haven't configured yet, the profile window displays a box showing the category's name, a brief summary of what it does, and a Configure button (see Figure 4-43). Click the Configure button to display the settings available for the category.

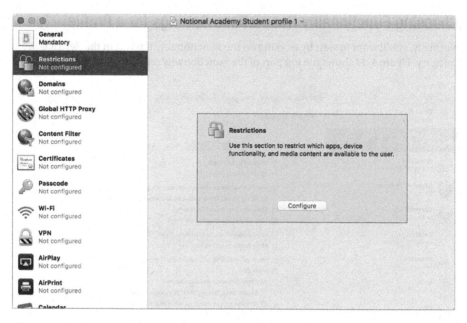

Figure 4-43. *For any category you haven't yet configured, click the Configure button in the summary box to display the settings available*

The following subsections explain each of the remaining categories in turn.

■ **Note**   As you move from one category to another, you may find that the category you leave displays a badge (a rounded rectangle containing a number) to its right. A yellow badge indicates an optional setting that you've left unset or for which you've specified an unusable value. A red badge indicates a required setting that you've left unset or specified an unusable value. Apple Configurator warns you about any red badges when you give the command to save the profile.

Configuring a Restrictions Payload in the Profile

The Restrictions category enables you to configure a huge swathe of settings, which this section explains. You click the three tabs—Functionality, Apps, and Media Content—at the top of the Restrictions category to choose the subcategory of restrictions settings you want to work with.

Choosing Functionality Restrictions Settings for a Profile

Normally, you'll want to start by working on the Functionality tab within the Restrictions category. Figure 4-44 shows the top part of the Functionality tab.

Figure 4-44. *Configure the settings on the Functionality tab in the Restrictions category in a profile in Apple Configurator to specify which functionality is available and which is restricted*

■ **Note** You'll notice that some of the settings in the Restrictions category are marked as "(supervised only)." This means that they apply only to iPads that are supervised using an MDM solution.

These are the settings you can configure on the Functionality tab in the Restrictions category:

- *Allow use of camera*: Select this check box to allow the user to use the iPad's camera.

- *Allow FaceTime*: Select this check box to allow the user to use the FaceTime app. This check box is available only if you select the "Allow use of camera" check box.

- *Allow screenshots and screen recording*: Select this check box if you want the user to be able to take screenshots (by pressing the Sleep/Wake button and the Home button together) and to record videos showing what's happening on the screen.

- *Allow screen observation by Classroom (supervised only)*: Select this check box if you want the iPad's screen to be observable by the Apple Classroom app. This check box is available only if you select the "Allow screenshots and screen recording" check box.

- *Allow AirDrop (supervised only)*: Select this check box to allow the user to use the AirDrop feature to send files to or receive files from other iOS devices or Macs.

- *Allow iMessage (supervised only)*: Select this check box to allow the user to send and receive instant messages via Apple's iMessage service.

- *Allow Apple Music (supervised only)*: Select this check box to allow the user to use the Apple Music service.

- *Allow Radio (supervised only)*: Select this check box to allow the user to use the Apple Radio service.

- *Allow voice dialing when device is locked*: Select this check box to allow the user to place FaceTime audio or video calls when the iPad is locked. This setting is more useful for the iPhone, which may need to make emergency or other urgent phone calls when locked, than for the iPad.

- *Allow Siri*: Select this check box to allow the user to use the Siri voice assistant feature. Clearing this check box disables the next three check boxes.

- *Allow Siri while device is locked*: Select this check box if you want to let the user use Siri while the iPad is locked. This check box is available only if you select the Allow Siri check box.

- *Enable Siri profanity filter (supervised only)*: Select this check box if you want to turn on Siri's feature that attempts to detect and avoid profanity in results Siri returns. This check box is available only if you select the Allow Siri check box.

- *Show user-generated content in Siri (supervised only)*: Select this check box if you want Siri to include user-generated content in search results. This check box is available only if you select the Allow Siri check box.

- *Allow Siri Suggestions*: Select this check box if you want the Siri Suggestions box to appear on the Search screen.

- *Allow iBooks Store (supervised only)*: Select this check box to allow the user to access the iBooks Store.

- *Allow installing apps*: Select this check box to allow the user to install apps on the iPad. Clearing this check box disables the next two check boxes.

- *Allow installing apps using App Store (supervised only)*: Select this check box to allow the user to install apps from the App Store. This check box is available only when the Allow installing apps check box is selected.

- *Allow automatic app downloads (supervised only)*: Select this check box if you want the iPad to be able to download apps automatically. This check box is available only when the "Allow installing apps" check box is selected.

- *Allow removing apps (supervised only)*: Select this check box to allow the user to remove apps from the iPad.

- *Allow in-app purchases*: Select this check box to allow the user to make in-app purchases, such as buying extra features for apps or boosts for games.

- *Require iTunes Store password for all purchases*: Select this check box if you want to force the user to enter a password for each purchase from the iTunes Store.

- *Allow iCloud backup*: Select this check box to allow the user to back up the iPad to iCloud.

■ **Caution**   Backing up many iPads to iCloud can consume a lot of bandwidth. You may want to clear the "Allow iCloud backup" check box to reduce the amount of bandwidth the iPads use.

- *Allow iCloud documents and data*: Select this check box to allow the user to store documents and data in iCloud.

- *Allow iCloud Keychain*: Select this check box to allow the user to use the iCloud Keychain feature for storing password, credit card information, and other sensitive data securely online.

- *Allow managed apps to store data in iCloud*: Select this check box to allow managed apps to store data in iCloud. Managed apps are apps managed by MDM solutions.

- *Allow backup of enterprise books*: Select this check box to allow the iPad to back up enterprise books. *Enterprise books* are books distributed by an organization (such as your school).

- *Allow notes and highlights sync for enterprise books*: Select this check box to allow the iPad to sync notes and highlights the user has added to enterprise books.

- *Allow iCloud Photo Sharing*: Select this check box to allow the user to use the iCloud Photo Sharing feature, which enables sharing the user's own photos with other iCloud users and viewing those photos that other users share.

- *Allow iCloud Photo Library*: Select this check box to allow the user to use the iCloud Photo Library feature, storing all the photos and videos in iCloud.

■ **Caution**   iCloud Photo Library can take up a huge amount of bandwidth, so you'll normally want to clear the Allow iCloud Photo Library check box.

- *Allow My Photo Stream (disallowing can cause data loss)*: Select this check box to allow the user to use the My Photo Stream feature, which stores up to 1,000 of the most recent photos in iCloud. The "disallowing can cause data loss" phrase means that if the user has been using My Photo Stream, disallowing it may cause some photos to be deleted.

- *Allow automatic sync while roaming*: Select this check box if you want the iPad's apps to be able to sync via the cellular connection. This setting applies only to Wi-Fi–and-cellular iPads, not to Wi-Fi–only iPads.

- *Force encrypted backups*: Select this check box to force the iPad to use encryption for any backups.

- *Force limited ad tracking*: Select this check box to limit tracking by advertisers. This is the equivalent of setting the Location-Based Apple Ads switch to Off on the System Services screen in the Settings app. You may well want to enable this setting.

- *Allow Erase All Content and Settings (supervised only)*: Select this check box to allow the Erase Data switch on the Touch ID & Passcode screen in the Settings app to be set to On.

- *Allow users to accept untrusted TLS certificates*: Select this check box to allow users to accept untrusted Transport Layer Security (TLS) certificates. Normally, you would not want users to be able to accept untrusted TLS certificates.

- *Allow automatic updates to certificate trust settings*: Select this check box to allow the iPad to automatically update digital certificates. This is normally helpful.

- *Allow trusting new enterprise app authors*: Select this check box to allow the user to "sideload" apps onto the iPad. *Sideloading* means installing apps from unofficial sources. Normally, you would clear this check box to prevent the user from installing unapproved apps.

- *Allow installing configuration profiles (supervised only)*: Select this check box to allow the user to install configuration profiles—for example, to connect the iPad to a Wi-Fi network or to a VPN.

- *Allow modifying account settings (supervised only)*: Select this check box to allow the user to modify account settings on the iPad.

- *Allow modifying Bluetooth settings (supervised only)*: Select this check box to allow the user to modify Bluetooth settings—for example, to connect a keyboard or a Bluetooth headset.

- *Allow modifying cellular data app settings (supervised only)*: Select this check box to allow the user to modify the settings on the Cellular Data screen. These settings control which apps can transfer data over the cellular connection; they don't apply to Wi-Fi-only iPads.

- *Allow modifying device name (supervised only)*: Select this check box to allow the user to modify the iPad's name. If you use the names as a means of identifying the iPads, you'll want to clear this check box.

- *Allow modifying Find My Friends settings (supervised only)*: Select this check box to allow the user to change the Find My Friends settings.

- *Allow modifying notification settings (supervised only)*: Select this check box to allow the user to change settings on the Notifications screen in the Settings app.

- *Allow modifying passcode (supervised only)*: Select this check box to allow the user to change the passcode on the iPad. The ability to change the passcode includes being able to change the type of passcode, such as changing from a six-digit passcode to a four-digit passcode. When this check box is cleared, the following check box is unavailable.

- *Allow modifying Touch ID fingerprints (supervised only)*: Select this check box to allow the user to add and remove Touch ID fingerprints. This check box is available only when the "Allow modifying passcode (supervised only)" check box is selected.

- *Allow modifying restrictions (supervised only)*: Select this check box to allow the user to modify the restrictions set on the iPad.

- *Allow modifying Wallpaper (supervised only)*: Select this check box to allow the user to change the wallpaper applied to the Home screen and the lock screen.

- *Allow pairing with non-Configurator hosts (supervised only)*: Select this check box to allow the user to pair the iPad with a computer via iTunes. Clear this check box if you want the iPad to be managed only by Apple Configurator.

- *Allow documents from managed sources in unmanaged destinations*: Select this check box if you want to allow the user to open documents from managed sources in unmanaged apps. Clear this check box if you want to restrict documents from managed sources to being opened by managed apps.

- *Allow documents from unmanaged sources in managed destinations*: Select this check box if you want to allow the user to open documents from unmanaged sources in managed apps. Clear this check box if you want managed apps to be able to open only documents from managed sources.

- *Treat AirDrop as unmanaged destination*: Select this check box to make the iPad treat AirDrop as an unmanaged destination.

- *Allow Handoff*: Select this check box to enable the Handoff feature, which lets the user resume on one iOS device or Mac a task that was started on another iOS device or Mac that uses the same iCloud account. For example, the user might start writing an e-mail message on the iPad and then continue writing it on an iPhone.

- *Allow sending diagnostic and usage data to Apple*: Select this check box to allow the iPad to send diagnostic data and usage data to Apple. The data is anonymized, so it shouldn't normally pose a security threat. When this check box is cleared, the following check box is unavailable.

- *Allow modifying diagnostics (supervised only)*: Select this check box to allow the user to change settings on the Diagnostics & Usage screen in the Settings app. This check box is available only if the "Allow sending diagnostic and usage data to Apple" check box is selected.

- *Allow Touch ID to unlock device*: Clear this check box if you want to disable the Touch ID feature.

- *Force Apple Watch wrist detection*: This check box enables you to forcibly enable the Wrist Detection feature on an Apple Watch. (Wrist Detection locks the Apple Watch when the wearer removes it.) This check box is only for the iPhone.

- *Allow pairing with Apple Watch (supervised only)*: This check box enables you to control whether an iPhone can pair with an Apple Watch.

- *Require passcode on first AirPlay pairing*: Select this check box if you need to make the user enter a passcode when pairing the iPad with an AirPlay device. This feature enables you to prevent the iPad from connecting to unauthorized AirPlay devices.

- *Allow predictive keyboard (supervised only)*: Select this check box to allow the user to use the predictive keyboard feature.

- *Allow auto correction (supervised only)*: Select this check box to allow the user to use auto-correction, which automatically corrects typos and expands text shortcuts.

- *Allow spell check (supervised only)*: Select this check box to allow the user to use the spell check feature.

- *Allow Define (supervised only)*: Select this check box to allow the user to use the Define feature, which searches for a definition of the word the user double-taps.

- *Allow Wallet notifications in Lock screen*: Select this check box to allow Wallet notifications to appear on the lock screen.

- *Show Control Center in Lock screen*: Select this check box to allow the user to display Control Center from the lock screen (without unlocking the iPad).

- *Show Notification Center in Lock screen*: Select this check box to allow notifications other than Wallet notifications to appear on the lock screen.

- *Show Today view in Lock screen*: Select this check box to allow the user to access Today View from the lock screen (without unlocking the iPad).

Choosing Apps Restrictions Settings for a Profile

Once you finish working on the Functionality tab of the Restrictions category, click the Apps tab to display its controls (see Figure 4-45). Here, you can configure the following settings:

- *Allow use of iTunes Store*: Select this check box to allow the user to use the iTunes Store.

- *Allow use of News (supervised only)*: Select this check box to allow the user to use the News app.

- *Allow use of Podcasts (supervised only)*: Select this check box to allow the user to use the Podcasts app.

- *Allow use of Game Center (supervised only)*: Select this check box to allow the user to use Game Center features. When this check box is cleared, the following two check boxes are disabled.

- *Allow multiplayer gaming (supervised only)*: Select this check box to allow the user to play multiplayer games via Game Center. This check box is available only when the "Allow use of Game Center (supervised only)" check box is selected.

- *Allow adding Game Center friends*: Select this check box to allow the user to add friends in Game Center. This check box is available only when the "Allow use of Game Center (supervised only)" check box is selected.

- *Allow use of Safari*: Select this check box to allow the user to use the Safari web browser. When this check box is cleared, the following four check boxes and the Accept Cookies pop-up menu are unavailable.

- *Enable AutoFill*: Select this check box to allow the user to use the AutoFill feature, which can automatically fill in fields in web forms—for example, entering the name and address from a specified contact record. This check box is available only when the "Allow use of Safari" check box is selected.

- *Force fraud warning*: Select this check box to turn on the Fraudulent Website Warning feature in Safari. (You can turn on this feature manually by setting the Fraudulent Website Warning switch to On in the Privacy & Security box in Safari's preferences.) This check box is available only when the "Allow use of Safari" check box is selected.

- *Enable JavaScript*: Select this check box to enable JavaScript in Safari. This check box is available only when the "Allow use of Safari" check box is selected.

- *Block pop-ups*: Select this check box to apply pop-up blocking
  in Safari. This is usually a good idea. (You can control pop-up
  blocking manually by setting the Block Pop-Ups switch in the
  General box in Safari's preferences.) This check box is available
  only when the "Allow use of Safari" check box is selected.

- *Accept cookies*: In this pop-up menu, choose how to handle
  cookies that websites try to set. Your choices are Never, From
  current website only, From websites I visit, and Always.

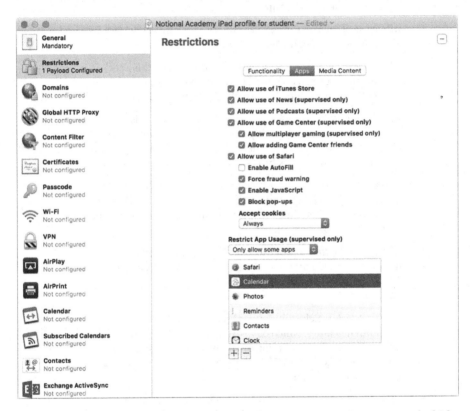

Figure 4-45. *Use the controls on the Apps tab in the Restrictions category to control which apps the user can run*

WHICH COOKIES SHOULD YOU LET THE IPADS ACCEPT?

You may find it hard to decide among the four choices—Never, From current website only, From websites I visit, and Always—in the "Accept cookies" pop-up menu on the Apps tab of the Restrictions category. Cookies have a bad reputation, but many websites rely on them, so it's not usually wise to select the Never item, because it may prevent websites from working correctly. The "From current website only" item also tends to be too restrictive. On the other hand, the Always item, which allows cookies both from sites that the user visits and third-party cookies attached to those sites, is seldom a good choice, because third-party cookies are typically used for advertising and tracking users from site to site.

Normally, the best choice is the "From websites I visit" item, which allows cookies from the sites that the user visits (also called first-party cookies) but not the third-party cookies.

- *Restrict App Usage (supervised only)*: In this pop-up menu, choose "Allow all apps," "Do not allow some apps," or "Only allow some apps," as needed. If you choose "Do not allow some apps" or "Only allow some apps," add each app to the list box by clicking the Add (+) button, using the "Choose an app" dialog to identify the app, and then clicking the Choose button. If you add an app that you want to remove, click the app in the list box, and then click the Remove (–) button. The "Choose an app" dialog shows both system apps and apps on the App Store.

Choosing Media Content Restrictions Settings for a Profile

Next, click the Media Content tab in the Restrictions category to display its controls (see Figure 4-46). On this tab, you can configure the following settings:

- *Ratings region*: In this pop-up menu, choose the country or region whose ratings system you want to use. For example, choose United States.

- *Movies*: In this pop-up menu, choose Allow All Movies, Don't Allow Movies, or one of the available ratings. For example, for the United States region, you can choose G, PG, PG-13, R, or NC-17.

- *TV Shows*: In this pop-up menu, choose Allow All TV Shows, Don't Allow TV Shows, or one of the available ratings.

- *Apps*: In this pop-up menu, choose Allow All Apps, Don't Allow Apps, or one of the age ratings, such as 12+.

- *Allow playback of explicit music, podcasts & iTunes U media*: Clear this check box if you want to prevent the Music, Podcasts, and iTunes U apps from playing back media marked as Explicit.

- *Allow explicit sexual content in iBooks Store*: Clear this check box if you want the iBooks Store to hide books that are marked as containing explicit sexual content.

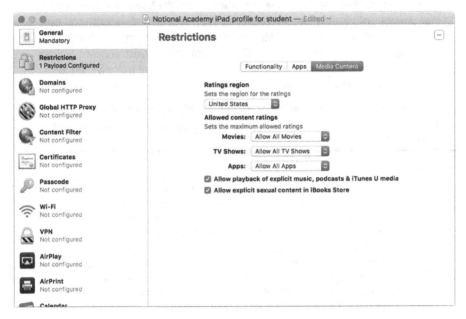

Figure 4-46. *On the Media Content tab of the Restrictions category, you can choose the ratings region, specify the allowed content ratings for movies, TV shows, and apps, and decide whether to let the iPad play explicit content*

Configuring a Domains Payload in the Profile

Apple Configurator enables you to configure unmarked e-mail domains, managed Safari web domains, and Safari Password Autofill domains in a profile. Here's what these three types of domains are:

- *Unmarked e-mail domain*: A domain you specify as being one from which the iPad should receive e-mail without marking its address. The Mail app marks the e-mail address of any message coming from a domain that you haven't specified as an unmarked e-mail domain.

- *Managed Safari web domain*: A domain you specify as being one that Safari should consider to contain managed documents.

- *Safari Password Autofill domain*: A domain for which Safari's Password Autofill feature can save passwords.

To configure domains, click the Domains category in the sidebar to display the Domains pane. If the Configure button appears, as it does until you start configuring domains, click it to display the Domains controls. As you can see in Figure 4-47, this contains three boxes: the Unmarked E-mail Domains box, the Managed Safari Web Domains box, and the Safari Password Autofill Domains (supervised only) box. Below each box is an Add (+) button that you can click to add a domain and a Remove (-) button that you can click to remove the selected domain.

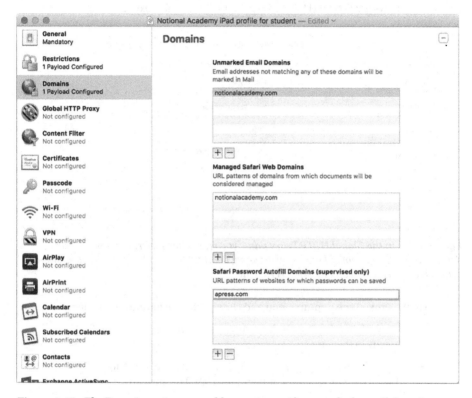

Figure 4-47. *The Domains category enables you to specify unmarked e-mail domains, managed Safari web domains, and Safari Password Autofill domains*

Configuring a Global HTTP Proxy Payload in the Profile

The Global HTTP Proxy category enables you to specify a proxy server that the iPad will use for all HTTP traffic. For example, your school may use a proxy server to restrict access to unapproved websites and to cache data for approved websites so that it can return their data more rapidly to clients and reduce use of Internet bandwidth.

To set up the global HTTP proxy payload, click the Global HTTP Proxy category in the sidebar, and then click the Configure button to display the Global HTTP Proxy pane. Figure 4-48 shows the Global HTTP Proxy pane for a manual proxy server.

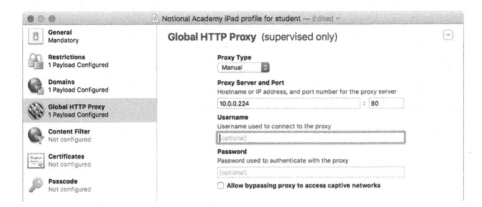

Figure 4-48. *In the Global HTTP Proxy pane, you can either specify the proxy server's details manually, as shown here, or by directing the iPad to the URL of a proxy server that contains a proxy auto-configuration (PAC) file*

Go to the Proxy Type pop-up menu and choose Manual or Auto, as needed:

- *Manual*: Choose Manual for a proxy server whose details you'll specify in the pane.

- *Auto*: Choose Auto if you want to direct the iPad to a URL to download a proxy auto-configuration (PAC) file instead.

If you choose Manual in the Proxy Type pop-up menu, configure the following settings to specify the details:

- *Proxy Server and Port*: Type the hostname or IP address of the proxy server in the left box and the port number (such as 80) in the right box.

- *Username*: If the proxy server is set to require a username and password, type it in this box.

- *Password*: Type the password for the username in this box.

- *Allow bypassing proxy to access captive networks*: Select this check box to allow the iPads to connect to known wireless networks without going through the proxy server.

If you choose Auto in the Proxy Type pop-up menu, configure the following settings in the Global HTTP Proxy pane, whose contents change (see Figure 4-49) when you select Auto:

- *Proxy PAC URL*: Type or paste the URL at which the PAC file is located.

- *Allow direct connection if PAC is unreachable*: Select this check box if you want the iPad to connect directly to URLs if it can't obtain the PAC. Having the iPad connect directly can be a good idea, because doing so enables the iPad to ride out temporary glitches in the system, but it may hide from you the fact that the proxy server isn't working.

- *Allow bypassing proxy to access captive networks*: As for a proxy server you configure manually, select this check box to allow the iPads to connect to known wireless networks without going through the proxy server.

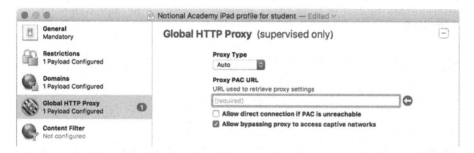

Figure 4-49. *For automatic proxy configuration, choose Auto in the Proxy Type pop-up menu, and then enter in the Proxy PAC URL box the URL at which the iPad will find the proxy auto-configuration (PAC) file*

Configuring a Content Filter Payload in the Profile

The Content Filter feature enables you to apply one of three types of filter to the iPads:

- *Plugin (Third Party App)*: You can configure a third-party filter service to provide the filtering. If your school uses a compatible third-party filtering service, you'll likely want to use it.

- *Built-in: Limit Adult Content*: This built-in filter lets you list specific URLs that are permitted and URLs that are blocked. The filter automatically block sites that identify themselves as having adult content, but you can block additional sites as needed. Use this filter type if your school doesn't have a compatible third-party filtering service and your students will need to browse the Web to research topics.

- *Built-in: Specific Websites Only*: This built-in filter lets you list specific URLs that are allowed. These URLs appear as bookmarks and are the only sites the iPad can access. This filter type is good for providing students with a short list of authorized URLs and preventing them from going to other sites.

■ **Caution**   Each content filter type works only for supervised iOS devices.

To set up a Content Filter payload, click the Content Filter category in the sidebar, and then click the Configure button that appears at first in the Content Filter pane. The Content Filter pane then displays the remaining controls.

Configuring the Built-in: Limit Adult Content Filter

If you want to use the Built-in: Limit Adult Content filter, open the Filter Type pop-up menu and click the Built-in: Limit Adult Content item. You'll see the controls shown in Figure 4-50.

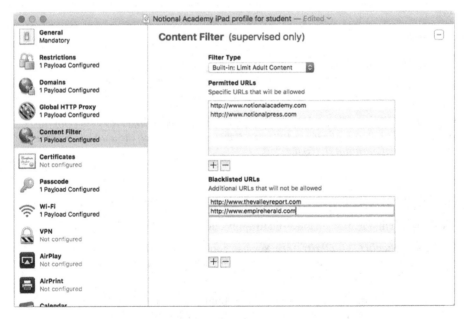

Figure 4-50. *The Limit Adult Content filter enables you to add a list of specifically permitted URLs and a list of extra blacklisted URLs to the list the filter already contains*

In the Permitted URLs box, set up the list of URLs that you want to permit even if the filter would normally block them. Click the Add (+) button to add a new line, type or paste the URL, and then press the Return key.

■ **Note**   Each URL must start with either http:// or https://.

Next, go to the Blacklisted URLs box and set up the list of URLs you want to disallow, even if the filter would normally allow them.

Configuring the Built-in: Specific Websites Only Filter

If you want to allow users to visit only specific websites, open the Filter Type pop-up menu and click the Built-in: Specific Websites Only item. The Content Filter pane displays the controls for specifying the websites (see Figure 4-51).

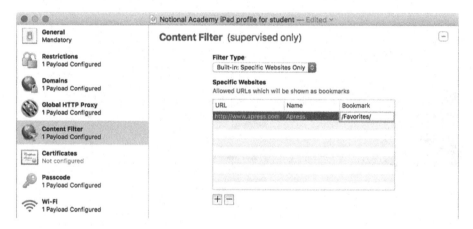

Figure 4-51. *The Specific Websites Only content filter enables you to limit the iPad to reaching only the websites you specify. You create a bookmark for each website, giving quick access to it.*

You can then create the list of allowed websites in the Specific Websites box like this:

1.   Click the Add (+) button to start creating a new entry.

2.   Type or paste the URL in the URL column.

3.   Type the display name for the bookmark in the Name column.

4.   If you want to put the bookmark in a folder, type the folder name and path in the Bookmark column. For example, type /Favorites/ to put the bookmark in the Favorites folder.

Configuring a Third-Party Filter

Apple Configurator also enables you to set the iPad to use a third-party filter. To do so, open the Filter Type pop-up menu in the Content Filter pane, and then click the Plugin (Third Party App) item. The Content Filter pane displays the controls for configuring the third-party filter (see Figure 4-52).

Figure 4-52. *The Plugin (Third Party App) filter type enables you to direct the iPad to use a third-party filtering service*

■ **Note**   If the third-party filter requires the iPad to use a digital certificate to authenticate itself with the filtering service, add the certificate to the profile's Certificates payload before setting up the Content Filter payload. You can then choose the certificate in the Certificate pop-up menu in the Content Filter payload.

Configure the controls on the Content Filter screen following the instructions from the provider of the filtering service. The following two fields are required:

- *Filter Name*: In this text box, type the name you want the app itself and the device to show for the filter.

- *Identifier*: In this text box, type the bundle identifier for the filter app.

All the other fields and controls are optional, but you'll typically need to fill in values or choose settings for some of them.

If the filtering service provider requires you to use a digital certificate to authenticate the devices that use the service, open the Certificate pop-up menu and choose the appropriate certificate that you've already added to the Certificates payload for this profile.

Configuring a Certificates Payload in the Profile

The Certificates category in Apple Configurator enables you to add one or more payloads, each containing a digital certificate in the PKCS1 format or the PKCS12 format, to the profile. You can use the digital certificates for authentication to services such as Wi-Fi networks, VPNs, or content filtering services. A digital certificate enables you to authenticate a device securely without the user having to type a complicated password or passcode.

To get started adding certificates, click the Certificates category in the sidebar, and then click the Configure button in the Certificates pane. Unlike with most of the other categories, the hidden controls don't appear at first; instead, a dialog for selecting the certificate opens. Navigate to the folder that contains the certificate, click the certificate file, and then click the Open button.

The certificate's details then appear in the Certificate pane (see Figure 4-53), and you can complete the payload by entering the certificate name and password:

- *Certificate Name*: In this box, edit the existing name (which comes from the certificate file's name) as needed or type a new name. For example, you might want to enter a description of the certificate (such as Certificate for VPN Connections) rather than the filename.

- *Password*: In this box, type the password that protects the certificate file. This is the password set in the certificate file itself.

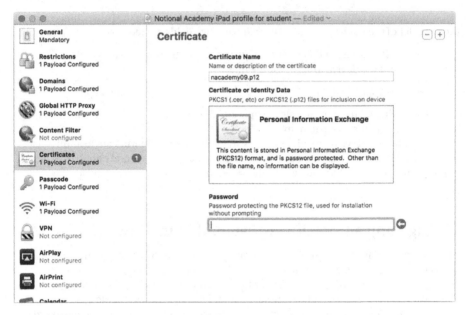

Figure 4-53. *In the Certificate pane, rename the certificate with a descriptive name if needed, and type the password that protects the certificate file*

Once you've added one certificate payload to the profile, you can click the Add (+) button in the upper-right corner of the Certificate pane to add another certificate payload.

Configuring a Passcode Payload in the Profile

The Passcode category (see Figure 4-54) enables you to enforce your choice of password policies on the iPad. Your options include choosing whether to allow simple passcodes (such as 1111 or 1234), setting the minimum password length, specifying the maximum time before the device automatically locks, and forcing periodic password changes.

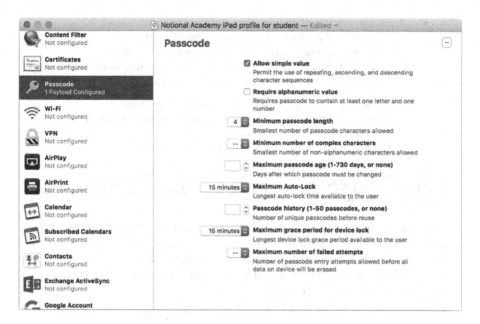

Figure 4-54. *Configure a passcode payload to apply your choice of passcode policities to the iPad*

These are the settings you can configure in the Passcode pane:

- *Allow simple value*: Select this check box if you want to let users use simple password values, such as 9999, 1234, or 9876. iOS bars simple passwords by default because they're too easy to crack, but you may find them convenient for iPads that remain in the classroom.

- *Require alphanumeric value*: Select this check box if you want to force users to use alphanumeric characters in the passcode. This setting is good for enterprise security but is likely overkill for iPads used by students in the classroom. Alphanumeric passcodes take more effort to enter than numeric passcodes, because the user must switch among keyboards, so you probably won't want to use them unless the user can normally unlock the iPad using Touch ID.

- *Minimum passcode length*: In this pop-up menu, select the minimum passcode length. You can either choose no minimum (the -- setting) or a value between 1 and 16. For iPads that will remain in the classroom, or at least within the school, four characters may be an effective minimum. For iPads that leave the school, use the iOS default of six characters as a workable minimum unless you need tighter security—in which case, use a higher value, such as 10.

- *Minimum number of complex characters*: For enterprise-level security, open this pop-up menu and choose the minimum number of non-alphanumeric characters the passcode must contain. Your choices are 1, 2, 3, and 4. For in-school use, leave this pop-up menu set to no minimum (the -- setting).

- *Maximum passcode age (1–730 days, or none)*: If you need to force users to change password periodically, enter the maximum permitted password age in days in this box. For normally use, leave this option set to no maximum age (the -- setting).

SHOULD YOU FORCE PERIODIC PASSCODE CHANGES?

Forcing users—and administrators!—to change passwords or passcodes regularly used to be staple advice, but most security experts now recommend against it. Many users responded by creating pattern-based password sequences (such as PwNov017!, PwDec017!, and so on) that scraped over the security hurdles but were easy to predict if seen or even hinted at.

Current advice is to *not* force password changes by setting a maximum password age, but to require passwords that are complex enough to be hard to crack. If you ever have reason to believe that a passcode has been compromised, you must change it immediately.

- *Maximum Auto-Lock*: In this pop-up menu, choose the maximum length of time the user can set for the Auto-Lock setting on the Display & Brightness screen in the Settings app. You can choose no maximum (the -- setting) or 1 minute, 2 minutes, 3 minutes, 4 minutes, 5 minutes, 10 minutes, or 15 minutes.

■ **Tip**　For iPads that go outside the school, set a short Maximum Auto-Lock setting, such as 1 or 2 minutes, to reduce the risk of the iPad being lost or stolen with its screen unlocked. For iPads that stay within the school, choosing the best Maximum Auto-Lock setting for your school's iPads is trickier. On the one hand, setting a maximum of even 15 minutes is useful for making sure the iPad doesn't get left with its screen on, running down the battery. On the other hand, having the iPads lock automatically during pauses in a lesson can cause disruptions, especially if the students don't know the passcodes to unlock them. You can mitigate this problem by setting the Maximum grace period for device lock to a modest interval, such as 5 minutes or 15 minutes.

- *Passcode history (1–50 passcodes, or none)*: In this box, you can enter the number of previous passcodes that you want the iPad to retain and block from future use. Leave the box blank if you want to allow users to reuse their existing passcodes or recent passcodes.

- *Maximum grace period for device lock*: In this box, enter the length of time that the user can unlock the iPad without having to enter the passcode. Your choices are no maximum (the -- setting), Immediately, 1 minute, 5 minutes, 15 minutes, 1 hour, or 4 hours. This is the equivalent of the Require Passcode setting on the Touch ID & Passcode screen in the Settings app, although that setting works only when the iPad Unlock switch in the Use Touch ID For box is set to Off. (Setting the iPad Unlock switch to On makes the iPad set the Require Password setting to Immediately.)

- *Maximum number of failed attempts*: In this pop-up menu, you can set the maximum number of failed passcode entries to allow before erasing the iPad's contents. This is equivalent to setting the Erase Data switch on the Touch ID & Passcode screen in the Settings app, except that the Erase Data feature uses a set value of 10 failed attempts; with the Maximum number of failed attempts setting, you can use a lower value if necessary.

■ **Caution**   The Maximum number of failed attempts setting is highly useful for enterprise devices that contain sensitive information, because it enables you to ensure that the iPad erases its contents after the specified number of failed password attempts, which you can set as low as 2 if you need hair-trigger wiping. You're less likely to need this setting for iPads in schools; even if your school's students have iPads as personal devices, you're probably better off requiring strong passcodes than enabling automatic erasure that can be triggered by students larking around or by a sibling's curiosity.

Configuring a Wi-Fi Payload in the Profile

The Wi-Fi category enables you to create payloads that set up Wi-Fi networks automatically on the iPad. This is a convenient way of making sure the iPad can connect to all the appropriate networks at your school.

To get started configuring the Wi-Fi payloads, click the Wi-Fi category in the sidebar, and then click the Configure button in the Wi-Fi pane to display the Wi-Fi controls (shown in Figure 4-55 with some settings chosen).

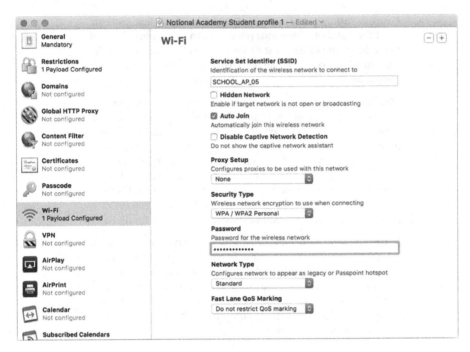

Figure 4-55. *Use the Wi-Fi pane to configure each Wi-Fi network you want the iPad to be able to use*

UNDERSTANDING HOTSPOT, CAPTIVE, AND PRIVATE NETWORKS

To make the most of iOS's networking capabilities, you need to understand the terms for different types of Wi-Fi networks and how iOS handles them.

First, a *captive network* is a network that, when a device connects to it, forces the device to display a particular web page, such as a login page. For example, when you go to connect an iPad to a captive network, Safari opens automatically and displays the login page so that you can provide your credentials and start using the network. When an iOS device connects to a captive network, the iOS Captive Network Assistant runs behind the scenes, managing the login process.

Second, iOS divides networks into two major categories—hotspot networks and private networks:

- *Hotspot network:* A Wi-Fi network that uses the HS2.0/Passpoint standard, captive network, or EAP-SIM network. (EAP-SIM is the acronym for Extensible Authentication Protocol Subscriber Identity Module, a standard for authenticating a device by using its Subscriber Identity Module card, usually called a SIM card.)

- *Private network*: Any Wi-Fi network that isn't a hotspot, including iOS Personal Hotspot networks.

When trying to connect to a Wi-Fi network, iOS uses the network types in the following order:

1. The private network it used most recently

2. Another private network

3. A hotspot network

This is probably what you would expect, especially if you've used an iOS device extensively—but what if multiple networks are available? In this case, iOS prefers still private networks to hotspot networks, but it ranks each network type by the kind of security it uses. Specifically, iOS chooses the networks in the following order:

1. A private network that uses EAP security

2. A private network that uses WPA security

3. A private network that uses WEP security

4. A private network that uses no security (an unsecured or open network)

5. A hotspot network that uses HS2.0/Passpoint

6. A hotspot network that uses EAP security

7. A hotspot network that uses WPA security

8. A hotspot network that uses WEP security

9. A hotspot network that uses no security (an unsecured or open hotspot)

Entering the Essential Details for the Wi-Fi Network

To set up a Wi-Fi network, start by filling in the essential details:

- *Service Set identifier (SSID)*: Type the network's SSID (its name).

- *Hidden Network*: Select this check box if the Wi-Fi network is hidden. *Hidden* means that the network isn't broadcasting its SSID; this is also called a *closed network*.

- *Auto Join*: Select this check if the iPad should automatically connect to this network when the network is in range.

- *Disable Captive Network Detection*: Select this check box to disable the Captive Network Assistant, which otherwise runs automatically when the iPad tries to connect to a captive network.

■ **Note** You'll see that the Proxy Setup pop-up menu and the Security Type pop-up menu also appear. We'll get to these controls a little later in the chapter.

- *Network Type*: In this pop-up menu, choose the Standard item for a regular Wi-Fi network. Choose the Passpoint item for a Wi-Fi hotspot that uses the HS2.0/Passpoint standard. Choose the Legacy Hotspot item for a Wi-Fi hotspot that uses an older Wi-Fi standard.

- *Fast Lane QoS Marking*: In this pop-up menu, choose the Do not restrict QoS marking item if you want to disable restrictions on Quality of Service (QoS) marking. Choose the Restrict QoS marking item if you want to restrict QoS marking.

UNDERSTANDING QOS AND QOS MARKING

In computer networking, *Quality of Service* (QoS) means prioritizing traffic from apps, data types, or users deemed to be more important or time-critical over less important or less time-critical apps, data types, or users. For example, an administrator might assign high priority to an app that plays a video stream, because watching streaming video doesn't work if the data doesn't arrive in time or sufficiently in sequence. Similarly, Internet audio calls might receive high priority to avoid the audio breaking up.

By contrast, e-mail would typically receive low priority, because a modest delay in data transmission doesn't usually much matter to an e-mail message; nor does the order in which most of the data packets in the e-mail message arrive matter, as long as all the packets arrive in the end so that the e-mail client app can reassemble the message. So an administrator might assign e-mail to the best-effort queue (which gets data transferred once priority traffic allows) or the background queue (a lower priority still).

Quality of Service (QoS) marking lets an administrator prioritize traffic according to how important it is that the traffic arrive in real time. On some wireless networks that run on Cisco equipment, an administrator can configure a feature called *fast lane* that enables devices running iOS 10 or a later version to detect that the device can request special treatment for apps that use QoS marking. In brief, fast lane lets an iOS device use QoS marking on some apps while not using it on other apps. The Fast Lane QoS Marking pop-up menu in the Wi-Fi pane lets you choose whether to restrict QoS marking or disable restrictions on QoS marking.

Setting Up Custom Proxying for This Wi-Fi Network

If you need to set up proxying for this Wi-Fi network that's different from any proxying you set in the Global HTTP Proxy category, open the Proxy Setup pop-up menu and click the Manual item or the Automatic item, as needed. The Wi-Fi pane displays controls for setting up the proxying.

If you choose the Manual item in the Proxy Setup pop-up menu, fill in the following fields:

- *Server and Port*: Type the hostname or IP address of the proxy server in the left box and the port number (such as 80) in the right box. Both server and port are required.

- *Username*: If the proxy server is set to require a username and password, you can type it in this box.

- *Password*: If you enter a username, type the password for the username in this box.

If you choose the Automatic item in the Proxy Setup pop-up menu, configure these two settings:

- *Proxy Server URL*: Enter the URL at which the iPad will find the server and proxy auto-configuration (PAC) file.

- *Allow direct connection if PAC is unreachable*: Select this check box to let the iPad connect directly to URLs if it can't obtain the PAC. As with the same setting in the Global HTTP Proxy category, letting the iPad connect directly is convenient, because it enables the iPad to use the network even if the proxy server is down, but it may mean that users can access sites the proxy server would normally prevent them from accessing.

Creating Another Wi-Fi Payload

After you finish setting up one Wi-Fi payload, you can click the Add (+) button in the upper-right corner of the Wi-Fi pane to start creating another Wi-Fi payload. A second Wi-Fi pane appears below the first Wi-Fi pane, and you can fill in the details of the network.

Configuring VPN Payloads in the Profile

The VPN category enables you to add one or more payloads of settings that enable the iPad to connect to virtual private networks. iOS supports around a dozen types of VPNs, which is more than we can cover fully here, but we'll look at the settings for several of the most widely used types of VPNs.

■ **Note** A virtual private network (VPN—the abbreviation also stands for *virtual private networking*, the umbrella term for the technology) enables you to connect two computers or devices securely using encryption across an unsecure network. For example, you can use a VPN to enable students or teachers to connect securely to the school's network from outside the school (such as from home). You would get the details of the VPN from the VPN's administrator.

To get started creating VPN payloads, click the VPN item in the sidebar, and then click the Configure button in the VPN pane. The controls for setting up the VPN payload appear. The controls change depending on which VPN type you select in the Connection Type pop-up menu, and we'll look at several examples in the following sections. For now, configure these two settings:

- *Connection Name*: Type the name you want the iPad to display for the VPN connection. This is a descriptive name to help the user to choose the right VPN connection.

- *Connection Type*: Open this pop-up menu and choose the VPN type. As of this writing, the choices are IKEv2, IPSec, L2TP, PPTP (iOS 9 and OS X 10.11 and earlier), Cisco AnyConnect, Juniper SSL, Pulse Secure, F5 SSL, SonicWALL Mobile Connect, Aruba VIA, Check Point Mobile VPN, and Custom SSL.

The following sections give examples of continuing the configuration with three widely used VPN types: IPSec, L2TP, and Cisco AnyConnect.

Configuring an IPSec VPN

Once you select IPSec in the Connection Type pop-up menu, the following controls appear in the VPN pane (see Figure 4-56):

- *Server*: Type the hostname or IP address for the VPN server.

- *Account*: In this text box, type the username for authenticating the connection. You can leave this text box blank if you want the user to enter the name each time.

- *Password*: In this text box, type the password that goes with the username. You can leave this text box blank if you want the user to enter the password each time.

- *Machine Authentication*: In this pop-up menu, choose the Shared Secret/Group Name item if you want to use a shared secret or a group name for authentication. (Both a shared secret and a group name are text strings—in effect, passwords or passcodes.) Choose the Certificate item if you want to use a digital certificate instead; if so, skip the next two items in this list.

- *Group Name*: Type the group name for the connection.

- *Shared Secret*: Type the shared secret for the connection.

- *Prompt for Password*: Select this check box if you want to force the user to enter the password each time they use the VPN connection.

- *Proxy Setup*: If you need to configure a proxy server for this VPN connection, open this pop-up menu and choose the Manual item or the Automatic item, as appropriate. If you choose the Manual item, type the proxy server's address or hostname and port in the Server and Port boxes, and enter any authentication needed in the Authentication box and the Password box. If you choose the Automatic item, enter in the Proxy Server URL the URL at which the iPad will find the proxy settings.

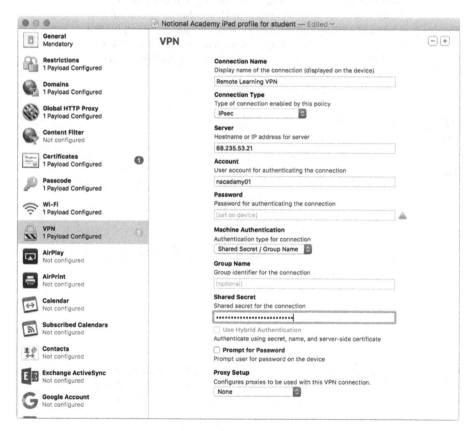

Figure 4-56. *Configuring an IPSec connection in the VPN pane*

If you select the Certificate item in the Machine Authentication pop-up menu, the controls in the lower part of the VPN pane change (see Figure 4-57). You can then configure the following settings as needed:

- *Identity Certificate*: In this pop-up menu, select the certificate to use the authenticate the VPN connection. You'll need to have added this certificate to the Certificates payload first.

- *Include User PIN*: Select this check box if you want iOS to make the user enter a PIN when establishing the VPN connection. iOS sends the PIN along with the other authentication information.

- *Enable VPN on Demand*: Select this check box if you want iOS to establish the VPN connection automatically when connecting to specific hosts or domains, or if you want iOS to skip using the VPN for specific hosts or domains. Click the Add (+) button below the list box to add a new entry, and then type the domain or hostname in the Match Domain or Host column. To control how iOS handles that domain or host, open the pop-up menu on that row in the On Demand Action column and choose the "Always establish" item, the "Never establish" item, or the "Establish if needed" item, as appropriate.

Figure 4-57. *If you select the Certificate item in the Machine Authentication pop-up menu, you can select the certificate for authentication, include a user PIN, and enable VPN on demand*

Configuring an L2TP VPN

When you select the L2TP item in the Connection Type pop-up menu, the following controls appear in the VPN pane (see Figure 4-58):

- *Server*: Type the hostname or IP address for the VPN server.

- *Account*: In this text box, type the username for authenticating the connection. You can leave this text box blank if you want the user to enter the name on the iPad.

- *User Authentication*: In this area, select the means of authentication. If the VPN uses a password, select the Password option button and type the password in the box next to it. If the VPN uses an RSA SecurID identifier for authentication, select the RSA SecurID option button.

- *Send all traffic through VPN*: Select this check box if you want the iPad to send all network traffic through the VPN. Leaving this check box cleared allows local network traffic to bypass the VPN.

- *Machine Authentication*: In this pop-up menu, choose the Shared Secret/Group Name item if you want to use a shared secret or a group name for authentication. Choose the Certificate item if you want to use a digital certificate instead; if so, skip the next two items in this list.

- *Group Name*: Type the group name for the connection.

- *Shared Secret*: Type the shared secret for the connection.

- *Use Hybrid Authentication*: Select this check box if you want authentication to use the group name, the shared secret, and a server-side certificate. You need to enter the group name and the shared secret to make this check box available.

- *Prompt for Password*: Select this check box if you want to make the user enter the password each time they use the VPN connection.

- *Proxy Setup*: If you need to configure a proxy server for this VPN connection, open this pop-up menu and choose the Manual item or the Automatic item, as appropriate. If you choose the Manual item, type the proxy server's address or hostname and port in the Server and Port boxes, and enter any authentication needed in the Authentication box and the Password box. If you choose the Automatic item, enter in the Proxy Server URL the URL at which the iPad will find the proxy settings.

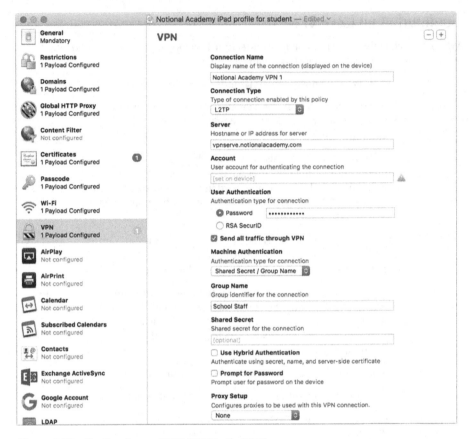

Figure 4-58. *Configuring an L2TP VPN in the VPN pane*

If you select the Certificate item in the Machine Authentication pop-up menu, the controls in the lower part of the VPN pane change. You can then configure the following settings as needed:

- *Identity Certificate*: In this pop-up menu, select the certificate to use the authenticate the VPN connection. This pop-up menu shows the certificates you've added to the Certificates payload.

- *Include User PIN*: Select this check box if you want iOS to make the user enter a PIN when establishing the VPN connection. iOS sends the PIN along with the other authentication information.

- *Enable VPN on Demand*: Select this check box if you want iOS to establish the VPN connection automatically when connecting to specific hosts or domains, or if you want iOS to skip using the VPN for specific hosts or domains. Click the Add (+) button below the list box to add a new entry, and then type the domain or hostname in the Match Domain or Host column. To control how iOS handles that domain or host, open the pop-up menu on that row in the On Demand Action column and choose the "Always establish" item, the "Never establish" item, or the "Establish if needed" item, as appropriate.

Configuring a Cisco AnyConnect VPN

When you select the Cisco AnyConnect item in the Connection Type pop-up menu, the controls explained in the following list appear in the VPN pane. Figure 4-59 shows the VPN pane with the Cisco AnyConnect item selected in the Connection Type pop-up menu and the Password+Certificate item selected in the User Authentication pop-up menu (so that you can see all the controls).

- *Server*: Type the hostname or IP address for the VPN server.

- *Account*: In this text box, type the username for authenticating the connection. You can leave this text box blank if you want the user to enter the name on the iPad.

- *Group:* In this text box, type the group to use for authenticating the connection. Leave this box blank if you want the group to be set on the iPad.

- *User Authentication*: In this pop-up menu, select the Password item, the Certificate item, or the Password+Certificate item, as appropriate. The controls in the lower part of the VPN pane change accordingly.

- *Password*: In this text box, type the password for authenticating the connection.

- *Enable VPN on Demand*: Select this check box if you want iOS to establish the VPN connection automatically when connecting to specific hosts or domains, or if you want iOS to skip using the VPN for specific hosts or domains. Click the Add (+) button below the list box to add a new entry, and then type the domain or hostname in the Match Domain or Host column. To control how iOS handles that domain or host, open the pop-up menu on that row in the On Demand Action column and choose the "Always establish," "Never establish," or "Establish if needed" item, as appropriate.

- *Disconnect on Idle*: In this pop-up menu, choose the time period after which to disconnect the VPN connection if it's been idle. Your choices are Never, 1 minute, 2 minutes, 5 minutes, 15 minutes, 30 minutes, and 1 hour.

- *Proxy Setup*: If you need to configure a proxy server for this VPN connection, open this pop-up menu and choose the Manual item or the Automatic item, as appropriate. If you choose the Manual item, type the proxy server's address or hostname and port in the

Server and Port boxes, and enter any authentication needed in the Authentication box and the Password box. If you choose the Automatic item, enter in the Proxy Server URL the URL at which the iPad will find the proxy settings.

- *Disconnect on idle*: To make the iPad disconnect the VPN connection after a specific period of idleness, open this pop-up menu, select the "After interval" item, and then specify the number of minutes and seconds in the boxes.

Figure 4-59. Configuring a Cisco AnyConnect VPN in the VPN pane

Configuring Another VPN Payload

After you finish configuring one VPN payload, you can click the Add (+) button in the upper-right corner of the VPN pane to start configuring another VPN payload. A second VPN pane appears below the first VPN pane, and you can enter the details of the VPN using the same techniques.

Configuring an AirPlay Payload in the Profile

The AirPlay category lets you create a payload containing passwords to enable an iPad to connect to password-protected AirPlay devices. If you want to restrict the iPad to connecting to only specific AirPlay devices, you can set up a whitelist of those devices, identified by their MAC addresses.

▓ **Tip**   To find the MAC address of an Apple TV, choose Settings ➤ General ➤ Network on the Apple TV and look at the Wi-Fi Address readout or the Ethernet Address readout on the Network screen. To find the MAC address or addresses of an AirPort Express, run AirPort Utility on a Mac, and then click the AirPort Express to display a pop-up window that shows the network name, IP address, and other information. Hold the pointer over the AirPort Express' name at the top of the pop-up window to display a second pop-up window that contains the model number and the MAC address for the Ethernet interface, the 2.4 GHz Wi-Fi interface, and the 5 GHz Wi-Fi interface.

To start creating an AirPlay payload, click the AirPlay category in the sidebar, and then click the Configure button in the AirPlay pane. The controls for configuring the payload appear in the AirPlay pane (shown in Figure 4-60 with some settings chosen).

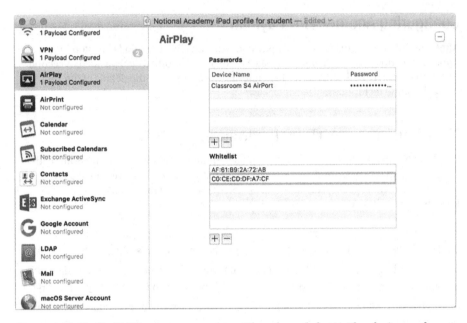

Figure 4-60. *In the AirPlay pane, you can provide passwords for AirPlay devices and create a whitelist of approved devices*

To add a password to the Passwords list, follow these steps:

1. Click the Add (+) button below the Passwords box. The "Choose an AirPlay destination to which the device can connect" dialog opens (see Figure 4-61).

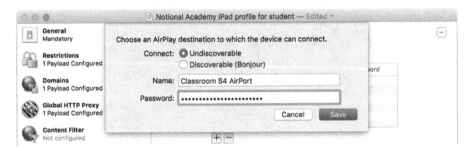

Figure 4-61. *In the "Choose an AirPlay destination to which the device can connect" dialog, identify the device, type the password, and then click the Save button*

2. In the Connect area, select the Undiscoverable option button if the AirPlay device isn't discoverable via the Bonjour network protocol. If the device is discoverable via Bonjour, select the Discoverable (Bonjour) option button instead; when you do this, a list box opens showing the available AirPlay devices.

3. If you selected the Undiscoverable option button, type the device's name in the Name box. If you selected the Discoverable (Bonjour) option button, click the device in the list box.

4. Type the device's password in the Password box.

5. Click the Save button. The device appears in the Passwords box in the AirPlay pane.

To add a device to the Whitelist box, follow these steps:

1. Click the Add (+) button under the Whitelist box. Apple Configurator adds a new line to the box.

2. Type the MAC address of the AirPlay device. Type just the letters and numbers, not the colons (or the hyphens that some devices show instead of colons).

3. Press the Return key. Apple Configurator validates the MAC address and separates its groups with colons.

Configuring an AirPrint Payload in the Profile

The AirPrint category lets you set up AirPrint printers for the iPad to use. Once the profile is installed, the iPad knows where to find the printers and can print to them without further setup.

To start creating an AirPrint payload, click the AirPrint category in the sidebar, and then click the Configure button in the AirPrint pane. The controls for configuring the payload appear in the AirPlay pane (shown in Figure 4-62 with one printer already added).

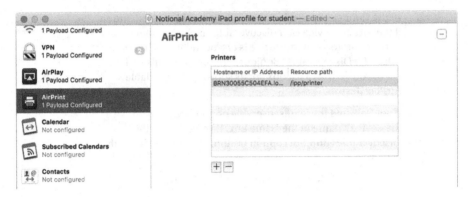

Figure 4-62. *Set up a payload of AirPrint-capable printers in the AirPrint pane*

Follow these steps to add a printer to the list in the Printers box:

1. Click the Add (+) button on the left below the Printers box. A dialog for adding a printer opens. Figure 4-63 shows this dialog with settings chosen.

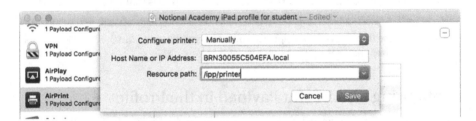

Figure 4-63. *In this dialog, open the Configure printer pop-up menu and see if the printer appears. If so, select it, and then select the IP address in the Host Name or IP Address pop-up menu; if not, enter the IP address and the resource path manually.*

2. Open the Configure printer pop-up menu and see if the printer you want to add appears on it. If so, select the menu item for the printer. If not, select the Manually item.

3. If you selected a printer in step 2, open the Host Name or IP Address pop-up menu and select the IP address for the printer (it may be selected already). If you selected the Manually item in step 2, type the printer's IP address in the Host Name or IP Address box (this control switches between being a pop-up menu and a text box). See the nearby sidebar "Getting the IP Address and Resource Path for an AirPort Printer" for information on getting the IP address and resource path.

4. In the "Resource path" box, enter the resource path for the printer. If you selected the printer in step 2, the resource path should be entered in this box already.

5. Click the Save button. The dialog closes, and the printer appears in the AirPrint pane.

■ **Note** If the Save button is unavailable when you're adding a printer manually, the problem is usually that you've entered the wrong IP address or resource path for a printer. Double-check your entries and correct any mistakes.

GETTING THE IP ADDRESS AND RESOURCE PATH FOR AN AIRPRINT PRINTER

To find the IP address and resource path for an AirPrint printer, follow these steps on a Mac connected to the appropriate network:

1. Click the Launchpad icon on the Dock to display the Launchpad screen.

2. Type *term* to display apps containing those letters.

3. Click the Terminal icon. A Terminal window opens.

4. Type *ippfind* and press the Return key. Terminal displays a list of printers found, such as the following line, where the first part (BRN30055C504EFA.local) is the printer name and the second part (/ipp/printer) is the resource path.

   ```
   ipp://BRN30055C504EFA.local.:631/ipp/printer
   ```

5. Type ping -c 5 followed by the printer name, and then press the Return key. (The -c 5 parameter tells the ping command to send five packets; if you don't specify this parameter, ping keeps sending packets until you press Ctrl-C to stop it.) Terminal returns the printer's IP address, as in the second and third lines here:

   ```
   ping -c 5 BRN30055C504EFA.local
   PING brn30055c504efa.local (192.168.1.69): 56 data bytes
   64 bytes from 192.168.1.69: icmp_seq=0 ttl=255 time=2.637 ms
   ```

You can now enter the IP address (such as 192.168.1.69) and the resource path (such as /ipp/printer) in the dialog in the AirPrint pane in Apple Configurator.

Configuring a Calendar Payload in the Profile

The Calendar category lets you create payloads of calendar settings that enable the iPad to connect to servers that use the CalDAV protocol. CalDAV is the acronym for Calendar Extensions to WebDAV, and WebDAV is Web Distributed Authoring and Versioning, a protocol for manipulating web content on remote servers. Various online calendars use CalDAV to provide calendar services.

CONFIGURING ACCOUNTS FOR INDIVIDUALS OR GROUPS

In some of the categories for configuring accounts, you can either create a payload for an individual user or a payload that will work with a group of users. As you'd imagine, a payload for an individual user belongs only in a profile for that user, so normally you'll want to create payloads for groups of users.

You can create a payload for a group or an individual in the Calendar category, the Subscribed Calendars category, the Exchange ActiveSync category, the LDAP category, and the Mail category. By contrast, in the Google Account category and the macOS Server Account category, you can create a payload only for an individual.

When creating a payload for a group of users, leave the Account Username box in the category blank, so that it shows the [set on device] prompt or the [optional] prompt. Likewise, leave the Account Password box blank. Each user then gets to fill in the appropriate account username and password when setting up their profile.

When you do need to configure a profile for an individual user, enter the account username in the Account Username box. You can then decide whether to enter the password in the payload as well or have the user enter it.

To get started creating a calendar payload, click the Calendar category in the sidebar, and then click the Configure button in the Calendar pane. The controls appear in the Calendar pane (see Figure 4-64), and you can set up the payload by configuring the following settings:

- *Account Description*: Type the descriptive name you want the iPad to display for the calendar account.

- *Account Hostname and Port*: Type the hostname or IP address of the CalDAV server in the left box and the port number in the right box. The default port number is 443 for connections that use SSL for security; you can turn SSL on or off by selecting or clearing the Use SSL check box at the bottom of the Calendar pane.

- *Principal URL*: Optionally, type or paste the Principal URL for the CalDAV account.

- *Account Username*: Optionally, type the username for the CalDAV account. Leave this field blank to have the user enter the username on the iPad.

- *Account Password*: If you enter the account username, enter the corresponding password. Otherwise, leave this field blank to have the user provide the password.

- *Use SSL*: Select this check box to make the CalDAV connections use SSL. This is normally a good idea for security unless the CalDAV server doesn't support SSL.

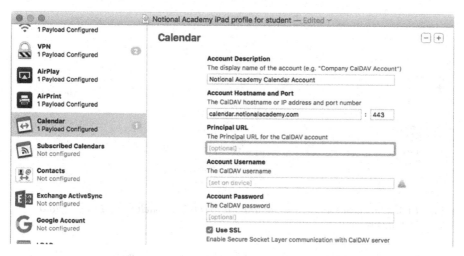

Figure 4-64. *Use the Calendar pane to set up one or more calendar payloads*

Configuring a Subscribed Calendars Payload in the Profile

The Subscribed Calendars category enables you to create payloads that add calendar subscriptions to the iPad. For example, you may want to add a calendar subscription to your school's main calendar, or to multiple calendars that the school maintains.

To get started creating a subscribed calendar payload, click the Subscribed Calendars category in the sidebar, and then click the Configure button in the Subscribed Calendars pane. The controls appear in the Subscribed Calendars pane (see Figure 4-65), and you can set up the payload by configuring the following settings:

- *Description*: Type the descriptive name you want the iPad to display for the calendar subscription.

- *URL*: Type or paste the URL that contains the subscribed calendar file.

- *Username*: Optionally, type the username needed for the subscription.

- *Password*: If you enter the username for the subscription, type the corresponding password.

- *Use SSL*: Select this check box to make the calendar connection use SSL. Usually, this is a good idea unless the calendar server doesn't support SSL.

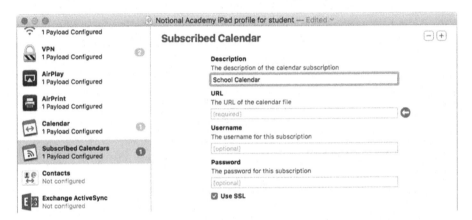

Figure 4-65. *Use the Subscribed Calendar pane to configure each subscribed calendar payload for the profile*

Configuring a Contacts Payload in the Profile

The Contacts category lets you add payloads containing settings for connecting to CardDAV servers. CardDAV is the acronym for vCard Extensions to WebDAV; it enables a client to manipulate contact data on a remote server. For example, you might configure a Contacts payload to enable iPads to connect to a school address book.

To get started configuring a contacts payload, click the Contacts category in the sidebar, and then click the Configure button in the Contacts pane. You can then configure the following controls in the Contacts pane (see Figure 4-66):

- *Account Description*: Type the descriptive name under which you want the account to appear on the iPad.

- *Account Hostname and Port*: Type the hostname or IP address of the CardDAV server in the left box and the port in the right box. The default port for secure connections is 443.

- *Principal URL*: In this text box, type or paste the Principal URL for the CardDAV account.

- *Account Username*: Optionally, type the username for the CardDAV account. Leave this field blank if you want the user to fill it in.

- *Account Password*: If you enter the username for the CardDAV account, type the account's password.

- *Use SSL*: Select this check box to make the iPad use SSL for communicating with the CardDAV server.

- *Communication Service Rules*: To specify the default app to use when calling contacts from the CardDAV account you're setting up, click the Choose button. In the "Choose an app" dialog that opens, type the app's name in the Search box, click the appropriate app in the list of results (see Figure 4-67), and then click the Choose button. The app then appears in place of the Choose button, with a Remove button that you can click if you want to change the app.

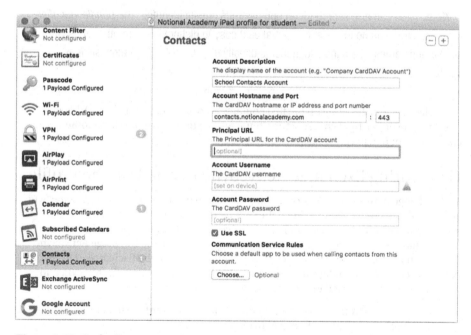

Figure 4-66. *In the Contacts pane, you can create payloads containing contacts accounts on CardDAV servers*

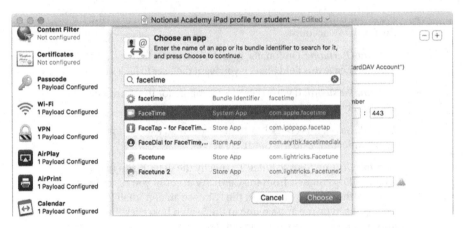

Figure 4-67. *Use the "Choose an app" dialog to select the default app for Communication Service Rules.*

■ **Note**   You can also search for an app using its bundle identifier. The *bundle identifier* gives the formal name of the app and makes it easy to distinguish from other apps with similar app names. The bundle identifier is usually in reverse-DNS notation, such as `com.apple.facetime`.

When you finish setting up the first contacts account, you can click the Add (+) button in the upper-right corner of the Contacts pane to start configuring another contacts account if necessary.

Configuring Exchange ActiveSync Payloads in the Profile

The Exchange ActiveSync category enables you to add one or more Exchange ActiveSync accounts to the profile. By preloading the settings on the iPad via the profile, you can ensure that the user can access her Exchange account without further configuration.

To start configuring Exchange ActiveSync payloads, click the Exchange ActiveSync category in the sidebar, and then click the Configure button in the Exchange ActiveSync pane. The controls for configuring the first payload then appear (see Figure 4-68), and you can set them as needed for the account:

- *Account Name*: Type the descriptive name you want the iPad to display for the Exchange ActiveSync account.

- *Exchange ActiveSync Host*: Type the name of the Microsoft Exchange Server to contact.

- *Use SSL*: Select this check box to make the iPad use SSL when communicating with the server. This is almost always a good idea, and the server may enforce the use of SSL anyway.

- *User*: Type the username for the account. You can type either the domain and the username (such as *main\jsmith*) or just the username (such as *jsmith*).

- *E-mail Address*: Type the e-mail address for the account.

- *Password*: Type the password for the account.

- *Past Days of Mail to Sync*: In this pop-up menu, choose how much mail to sync. Your choices are No Limit, 1 day, 3 days, 1 week, 2 weeks, and 1 month.

- *Authentication Credential Name*: Type the name or description for the credential that the iPad will use for ActiveSync.

- *Authentication Credential*: Open this pop-up menu and choose from it the appropriate certificate that you've already added to the Certificates payload.

- *Allow messages to be moved*: Select this check box if you'll allow the user to move messages from the Exchange account to another account.

- *Allow recent addresses to be synced*: Select this check box to allow this account to sync recent addresses across devices.

- *Allow Mail Drop*: Select this check box to allow the account to use the Mail Drop feature.

- *Use only in Mail*: Select this check box if you want to restrict this account to sending mail only via the Mail app. Clear this check box if you want the account to be able to send e-mail via other apps as well.

- *Enable S/MiME*: Select this check box to enable S/MIME (Secure/Multipurpose Internet Mail Extensions), a protocol for encrypting e-mail messages and signing them with digital certificates.

- *Communication Service Rules*: To specify the default app to use when calling contacts from the CardDAV account you're setting up, click the Choose button. In the "Choose an app" dialog that opens, type the app's name in the Search box, click the appropriate app in the list of results, and then click the Choose button. The app then appears in place of the Choose button, with a Remove button that you can click if you want to change the app.

Figure 4-68. *Configure one or more Exchange ActiveSync account payloads in the Exchange ActiveSync pane*

When you finish setting up the first Exchange ActiveSync account, you can click the Add (+) button in the upper-right corner of the Exchange ActiveSync pane to start configuring another Exchange ActiveSync account if necessary.

Configuring Google Account Payloads in the Profile

The Google Account category enables you to configure one or more payloads that each contain the settings for an individual Google account. The only required field is the e-mail address, but you can also specify the account description, the account name, and the default app to use for calling contacts from this account. You don't specify the password—instead, the user enters the password when signing in to the account.

■ **Note**   There are two things to note here. First, you're setting up an individual Google account, so you'll normally want to include Google Account payloads only in individual profiles. Second, installing Google accounts via profiles from Apple Configurator works only for devices that you supervise using Apple Configurator. If you use an MDM system to supervise the devices instead, you need to use install the profiles containing Google account payloads through that system.

In the Google Account pane (see Figure 4-69), you can configure the following settings to create the payload:

- *Account Description*: Optionally, type a descriptive name for the account (such as Google Account).

- *Account Name*: Optionally, type the username the way it should appear in the account.

- *E-mail Address*: Type the e-mail address of the Google account. This field is required.

- *Communication Service Rules*: To specify the default app to use when calling contacts from the CardDAV account you're setting up, click the Choose button. In the "Choose an app" dialog that opens, type the app's name in the Search box, click the appropriate app in the list of results, and then click the Choose button. The app then appears in place of the Choose button, with a Remove button that you can click if you want to change the app.

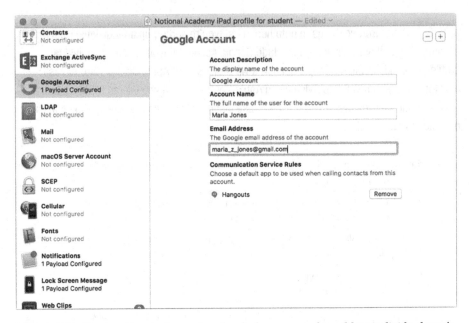

Figure 4-69. *Create a Google Account payload when you need to add an individual user's Google account to a profile*

If you need to set up another Google account, click the Add (+) button in the upper-right corner of the Google Account pane to display another Google Account pane. You can then fill in the settings for this account.

Configuring LDAP Payloads in the Profile

By creating an LDAP payload in a profile, you can set up an iPad to connect automatically to an LDAP server. The LDAP category enables you to create one or more LDAP payloads, as needed.

To get started creating an LDAP payload, click the LDAP category in the sidebar, and then click the Configure button in the LDAP pane. The LDAP pane then displays the rest of the controls (see Figure 4-70), and you can set up the account by configuring them. These are the controls:

- *Account Description*: Type the descriptive name to display for the LDAP account. This field is required.

- *Account Username*: Optionally, type the username for the individual LDAP account you're adding to the profile.

- *Account Password*: If you enter the account username, type the corresponding password in this box.

- *Account Hostname*: Type the hostname or IP address of the LDAP server.

- *Use SSL*: Select this check box if you want to make the iPad use SSL for connecting to the server. This is usually a good idea.

- *Search Settings*: In this box, set up any search bases for the LDAP server. To add a search base, click the Add (+) button on the left below the Search Settings box. Apple Configurator inserts a new line in the box containing default information, which you can then edit as needed. Type a description for the search base in the Description column. Open the pop-up menu in the Scope column and choose the Base item, the One Level item, or the Subtree item, as needed. Then edit the entry in the Search Base column to specify the search base.

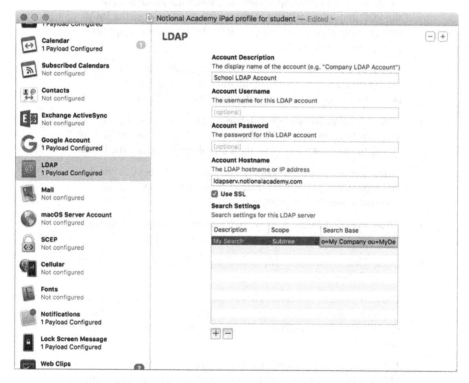

Figure 4-70. In the LDAP pane, you can set up one or more accounts for connecting to LDAP servers

If you need to set up another LDAP account, click the Add (+) button in the upper-right corner of the LDAP pane to display another LDAP pane. You can then configure the settings for that account as needed.

Configuring Mail Payloads in the Profile

The Mail category enables you to create payloads that set up an iPad to connect to POP3 and IMAP e-mail accounts.

To begin creating a Mail payload, click the Mail category in the sidebar, and then click the Configure button in the Mail pane. The controls then appear in the Mail pane (see Figure 4-71), and you can configure the account using them:

- *Account Description*: Type the descriptive name you want the iPad to display for the account.

- *Account Type*: In this pop-up menu, choose the IMAP item or the POP item to specify the account type. If you choose the IMAP item, the Path Prefix box appears. If the IMAP account requires a path prefix, type it here.

- *User Display Name*: In this box, you can type the name to display for the user if you're setting up an individual account. Leave this box empty to have the users enter names on the iPads.

- *E-mail Address*: In this box, you can type the e-mail address if you're setting up an individual account. Otherwise, leave this box empty to have the users enter their e-mail addresses on the iPads.

- *Allow user to move messages from this account*: Select this check box if you want to allow the user to move messages from this account to another account.

- *Allow recent addresses to be synced*: Select this check box to allow this account to sync recent addresses across devices.

- *Allow Mail Drop*: Select this check box to allow the account to use the Mail Drop feature.

- *Use only in Mail*: Select this check box if you want to restrict this account to sending mail only via the Mail app. Clear this check box if you want the account to be able to send e-mail via other apps as well.

- *Enable S/MiME*: Select this check box to enable S/MIME (Secure/Multipurpose Internet Mail Extensions), a protocol for encrypting e-mail messages and signing them with digital certificates.

Figure 4-71. *In the Mail pane, set up a payload for each IMAP or POP3 e-mail account you want to add to the profile*

In the lower part of the Mail pane, click the Incoming Mail tab button to display the controls for specifying the server and account for incoming mail. You can then configure these controls:

- *Mail Server and Port*: Type the hostname or IP address of the incoming mail server in the left box and the port in the right box.

■ **Note** Port 995 is the default port for POP3 using SSL, whereas port 110 is the default port for POP3 that doesn't use encryption. For IMAP, port 993 is the default port for SSL, port 143 is the default port for TLS, and port 143 is the default port for unencrypted mail. Some servers use different ports.

- *Username*: If you're setting up an individual account, you can enter it in this box. Leave this box empty if each user will enter the username on the iPad.

- *Authentication Type*: In this pop-up menu, choose the appropriate authentication type: Password, MDM Challenge-Response, NTLM, or HTTP MD5 Digest.

- *Password*: If you entered the username and selected Password in the Authentication Type pop-up menu, you can enter the password here.

- *Use SSL*: Select this check box to have the iPad use SSL when communicating with the incoming mail server. This is normally wise.

Click the Outgoing Mail tab button to display the controls for specifying the server and account for outgoing mail (see Figure 4-72). You can then configure these controls:

- *Mail Server and Port*: Type the hostname or IP address of the outgoing mail server in the left box and the port in the right box. Port 465 is the default port for SMTP using SSL, port 587 is the default for SMTP using TLS, and port 25 is the default port for SMTP that doesn't use encryption.

- *Username*: If you're setting up an individual account, you can enter it in this box. Leave this box empty if the user will enter the username.

- *Authentication Type*: In this pop-up menu, choose the appropriate authentication type: Password, MDM Challenge-Response, NTLM, or HTTP MD5 Digest.

- *Password*: If you entered the username and selected Password in the Authentication Type pop-up menu, you can enter the password here.

- *Outgoing password same as incoming*: Select this check box if the outgoing mail server uses the same password as the incoming mail server.

- *Use SSL*: Select this check box to have the iPad use SSL when communicating with the incoming mail server. This is normally wise.

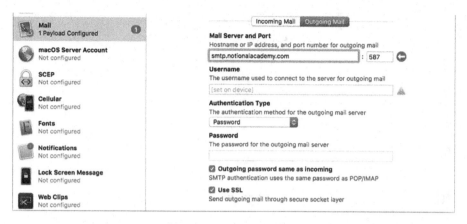

Figure 4-72. *Specify the details of the outgoing mail server on the Outgoing Mail tab at the bottom of the Mail pane*

Configuring a macOS Server Account Payload in the Profile

The macOS Server Account category enables you to configure one or more payloads containing the settings needed to access an account on a macOS server. Once you install the profile on an iPad, the user can view and edit existing documents on the server, move existing documents to the iPad, and create and save new documents.

■ **Note**   In the macOS category, the username is required, creating a payload containing the settings for a specific individual account. You can't create payloads that enable users to enter their own usernames.

To start creating a macOS Server Account payload, click the macOS Server Account category in the sidebar, and then click the Configure button in the macOS Server Account pane. The pane then displays its full set of controls (see Figure 4-73), and you can configure them to set up the first payload. These are the controls:

- *Account Description*: Type the descriptive name to display for the macOS server account.

- *Server Address*: Type the hostname, IP address, or URL of the macOS server.

- *User Name*: Type the username.

- *Password*: Optionally, type the password for the account.

- *Documents Server Port*: Type the port number to which the iPad should connect for the documents service.

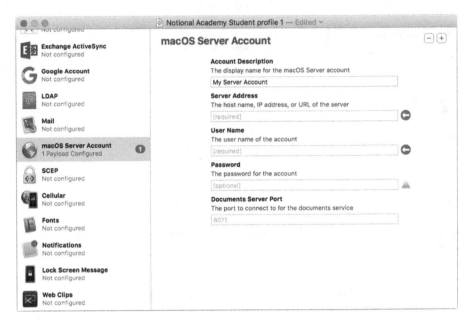

Figure 4-73. In the macOS Server Account pane, you can create one or more payloads containing the settings for a specific account

Configuring a SCEP Payload in the Profile

SCEP is the acronym for Simple Certificate Enrollment Protocol. The SCEP category lets you create one or more payloads that enable the iPad to get digital certificates from a certificate authority (CA). A *certificate authority* is a body that issues digital certificates for encryption and identification. Major certificate authorities include Symantec (which bought VeriSign, a leading CA), Comoda, GoDaddy, and GlobalSign.

To start configuring a SCEP payload, click the SCEP category in the sidebar, and then click the Configure button in the SCEP pane. The SCEP pane displays its full set of controls (see Figure 4-74), and you can configure them to set up the first payload. These are the controls:

- *URL*: Type or paste the base URL for the SCEP server in this box.

- *Name*: In this box, type the name of the instance the iPad will used when connecting to the SCEP server. The instance enables the server to distinguish between clients.

- *Subject*: In this box, you can type a name in the X.500 format.

- *Subject Alternative Name Type*: In this pop-up menu, you can choose which format to use for an alternative name for the SCEP server. Your options are None, RFC 822 Name, DNS Name, or Uniform Resource Identifier.

- *Subject Alternative Name Value*: In this box, type the alternative name, using the format you specified in the Subject Alternative Name Type pop-up menu.

- *NT Principal Name*: In this box, optionally type the NT principal name for the iPad to use when requesting the certificate.

- *Retries*: In this box, type the number of times the iPad should try to get the certificate from the SCEP server before giving up.

- *Retry Delay*: In this box, type the number of seconds to wait between retries.

- *Challenge*: In this box, you can type the pre-shared secret (in other words, the password or passcode) the iPad should use for automatic enrollment.

- *Key Size*: In this pop-up menu, select the size of the encryption key. Your choices are 1024 bits and 2048 bits.

- *Use a digital signature*: Select this check box if you want the iPad to use the key as a digital signature.

- *Use for key encipherment*: Select this check box if you want the iPad to use the key for enciphering data.

- *Fingerprint*: In this box, enter the SHA1 fingerprint or MD5 fingerprint of the CA's certificate. The iPad uses the fingerprint to confirm the authenticity of the CA when enrolling via HTTP. You can type or paste in the fingerprint, but if you have access to the CA's certificate, it's easier to click the Create from Certificate button, use the "Select a certificate file (PKCS1 format) to use its fingerprint" dialog to select the certificate file, and then click the Open button.

Figure 4-74. *In the SCEP pane, set up one or more payloads to enable the iPad to obtain certificates from a certificate authority via Simple Certificate Enrollment Protocol*

Configuring a Cellular Payload in the Profile

For cellular iPads, you can use the Cellular category to configure the Default APN (also called the Default/Attach APN) and the Data APN for the cellular connection. APN is the abbreviation for Access Point Name. An APN specifies where the iPad connects to the carrier's network.

■ **Caution**   Configure a Cellular payload to specify APNs only if your carrier tells you to do so. Otherwise, let the SIM card in each cellular iPad control the APNs to which the iPad connects.

To start creating a Cellular payload, click the Cellular category in the sidebar, and then click the Configure button in the Cellular pane. The Cellular pane displays controls for configuring the APNS. The controls change depending on which item you select in the Configured APN Type pop-up menu: the Default APN item, the Data APN item, or the Default and Data APNs item. Figure 4-75 shows the Cellular pane with the Default and Data APNs item selected in the Configured APN Type pop-up menu.

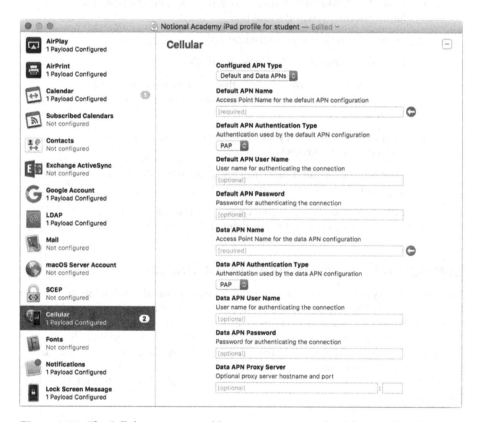

Figure 4-75. *The Cellular category enables you to create a payload that specifies the APNs through which a cellular iPad connects to the carrier's network. You'll normally not need to specify APNs.*

Configure these controls to set up a default APN with information you get from the carrier:

- *Default APN Name*: Type the APN's name in this box.

- *Default APN Authentication Type*: In this pop-up menu, choose the PAP item or the CHAP item, depending on your carrier's instructions. PAP is the acronym for Password Authentication Protocol. CHAP stands for Challenge Handshake Authentication Protocol.

- *Default APN User Name*: If your carrier told you to enter the username for authenticating the connection, type it in this box.

- *Default APN Password*: If your carrier told you to enter a password for the username, type it in this box.

Configure these controls to set up a data APN:

- *Data APN Name*: In this box, type the APN's name.

- *Data APN Authentication Type*: In this pop-up menu, choose the PAP item or the CHAP item, depending on your carrier's instructions.

- *Data APN User Name*: If your carrier told you to enter a username, type it in this box.

- *Data APN Password*: If your carrier told you to enter a password to go with the username, type it in this box.

- *Data APN Proxy Server*: If your carrier told you to enter a proxy server hostname and port, type them in these boxes.

Configuring a Fonts Payload in the Profile

The Fonts category enables you to configure one or more payloads containing the TrueType fonts and OpenType fonts you want to install on the iPad. You may need to install certain fonts to make sure documents display correctly.

To create a font payload, click the Fonts category in the sidebar, and then click the Configure button in the Fonts pane. In the Select Font dialog that opens, click the font, and then click the Select button. The font then appears in the Font pane.

If you need to create another font payload, click the Add (+) button to open the Select Font dialog again.

Configuring a Notifications Payload in the Profile

The Notifications category lets you configure a single payload that applies notifications settings to one or more apps. Much as when configuring notifications interactively, you can choose which apps can raise notifications, control whether the notifications appear in Notification Center and on the lock screen, control sounds and badges, and choose the style for unlocked alerts. A notifications payload applies only to supervised devices.

To get started, click the Notifications category in the sidebar, and then click the Configure button to display the Notifications pane (shown in Figure 4-76 with some settings already chosen). Then follow these steps:

1. Click the Add (+) button. The Choose an app dialog opens.

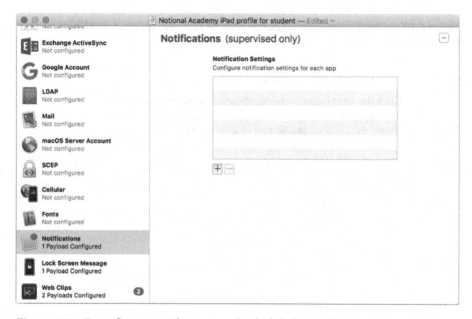

Figure 4-76. *To configure a notifications payload, click the Notifications category in the sidebar, click the Configure button, and then click the Add (+) button in the Notifications pane*

2. Type part or all of the app's name. You can also type its bundle identifier (the formal name) instead if you know the identifier. For example, if you need to find the Mail app, you can simply type *mail*. The "Choose an app" dialog displays a list of results (see Figure 4-77).

Figure 4-77. *In the "Choose an app" dialog, type the app's name or bundle identifier. Click the app in the list of results, and then click the Next button.*

3. Click the appropriate result.

4. Click the Next button. The Notification Settings dialog for the app appears. The app's name appears in quotes. Figure 4-78 shows the Notification Settings for "Mail" dialog.

Figure 4-78. *In the Notification Settings dialog for the app, choose which notifications to allow, and how any allowed notifications and alerts should appear*

5.   Select the Allow Notifications check box if you want to allow the app to raise notifications. Clearing this check box disables the next four check boxes, because they're relevant only if the app is allowed to raise notifications.

6.   Select the Show in Notification Center check box to include the app's notifications in Notification Center (on iOS 10) or Cover Sheet (on iOS 11).

7.   Select the Sounds check box if you want the iPad to play a sound to announce the notifications. You probably won't want these sounds in the classroom.

8.   Select the Badge App Icon check box if you want a badge (a red circle or rounded rectangle) showing the number of new notifications available in the app to appear on the app's icon.

9.   Select the Show on Lock Screen check box if you want the app's notifications to appear on the lock screen.

10. In the Unlocked Alert Style pop-up menu, choose the alert style for the app when the iPad is unlocked: None, Banners, or Alerts. *Banners* are the panels that appear at the top of the screen for a few seconds before automatically disappearing. *Alerts* are dialogs that remains onscreen until the user dismisses them.

11. Click the Save button to apply your changes. The Notification Settings dialog closes, and the app appears in the Notification Settings box in the Notifications pane (see Figure 4-79). You can then click the + button to start adding another app.

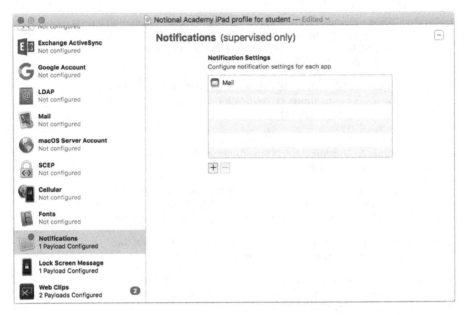

Figure 4-79. The app you configured appears in the Notifications Settings box in the Notifications pane. You can then click the Add (+) button to configure notifications for another app.

■ **Note**   If you need to edit the settings for an app you've added, double-click that app's entry in the Notification Settings box in the Notifications pane to open the Notification Settings dialog box for the app.

Configuring a Lock Screen Message Payload in the Profile

The Lock Screen Message category enables you to display a message and asset tag information on the iPad's lock screen. Both the message and the asset tag information are optional rather than required. The message is primarily for use if the iPad goes missing; the asset tag information is to help you identify the iPad easily.

Click the Lock Screen Message category in the sidebar, and then click the Configure button to display the controls in the Lock Screen Message pane (see Figure 4-80). You can then enter the message and asset tag information:

- *"If Lost, Return to..." Message*: In this box, type the message you want to have appear on the lock screen and in the login window.

- *Asset Tag Information*: In this box, type the identifying information for the iPad. This information appears at the bottom of the lock screen and the login window.

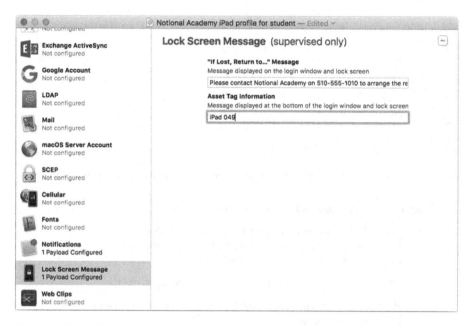

Figure 4-80. *In the Lock Screen Message pane, enter the text for the "If Lost, Return to..." message and any asset tag information to help you identify the iPad*

Configuring Web Clips Payloads in the Profile

Apple Configurator enables you to add web clips to an iPad to give the user quick access to specific websites. A *web clip* is an icon that appears on the iPad's Home screen, like an app icon, that makes the web browser display the address set in the web clip. Web clips are great for ensuring that your students can access key websites directly from the Home screen.

Each web clip counts as a single payload, but you can configure as many of them as you need. To set up the first web clips payload, click the Web Clips category in the sidebar, and then click the Configure button to display the Web Clip pane (shown in Figure 4-81 with some settings chosen).

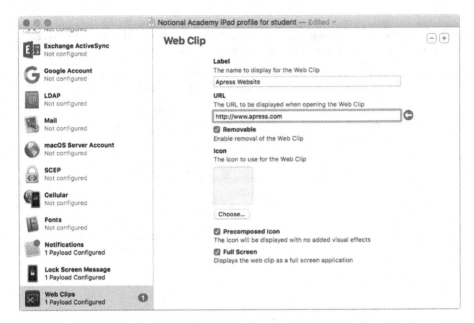

Figure 4-81. *In the Web Clip pane, set up each web clip you want to install on the iPad*

To set up a web clip, choose the appropriate settings for it:

- *Label*: Type a descriptive name for the web clip. Because the name appears on the Home screen, a long name will be truncated, so it's best to keep names short.

- *URL*: Type or paste the URL you want the web clip to open.

- *Removable*: Select this check box if you want to allow the user to remove the web clip.

- *Icon*: Click the Choose button to open an unnamed dialog for selecting the icon. Select the icon file, and then click the Open button.

- *Precomposed Icon*: Select this check box if you want the iPad to display the icon without added visual effects.

- *Full Screen*: Select this check box to make the web clip appear as a full-screen app when the user taps the icon. This is usually helpful.

When you finish setting up the first web clip, you can click the Add (+) button in the upper-right corner of the Web Clip pane to start creating another.

Saving the Changes to the Profile

If you've been working through the categories in order, you should now have finished creating the profile. Press Cmd-S or choose File ➤ Save from the menu bar to save the profile.

If the profile contains any errors when you try to save it, a dialog opens (see Figure 4-82) showing the number of errors. You can click the Save Anyway button to save the profile without fixing the errors, but usually it's best to click the Continue Editing button and fix the errors before you forget. Look for the red badges in the sidebar to see which categories contain the errors.

Figure 4-82. *This dialog warns you of any errors when you go to save the profile. To fix the problems, click the Continue Editing button, and then click each category in turn that shows a red badge, as the Wi-Fi category does here.*

Signing and Unsigning a Profile

When you finish creating a profile, you can sign the profile with a digital certificate to prevent further changes to the profile and to confirm who created the profile. To sign the profile, follow these steps:

1. With the profile open in the profile window, choose File ➤ Sign Profile. The dialog shown in Figure 4-83 opens.

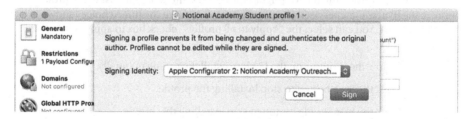

Figure 4-83. *You can sign a profile with a digital certificate to prevent changes to it*

2. Open the Signing Identity pop-up menu and click the appropriate identity.

3. Click the Sign button. The dialog closes, and a bar appears across the top of the profile window saying "This profile has been signed and cannot be edited."

4. If you need to make changes to the profile, choose File ➤ Unsign Profile to remove the signature. You can then edit the profile and sign it again when you finish.

Adding a Profile to an iPad

You can add a profile to an iPad either directly or by including the profile in a blueprint that you apply to the iPad. This section shows you how to add a profile directly; the next section discusses blueprints.

To add one or more profiles to one or more iPads, follow these steps:

1. Select the iPad or iPads in the device browser.

2. Click the Add button to display the Add pop-up menu, and then click Profiles. A dialog opens.

3. Navigate to the folder that contains the profile or profiles, and then select the profile or profiles.

4. Click the Add button. Apple Configurator starts installing the profiles.

■ **Note**   If the iPad is locked, Apple Configurator may prompt you to unlock it.

If a dialog opens saying that Configurator requires interaction to install the profile because the iPad is unsupervised (see Figure 4-84), you have the three choices shown in the following list. You can select the "Apply to all profiles" check box to apply your choice to all the profiles:

- Follow the prompts on the iPad to install the profile manually.

- Click the Stop button to stop installing the profile.

- Click the Skip Profile button to skip installing this profile.

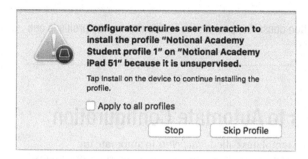

Figure 4-84. *If this dialog opens, you can continue the installation procedure on the iPad manually, skip the profile, or stop applying the profile. Select the Apply to all profiles check box if you want to take the same action with all the profiles that need user interaction.*

Removing a Profile from an iPad

You can remove a profile from an iPad in two ways:

1. *Apple Configurator*: Double-click the iPad in the device browser to display the Info view. Click the Profiles category in the sidebar, then click the profile and press the Delete key or choose Edit ➤ Delete from the menu bar. Click the Remove button in the confirmation dialog that opens.

2. *iPad*: Choose Settings ➤ General ➤ Profile to display the Profile screen. Tap the button for the appropriate profile to display the Profile screen, which shows the details of the profile. Tap the Delete Profile button, enter your authorization passcode (set in the General payload for the profile) in the Enter Passcode dialog, and then tap the Delete button in the Delete Profile dialog. If the Remove Protected Profile dialog opens (see Figure 4-85), type the removal passcode, and then tap the Delete button.

Figure 4-85. *If the profile's Security setting is With Authorization, you must type the removal password in the Remove Protected Profile dialog to remove the profile from the iPad*

■ **Note**   If the Delete Profile button doesn't appear on the Profile screen, the profile is one that you cannot remove.

Creating Blueprints to Automate Configuration

Apple Configurator lets you create templates called *blueprints* to automate the configuration of your iPads. In this section, we'll examine what a blueprint can contain, look at how to start creating a blueprint and adding items to it, and then apply the blueprint to the iPads that need it.

What Can a Blueprint Contain?

A blueprint can contain various items, including the following:

- Configuration profiles containing settings

- Apps you want to install

- MDM information and MDM supervision identity

- Administrative actions, such as enforcing Single App Mode on an iPad

Displaying the Blueprint Browser and Starting a New Blueprint

To work with blueprints in Apple Configurator, you use the blueprint browser. You can switch to the blueprint browser in any of these ways:

- *Toolbar*: Click the Blueprints button on the toolbar and then click Edit Blueprints on the pop-up menu.

- *Menu bar*: Choose View ➤ Edit Blueprints.

- *Keyboard or menu bar*: Press Cmd-B or choose File ➤ New Blueprint to switch to the blueprint browser and start creating a new blueprint.

If you used the third method to display the blueprint browser, you'll see a new blueprint with a default name such as Untitled or Untitled 1 (see Figure 4-86). If you used either other method, click the New button in the lower-left corner of the blueprint browser to start a new blueprint.

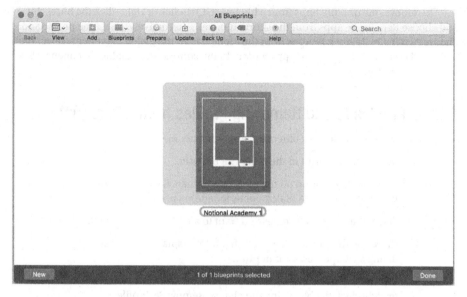

Figure 4-86. *Click the New button in the lower-left corner of the blueprint browser to start a new blueprint, type the name over the default name (such as Untitled), and press the Return key.*

Type the name for the blueprint over the default name, and then press the Return key or click elsewhere to apply the name.

■ **Note**   Don't click the Done button yet, because doing so closes the blueprint browser.

Adding Items to a Blueprint

Now that you've started a new blueprint, you can add apps and profiles to it. You can also modify the device's information and choose advanced settings.

Adding Apps to or Removing Apps from a Blueprint

To add apps to a blueprint, you use the same technique as for adding apps to an iPad. See the section "Adding Apps to or Removing Apps from an iPad or a Blueprint," earlier in this chapter, for details—but here's the short version: select the blueprint in the blueprint browser, click the Add button on the toolbar and click the Apps item on the pop-up menu. Select the app or apps in the dialog, and then click the Add button.

To remove one or more apps from a blueprint, Ctrl-click or right-click the blueprint and choose Remove ➤ Apps from the shortcut menu. Alternatively, select the profile and choose Actions ➤ Remove ➤ Apps from the menu bar. In the dialog that opens, select the apps, and then click the Remove Apps button. In the confirmation dialog that opens, click the Remove button.

Adding Profiles to and Removing Profiles from a Blueprint

To add one or more profiles to a blueprint, follow these steps:

1. Select the blueprint in the blueprint browser.

2. Click the Add button on the toolbar, and then click Profiles on the pop-up menu. A dialog opens for adding profiles.

3. Select the profile or profiles you want to add.

4. Click the Add button. Apple Configurator displays a progress dialog as it updates the blueprint.

5. To remove one or more profiles from a blueprint, Ctrl-click or right-click the blueprint and choose Remove ➤ Profiles from the shortcut menu, or click the profile and then choose Actions ➤ Remove ➤ Profiles from the menu bar. In the dialog that opens, select the profile or profiles, and then click the Remove Profiles button. In the confirmation dialog that opens, click the Remove button.

Modifying a Device's Information via a Blueprint

As you saw in the earlier section "Changing an iPad's Name, Wallpaper, or Home Screen," you can modify a device's name, Home screen and lock screen wallpapers, and Home screen layout by working on the device. You can also configure these changes in a blueprint to make the changes on the iPads to which you apply the blueprint.

To make these changes, select the blueprint in the blueprint browser and give the appropriate commands:

1. *Change the device name*: Choose Actions ➤ Modify ➤ Device Name from the menu bar or Modify ➤ Device Name from the shortcut menu.

2. *Change the wallpapers*: Choose Actions ➤ Modify ➤ Wallpapers from the menu bar or Modify ➤ Wallpapers from the shortcut menu.

3. *Change the Home screen layout*: Choose Actions ➤ Modify ➤ Home Screen Layout from the menu bar or Modify ➤ Home Screen Layout from the shortcut menu.

Choosing Advanced Settings for a Blueprint

You can choose advanced settings for a blueprint the same way you can choose advanced settings for an iPad. For example, you can add an Erase All Content and Settings command to a blueprint to erase the contents and apply default settings to an iPad, or you can add a Use Single App Mode command to make the iPad run in Single App Mode. See the earlier section "Choosing Advanced Settings for an iPad or a Blueprint" for details on the advanced settings.

Viewing the Information for a Blueprint

As mentioned earlier, when you add items to a blueprint, the blueprint's icon in the blueprint browser stubbornly stays the same, so you can't see what you've added. If you make any gross errors, such as trying to add a profile that you've already added to the blueprint, the blueprint browser will tell you what's wrong, but otherwise it restricts you to a laconic (some might say enigmatic) view.

When you want to get a quick overview of the contents of a blueprint, click the blueprint in the blueprint browser and give a Quick Look command by pressing the spacebar, choosing File ➤ Quick Look from the menu bar, Ctrl-clicking or right-clicking the selection and clicking the Quick Look item on the shortcut menu, or pressing the Cmd-Y keyboard shortcut. A pop-up window appears, showing brief details of the blueprint (see Figure 4-87). Click elsewhere or press the spacebar again when you want to dismiss the pop-up window.

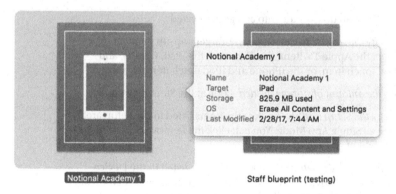

Figure 4-87. Give the Quick Look command (for example, press the spacebar) to display brief details of a blueprint's contents

To see the full details of what's in a blueprint, select the blueprint and choose File ➤ Get Info from the menu bar, Ctrl-click or right-click the blueprint and click Get Info on the shortcut menu, or select the blueprint and press the standard Cmd-I (Get Info) keyboard shortcut. The blueprint browser switches to Info view, which reveals the contents of the blueprint. Figure 4-88 shows an example of a blueprint in Info view.

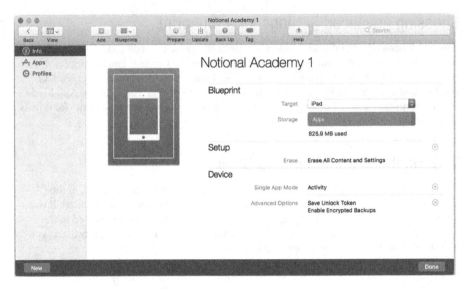

Figure 4-88. *Info view shows the contents of the selected blueprint. Click the Back (<)*
button at the left end of the toolbar to return to the blueprint browser.

As you can see, the sidebar shows different categories of items for the blueprint: Info,
Apps, and Profiles. As usual, you click the category you want to display in the main part of
the window.

Here's what you can do with the Info category selected:

- *Specify the target devices*: Open the Target pop-up menu and
  select the Apple TV item, the iPad item, the iPad, iPhone, and
  iPod touch item, or the iPhone and iPod touch item, as needed.

- *See the amount of storage needed*: Look at the Storage readout.

- *Verify the Setup settings*: Look at the items listed in the Setup area,
  such as Single App Mode. You can click the Remove (X) button to
  the right of an item to remove it.

- *Verify the Device settings*: Look at the items listed in the Device
  area, such as Advanced Options. To remove an item or a group of
  items, click the Remove (X) button to its right.

Similarly, you can review the items in the other categories by clicking the category in
the sidebar. The Apps category displays a straightforward grid of the apps you've added to
the blueprint, and the Profiles category displays a grid of the profiles in the blueprint. You
can remove an app or a profile by clicking it, pressing the Delete key, and then clicking
the Remove button in the confirmation dialog that opens.

To return from the Info view, click the Back button at the left end of the toolbar.

Duplicating a Blueprint

When you've set up a blueprint exactly the way you need it, you can duplicate it to give yourself a quick start on creating a similar one. To duplicate the blueprint, Ctrl-click or right-click the blueprint in the blueprint browser, and then click the Duplicate item on the shortcut menu.

Apple Configurator gives the duplicate blueprint the same base name, adding a space and 1 to the end of the name to differentiate it. You can then click the duplicate blueprint, click its name to display an edit box around it, type the new name, and press the Return key.

Applying a Blueprint to an iPad

When a blueprint is ready, you can apply it to the appropriate iPad or iPads. To do so, follow these steps:

1. In the device browser, select the iPad or iPads to which you'll apply the blueprint.

2. Click the Blueprints button on the toolbar, and then click the appropriate blueprint on the pop-up menu. Alternatively, choose Actions ➤ Apply from the menu bar, and then click the appropriate blueprint on the Apply submenu; or Ctrl-click or right-click in the selection, click the Apply item on the shortcut menu, and then click the blueprint on the Apply submenu. A confirmation dialog opens (see Figure 4-89).

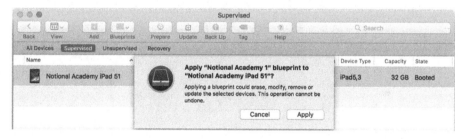

Figure 4-89. *Click the Apply button in this dialog to confirm you want to apply the blueprint to the iPad or iPads*

3. Click the Apply button. Apple Configurator applies the blueprint to the iPad.

Deleting a Blueprint

To delete a blueprint you no longer need, follow these steps:

1. Switch to the blueprint browser. For example, click the Blueprints button on the toolbar and then click Edit Blueprints on the pop-up menu.

2. Select the blueprint or blueprints you want to delete. For example, click a blueprint.

3. Press the Delete key on the keyboard or choose Edit ➤ Delete from the menu bar. A confirmation dialog opens.

4. Click the Remove button. Apple Configurator deletes the blueprint.

Summary

In this chapter, you've learned to use Apple Configurator to configure iPads automatically. You now know what you can do with Apple Configurator, how to install and configure the app, and how to perform the various actions it enables you to take. You've also learned how to create blueprints, how to add apps, profiles, and advanced settings to them, and how to apply blueprints to iPads.

In the next chapter, we'll look at how to manage iPads with Apple School Manager.

CHAPTER 5

■ ■ ■

Managing iPads with Apple School Manager

In this chapter, you'll learn about Apple School Manager, Apple's turnkey service for managing Macs and iOS devices in schools and similar institutions. This chapter explains what you need to know about Apple School Manager to use it effectively—starting with the fact that you may not need to use Apple School Manager directly at all if your school uses a mobile device management (MDM) solution that integrates with Apple School Manager.

I'll start by covering the essentials of Apple School Manager: what it is, what you can do with it, and the roles it includes for school staff and students. I'll then cover how to sign your school up for Apple School Manager, how to get started by running Setup Assistant, how to work with locations, user accounts, and classes, how to assign roles to user accounts, and how to manage devices.

Understanding the Essentials of Apple School Manager

Apple School Manager is a service that Apple provides to help schools deploy Macs and iOS devices. Via Apple School Manager, you can configure devices to be enrolled automatically in your MDM solution, you can create accounts for your school's staff and students, and you can buy content to deploy on the devices.

Understanding the Two Ways to Access Apple School Manager

You can access Apple School Manager in either of two ways:

- *Directly through the web-based portal*: You can log in to Apple School Manager through the web-based portal on pretty much any computer. You then use Apple School Manager to manage your iPads (or other devices) as explained in the main part of this chapter.

© Guy Hart-Davis 2017
G. Hart-Davis, *Deploying iPads in the Classroom*,
https://doi.org/10.1007/978-1-4842-2928-6_5

■ **Note**　The Apple School Manager web-based portal supports Safari 7.1.7 or later versions on macOS or OS X, Google Chrome 40 or later versions on various operating systems, and Microsoft Edge 25.10 or later versions on Windows.

- *Indirectly through an MDM solution*: Many MDM solutions for managing iOS devices and Macs feature integration with Apple School Manager. In this approach, you enter your Apple School Manager details into your MDM solution and then use the MDM solution to manage the devices. The MDM solution implements the changes in Apple School Manager as needed.

Actions You Can Take with Apple School Manager

With Apple School Manager, you can take a wide range of actions, including the following:

- Create accounts for staff and students
- Assign accounts to different roles, such as Administrator, Manager, Teacher, or Student
- Define permissions for those roles
- Manage your school's devices

■ **Note**　Apple introduced Apple School Manager with iOS 9.3 in January 2016. If your iPads are running an older version of iOS, you'll need to upgrade to at least iOS 9.3—and preferably a later version, such as the current version—if you want to use Apple School Manager with them.

Understanding Roles in Apple School Manager

Apple School Manager supports nine different roles that control what different types of users can do within the system. You'll learn the details of roles and their privileges in the section "Assigning Roles to Accounts," later in this chapter, but at this point it's helpful to know a little about the different roles and which other roles (if any) each role can affect.

These are the nine roles, in order from the most powerful to the least powerful:

- *Administrator*: The Administrator runs the system and can make changes to other Administrators and all the other roles.
- *Site Manager*: A Site Manager manages an Apple School Manager site (a location) and can make changes to other Site Managers and all other roles except Administrator.

- *People Manager*: A People Manager can make changes to other People Managers and all other roles except Administrator.

- *Device Manager*: A Device Manager can make changes to devices but not to other roles.

- *Content Manager*: A Content Manager manages content (such as apps and books) but can't make changes to any roles.

- *Manager*: A Manager can make changes to the Teacher, Staff, and Student roles.

- *Teacher*: A Teacher can make changes to only the Student role.

- *Staff*: A Staff member can't make changes to any roles.

- *Student*: A Student can't make changes to any roles.

Signing Your School Up for Apple School Manager

If your school isn't signed up for Apple School Manager, you can sign it up relatively easily. You first fill in an application form online. Apple reviews your application and, assuming your school qualifies for the program, confirms it. You can then complete the enrollment process.

■ **Note**　If your school is already part of the Apple Deployment Program, sign in with your existing account instead of creating a new account. Then click the Upgrade Now button on the Upgrade to Apple School Manager screen to upgrade your account to Apple School Manager.

Enrolling Your School in Apple School Manager

To enroll your school in Apple School Manager, go to the Apple School Manager home page at school.apple.com. Click the "Not enrolled? Enroll your institution now" link, and then follow the prompts to create a new account. You'll need to provide the following information:

- Your school's location, full address, and phone number

- Your school's legal name

- Your school's type (K–12 or higher education)

- Your school's website (used for verification and to prepopulate Managed Apple IDs)

- Your first name, last name, and job title (a job title without a name isn't acceptable)

- Your work e-mail address

> ■ **Note** The work e-mail address you provide must not be associated with an iTunes account or an iCloud account. It also must not have been used as an Apple ID for another Apple service.

- The name, work e-mail address, and job title of a verification contact, such as the principal or the Head of IT (assuming that's not you)

Getting the Verification Contact to Grant You Administrator Access

After you submit your application for enrollment, Apple reviews the information and phones your verification contact to confirm the information you've provided. Assuming all is well, Apple School Manager sends the verification contact an e-mail message with the subject line "Thank you for verifying your institution." This message contains a Confirm [Your Name] button that the verification contact can click to confirm you as the administrator, plus a Choose Someone Else link that the verification contact can click to confirm someone other than you instead.

The message also contains a check box for the verification contact to check. This check box approves the administrator (I'm assuming that's you) as having the authority to sign the Apple School Manager terms and conditions on the school's behalf.

Once your verification contact has jumped through these hoops, you (the administrator) receive an e-mail message titled "Enrollment Complete" from Apple School Manager.

Setting Up Your Managed Apple ID

When you receive the "Enrollment Complete" message, click the Get Started button in it. Your default web browser opens to the page for creating a Managed Apple ID. You'll need to set up a secure password, enter your date of birth, provide a mobile phone number, and then enter the verification code sent to your phone.

Running Setup Assistant

Apple School Manager includes a Setup Assistant feature that helps you get started. You can either connect your school's Student Information System (SIS) to your Apple School Manager account and import data directly from it—by far the easier approach—or load your data into Apple's CSV templates and upload them to Apple School Manager via Secure File Transport Protocol (SFTP). Whichever approach you take, Setup Assistant also enables you to add your institution's details to your school's Apple School Manager account.

■ **Note** CSV is the abbreviation for *comma-separated values*, a format that's widely used to interchange text-only data such as database records. Each field is separated from the next field by a comma.

Importing Student, Staff, and Class Data from Your School's SIS

If your school uses an SIS, you'll normally want to connect it to Apple School Manager so that you can copy information from the SIS to Apple School Manager. When you make the first connection to the SIS, you copy the data on students, staff, and classes to Apple School Manager. Thereafter, Apple School Manager receives updates from the SIS every 24 hours, automatically adding any information that has been updated.

To connect to your school's SIS, follow these steps:

1. If you don't currently have Setup Assistant open, click your name in the upper-right corner of the screen, and then click Setup Assistant on the pop-up menu to open Setup Assistant.

2. Go to the Find Students, Staff, and Classes heading, and then click the Add (+) button.

3. Click Student Information System (SIS). The pop-up menu opens.

4. Click the type of SIS your school uses.

5. Click the Connect button. A screen for connecting to that type of SIS appears.

6. Fill in the required information (this depends on the type of SIS).

7. Click the Connect button. Apple School Manager establishes the connection and then copies information from the SIS.

■ **Note** If Apple School Manager gives any errors when copying information from the SIS, correct the data in the SIS, and then try connecting Apple School Manager to it again.

8. When Apple School Manager has copied the data, click the Review Data button to display the data that will be added to Apple School Manager.

9. Review the data to make sure it looks correct.

10. Click the Confirm button to confirm adding the data to Apple School Manager.

Uploading Data to Apple School Manager via SFTP

If your school doesn't have an SIS, or has an SIS that isn't directly compatible with Apple School Manager, you can upload data to Apple School Manager via Secure File Transport Protocol (SFTP). The data needs to be in CSV files, which you can create from most database and spreadsheet apps. Apple School Manager provides template files to help ensure you get the data in the format needed.

Getting the SFTP Information

The first step in setting up the SFTP connection to Apple School Manager is running Setup Assistant and getting the SFTP information you need. To do so, follow these steps:

1. If you don't currently have Setup Assistant open, click your name in the upper-right corner of the screen, and then click Setup Assistant on the pop-up menu to open Setup Assistant.

2. Go to the Find Students, Staff, and Classes heading, and then click the Add (+) button.

3. Click the Set Up SFTP button. A screen appears showing the URL, username, and password to use for uploading files to Apple School Manager via SFTP, plus a Download Templates button for downloading the CSV templates.

4. Note the SFTP information, or enter it directly in the FTP app you will use.

Downloading and Filling Out the CSV Templates

Next, download the CSV templates and fill them out with the information on your school's students, staff, and classes. To download the CSV template files, click the Download Templates button.

There are six CSV template files:

- *Students template*: You use this template for uploading data on student accounts.

- *Staff template*: You use this template for uploading data on staff accounts, including teachers.

- *Courses template*: You use this template for uploading course information.

- *Classes template*: You use this template for uploading class information.

- *Rosters template*: You use this template for uploading class rosters.

- *Locations template*: You use this template for uploading location information.

How to Fill Out the Templates

How you fill out the Apple School Manager templates will depend on how your school stores the data you will need to upload. The following list summarizes your choices:

- *Student Information System (SIS)*: If your school has an SIS that's not directly compatible with Apple School Manager, you should be able to export information from the SIS to CSV files. You'll probably need to map the fields manually, specifying which field in the CSV file receives the data from which field in the SIS, to get the fields in the right order in the CSV files.

■ **Note**　If your school has an SIS that's directly compatible with Apple School Manager, you'll normally be better off linking the SIS to Apple School Manager rather than messing around with the templates.

- *Other database*: If your school stores information in a database rather than an SIS, you should be able to export the required information to CSV files. Again, you'll need to map the fields manually to get them in the right order.

- *Excel workbook*: If your school stores information in an Excel workbook, you can set up worksheets that pull together the appropriate fields in the right order, and then use the Save As command to save them to CSV files.

- *Manually*: Although it's possible to fill out the CSV templates manually in a spreadsheet app (or even a word processing app), doing so is so laborious that it's rarely worthwhile other than for testing Apple School Manager.

Filling Out the Students Template

The Students template enables you to import your school's student accounts into Apple School Manager. Table 5-1 explains the fields in the Students template. There are four required fields: person_id, first_name, last_name, and location_id. Of these fields, only person_id must be unique.

Table 5-1. *Fields in the Students Template*

Field	Explanation	Example	Required?	Unique?
person_id	A number that identifies the student uniquely in your SIS or database. You use the same person_id value in the Rosters template and the Classes template.	ABBAD61E-7E99-551A-CBA8-FECF3812919D1	Yes	Yes
person_number	Your institution's badge number or ID number for the student.	42	No	No
first_name	The student's first name	Alice	Yes	No
middle_name	The student's middle name or middle initial	A	No	No
last_name	The student's last name	Abrahams	Yes	No
grade_level	The student's grade level	8	No	No
email_address	The student's e-mail address	a_abrahams@notionalacademy.com	No	No
sis_username	The student's username in your school's SIS or database	a_abrahams	No	No
password_policy	The passcode policy to apply: 8 for a standard, eight-digit passcode; 6 for a six-digit passcode; 4 for a four-digit passcode. 8 digits gives fairly strong security; 6 gives moderate security; and 4 gives low security but is much easier for students to remember.	6	No	No
location_id	The location ID for the school or department to which the student belongs. A student can have up to 15 locations.	FEDCBA21-179E-551A-CBA8-FECD826183EA	Yes	No

Filling Out the Staff Template

The Staff template enables you to import your school's staff accounts into Apple School Manager. As you can see in Table 5-2, many of the fields in the Staff template are the same as those in the Students template. In the Staff template, too, the key field is the person_id field, which must be unique for each person in the school.

Table 5-2. *Fields in the Staff Template*

Field	Explanation	Example	Required?	Unique?
person_id	A number that identifies the staff member uniquely in your SIS or database. You use the same person_id value in the Rosters template and the Classes template.	ABCDEF12-789F-123A-CBA8-FECF3812919D1	Yes	Yes
person_number	Your institution's badge number or ID number for the staff member.	42	No	No
first_name	The staff member's first name	Bill	Yes	No
middle_name	The staff member's middle name or middle initial	B	No	No
last_name	The staff member's last name	Brown	Yes	No
email_address	The staff member's e-mail address	b_brown@notionalacademy.com	No	No
sis_username	The staff member's username in your school's SIS or database	b_brown	No	No
password_policy	The passcode policy to apply. For staff, you should use 8 to require a standard, eight-digit passcode.	8	No	No
location_id	The location ID for the school or department to which the staff member belongs. A staff member can have up to 15 locations.	FEDCBA21-179E-551A-CBA8-FECD826183EA	Yes	No

Filling Out the Courses Template

The Courses template enables you to upload information on your school's courses to Apple School Manager. Table 5-3 explains the fields in the Courses template. This template has two required fields: course_id (which links classes to the courses that contain them) and location_id (which specifies the location to which the course belongs).

Table 5-3. *Fields in the Courses Template*

Field	Explanation	Example	Required?	Unique?
course_id	A number that identifies the course uniquely in your SIS or database. You use the same course_id value in the Classes template.	CDEFAB22-E888-6AAB-B22B-ABAB3812	Yes	Yes
course_number	Your school's ID number for the course.	ELIT101	No	No
course_name	The name of the course	English Literature 101	No	No
location_ID	The location ID for the school or department to which the course belongs.	FEDCBA21-179E-551A-CBA8-FECD826183EA	Yes	No

Filling Out the Classes Template

The Classes template enables you to upload information on your school's classes to Apple School Manager. A class is one of the components of a course and is linked to the course by the course_id field, which is required. Also required are the class_id field, which identifies the class uniquely in the school's system, and the location_id field, which specifies the location to which the class belongs. Table 5-4 explains the fields in the Classes template.

Table 5-4. *Fields in the Classes Template*

Field	Explanation	Example	Required?	Unique?
class_id	A number that identifies the class uniquely in your SIS or database. You use the same class_id value in the Rosters template.	C44D33AF-B99C-7DBD-B66C-2646ACFEBA	Yes	Yes
class_number	Your school's ID number for the course.	51	No	No
course_id	The course_id number of the course to which the class belongs.	CDEFAB22-E888-6AAB-B22B-ABAB3812	Yes	No

(continued)

Table 5-4. *(continued)*

Field	Explanation	Example	Required?	Unique?
instructor_id	The person_id number of the first (or only) teacher for this class.	ABCDEF12-789F-123A-CBA8-FECF3812919D1	No	No
instructor_id_2	The person_id number of the second teacher for this class.	ABCDEF12-888E-123A-CBA8-FECF3812919D1	No	No
instructor_id_3	The person_id number of the third teacher for this class.	ABCDEF12-611C-123A-CBA8-FECF3812919D1	No	No
location_id	The location ID for the school or department to which the class belongs.	FEDCBA21-179E-551A-CBA8-FECD826183EA	Yes	No

Filling Out the Rosters Template

The Rosters template lets you import your class rosters into Apple School Manager. In Apple School Manager, a *roster* is a record that allocates one student to the specified class—it's not the complete list of students in a class. Each student in that class needs his or her own roster.

Table 5-5 explains the fields in the Rosters template, which has three required fields: roster_id, class_id, and student_id.

Table 5-5. *Fields in the Rosters Template*

Field	Explanation	Example	Required?	Unique?
roster_id	A number that identifies the roster uniquely in your SIS or database.	6648ACDC-8181-8AD8-911E-3628383AC	Yes	Yes
class_id	The number that identifies the class uniquely in your SIS or database.	C44D33AF-B99C-7DBD-B66C-2646ACFEBA	Yes	No
student_id	The person_id number of the student allocated to the class.	ABBAD61E-7E99-551A-CBA8-FECF3812919D1	Yes	No

■ **Note** If you're creating rosters information manually, there's a complication you need to understand: each `roster_id` value needs to be unique within your school. For the roster of a class that contains 30 students, you need 30 unique `roster_id` values, each on its own row and accompanied by the `class_id` number of the class and the `student_id` number of a student. Similarly, each other class needs a unique `roster_id` value for each student. One way to create unique `roster_id` values is to use the `uuidgen` command in a shell script in a Terminal window on macOS.

Filling Out the Locations Template

The Locations template enables you to import your school's locations into Apple School Manager. This is the simplest of the templates, and you should be able to fill it out quickly. Table 5-6 explains the two fields in the Rosters template.

Table 5-6. *Fields in the Locations Template*

Field	Explanation	Example	Required?	Unique?
location_id	A number that identifies the location uniquely in your SIS or database. You use the location_id number in the Students template, the Staff template, the Courses template, and the Classes template	FEDCBA21-179E-551A-CBA8-FECD826183EA	Yes	Yes
location_name	The name of the location	Notional Academy campus	Yes	No

Uploading the Information via SFTP

After filling in the CSV templates, compress them into a zip archive. For example, on macOS, open a Finder window to the folder that contains the CSV templates, select the templates, and then choose File ➤ Compress 6 Items from the menu bar. This creates a file named `Archive.zip`. You can rename it if you want, but you don't need to.

Next, establish an SFTP connection using the information you noted earlier. You'll need to use a third-party app, such as Forklift on macOS or FileZilla on Windows, Linux, or macOS. Drag the zip archive file to the Dropbox folder, and drop it there. (Just to be clear: *Dropbox* here is the name of the folder in Apple School Manager—it has nothing to do with the Dropbox online file-transfer service.)

Once you've done this, return to the Apple School Manager window and click the Continue button. When the file has uploaded, Apple School Manager warns you if it contains errors. If so, you'll need to fix them, create a new zip archive, and then upload it. You can leave the previous zip archive file on the Apple SFTP server—Apple School Manager uses the new file you upload.

When you've successfully uploaded data without errors, you can click the Review SFTP Data button to review the data.

Adding Other Institution Details in Setup Assistant

After you finish importing or uploading data, Setup Assistant displays a screen where you can add further data about your school:

- *Tax Status*: Click the Add (+) button next to the Add Institution Details heading, then click Add Tax Status. In the Add Tax Status pop-up menu, click the appropriate status. Then enter your Apple Customer Number or your Certificate ID to enable Apple to verify the tax information.

- *Find Devices*: Enter your Apple Customer Number or your reseller's or carrier's Apple Reseller ID to let you associate devices with your MDM solution.

Click the Save button when you finish adding information in Setup Assistant.

Configuring Managed Apple IDs in Setup Assistant

Apple School Manager gives you tools for working with Managed Apple IDs, the identifiers that students and staff use to sign in to their iPads, to authenticate themselves for Apple services, or to work with Apple School Manager. Whereas standard Apple IDs are owned and managed by individual users, Managed Apple IDs are owned and managed by schools.

UNDERSTANDING APPLE'S RECOMMENDED FORMAT FOR MANAGED APPLE IDS

To reduce confusion, Apple recommends that you set up your school's Managed Apple IDs with a different format than that used for the students' and staff's regular e-mail addresses. The confusion arises from the fact that, if you use the regular e-mail addresses, the students will need to remember two passcodes for the same address: the original passcode for e-mail, plus the passcode for the Managed Apple ID.

So, for a school with the domain `notionalacademy.com`, you might want to use e-mail addresses such as `a_abrahams@notionalacademy.com` and `b_brown@notionalacademy.com`, but Apple recommends including the text `appleid.` after the @ sign, giving Managed Apple IDs such as `a_abrahams@appleid.notionalacademy.com` and `b_brown@appleid.notionalacademy.com`.

Apple School Manager creates Managed Apple IDs when you import user accounts from your school's SIS, import CSV files via SFTP, or create user accounts manually. To choose the format for the Managed Apple IDs, follow these steps in Setup Assistant:

1. Click the Add (+) button next to the Create Accounts and Classes heading.

2. Click the Change Settings button to open the settings for editing in the Format window.

3. In the Domain box, enter the school's domain (such as `notionalacademy.com`).

4. Select the "Include 'appleid' in the Domain" option if you want to place `appleid.` before the domain name. This is normally a good idea.

5. Click the Save Format button. The Format window closes, returning you to Setup Assistant.

6. Click the Preview Accounts and Classes button to view the list of Managed Apple IDs that the settings you've chosen will generate.

7. Click the Create Managed Apple IDs button to begin generating the Managed Apple IDs.

Working with Locations

Apple School Manager ties user roles to locations. For example, a staff member can be an Administrator in one location and a Teacher in another location.

Apple School Manager walks you through the process of creating your school's initial location when you sign up for the service. You can subsequently add other locations as needed.

To work with locations, click the Locations item in the sidebar. The list of existing locations appears. You can then take the following actions:

- *Add a location*: Click the Add New Location button toward the top of the screen. Enter the details for the new location, and then click the Save button.

- *Edit your school's default password policy location information*: Click the appropriate location, and then click the Edit button (the blue circle showing a pencil icon). Select the default password policy you want to apply, and then click the Save button.

- *Delete a location and transfer its data to another location*: Click the location you want to delete, and then click the Delete Location button. Click the Choose a Transfer Location pop-up menu, and then click the location to which you want to transfer the information from the location you're deleting. Click the Continue button to effect the transfer and the deletion, and then click the Done button.

Working with User Accounts and Classes

When you are using Apple School Manager to manage your school's deployment of devices directly, you can set up user accounts either by creating them manually or by copying or uploading existing information.

You can also create classes manually if necessary by specifying the students and teacher (or teachers) that make up each class.

Working with User Accounts

This section looks at how to create user accounts manually, how to create Administrator and Manager accounts, and how to edit user accounts. I'll also cover how to deactivate and reactivate user accounts, how to delete user accounts you've created manually, how to inspect user accounts, and how to reset the verification phone number for an account.

WHAT INFORMATION DOES A USER ACCOUNT CONTAIN?

A user account can contain the following information:

- The account's status (New, Active, Deactivated, Locked, or Passcode Reset)

- The first name, middle initial or name, and last name of the user

- The user's Managed Apple ID

- The user's role and location

- The Managed Apple ID passcode policy applied to the account

- The grade level for a student

- The e-mail address for the user

- The Person Number and the Person ID

Creating a User Account Manually

If you're not copying user account information from your school's SIS or uploading the information in CSV files, you can create user accounts manually. To do so, follow these steps:

1. Click the Accounts item in the sidebar.

2. Click the Add New Account button to display the fields for creating a new account.

3. Enter the first name and last name. This information is required.

4. Enter the middle initial or middle name if appropriate. This information is optional.

5. Select the appropriate role for the account. For example, select the Student role for a student. This information is required.

6. Select the location for the account. This information is required.

7. Enter the Managed Apple ID for the account. This information is also required.

8. Enter the grade level if appropriate. This information is optional.

9. Enter the e-mail address if appropriate. This information is also optional.

10. Enter the Person ID if necessary. This information is also optional.

■ **Note** A Person ID is a unique identifier used to identify the user in your school's SIS. A Person Number is a unique alphanumeric identifier used to identify the user account.

---

11. Enter the Person Number if appropriate. This information, too, is optional.

12. Enter the SIS username, if appropriate. This is also optional.

13. Click the Save Person button in the lower-right corner of the screen.

Creating Administrator Accounts and Manager Accounts

Apart from the Administrator account with which you initially set up your school's Apple School Manager account, you can create up to four more Administrator accounts. For security, you'll normally want to set up at least one other Administrator account in case you get locked out of your account.

The process for creating an Administrator account is the same as creating a user account (see the previous section): you click the Accounts item in the sidebar, click the Add New Account button, and then fill in the fields. The key difference is that you select the Administrator role for the account.

Similarly, you can create accounts in the five Manager roles—Manager, Site Manager, People Manager, Device Manager, and Content Manager—by selecting the appropriate Manager role for each account.

Editing User Accounts

When you need to change the information in a user account, you can edit the user account by clicking the Accounts item in the sidebar, selecting the account, and then clicking the Edit button (the blue circle showing a pencil icon). Make the changes needed (but see the next Caution), and then click the Save button to save them.

■ **Caution** Be careful when editing an account that you've imported from your school's SIS or uploaded as a CSV file. In these accounts, you can safely edit only the Managed Apple ID field, the Role field, and the Passcode field. Editing any other fields changes the account to a manually created account, which prevents you from updating it with new information from the SIS or a CSV file.

CONVERTING EXISTING ACCOUNTS TO MANAGER AND ADMINISTRATOR ACCOUNTS

Besides creating new Administrator accounts and Manager accounts, you can also convert an existing account to a Manager account, and you can convert any Manager account that you've created manually to an Administrator account.

To convert an account to a Manager account, click the Accounts item in the sidebar, select the account (search for it if necessary), and then click the Edit button (the blue circle showing a pencil icon). With the account open for editing, select the appropriate Manager role and the location in which the user will exercise the role, and then click the Save button.

To convert a Manager account to an Administrator account, open the Manager account for editing, select the Administrator role and the appropriate location, and then click the Save button.

Deactivating and Reactivating User Accounts

You may sometimes need to deactivate a user account to prevent that user from signing in with their Managed Apple ID. To deactivate a user account, follow these steps:

1. Click the Accounts item in the sidebar.

2. Click the user account you want to deactivate. Search for the account if necessary.

3. Click the Deactivate Account button.

4. Click the Done button.

▪ **Note**   You can also deactivate multiple user accounts at once. To do so, click the Accounts item in the sidebar, and then select each user account you want to deactivate. In the Account Status row, click the Change button, and then click the Deactivate item on the pop-up menu. Click the Continue button, and then click the Done button.

▪ **Caution**   Apple School Manager automatically deletes any account that you leave deactivated for more than 30 days, so it's a good idea to review account status once every week or two.

When you need to reactivate a user account, follow the same steps as for deactivating a user account, but click the Reactivate Account button instead of the Deactivate Account button. You can also reactivate multiple user accounts at the same time by selecting the accounts, clicking the Change button in the Account Status row, and then clicking the Reactivate item on the pop-up menu. Finish by clicking the Continue button and then clicking the Done button.

Deleting User Accounts You Have Created Manually

You can delete user accounts that you've created manually in Apple School Manager, but you can't delete user accounts that have been created automatically.

To delete a user account, follow these steps:

1. Click the Accounts item in the sidebar.

2. Click the user account you want to delete. You can search for the account to locate it.

3. Click the Delete button. A confirmation dialog opens.

4. Click the Delete button to confirm the deletion.

5. Click the Done button.

▪ **Note**   You can delete multiple user accounts if necessary. To do so, click the Accounts icon in the sidebar, and then select each user account you want to delete. In the Account Status row, click the Change button, and then click the Delete item on the pop-up menu. Click the Continue button to confirm the deletion, and then click the Done button.

Inspecting a User Account

Apple School Manager includes an Inspect feature for inspecting the contents of a specific Managed Apple ID, enabling you to check that a device configured for multiple users is being used in compliance with your school's policies. To inspect an account, you must hold a higher role in Apple School Manager than the account: For example, a Manager can inspect the Teacher, Staff, and Student roles, a Teacher can inspect only the Student role, and an Administrator can inspect all the roles below Administrator.

Apple School Manager requires you to create an inspection Managed Apple ID and a custom password for each inspection. Follow these steps to create these credentials:

1. Click the Accounts item in the sidebar.

2. Click the user account you want to inspect. Search for the account if necessary.

3. Click the Inspect icon (the blue circle showing an eye icon).

4. Click the Continue button. The inspection Managed Apple ID and password appear.

5. Note the Managed Apple ID and password.

6. Click the Done button.

You can now use the inspection Managed Apple ID and password to inspect the user account. You have 15 minutes to do so before the credentials expire.

Resetting the Verification Phone Number for an Account

For security, Apple School Manager requires a six-digit verification code to supplement the Managed Apple ID account passcode for each user account that has Administrator, Manager, Staff, or Teacher roles. This code is sent to the phone number you've associated with the user account.

When you need to reset the phone number for an account, follow these steps:

1. Click the Accounts item in the sidebar.

2. Click the user account for which you want to reset the verification phone number. Search for the account if necessary.

3. Click the Reset Phone Number button.

4. Click the Reset button to confirm the change.

The next time the user signs in to their account, Apple School Manager prompts them to add the new phone number.

ADDING MULTIPLE VERIFICATION PHONE NUMBERS FOR KEY ROLES

If you need to lock down key roles in Apple School Manager, you can add extra verification phone numbers. For example, you may want to layer extra security onto your Administrator accounts and some Manager accounts.

To do this, go to the Apple ID website, `http://appleid.apple.com`, and sign in using your Managed Apple ID. Go through Two-Step Verification if prompted—for example, get a code sent to your trusted iPhone or iPad, and then enter that on the website.

Next, go to the Security section of the page, and click the Edit button on the right side. Under the Trusted Phone Numbers heading, click the Add Another Phone Number button to display the Enter a Phone Number That Can Receive Text Messages dialog, enter the phone number, and then click the Continue button. When the six-digit code appears, type it in, and then click the Verify button.

Managing Passcodes

You'll need to spend some of your time in Apple School Manager managing passcodes for your school's user accounts. This section first briefly examines how Apple School Manager uses passcodes to secure accounts. I'll then cover how you set passcode policies in Apple School Manager, create new sign-ins for user accounts you've imported or created, and reset passcodes when users forget them.

Understanding How Apple School Manager Uses Passcodes

When you import user accounts or create them manually, you create a temporary passcode for each account. This passcode is good only for the user to sign in with the account's Managed Apple ID—as soon as the user is signed in, Apple School Manager walks them through the process of setting their own passcode.

Any student (someone with a user account assigned the Student role) can sign in on devices listed in Apple School Manager using their Managed Apple ID and passcode. For devices not listed in Apple School Manager, a student can sign in using their Managed Apple ID, passcode, and a six-digit verification code.

Apple School Manager has tighter security for accounts that have the Administrator, Manager, Staff, or Teacher roles. These accounts require not only the Managed Apple ID passcode but also a six-digit verification code. Once you've entered this verification code on a device, you don't need to enter it again for 30 days.

Setting Passcode Policies for Apple School Manager

Apple School Manager supports three passcode policies that you can apply to roles:

- Standard passcode containing at least eight characters (letters and numbers)

- Six-digit passcode

- Four-digit passcode

Accounts with the Student role can use any of the three passcode policies, but you can enforce a particular policy if your school so prefers. Accounts with the Administrator, Manager, Staff, or Teacher roles should use a standard passcode; you can change this, but it's better if you don't.

To control which passcode policy your school's accounts with the Student role use, follow these steps:

1. Click the Accounts item in the sidebar.

2. Select the account or accounts you want to affect. If you select multiple accounts, they must all have the same role.

3. Click the Edit button (the blue circle showing a pencil icon).

4. Click the Passcode Policy pop-up menu, and then click the passcode policy you want to apply.

5. Click the Save button to save the changes.

Creating New Sign-Ins for User Accounts

After importing user accounts into Apple School Manager, or creating new user accounts directly in Apple School Manager, you need to create a temporary passcode for each account and communicate it to each user. The users can then sign in to their user accounts for the first time, and create new passcodes for themselves when Apple School Manager prompts them to do so.

To create new sign-ins for user accounts, follow these steps:

1. Click the Accounts item in the sidebar.

2. Select the user account or user accounts for which you want to create the new sign-ins.

3. If you selected a single account, click the Create Sign-In button. If you selected multiple accounts, go to the Sign-Ins row and click the Create button.

4. When Apple School Manager prompts you how to communicate the passcodes, click the .CSV and PDF button or the Send as an Email button, as needed:

    - *.CSV and PDF*: Click the Download button, and then click the 8-Up PDF button, the 1-Up PDF button, or the .CSV button, as needed.

■ **Note**   The 8-Up PDF option creates pages containing 8 users (or, on the last sheet, however many are left, fewer than 8). You can print the PDF, cut up the sheets of paper, and distribute the sections to the users. The 1-Up PDF option creates a full page for each user. The .CSV option creates a comma-separated values file containing five columns: Managed Apple ID, First Name, Middle Name, Last Name, and Initial Passcode.

- *Send as an Email*: Select or deselect the option for displaying the user's photo in the e-mail message, and then click the Email button. Apple School Manager sends a message containing the Managed Apple ID and the initial passcode to the e-mail address listed in the user account.

Resetting a Forgotten Passcode

If a user forgets their passcode, you can reset it. Resetting the passcode gives the user a temporary passcode, and when they log in with the temporary passcode, Apple School Manager prompts them to create a new passcode.

To reset a passcode, follow these steps:

1. Click the Accounts item in the sidebar.

2. Click the user account for which you want to reset the passcode. As usual, you may want to search to locate the account.

3. Click the Reset Passcode button.

■ **Note**   You can reset the passcodes for multiple user accounts at once if necessary. Click the Accounts item in the sidebar, select each user account you want to affect, and then click the Create button in the Sign-Ins row.

---

4. When Apple School Manager prompts you how to communicate the passcodes, click the .CSV and PDF button or the Send as an Email button, as needed:

   - *.CSV and PDF*: Click the Download button, and then click the 8-Up PDF button, the 1-Up PDF button, or the .CSV button, as needed.

- *Send as an Email*: Select or deselect the option for displaying the user's photo in the e-mail message, and then click the Email button. Apple School Manager sends a message containing the Managed Apple ID and the initial passcode to the e-mail address listed in the user account.

Sending Verification Codes to Students

Apple School Manager enables you to send a verification code that permits a student to sign in using their Managed Apple ID to an iPad running Shared iPad, to the iCloud service using Safari, or to the iCloud preferences pane on a Mac.

To send a verification code, follow these steps:

1. Click the Accounts item in the sidebar.

2. Select the user account that needs the verification code.

3. Click the Verification Code button.

4. When Apple School Manager prompts you how to communicate the verification code, click the .CSV and PDF button or the Send as an Email button, as needed:

   - *.CSV and PDF*: Click the Download button, and then click the 1-Up PDF button or the .CSV button, as needed.

   - *Send as an Email*: Click the Send as an Email button. Apple School Manager sends a message containing the Managed Apple ID and the verification code to the e-mail address listed in the user account.

■ **Note** You can send verification codes to multiple user accounts if need be. Click the Accounts item in the sidebar, select each user account that needs a verification code, and then click the Create button in the Verification Codes row. You can then choose between the .CSV and PDF option (which includes the capability to create an 8-Up PDF) and the Send as an Email option, which sends an e-mail message containing the verification code to each user.

Working with Classes

Your school may create all classes in its MDM solution. If so, you won't need to create classes manually. Otherwise, you can create classes manually as needed by specifying the students and teacher (or teachers) that make up each class.

Creating a Class Manually

To create a class manually, follow these steps:

1. Click the Classes item in the sidebar.

2. Click the Add New Class button. A screen for creating the class appears.

3. Type the course name. This is an optional field—if you enter the name, it becomes part of the class name.

4. Type the class ID. This is an optional field.

5. Type the class number. This is an optional field.

6. Add students to the class. These too are optional, but you'll need to add some students sooner or later.

7. Add one or more teachers to the class. Teachers are also optional while you're creating the class.

8. Enter the location for the class. This is a required field that specifies which of your defined locations the class takes place in.

9. Click the Save button. Apple School Manager creates the class, and it appears in the Classes list.

Searching the Classes Table

You can search the Classes table when you need to find specific information, such as a particular class, all the classes in a subject, or all the classes for a given teacher.

To search the Classes table, follow these steps:

1. Click the Classes item in the sidebar.

2. Click the Filter button if you need to filter the table.

3. Click the field you want to search.

4. Type your search term. The search results appear.

5. If you've searched for a class, you can click the Show button (the blue circle showing a magnifying glass) to display the students in the class.

Editing a Class You've Created

If you've created a class, you can edit it as needed. To do so, follow these steps:

1. Click the Classes item in the sidebar.

2. Click the class you want to edit. Search for the class if necessary.

3. Click the Edit button (the blue circle showing a pencil icon) to open the class for editing.

4. To add students, click the Add button in the Students section, click the appropriate student or students, and then click the Continue button.

5. To change the location of the class, select the new location.

6. When you finish making changes to the class, click the Save button. Apple School Manager saves the changes to the class.

■ **Tip** You can save time by adding one or more students to multiple classes at the same time. Click the Classes item in the sidebar, and then select the classes you want to affect. Click the Add button, select the appropriate student or students, and click the Continue button. As usual, click the Save button when you finish making changes.

Deleting a Class You've Created

You can delete any class you've created. To do so, follow these steps:

1. Click the Classes item in the sidebar.

2. Click the class you want to delete. You can search for the class if necessary.

3. Click the Delete Class button. A confirmation dialog opens.

4. Click the Delete button. Apple School Manager deletes the class.

Assigning Roles to Accounts

Apple School Manager supports various different roles, such as Administrator, Teacher, Staff, and Student. Some of the roles can make changes to other roles. For example, the Teacher role can make changes to the Student role, whereas the Student role can't make changes to another role; the Administrator role can make changes to all the other roles. To control what a particular user account can do, you assign the appropriate roles to the user account.

■ **Note** Each role is tied to a location, so you can give a person different roles for different locations. For example, you might assign a staff member the Teacher role for one location and a different role, such as Manager or Staff, at another location.

Understanding the Roles and Their Privileges

Table 5-7 shows the roles that Apple School Manager supports and the roles (if any) that each role can manipulate.

Table 5-7. *Apple School Manager roles*

Role	Can Manipulate These Other Roles
Administrator	Other Administrators Site Manager People Manager Device Manager Content Manager Manager Teacher Staff Student
Site Manager	Other Site Managers People Manager Device Manager Content Manager Manager Teacher Staff Student
People Manager	Other People Managers Site Manager Device Manager Content Manager Manager Teacher Staff Student
Device Manager	None
Content Manager	None
Manager	Teacher Staff Student
Teacher	Student
Staff	None
Student	None

Each role has a collection of *privileges*, or authorizations to take specific actions. Table 5-8 explains the privileges assigned to the Administrator, Site Manager, People Manager, Device Manager, Content Manager, and Manager roles.

Table 5-8. Apple School Manager Privileges for Administrator and Manager Roles

Privilege	Administrator	Site Manager	People Manager	Device Manager	Content Manager	Manager
Basic Privileges						
Use Managed Devices	Required	Required	Required	Required	Required	Required
Use Managed Apps and Books	Required	Required	Required	Required	Required	Required
Sign In to icloud.com with a Managed Apple ID	Required	Required	Required	Required	Required	Required
Accept Apple School Manager Terms and Conditions	Required	Always off	Always off	Always off	Always off	Always off
Edit Privileges for Other Roles	Required	Required	Required	Always off	Always off	Always off
Transfer App and Book Licenses Between Locations	Required	Always off	Always off	Always off	Always off	Always off
Add Apple Customer Numbers and DEP Reseller IDs	Required	Always off	Always off	Always off	Always off	Always off
Set Institution's Tax Status Information	Required	Always off	Always off	Always off	Always off	Always off
Privileges for Configuring Institution Settings						
Configure SIS Information	Required	Required	Required	Always off	Always off	Always off
Create, Edit, and Delete Locations	Required	Required	Required	Always off	Always off	Always off
Set the Default Managed Apple ID User Name Format	Required	Required	Required	Always off	Always off	Always off

(continued)

355

Table 5-8. (*continued*)

Privilege	Administrator	Site Manager	People Manager	Device Manager	Content Manager	Manager
Set the Default Passcode Policy for New Students	Required	Required	Required	Always off	Always off	Always off
Privileges for Managing Device Settings						
Manage MDM Servers	Required	Required	Always off	Required	Always off	Always off
Add, Assign, and Remove Devices	Required	Required	Always off	Required	Always off	Always off
Privileges for Managing Apple IDs						
Create, Edit, and Delete Managed Apple IDs	On by default	On by default	On by default	Always off	Always off	On by default
Assign Roles to Users	On by default	On by default	On by default	Always off	Always off	On by default
Change Students' Passcode Policies	On by default	On by default	On by default	Always off	Always off	On by default
Generate AppleCare Support PIN for Users	On by default	On by default	On by default	Always off	Always off	On by default
Change Account Status of Users	On by default	On by default	On by default	Always off	Always off	On by default
Privileges for Performing and Viewing Account Inspection						
Inspect User Accounts	On by default	On by default	On by default	Always off	Always off	On by default
View Account Inspection Log	On by default	On by default	On by default	Always off	Always off	On by default

Privileges for Classes, Passcodes, and Verification Codes

Create, Edit, and Delete Classes	On by default	On by default	Always off	Always off	On by default
Reset Passcodes for Users	On by default	On by default	Always off	Always off	On by default
Generate Verification Codes for Students	On by default	On by default	Always off	Always off	On by default
Privileges for Managing Content, Apps, and Books					
Buy Apps and Books	On by default	Always off	Always off	On by default	Off by default
View App and Book Store	On by default	Always off	Always off	On by default	On by default
Contribute to Institution's iTunes U Public Website	On by default	Always off	Always off	Always off	On by default
Request, Connect, or Publish to Institution's iTunes U Public Site Manager	On by default	Always off	Always off	Always off	On by default
Reassign Licenses for Apps and Books	On by default	Always off	Always off	On by default	On by default
Hold Unassigned Licenses for Apps and Books	On by default	Always off	Always off	On by default	On by default

Table 5-9 explains the privileges assigned to the Teacher, Staff, and Student roles.

Table 5-9. *Apple School Manager Privileges for the Teacher, Staff, and Student Roles*

Privilege	Teacher	Staff	Student
Use Managed Devices	Required	Required	Required
Sign In to icloud.com with a Managed Apple ID	Required	Required	Required
Use Managed Apps and Books	Required	Required	Required
Inspect Student Accounts	On by default	—	—
View Account Inspection Log	On by default	—	—
Create, Edit, and Delete Classes	Off by default	—	—
Reset Passwords for Students	On by default	—	—
Generate Verification Codes for Students	On by default	—	—
View App and Book Store	Off by default	—	—
Contribute to Institution's iTunes U Public Website	On by default	—	—

Viewing and Editing the Privileges for a Role

When you need to find out which privileges a particular role has, you can view the roles assigned to the account, and edit them if necessary.

■ **Note** To view and edit roles, you need to be logged in with an account that has the privileges needed to manipulate the roles. Normally, you'd use an account that has the Administrator, Site Manager, People Manager, or Manager role.

To view the privileges for a role, and edit the privileges if necessary, follow these steps:

1. Click the Roles item in the sidebar.

2. Click the role you want to examine. The privileges for the role appear.

3. If you want to see the accounts to which this role has been applied, click the Show button (the blue circle showing a magnifying glass).

4. If you need to edit the privileges for the role, click the Edit button (the blue circle showing a pencil icon). You can then check the check box for a privilege you want to add, or uncheck the check box for a privilege you want to remove. When you finish, click the Save button to save your changes.

■ **Note**   At the risk of stating the obvious, changing the privileges for a role changes the privileges for all the accounts to which you've applied the role. If you need to give more privileges to a particular account without giving them to other accounts, you're usually better off applying to that account a role that confers those privileges rather than adding privileges to an existing role applied to that account.

Assign a Role to an Account

To assign a role to an account, follow these steps:

1. Click the Accounts item in the sidebar.

2. If you'll need to filter your search results, click the Filter button on the Search bar.

3. Click in the Search People field.

4. Type your search criteria. The search results appear.

5. Select the account or accounts you want to affect.

6. Click the Edit button (the blue circle showing a pencil icon) to open the accounts for editing.

7. Click the role and location you want to assign to the account.

8. Click the Save button to save your changes.

Managing Your School's Devices with Apple School Manager

Apple School Manager makes it easy to enroll and deploy iOS devices that your school has acquired from Apple, an Apple Authorized Reseller, or carrier. You can enroll devices without having to physically prepare them at all: instead, you can order the devices from Apple and have them shipped to the users. When the users activate the devices, the devices are automatically enrolled in your school's MDM solution, and the management settings, apps, and books you've specified are installed automatically on the devices.

Setting Up Your Suppliers in Apple School Manager

If your school will purchase iPads from Apple Authorized Resellers or from carriers, you need to get the appropriate information in place to make the iPads show up in Apple School Manager.

First, tell the reseller or carrier your school's DEP Customer ID, and add the reseller's or carrier's DEP Reseller ID to your account profile, as explained in the next list. The DEP Customer ID is your school's unique identifier. It enables the reseller to submit the devices you buy for enrollment in the Device Enrollment Program and in Apple School Manager.

To add an reseller's or carrier DEP Reseller ID to your Apple School Manager account, follow these steps:

1. Click the Locations item in the sidebar. The list of locations appears.

2. Click the location you want to affect. You can search for it if necessary.

3. Click the Settings button.

4. Click the Device Purchases button.

5. Click the Add button next to Apple Reseller Number.

■ **Note**   If the Add button doesn't appear, or if it's dimmed and unavailable, your Apple School Manager account may already contain the relevant information.

---

6. Type or paste in the reseller number.

7. Click the Save button.

Tracking Your Device Orders

After you place an order for devices (such as iPads) with an Apple Authorized Reseller or a carrier, the reseller or carrier updates Apple with details of the devices. Apple School Manager sends you (assuming you're the administrator) e-mail messages to let you know the progress of the order.

■ **Note**   The Apple School Manager messages come from the address `noreply@email`
`.apple.com`. Add this address to your contacts or to a whitelist to make sure the messages don't go into your Junk folder.

The e-mail messages have the five subject lines shown in the following list:

- *Devices Submitted*: This message tells you that the reseller or carrier has submitted the order.

- *Devices Pending*: This message alerts you to the fact that you need to add the reseller or carrier's DEP Reseller ID to your Apple School Manager account.

- *Devices Available*: This message lets you know that the devices are available to be enrolled in your Apple School Manager account.

- *Submission Errors*: This message warns you that the reseller's or carrier's submission to Apple contained errors and that you need to follow up with the reseller or carrier to sort out the problem.

- *Devices Removed*: This message tells you that one or more devices have been removed from the order submitted by the reseller or carrier. You'll see this message if you return all or some of the devices in an order to the reseller or carrier.

Managing Your MDM Servers for Assigning Devices

To assign your devices, you must set up one or more MDM servers, communicate their identity to Apple, and authorize them by installing a server token (a digital identifier) on each server. How you transfer the token depends on the MDM solution you're using.

■ **Note**   Server tokens last only for a year, so you'll need to replace them every year with new tokens that you generate and download through Apple School Manager. Most MDM solutions warn you when your server tokens are about to expire, but some solutions don't, so it's a good idea to keep a log of when you install server tokens and when you replace them.

Adding an MDM Server

Follow these steps to add an MDM server to your Apple School Manager account:

1. Click the MDM Servers item in the sidebar.

2. Click the Add New MDM Server button.

3. Type a unique name for the server.

■ **Note** You don't need to use fully qualified domain names (such as `mdmserver1` `.notionalacademy.com`) for your MDM servers if you don't want to. If you prefer, you can create descriptive names based on where the servers are located, such as `Main Building MDM Server 1`.

---

4. Select the public key certificate file, and then click the Upload button.

5. Click the Save button.

6. Click the Get Token button, and then click the Get Server Token item on the pop-up menu.

7. Upload the server token to the appropriate MDM server, following your MDM vendor's instructions.

8. Click the Set as Default button if you want this server to be the default MDM server for devices you purchase from now on.

Editing and Deleting MDM Servers

Sooner or later, you'll likely need to edit the details for an MDM server. To do so, click the MDM Servers item in the sidebar, and then click the server you want to affect. You can then take the following actions on the server:

- View the server's details, including the public key certificate, the server token, and the last connected IP address.

- View the assigned devices by device type and quantity, and download a comma-separated values file containing the assigned devices' serial numbers.

- Rename the server.

- Make the server the default server, or change the default from this server to another server.

- Upload a public key certificate.

- Generate and download a new server token.

To delete an MDM server, follow these steps:

1. Click the MDM Servers item in the sidebar.

2. Click the server you want to delete.

3. Click the Delete Server button.

4. Click the OK button in the confirmation dialog that opens.

5. Click the MDM server to which you want to reassign the devices.

6. Click the Reassign & Delete button.

Assigning Your Devices to Your MDM Servers

After your reseller or carrier ships your order, you can use the order number to assign some or all the devices in the order to one of your MDM servers. To assign devices, follow these steps:

1. Click the Device Assignments item in the sidebar.

2. Click the button for the device assignment method you want to use. You have three options:

   - *Serial Number*: Enter the serial number of each device, separated by commas. This method is usually convenient only for small numbers of devices.

   - *Order Number*: Enter the order number. This is usually the most convenient way of assigning large numbers of devices.

   - *Upload CSV File*: Select the comma-separated values (CSV) file that contains the serial numbers for the devices you want to add.

■ **Tip** If you need to split the devices in an order between your MDM servers, download a CSV file containing all the s erial numbers in the order, and then divide that CSV file into smaller files containing the groups of devices you need.

---

3. Click the Perform Action pop-up menu, click the Assign to Server item on the pop-up menu, and then click the appropriate server.

4. Click the Done button.

■ **Note** If you have an Apple Authorized Service Provider replace an iPad or other iOS device that was enrolled in Apple School Manager, you can normally enroll the replacement device. You can identify the device using its order number, which starts with R because it is a replacement. Assign the device manually to your MDM server.

REVIEWING YOUR SCHOOL'S DEVICE ASSIGNMENTS

When you need to see which devices are assigned where, click the Assignment History item in the sidebar to display the list of assignments. Then click the Details button on an assignment to display the details for that assignment. You can then see the following details:

- The number of devices in the assignment

- The order numbers for the devices

- The date each device was assigned or unassigned

- The MDM server to which each device is assigned

- Who assigned each device to the MDM server

Click the Download button if you want to download a CSV file containing the serial numbers of the devices in the assignment.

Unassigning and Reassigning Devices

If you move a device from one location to another, you can unassign the device from its current MDM server and assign it to another MDM server.

To unassign a device, follow these steps:

1. Click the Device Assignments item in the sidebar.

2. Click the button for the device unassignment method you want to use. Your options are the same as for assigning devices:

   - *Serial Number*: Enter the serial number of each device, separated by commas. Use this method for unassigning small numbers of devices.

   - *Order Number*: Enter the order number. Use this method for unassigning a whole order's worth of devices.

   - *Upload CSV File*: Select the comma-separated values (CSV) file that contains the serial numbers for the devices you want to unassign. This is often the most convenient method of unassigning devices.

3. Click the Perform Actions pop-up menu, and then click the Unassign Devices item on the pop-up menu.

4. Click the Done button.

After unassigning the devices, you can reassign them by assigning them to a different MDM server.

Releasing Devices from Apple School Manager

When you no longer need to manage a device with Apple School Manager, you can *release* the device, removing it permanently from the Apple School Manager system. Apple School Manager's terms and conditions require schools to release any devices that they no longer own. If, for example, your school transfers ownership of iPads to students when they leave the school, you'll need to release those iPads from Apple School Manager.

■ **Caution**   You can never add back a device that you've released from Apple School Manager, so don't be tempted to try out the command.

To release one or more devices from Apple School Manager, follow these steps:

1. Click the Device Assignments item in the sidebar.

2. Click the button for the device release method you want to use. Your options for identifying the devices should seem familiar by now:

    -   *Serial Number*: Enter the serial number of each device, separated by commas. Use this method for releasing individual devices or small groups of devices.

    -   *Order Number*: Enter the order number. Use this method for releasing a whole order's worth of devices.

    -   *Upload CSV File*: Select the comma-separated values (CSV) file that contains the serial numbers for the devices you want to release. This method tends to give you the greatest flexibility.

3. Click the Perform Actions pop-up menu, and then click the Release Devices item on the pop-up menu.

4. Click the Done button. A confirmation dialog opens.

5. Select the I Understand That This Cannot Be Undone check box.

6. Click the Release button.

7. Click the OK button. Apple School Manager releases the devices.

Summary

In this chapter, you've learned about Apple School Manager, Apple's one-stop solution for deploying and managing Macs and iOS devices in schools. You now know when to work directly in Apple School Manager and when to work indirectly through your MDM solution instead. When working directly in Apple School Manager, you know how to sign up your school, run Setup Assistant to get started, and work with locations, user accounts, classes, roles, and devices.

In the next chapter, we'll look at how to manage iPads using MDM tools.

CHAPTER 6

■ ■ ■

Managing iPads with Mobile Device Management

This chapter discusses how to manage your school's iPads with mobile device management (MDM) solutions. MDM enables you to automate many aspects of deploying, configuring, and controlling iPads, so if your school has any serious deployment of iPads, you'll likely be using MDM.

Many different MDM solutions are available, most of which work with not only iOS devices (such as iPads) but also with other operating systems for mobile devices, such as Android, Windows, macOS, and Windows Phone. There's a good chance that your school has already implemented an MDM solution—in which case, you'll presumably want to use that solution for managing your iPads rather than layering another MDM solution on top.

I don't know which (if any) MDM solution your school is using, and there's no way this chapter can cover all of them—so the chapter takes a more general approach. We'll start by getting an overview of the MDM solutions available for managing iPads and discussing the key differences among them, in case your school doesn't have an MDM solution and you need to choose one. We'll then look at key aspects of what you can do to iPads using MDM solutions, using a couple of MDM solutions for examples. This coverage is also general, because although most MDM solutions have similar capabilities, they implement those capabilities in different ways.

Understanding and Choosing Mobile Device Management Solutions for iPad

As discussed in earlier chapters, Apple has built various management capabilities into iOS. You can use Apple Configurator and Apple School Manager to tap into these management capabilities, but you can also use third-party MDM solutions. For example, you can use MDM to set up an iPad automatically, apply profiles and other restrictions to the iPad over the air, locate an iPad if it goes missing, or even wipe a lost iPad remotely.

As of this writing, many different MDM solutions are available that include capabilities for managing Apple devices; most tools work for both Macs and iOS devices, because macOS also contains extensive management capabilities, and many work for other mobile operating systems as well. In this chapter, we'll concentrate on MDM solutions for iOS, because this book is about deploying the iPad.

© Guy Hart-Davis 2017
G. Hart-Davis, *Deploying iPads in the Classroom*,
https://doi.org/10.1007/978-1-4842-2928-6_6

You'll find that most of the MDM tools offer similar functionality with iPads. That's because Apple has made iOS expose a certain set of capabilities to MDM tools, and most MDM vendors implement all those capabilities so as to compete effectively with each other.

If you need to choose an MDM solution for your school, your starting point will likely be the number of iPads and other devices your school plans to deploy. Chances are, the more devices you need to manage, the heavier-duty your MDM will need to be, because heavier-duty MDM gives you more management capabilities and can reduce the amount of time and effort you need to expend.

Apart from the number of devices, you'll probably want to concentrate on four key differentiating points when choosing an MDM solution:

- *Cloud-based MDM versus server-based MDM*: Some MDM solutions work entirely in the cloud: you log in via a web browser on whichever computer or device you happen to be using, and perform all your administration through the browser. The data is stored in the cloud. Other MDM solutions require you to run an app on a server locally. Some server-based MDM solutions also let you store data in the cloud.

- *Client operating systems*: Some MDM solutions can handle not only iOS but also Android, Windows, macOS, and other operating systems, such as Windows Phone and Chrome OS. If you're choosing an MDM solution for your school, you'll presumably want it to be able to handle all the operating systems you're currently using and any you plan to add in the foreseeable future.

- *Cost*: Some MDM solutions have straightforward pricing, such as $2 per device per month; some have different levels of per-device-per-month pricing to let you choose the features you need. For other MDM solutions, costs are much more opaque, and you may need to specify your school's requirements before you can learn the price.

- *Support for education features in iOS 9.3 and later versions*: iOS 9.3, released in January 2016, added support for Apple School Manager (discussed in Chapter 5), for the Shared iPad feature (discussed in Chapter 5), and for the Classroom app (discussed in Chapter 8). If you need to use any of these features, you'll need an MDM solution that supports them. Table 6-1 summarizes the MDM solutions that Apple identifies as fully supporting the education features in iOS 9.3 and later versions.

Table 6-1. *MDM Solutions Compatible with Education Features in iOS 9.3 and Later Versions*

MDM Solution	Vendor	Website	Client Operating Systems	Cloud or Server
VMWare AirWatch	VMWare	www.air-watch.com	iOS, Android, Chrome, Windows, macOS, Tizen, QNX, Windows CE	Server
Cisco Meraki	Cisco Systems	meraki.cisco.com	iOS, Android, Windows, macOS, Windows Phone, Chrome OS	Cloud
FileWave	FileWave	www.filewave.com	iOS, Android, macOS, Windows	Server
ZuluDesk	ZuluDesk BV	www.zuludesk.com	iOS, macOS	Cloud
HEAT LANrev	Ivanti	www.heatsoftware.com	iOS, Android, Windows, macOS, Windows Phone	Server
Mobile Manager	Lightspeed Systems	www.lightspeedsystems.com	iOS, Android, Chrome, macOS, Windows	Cloud
Mosyle Manager	Mosyle	www.manager.mosyle.com	iOS, macOS	Cloud
TabPilot	TabPilot	www.tabpilot.com	iOS, Android, macOS	Cloud
JAMF Pro	JAMF Software	www.jamf.com	iOS, macOS	Cloud or server

■ **Note** Various MDM solutions have changed hands and names over the past few years. For example, in November 2012, Cisco Systems bought Meraki; in January 2014, VMWare bought AirWatch; and in January 2017, LANDESK and HEAT Software merged to form Ivanti (www.ivanti.com). Also in early 2017, JAMF Software renamed Casper Suite to Jamf Pro and Bushel to Jamf Now. So, if any of the MDM solutions or the websites seems to have gone missing, try searching to see if it has been bought, consolidated, or renamed.

Setting Up, Navigating, and Configuring Your MDM Solution

If you're adding MDM to your school, you'll need to set up the MDM solution you've chosen, work out how to navigate its interface, and configure it with essential data and digital certificates. As you'd imagine, setup, navigation, and configuration vary hugely depending on the MDM solution, so this section skates briefly over these topics, providing a few examples.

Setting Up Your MDM Solution

Not surprisingly, setting up your MDM solution is entirely different for server-based MDM than for cloud-based MDM. For example, for the server-based VMWare AirWatch, you'll need to choose which of several deployment configurations to use—single-server, multi-server, or a hybrid configuration—and then install the server software on suitable machines. By contrast, with a cloud-based MDM solution such as Meraki Systems Manager, you just need to log into your school's account via a web browser.

Navigating Your MDM Solution

Once you're logged in to your MDM solution, you'll need to come to grips with its interface. There's too much variation here to cover sensibly, but the MDM vendors usually try to make navigation as straightforward as possible. Here are two examples:

- *TabPilot*: The TabPilot control center is called Control Tower. The sidebar on the left side of the window gives you access to the Dashboard screen (shown in Figure 6-1), the collapsible Organization pane, the collapsible Location pane, and the Status screen.

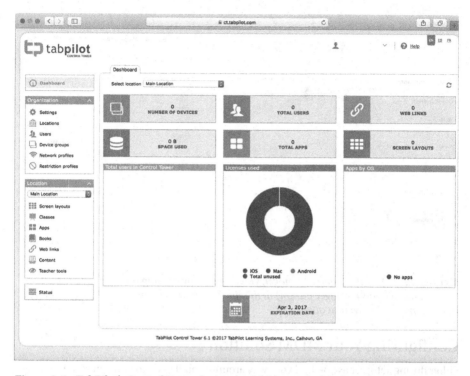

Figure 6-1. *TabPilot's Control Tower features a sidebar on the left that gives you access to the Dashboard, items in the Organization category, items in the Location category, and the Status screen*

- *Meraki Systems Manager*: You access most of the commands by clicking the Systems manager button or the Organization button in the sidebar on the left of the window and then making a choice in the pop-up panel that opens. Figure 6-2 shows Meraki Systems Manager with the Systems manager pop-up panel open, which gives access to three categories of commands: the Monitor category, the MDM category, and the Configure category.

Figure 6-2. *In Meraki Systems Manager, you navigate by clicking the appropriate button (such as the Systems manager button) in the sidebar on the left and then making a choice from the pop-up panel that opens*

Configuring Your MDM Solution

Either during setup or as you find your way around, you'll need to perform some configuration in your MDM solution. Again, the specifics vary depending on the MDM solution, but you'll normally need to enter information about your organization, choose security settings, and so forth.

First, locate the settings you need. For example, in Meraki Systems Manager, you click the Organization tab on the left to display the Organization pop-up panel (see Figure 6-3). You can then go to the Configure column on the right of the pop-up panel and click the appropriate button, such as the Settings button, to bring you to the settings screen, such as the Meraki Systems Manager Settings screen shown in Figure 6-4.

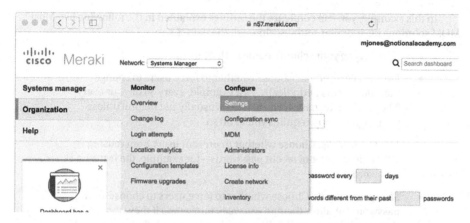

Figure 6-3. *In your MDM solution, navigate to the area for configuring settings. For example, in Meraki Systems Manager, click the Organization button in the sidebar, and then click the Settings button in the Configure column*

Figure 6-4. *This Settings screen in Meraki Systems Manager enables you to configure organization, security, SAML configuration, administration, privacy, SNMP, and Dashboard API access settings*

In this example, you can configure the settings explained in the following list. Most MDM solutions have similar settings, although the names vary.

- *Name*: Type your school's name in this box.

- *Password expiration*: Choose whether to force users to change their passwords periodically—for example, every 30 days or every 90 days. Forcing password changes is usually not helpful unless your organization requires you to do so.

- *Used passwords*: Choose whether to prevent users from reusing a specific number of recent passwords—for example, the last 10 passwords.

- *Strong passwords*: Choose whether to force users to choose strong passwords or allow them to use weak passwords if they want. If users will keep any sensitive or valuable data on their iPads, strong passwords are a must.

- *Account lockout*: Choose whether to lock a user account after a specific number of failed login attempts. Setting an account lockout is good for security, but you'll need to allow the user a reasonable number of attempts to type the credentials accurately.

- *Idle timeout*: Choose whether to log users out automatically after a specific number of minutes of activity.

- *Two-factor authentication*: Choose whether to force users to set up and use two-factor authentication. Two-factor authentication is a great security measure for iPads that go beyond the school's boundaries. If the iPads remain within the school, you likely don't need to use two-factor authentication.

- *Login IP ranges*: Choose whether to restrict access to the MDM solution to IP addresses in those ranges that you specify. This feature can help you to reduce the risk of unauthorized access to your MDM solution.

- *SAML SSO*: Choose whether to use Security Assertion Markup Language (SAML) for authenticating users and providing a means of Single Sign-On (SSO). If you choose the SAML SSO Enabled item in the SAML SSO pop-up menu, click the Add a SAML IdP link to add a SAML Identity Provider.

- *Licensing notifications*: Choose whether to send licensing notifications only to administrators in your organization.

- *Block Meraki support*: Choose whether to block Meraki's support from viewing your organization.

- *SNMP Version 2C*: Choose whether to enable or disable Simple Network Management Protocol (SNMP) version 2C.

- *SNMP Version 3*: Choose whether to enable or disable SNMP version 3.

- *SNMP IP Restrictions*: Choose whether to restrict SNMP to specific IP addresses or ranges, or to allow SNMP queries from all IP addresses.

- *Dashboard API access*: Choose whether to enable access to the Cisco Meraki Dashboard API.

As another example, in TabPilot's Control Tower, you click the Settings button in the Organization pane in the sidebar to display the Settings screen (see Figure 6-5). Here, you can click the seven tabs across the top to configure the following categories of settings:

- *System*: On this tab, you can choose which country's Apple App Store to use (for example, United States) and enable or disable the Apple Classroom app.

- *Permissions*: On this tab (shown in Figure 6-5), you can specify the permissions for the Teacher group, the Technician group, the Location Admin group, and the Organization Admin group.

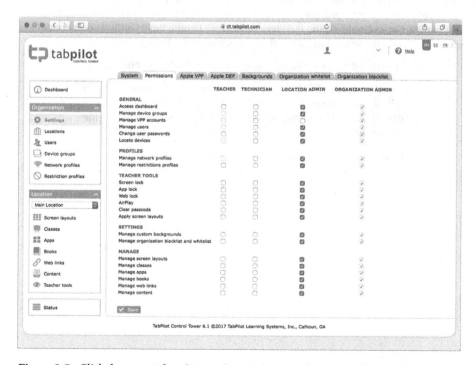

Figure 6-5. *Click the seven tabs—System, Permissions, Apple VPP, Apple DEP, Backgrounds, Organization whitelist, and Organization blacklist—across the top of TabPilot's Control Tower to access different categories of settings*

- *Apple VPP*: On this tab, you can add your school's membership in Apple's Volume Purchase Program.

- *Apple DEP*: On this tab, you can add your school's membership in Apple's Device Enrollment Program. You can also control which setup screens the iOS Setup Assistant displays when an iPad is being set up.

- *Backgrounds*: On this tab, you can upload and manage background images to use in screen layouts.

- *Organization whitelist*: On this tab, you can build a whitelist of websites your school permits access to.

- *Organization blacklist*: On this tab, you can build a blacklist of websites that your school blocks.

Downloading a Signed Certificate from Apple

Depending on the MDM solution, you may need to add a signed certificate (a digital identifier) from Apple before you can start managing iOS devices or Macs. If so, the MDM solution normally provides easy-to-follow steps for requesting the certificate and installing it. For example, Figure 6-6 shows the APNS (Apple Push Notification Service) screen in Meraki Systems Manager, which walks you through these three steps:

- Downloading a Certificate Signing Request (CSR for short).

- Going to Apple's Push Certificates Portal, uploading the CSR (thus telling Apple which MDM vendor you want to use), and then downloading the push certificate. The certificate has the .pem file extension.

- Uploading the push certificate to the MDM vendor.

Figure 6-6. *You may need to add a signed certificate from Apple before you can start using MDM. The MDM vendor typically walks you through the process of getting and adding the certificate*

Once you've done this, you'll typically see confirmation that the push notification certificate is configured correctly. Figure 6-7 shows the screen you see in Meraki Systems Manager.

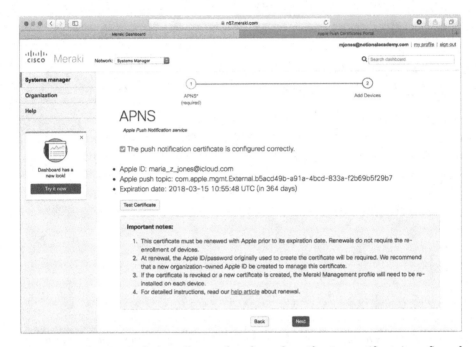

Figure 6-7. *The MDM solution tells you when the push notification certificate is configured correctly*

Managing iPads with MDM

Once you've set up your MDM solution and configured its settings, you should be ready to start managing your school's iPads. This section shows actions that you can take with a typical MDM solution, again using Meraki Systems Manager and TabPilot for examples. As in the rest of this chapter, exactly what you can do will depend on the MDM solution you're using.

Enrolling iPads in Your MDM Solution

Once you've added any push notification certificate needed for your MDM solution to work (as discussed in the previous section), you can start enrolling your iPads in the MDM solution. Depending on the MDM solution, you can usually enroll an iPad in any of several ways:

- Manually

- Using Apple Configurator

- Using DEP

Enrolling an iPad Manually

The first way of enrolling iPads in your MDM solution is enrolling them manually. This example uses Meraki Systems Manager:

1. Click the Systems manager button in the sidebar to display the pop-up panel.

2. Click the Clients button in the Monitor column to display the Client list screen.

3. Click the Add Devices button. The Add Devices screen appears (see Figure 6-8), offering you the choice between using the Mobile Browser method and the iOS App method. The Mobile Browser method uses a browser app (such as Safari) on the iPad; the iOS App method involves installing a custom app on the iPad. In this example, we'll use the Mobile Browser method.

Figure 6-8. *From the Add Devices screen in Meraki Systems Manager, you can add an iPad by navigating to the Meraki website and entering a network ID or by scanning a QR code in the SM iOS app*

4. On the iPad, press the Home button to display the Home screen, and then tap the Safari icon to open Safari.

5. Tap in the address box, type *m.meraki.com*, and then tap the Go button on the keyboard. The Meraki SM Setup screen appears (see Figure 6-9).

Figure 6-9. On the Meraki SM Setup screen, tap in the box, type the Network ID shown on the Mac you're using for administering Meraki Systems Manager, and then tap the Register button

6. Tap in the box and type the Network ID shown in the Mobile Browser box on the Add Devices screen. (The Add Devices screen is on the Mac.)

7. Tap the Register button. Meraki begins installing a profile on the iPad. The Settings app opens and displays the Install Profile dialog (see Figure 6-10).

Figure 6-10. In the Install Profile dialog in the Settings app, you can tap the More Details button to view more details about the profile, or simply tap the Install button to proceed with the installation

8. To see the details of the profile you're installing, tap the More Details button. A dialog called Meraki Management (the name of the profile) opens, showing the contents of the profile (see Figure 6-11).

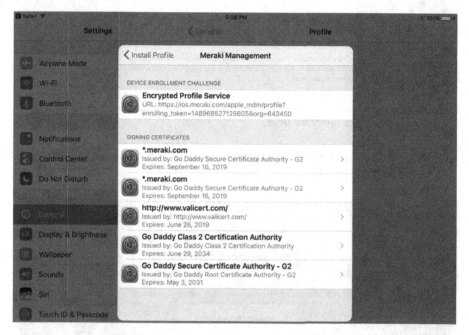

Figure 6-11. *You can display the Meraki Management dialog to view the contents of the profile. From here, you can tap one of the buttons in the Signing Certificates box to display the details of the certificate*

9. Optionally, tap one of the buttons in the Signing Certificates box to display the details of that certificate. Tap the Back (<) button in the upper-left corner when you're ready to return to the Meraki Management dialog.

10. When you finish viewing the contents of the profile, tap the Install Profile (<) button to return to the Install Profile dialog.

11. Tap the Install button. The Enter Passcode dialog opens.

12. Type your login passcode for the iPad to authorize installing the profile. A second Install Profile dialog opens.

13. Tap the Install button. The iPad enrolls the Meraki certificates and then displays the Warning dialog (see Figure 6-12) to let you know that installing the profile will allow the administrator to remotely manage the iPad.

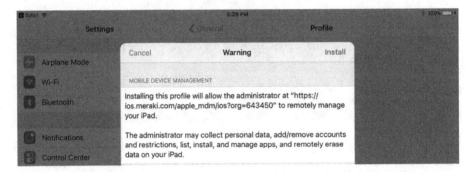

Figure 6-12. *The Warning dialog makes sure you know that installing the profile will enable remote management of the iPad*

14. Tap the Install button. The Remote Management dialog opens (see Figure 6-13).

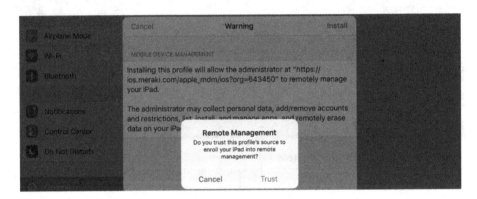

Figure 6-13. *Tap the Trust button in the Remote Management dialog*

15. Tap the Trust button. The Profile Installed dialog opens (see Figure 6-14), confirming that the profile has been installed.

Figure 6-14. *The Profile Installed dialog opens to confirm that you have installed the profile on the iPad*

16. Tap the Done button. The iPad then displays the Safari window again (see Figure 6-15), where the Meraki SM Setup page confirms that registration is complete.

Figure 6-15. *The Meraki SM Setup page in Safari confirms that registration is complete for this iPad*

You can now start managing the iPad with Meraki Systems Manager.

Enrolling an iPad Using Apple Configurator

Some MDM solutions enable you to enroll an iPad by downloading a profile and installing it using Apple Configurator. The following example illustrates this process using TabPilot.

1. Click the Device Groups button in the Organization pane in the sidebar to display the Device Groups screen (see Figure 6-16).

Figure 6-16. *On the Device Groups screen in TabPilot Control Tower, click the device group into which you want to enroll the iPad*

Note Enrolling an iPad using Apple Configurator in TabPilot requires you to select a device group. If you haven't yet created any device groups, click the Create button on the Device Groups screen to start creating a new device group. For example, you might create a device group for a class or for a classroom.

---

2. Click the device group into which you want to enroll the iPad. The screen for the device group appears.

3. Click the Device group details tab to display its contents (see Figure 6-17).

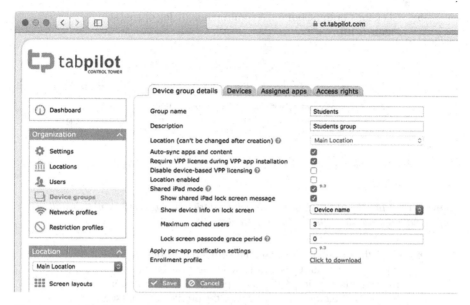

Figure 6-17. *On the Device group details tab for the device group, click the "Click to download" link on the Enrollment profile line*

4. Click the "Click to download" link on the Enrollment profile line. Safari downloads the enrollment profile, which causes the System Preferences app to open and display a dialog prompting you to install the profile (see Figure 6-18).

Figure 6-18. *In this dialog, you can click the Show Profile button to display the profile details or click the Continue button to install the profile*

5. Click the Continue button. A confirmation dialog opens (see Figure 6-19).

Figure 6-19. *Click the Install button in the confirmation dialog if you want to install the profile, making your Mac trust the MDM provider*

6. Click the Install button, and then authenticate yourself by typing your account password and clicking the OK button in the authentication dialog that opens. The Profiles screen in System Preferences then displays the profile's details (see Figure 6-20).

Figure 6-20. *The Profiles screen shows the details of the profile you installed*

7. In Apple Configurator, select the iPad or iPads you want to enroll.

8. Choose Actions ➤ Add ➤ Profiles from the menu bar to open the dialog for selecting profiles.

9. Click the profile you downloaded. You'll normally find it in your Downloads folder unless you've put it elsewhere. The file will have a name such as `enroll.mobileconfig`.

10. Click the Add button. Apple Configurator adds the profile to the iPad.

Enrolling an iPad via DEP

If your school is signed up for Apple's Device Enrollment Program (DEP), you can use DEP as the easiest way to enroll iPads in your MDM solution.

Before you can enroll iPads using DEP, you must enter your DEP account in your MDM solution. How you do this depends on the MDM solution. For example, as you saw earlier in this chapter, in TabPilot Control Tower, you click the Settings button in the Organization pane in the sidebar, click the Apple DEP tab on the tab bar to display the Apple DEP controls, and then click the Add button.

Once you've configured the DEP account, enrollment takes place automatically during setup. After you power on the iPad, you choose the language on the Language screen, choose the region on the Region screen, and connect to a Wi-Fi network on the Wi-Fi screen as usual. When the iPad is connected to the Wi-Fi network, a message appears saying that your institution will automatically configure the iPad. iOS then downloads and installs the MDM profile and walks you through the remaining setup steps.

Viewing a List of Clients

Once you've enrolled your iPads in the MDM solution, they show up in the MDM solution's client list. How you reach the client list depends on the MDM solution, but it's usually easy enough to find. For example, in Meraki Systems Manager, you can click the Systems Manager button in the sidebar and then click the Clients button in the Monitor column of the Systems Manager pop-up panel to display the Client list screen (see Figure 6-21).

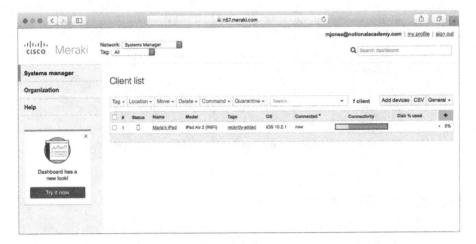

Figure 6-21. *From the Client list screen in Meraki Systems Manager, you can quickly manipulate one or more devices with a single action. You can also display details for a particular device*

From a client list, you can take actions such as these:

- *Select the clients you want to affect*: Select the check box for each client.

- *View details for a client*: Click the client in the Client list to display the details screen (see Figure 6-22).

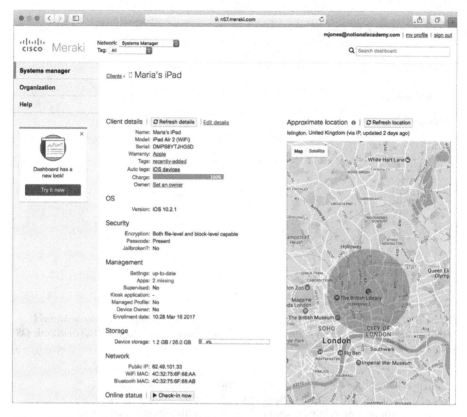

Figure 6-22. *Display the details screen for a client to zero in on specific information*

- *Apply or remove tags*: Use the tag controls, such as the Tag pop-up menu in Meraki Systems Manager, to apply tags to the clients or to remove existing tags.

- *Set or clear the location*: Use the location controls, such as the Location pop-up menu in Meraki Systems Manager, to work with the clients' locations.

- *Move the clients from one network to another*: Use a Move command, such as the Move pop-up menu in Meraki Systems Manager, to move the selected clients to a different network as needed.

- *Give commands and enable features*: Use a feature for giving commands, such as the Command pop-up menu in Meraki Systems Manager (see Figure 6-23), to give commands such as Reboot, Shut Down, Enable Single App Mode, Install available OS updates, Sync apps, or Sync profiles.

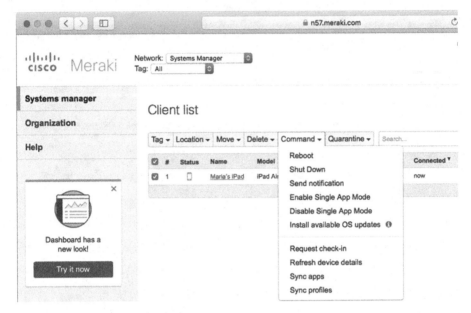

Figure 6-23. *From a command feature, such as the Command pop-up menu in Meraki Systems Manager, you can give commands such as Reboot, Shut Down, Install available OS updates, or Sync apps*

- *Quarantine a client*: Use a quarantine feature, such as the Quarantine pop-up menu in Meraki Systems Manager, to give quarantine-related commands, such as authorizing the use of a file that has been quarantined or running a selective wipe of quarantined files.

Viewing an iPad's Device Management or Removing Management

Working on an iPad, you can quickly view which device management (if any) has been applied. If the device management is not locked in place, you can remove it.

To view the device management, press the Home button to go to the Home screen and choose Settings ➤ General ➤ Device Management. On the Device Management screen (see Figure 6-24), you can tap the button in the Mobile Device Management box to display the details of the device management (see Figure 6-25).

Figure 6-24. *On the Device Management screen in the General category of the Settings app on the iPad, tap the button in the Mobile Device Management box to display the Profile screen*

Figure 6-25. *The Profile screen shows the details of the profile applied for device management*

If the Remove Management button appears, you can tap it to start removing the device management. Authenticate yourself by typing your passcode for the iPad in the Enter Passcode dialog that opens, and then tap the Remove button in the Remove Management dialog that opens next (see Figure 6-26).

Figure 6-26. *Tap the Remove button in the Remove Management dialog to remove the device management from the iPad*

After iOS removes the management, the Profile screen appears, either showing any remaining profiles that are installed or (if there are none) the readout "No profiles are currently installed."

Separating Devices into Different Groups

MDM solutions typically enable you to separate your devices into different groups so that you can treat them differently. For example, you can assign specific apps or access rights to a group so that all the group's devices have those apps and rights.

Using groups can greatly simplify administration, so you'll likely want to look into the grouping features your MDM solution offers. Different MDM solutions not only use different terms for grouping but also provide different capabilities. Here are three examples:

- *Jamf Pro*: Jamf Pro enables you to create smart mobile device groups and static mobile device groups. The smart groups draw in all the devices that match the criteria you specify, like a Smart Playlist in iTunes. The static groups contain only those devices that you specifically assign to them, like non-smart playlists in iTunes.

- *TabPilot*: TabPilot provides device groups to which you assign devices. Each device can belong to only one device group at a time, but you can move devices from one device group to another as needed.

- *Meraki Systems Manager*: Meraki Systems Manager provides tags that you can apply either manually or dynamically. As an administrator, you can create tags manually—for example, you might create tags such as "Classroom_25" or "Library"—but Meraki Systems Manager also automatically generates tags based on device type (for example, "iOS devices" and "Android devices"), geofencing (such as "Geofencing - compliant devices"), and security policies.

Creating and Managing Users

MDM solutions enable you to create user accounts for different user types, such as administrators, technicians, teachers, and students. You can assign different capabilities, roles, and permissions to the different user types.

As with most of this chapter, the specifics depend on the MDM solution you're using. For example, TabPilot divides users into Control Tower users, School users, and Apple School Manager users. Control Tower users are people who can log into Control Tower to perform administrative functions. TabPilot has four types of user roles: Organization Admin, Location Admin, Technician, and Teacher. School users are students who won't need to perform any administration and so won't need access to Control Tower. Apple School Manager users are users added through Apple School Manager. Figure 6-27 shows the School users tab of the Users screen in TabPilot Control Tower, from which you can add and delete users.

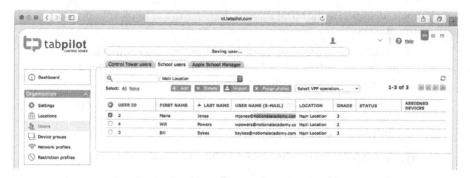

Figure 6-27. *To work with users in TabPilot Control Tower, you click the Users button in the Organization list in the sidebar, and then click the Control Tower users tab or the School users tab on the Users screen*

■ **Tip** Instead of adding users manually, you may be able to create them quickly by importing a list that you output from your school's registration database. For example, TabPilot enables you to import a list from a comma-separated values (CSV) file.

Managing Apps

MDM solutions enable you to manage apps on your iPads automatically. You can typically add apps in three ways:

- Add commercial apps through Apple's Volume Purchase Program (VPP)
- Add commercial apps directly from the App Store
- Add enterprise apps from your school

Assigning Apps with Volume Purchase Program

Most MDM solutions enable you to distribute and manage apps bought with Apple's Volume Purchase Program, or VPP. VPP is usually the easiest and most efficient way to handle commercial apps for many iPads.

To use VPP, you need to set up your school's VPP account in the MDM solution. This is a straightforward process that involves downloading the VPP service token file (an electronic identifier) to the MDM solution. Here are two examples of where to perform this process:

- *Meraki Systems Manager*: Click the Systems manager button in the sidebar, and then click the VPP button in the MDM column of the Systems manager pop-up panel.

- *TabPilot Control Tower*: In the Organization box, click the Settings button to display the Settings screen, and then click the Apple VPP tab on the tab bar.

After setting up VPP, you can distribute VPP licenses in either of two ways:

- *Assign licenses to iOS devices*: This method uses an iOS device's serial number to identify the device uniquely. Using this method, you can push apps to a device without the device having a user signed in using an Apple ID. With supervised devices, you can install apps "silently"—without the user being notified. You'd typically use this method with iPads kept in the classroom and shared among students.

- *Assign licenses to users*: This method requires a user to be signed in on the iPad with an Apple ID. You'd typically use this method with iPads issued to students.

■ **Note**   There's actually a third way to distribute VPP licenses: you can distribute codes that users then redeem. But Apple has deprecated this way of distributing VPP licenses—in other words, Apple has recommended people no longer use this method—and the other two methods are usually better.

Adding Apps from the App Store

You can also add apps from the App Store. This capability is useful both if you school doesn't have a VPP account and when you want to add individual apps to iPads.

For example, in TabPilot Control Tower, you click the Apps button in the Location list in the sidebar to display the Apps screen. You can then click the Add app button to display the Add app dialog (see Figure 6-28). Here, you can click the VPP Apps tab or the App Store tab to display the appropriate controls, search for an app, select its check box, and then click the Add button to add it. Select the Free only check box if you want to restrict the search to free apps.

Figure 6-28. *In TabPilot Control Tower, you can search for apps on the App Store, optionally limiting results to free apps only. When you find an app you want to add, select its check box and click the Add button*

Adding Enterprise Apps

If your school has developed apps in-house for teachers or students, you can distribute them as enterprise apps. For example, in Meraki Systems Manager, you go to the Apps screen, click the Add new button, and then click the iOS enterprise app item on the pop-up menu. This brings you to the Enterprise iOS App screen (see Figure 6-29), where you identify the app, upload it to Meraki, and specify the devices on which to install the app and which options to use for the installation.

Figure 6-29. *You can use the Enterprise iOS App screen in Meraki Systems Manager to upload an enterprise app to your account so that you can load it onto your school's iPads*

Working with Profiles

To configure your school's iPads, you can apply profiles to them via your MDM solution. Most MDM solutions enable you to create new managed profiles and upload profiles you've created in Apple Configurator. Depending on the MDM solution, you may be able to create profiles that are specific to that MDM solution and Apple-specific profiles.

■ **Note**   See the section "Working with Configuration Profiles" in Chapter 4 for details on creating profiles in Apple Configurator.

For example, in Meraki Systems Manager, you start working with profiles by clicking the Systems manager button in the sidebar, and then clicking the Settings button in the MDM column. On the "Profiles & settings" screen, click the "Create a profile" button to start creating a profile. You can then set the profile's name, description, removal policy, and scope on the Profile configuration tab (see Figure 6-30). (The *scope* specifies the devices to which the profile applies—for example, All Devices, or just specific devices.)

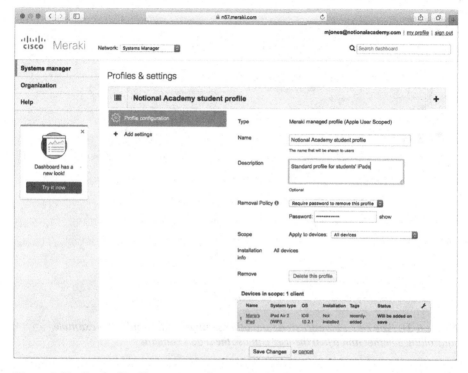

Figure 6-30. *On the "Profiles & settings" screen in Meraki Systems Manager, enter the name and description for the profile, specify its removal policy, and choose which devices to apply it to*

Next, click the Add settings tab and add restrictions to the profile (see Figure 6-31). Meraki Systems Manager breaks up the restrictions into different categories than Apple Configurator, but you can search to find the restrictions you need.

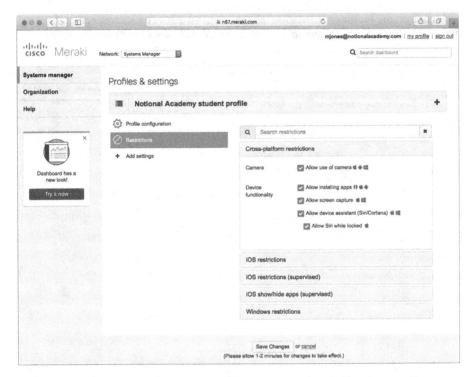

Figure 6-31. You can add restrictions and other settings to the profile—for example, controlling whether and when the user can use the iPad's cameras

Scheduling Software Updates

Most MDM solutions enable you to manage updates to iOS on iPads you've enrolled in the MDM solution via DEP. This feature enables you to keep your school's iPads up to date no matter where the iPads are physically located.

For example, in Meraki Systems Manager, display the Client list screen by clicking the Systems manager button in the sidebar and then clicking the Clients button in the Monitor column in the pop-up panel. You can then select the check box for each iPad you want to update, click the Command pop-up button, and then click the Install available OS updates item on the pop-up menu. In the confirmation dialog that opens, click the OK button to proceed.

■ **Tip** If the iPads are on the same network, it's usually a good idea to stagger the updates over a few hours to avoid bandwidth problems.

Tracking Misplaced iPads with Lost Mode

Most MDM solutions enable you to use the Lost Mode feature to track down managed iPads that have gone missing. You need to enable Lost Mode before you can use it, and—if you get the iPad back—disable Lost Mode afterward.

As you'd expect, different MDM solutions implement Lost Mode differently, but here's an example using TabPilot:

1. In Control Tower, click the Device groups button in the Organization list to display the Device groups screen.

2. Click the group that contains the iPad you want to affect. The screen for the device group appears, showing the iPads in the device group.

3. Click the iPad to display its details screen. The Device details tab appears at first by default (see Figure 6-32).

Figure 6-32. *On the Device details tab for an iPad in TabPilot Control Tower, you click the Lost mode button to enable Lost Mode so that you can track the iPad's location*

4. Click the Lost mode button at the bottom of the screen. The "Lost mode" dialog opens (see Figure 6-33).

Figure 6-33. *In the "Lost mode" dialog in TabPilot Control Tower, enter your contact phone number, a message to whoever finds the iPad, and any footnote needed*

5. In the Phone number box, type your contact phone number.

6. In the Message box, type a message to the person who finds the iPad—for example, asking him or her to call the phone number to arrange the iPad's return.

7. In the Footnote box, type any extra information needed.

8. Click the Lost mode button. TabPilot Control Tower sends the command to put the iPad into Lost mode. The iPad's screen displays the phone number, message, and any footnote you set.

9. Click the Save button to save the changes.

Once you've enabled Lost mode, you can learn the iPad's location by clicking the Device Location tab at the top of the details screen for the iPad, and then looking at the map that appears.

After you recover the iPad, you turn off Lost mode by clicking the "Disable lost mode" button on the Device details tab on the details screen for the iPad.

Summary

In this chapter, you've learned about using MDM solutions to manage your school's iPads. You now know which MDM solutions fully support the education features in iOS 9.3 and later versions. The specifics for most of the actions you can take with MDM vary depending on the MDM solution, but we've looked at examples of how you perform some of the most common actions.

In the next chapter, we'll look at how to connect the iPads to files, printers, and other resources on the school network.

CHAPTER 7

■ ■ ■

Accessing Files and Printing Documents

In this chapter, we'll look at how to connect your school's iPads to local storage and online storage for accessing existing files and creating new files. We'll also cover how to print documents from iPads to your school's printers.

We'll start with local storage, which is typically the best bet for class-based iPad deployments. We'll cover connecting to shared folders on both Windows Server and macOS Server. For macOS Server, we'll also examine how to configure the File Sharing service to provide personal folders for iPad users and how to configure the Caching service to cache data and speed up network performance. After that, we'll move on to online storage, which is usually the best choice for one-to-one deployments. We'll go through the four leading online storage services—iCloud Drive, Microsoft OneDrive, Dropbox, and Google Drive—and how you access them on iPads. Finally, we'll cover what you need to know about printing.

Accessing Files on Local Storage

For class-based iPad deployments, you'll normally want to provide local storage for sharing files so that students can quickly access the files without burdening your school's Internet connection. In this section, we'll look first at how to access files in shared folders on Windows Server before moving on to look at accessing files in shared folders on macOS Server. We'll also go through how to set up the Caching service on macOS Server to speed up file access.

Accessing Shared Folders on Windows Server

If your school uses Windows Server to share files, you can set up your school's iPads to access those files.

Windows Server typically shares files via SMB, the Server Message Block protocol. As of this writing, iOS doesn't include a feature for connecting to SMB shares, even in the new Files app included in iOS 11, so you'll need to use a third-party app to make the connection. This section uses the FileExplorer app as an example.

© Guy Hart-Davis 2017
G. Hart-Davis, *Deploying iPads in the Classroom*,
https://doi.org/10.1007/978-1-4842-2928-6_7

Getting the FileExplorer App

To get started, install the FileExplorer app on the iPad, either by using the App Store app on the iPad itself or by using Apple Configurator or an MDM solution.

■ **Note** FileExplorer comes in two versions, a free version (called FileExplorer) that's limited to connecting to a single Windows share, and a paid version (called FileExplorer Pro, for $4.99) without limitations. You may want to use the free version to evaluate FileExplorer, but if you decide to use the app seriously, you will likely need to upgrade to FileExplorer Pro.

Once the app is installed, launch FileExplorer by tapping the FileExplorer icon on the Home screen. The FileExplorer screen appears (see Figure 7-1).

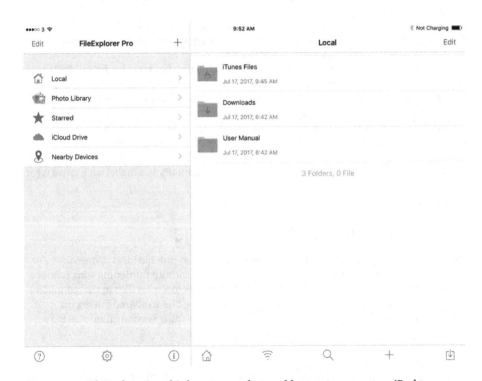

Figure 7-1. *FileExplorer is a third-party app that enables you to connect an iPad to various systems, including shared folders on Windows Server*

Connecting FileExplorer to a Windows Server Share

To connect FileExplorer to a Windows Server share, tap the New Connection (+) button at the top of the left pane in FileExplorer. The New Connections dialog opens (see Figure 7-2).

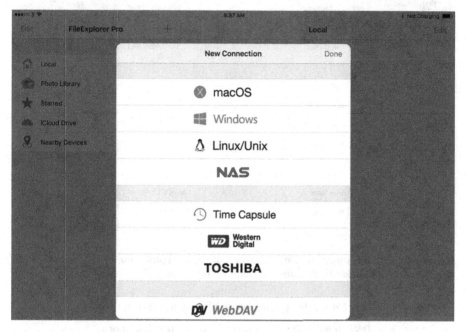

Figure 7-2. *In the New Connection dialog in FileExplorer, tap the Windows button to start connecting to a Windows Server share*

Tap the Windows button. A dialog opens showing fields for making the connection (see Figure 7-3). You can now connect to the shared folder in one of these ways:

- *Fill in the fields*: If you want to control the various aspects of the connection, fill in all the required fields in the Connection section, fill in optional fields as needed in the Connection section and the Connect As section, and set the various switches. Then tap the Save button. The following list explains the fields:

  - *Display Name*: Type the descriptive name you want FileExplorer to display for the share. This field is optional, but it's usually helpful to enter a name that makes clear what the shared folder is and what the user will find there.

405

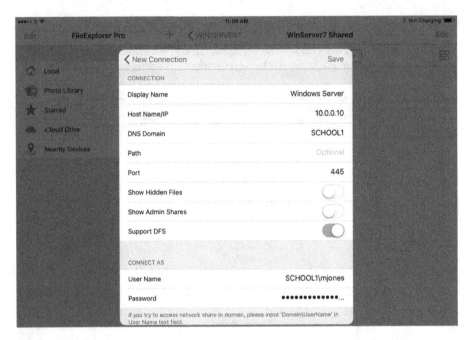

Figure 7-3. *You can control the various aspects of the new connection by entering the details in the Connection section and the Connect As section of this dialog*

- *Host Name/IP*: Type the server's hostname or IP address.

- *DNS Domain*: If the Windows Server system is part of a domain, enter the domain name in this field.

- *Path*: In this optional field, enter the path to the shared folder.

- *Port*: Enter the port for connecting to the share. The default port for connecting to SMB over TCP/IP is 445.

- *Show Hidden Files*: Set this switch to On if you want FileExplorer to display hidden files in the shared folder. You may want to do this for administrators, but users don't normally need to see hidden files.

- *Show Admin Shares*: Set this switch to On if you want FileExplorer to display Windows Server's hidden administrative share points. Normally, you'd want to do this only for administrators, not for users.

- *Support DFS*: Set this switch to On if you want FileExplorer to support DFS, the Distributed File System. You'd want to do this if the Windows Server system uses DFS to present a single view of shared folders that are located on different servers.

- *User Name*: Type the username for the connection—the user's username on the Windows server. If the iPad is connecting as a domain member, enter the username preceded by the domain name and a backslash, such as *SCHOOL1\mjones*.

■ **Note** The User Name and Password fields are marked as optional because you can choose whether to store this information in the connection. Normally, storing the information in the connection is helpful, because it enables the iPad to connect to the shared folder thereafter without having to re-enter the username and password. If you don't save the username and password in the connection, the user must enter them on the iPad when connecting to the shared folder.

- *Password*: Type the password corresponding to the username.

- *Tap the server's button in the Network Neighborhood section*: The Network Neighborhood section at the bottom of the dialog shows a button for each server or shared folder that the FileExplorer app has detected (see Figure 7-4). To connect to the server or shared folder using default settings, tap the appropriate button. In the Connect As dialog that opens (see the left screen in Figure 7-5), tap the Registered User button to connect using a user account. In the Login dialog that then opens (see the right screen in Figure 7-6), type the user's username and password for the Windows server, and then tap either the Login button (to log in without saving the credentials) or the Save & Login button (to log in and save the credentials).

Figure 7-4. You can also connect to a server or shared folder by tapping its name in the Network Neighborhood section at the bottom of the dialog

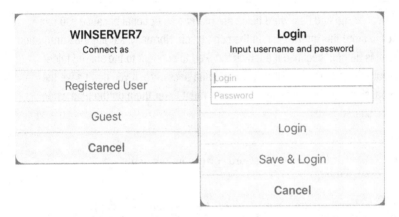

Figure 7-5. Tap the Registered User in the Connect As dialog (left) to connect using a user account. In the Login dialog (right), type the username and password, and then tap either the Login button or the Save & Login button, as needed

Working with Files on a Windows Server Shared Folder

Once you've connected FileExplorer to the Windows Server shared folder, the shared folder appears in the right pane in FileExplorer (see Figure 7-6). Tap the shared folder to display its contents.

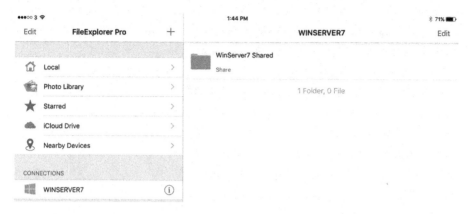

Figure 7-6. *Tap the shared folder to display its contents*

The list of folders and files in the shared folder appears (see Figure 7-7). As usual, you can tap a folder to display its contents.

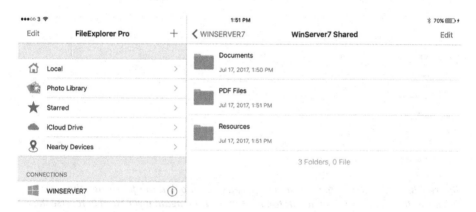

Figure 7-7. *Tap a folder in the right pane of FileExplorer to display the folder's contents*

Once you've opened a folder, the list of files appears (see Figure 7-8). You can navigate the list of files by scrolling up and down, but you can also pull down on the screen a little way to display a toolbar of buttons above the file list (see Figure 7-9). You can then tap the Name, Date, Size, or Type button to sort the files by that attribute. An arrow indicates the sort field, pointing up for an ascending sort (alphabetical order, low numbers to high, early dates to later dates) or down for a descending sort. Tap the same button again to switch between ascending sort order and descending sort order.

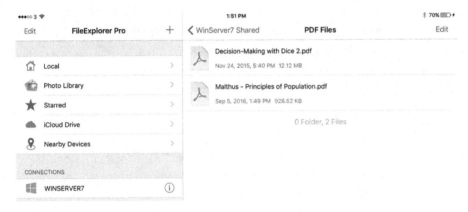

Figure 7-8. *After opening the appropriate folder, you can tap a file to open it in the default app*

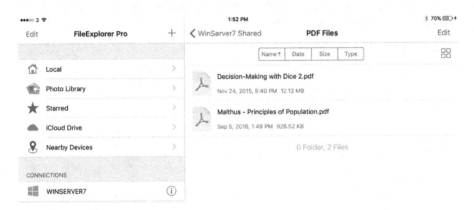

Figure 7-9. *Pull down on the screen to display a toolbar of buttons for sorting the files. Tap the button for the sort you want; tap the same button again if you need to reverse the sort order.*

You can tap a file to open it in the default app. To take other actions, swipe left on the file to display the four icons shown in Figure 7-10. You can then take the following actions:

- *Open the file in another app*: Tap the Share button to display the Share panel (shown on the left in Figure 7-11), and then tap the Open In button. In the Open In panel (shown on the right in Figure 7-11), tap the app you want to use.

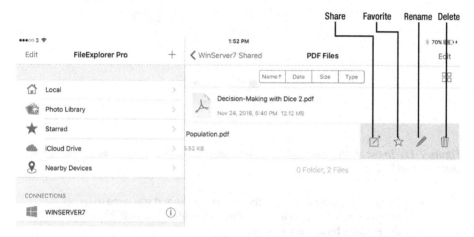

Figure 7-10. Swipe left on a file to display the Share, Favorite, Rename, and Delete buttons

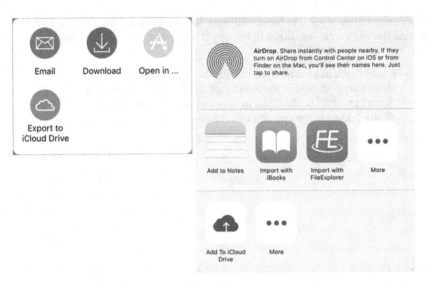

Figure 7-11. *In the Share panel (left), tap the Open In button, and then tap the app in the Open In panel (right)*

- *Make the file a Favorite*: Tap the Favorite button. If you need to remove Favorite status from the file, swipe left again, and then tap the Favorite button once more.

- *Rename the file*: Tap the Rename button to display the Rename dialog. Type the new name, and then tap the OK button.

- *Delete the file*: Tap the Delete button to display the Delete dialog, and then tap the Delete button in it.

Accessing Files on macOS Server Shared Folders

In this section, we'll go through how to connect iPads to shared folders on macOS Server. macOS Server is designed to work with iOS devices, so we'll dig into the topic in depth. First, I'll cover setting up file sharing on macOS Server, including setting the File Sharing service to create personal folders for iOS users. Then I'll examine how to use an iPad to access files in shared folders on macOS Server.

■ **Note**   macOS Server also provides a Caching service that you can use to speed up access to files. I cover Caching service in the next main section.

Setting Up File Sharing on macOS Server

In this section, we'll look at how to set up the File Sharing service on macOS Server to provide file storage accessible to your school's iPads. You can set up both personal folders—a folder for each iOS user who connects to the server, and accessible only by that user—and shared folders that all users or multiple users can access.

Enabling the File Sharing Service

Your first move is to enable the File Sharing service on macOS Server if it's not already enabled. On the Mac that's running macOS Server, follow these steps to enable File Sharing:

1. In the Server app, go to the Services category in the sidebar. If the Services category is collapsed, move the pointer over the Services heading, and then click the Show button to expand the Services category.

2. Click the File Sharing item in the Services category to display the File Sharing pane (see Figure 7-12).

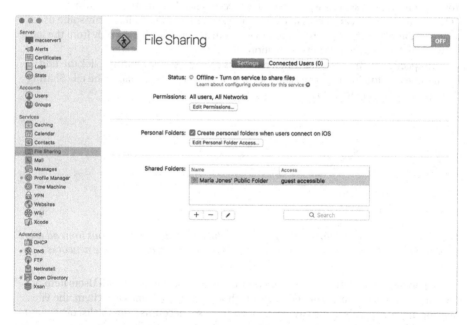

Figure 7-12. *In the File Sharing pane in macOS Server, set the switch in the upper-right corner to On to enable the File Sharing service*

3. Set the switch in the upper-right corner to On. macOS Server turns on the File Sharing service, and the Status readout shows the name under which the server appears in the Finder sidebar (see Figure 7-13).

Figure 7-13. *When you turn on the File Sharing service, the Status readout shows the name under which the server appears in the Finder sidebar*

Controlling Which Users and Which Networks Can Access File Sharing

Your next move is to specify which users can access File Sharing, and from which networks those users can access it. For example, you may want to allow only some users to access File Sharing, or you may want to let them access File Sharing only from the local network, not across an Internet connection.

To specify which users and which networks can access File Sharing, click the Edit Permissions button in the Permissions section of the File Sharing pane. The File Sharing dialog opens (see Figure 7-14).

Figure 7-14. *In the File Sharing dialog, choose whether to allow connections from all users or only specific users; and from all networks, private networks, or only some networks*

Open the Allow Connections From pop-up menu and choose the All Users item or the Only Some Users item, as needed. If you choose the Only Some Users item, the File Sharing dialog expands to display a box for adding user accounts from the list of accounts set up on the macOS Server system (see Figure 7-15).

Figure 7-15. *If you select Only Some Users in the Allow Connections From pop-up menu, click the Add (+) button and add each user to the box that appears*

Set up the list of accounts by clicking the Add (+) button, typing the start of a username, selecting the appropriate match in the list that appears, and then pressing the Return key.

Next, specify the networks from which those users are allowed to connect to File Sharing. Open the When Connecting From pop-up menu, and then click the appropriate item:

- *All Networks*: Select this item to allow the specified users to connect from all networks.

- *Private Networks*: Select this item to allow the specified users to connect only from private networks—that is, networks that use the private IP address ranges.

UNDERSTANDING PRIVATE IP ADDRESS RANGES

There are three private IP address ranges:

- 10.0.0.0–10.255.255: This is a single class A network that contains 16,777,216 IP addresses.

- 172.16.0.0–176.31.255.255: This is 16 contiguous class B networks that contain 1,048,576 IP addresses.

- 192.168.0.0–192.168.255.255: This is 256 contiguous class C networks that contain 65,536 IP addresses.

Normally, your school will already be using one of these private address ranges. Selecting the Private Networks item in the When Connecting From pop-up menu sets File Sharing to accept connections from whichever of these private address ranges the school is using.

- *Only Some Networks*: Select this item to allow the specified users to connect only from the networks you specify.

When you select the Only Some Networks item, the File Sharing dialog expands to show a box for the networks (see Figure 7-16). The Private Networks item appears in the list automatically and is selected at first; you can remove this item by clicking the Remove (–) button or by clicking the Add (+) button and then clicking the This Mac button instead.

Figure 7-16. *When you select the Only Some Networks item in the When Connecting From pop-up menu, you can choose among Private Networks, This Mac, and one or more new networks you create*

To add another network, follow these steps:

1. Click the Add (+) button to open the pop-up menu, and then click the Create a New Network item. The Create a New Network dialog opens (see Figure 7-17).

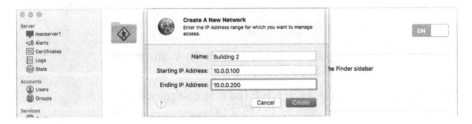

Figure 7-17. *In the Create a New Network dialog, enter the name for the network, type the starting IP address and ending IP address, and then click the Create button*

2. Type the name for the new network in the Name box.

3. Type the starting IP address, such as *10.0.0.100*, in the Starting IP Address box.

416

4. Type the ending IP address, such as *10.0.0.200*, in the Ending IP Address box.

5. Click the Create button.

The new network appears in the box in the File Sharing dialog, and you can add other new networks if needed.

When you finish specifying which connections and networks to allow, click the OK button to close the File Sharing dialog and return to the File Sharing pane.

Setting File Sharing to Create Personal Folders and Configuring Access to Them

Next, in the Personal Folders section of the File Sharing pane, select the Create Personal Folders When Users Connect on iOS check box if you want macOS Server to automatically create a personal folder for each user who connects to the server using an iOS device. Given that you're deploying iPads, you'll normally want to do this.

If you're just using iPads (or other iOS devices) and macOS Server, this is all you need do to connect the iPads so that they can create personal folders. But if you're using other platforms, you may need to allow them access to the personal folders as well. To control access to the personal folders, follow these steps:

1. Click the Edit Personal Folder Access button in the File Sharing pane. The Personal Folder Access dialog opens (see Figure 7-18).

Figure 7-18. *In the Personal Folder Access dialog, specify which protocols to permit to access personal folders by selecting the SMB, AFP, and WebDAV check boxes, as needed. Select the Only Allow Encrypted Connections check box if you want to permit only encrypted connections.*

2. On the Access row, select the appropriate check boxes:

   - *SMB*: Select this check box to permit connections to the personal folders via the Server Message Block (SMB) protocol. SMB is the protocol Windows normally uses for accessing files on other computers.

   - *AFP*: Select this check box to permit connections to the personal folders via the Apple File Protocol (AFP) protocol. AFP is the protocol macOS and OS X use by default for accessing files on other computers.

417

- *WebDAV*: Select this check box to permit connections to the personal folders via the Web Digital Authoring and Versioning (WebDAV) protocol. WebDAV is a protocol that's widely used for accessing files across an Internet connection rather than a local network connection.

3. On the Security row, select the Only Allow Encrypted Connections check box if you want to permit only encrypted connections to the personal folders. Selecting this check box makes the AFP check box on the Access row dimmed and unavailable.

4. Click the OK button to close the Personal Folder Access dialog and return to the File Sharing pane.

Setting Up Shared Folders

You can also set up shared folders accessible by all—or some of—the users. To do so, use the controls below the Shared Folders box in the File Sharing pane like this:

- *Add a shared folder*: Click the Add (+) button below the Shared Folders box. An unnamed dialog for selecting the folder opens. Navigate to the folder you want to share, and then click the Choose button. The folder appears in the Shared Folders box, and you can edit it as explained in the next bulleted paragraph.

■ **Note**   You can click the New Folder button in the unnamed dialog to create a new folder within the current folder.

■ **Tip**   For performance, Apple recommends putting shared folders on a separate drive from system drive of the Mac running macOS Server. For example, you might use a second hard drive or an external hard drive.

- *Edit a shared folder*: Click the shared folder you want to edit, and then click the Edit button (the button with the pencil icon). A dialog opens showing the folder's details (see Figure 7-19). You can then take the following actions:

    - *Change the display name of the shared folder*: Click in the Name box and edit the name. This changes only the name that users see for the folder. The folder's name in the file system remains the same.

- *Browse the folder*: Click the Browse button. If you've made any changes, macOS Server prompts you to save them. macOS Server then closes the dialog, selects the server in the Server list in the sidebar, and displays the Storage tab with the folder highlighted.

- *Change access to the folder*: In the Access area, select or clear the check boxes as needed. Select the iOS check box to allow iOS devices to access the shared folder. Select the SMB check box to allow access via SMB, such as from Windows PCs. Select the AFP check box to allow access via Apple File Protocol, the native Mac protocol; this check box is unavailable if you select the Only Allow Encrypted Connections check box.

- *Change permissions for the folder*: Use the controls in and below the Permissions box to set up the permissions for the folder. To add a user or group from the macOS Server system, click the Add (+) button below the Permissions box, start typing the username or group name on the new line that appears in the box, select the user or group from the list of matches, and then press the Return key. To remove a user or group, click the user or group in the Permissions box and then click the Remove (-) button. To change the permissions for a user or group, click the pop-up menu on the appropriate row in the Permissions box, and then click the appropriate item, such as Read & Write, Read Only, Write Only, or No Access.

■ **Note** The Write Only permission is for folders used as dropboxes. A user can copy or move files to a Write Only folder, but can't view the contents of the folder.

Figure 7-19. When you open a shared folder for editing, you can change the name, specify access types, and grant and revoke permissions

- *Remove a shared folder*: Click the shared folder you want to remove, and then click the Remove (–) button below the Shared Folders box. The Are You Sure You Want to Remove the Selected Share Point? dialog opens (see Figure 7-20). Click the Remove button to remove the shared folder.

Figure 7-20. Click the Remove button in the Are You Sure You Want to Remove the Selected Share Point? dialog

When you finish configuring the shared folder, click the OK button to close the dialog and save the changes.

Using an iPad to Access Files on macOS Server

After setting up personal folders, shared folders, or both on macOS Server, you can connect an iPad to the server. You do this by setting up a macOS Server account on the iPad. You can set up the account either by working directly on the iPad, as explained in the next subsection, or by using policy, as discussed in the second subsection.

Connecting an iPad to macOS Server Manually

To connect an iPad to macOS Server manually, follow these steps on the iPad:

1. Choose Home ➤ Settings ➤ Mail to display the Mail screen in the Settings app.

2. Tap the Accounts button to display the Accounts screen (see Figure 7-21).

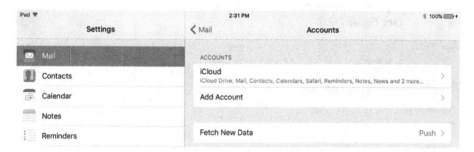

Figure 7-21. *On the Accounts screen in the Settings app, tap the Add Account button to start adding a macOS Server account*

3. Tap the Add Account button to display the Add Account screen (see Figure 7-22).

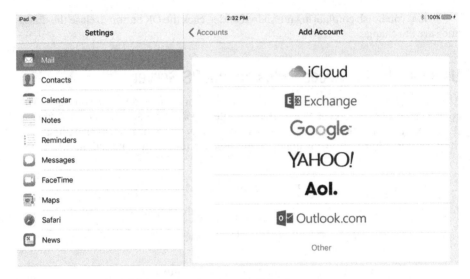

Figure 7-22. On the Add Account screen, tap the Other button

    4. Tap the Other button to display the Other screen (see Figure 7-23).

Figure 7-23. On the Other screen, tap the Add macOS Server Account button

    5. Tap the Add macOS Server Account button to open the macOS Server dialog (see Figure 7-24).

Figure 7-24. In the macOS Server dialog, tap the server you want to connect the iPad to

6. Tap the appropriate button:

- If the macOS server appears by name, tap its button. A dialog opens (see Figure 7-25). Enter the user's username for the macOS Server system and the corresponding password; if you want, edit the Description field to make the name more descriptive or more helpful, and then tap the Next button.

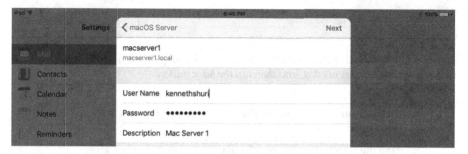

Figure 7-25. *In the dialog for a server whose name appears, type the username and password, edit the server's description if desired, and then tap the Next button*

- If the server doesn't appear by name, tap the Other button to display the dialog shown in Figure 7-26. Tap the Host Name field and type the server's hostname or IP address. Tap the User Name field and type the username, then tap the Password field and type the password. iOS automatically enters in the Description field a description derived from the Host Name field; you can edit this to make the name more descriptive or more helpful. When you finish, tap the Next button. iOS attempts to establish a connection to the server.

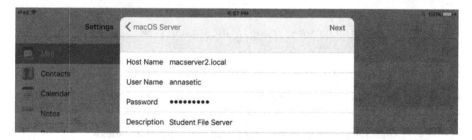

Figure 7-26. *In this dialog, type the name of the macOS server, enter the username and password, improve the description if necessary, and then tap the Next button*

7. Once the iPad has connected to the server, the macOS Server dialog opens (see Figure 7-27).

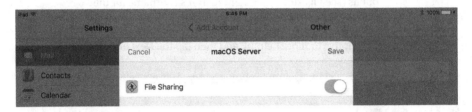

Figure 7-27. *In the macOS Server dialog, set the File Sharing switch and any other switches to On or Off, as needed, and then tap the Save button*

8. Set each switch, such as the File Sharing switch, to On or Off, as needed.

9. Tap the Save button to close the macOS Server dialog and save the connection. The server appears in the Accounts pane (see Figure 7-28).

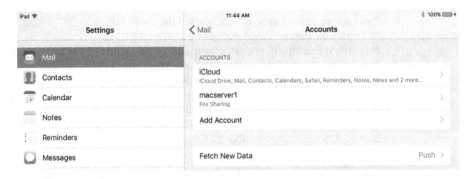

Figure 7-28. *A button for the server appears in the Accounts pane*

Connecting an iPad to macOS Server via Policy

Connecting an iPad to macOS Server manually is useful sometimes, but you'll normally want to use policy instead, either with Apple Configurator or with an MDM solution:

- *Apple Configurator*: Install on the iPad a profile that includes a macOS Server Account payload. See the section "Configuring a macOS Server Account Payload in the Profile" in Chapter 4.

- *MDM solution*: Use the MDM solution to install a profile that includes a macOS Server Account payload. How you do this depends on the MDM tool.

■ **Note**   Normally, you'll create a payload in a profile to set up multiple iPads. In this case, each user will enter the username and password for the macOS Server account manually when installing the profile. In special cases, you may need to create a custom payload containing a payload for an individual user that includes that user's username and password. Doing so is more labor intensive but makes setting up the macOS Server account that much easier for the user.

Using Shared Folders on a macOS Server

Once you've connected an iPad to macOS Server, you can use the server's shared folders from any app that supports document management. Here's an example using Apple's Pages app:

1. Launch the Pages app. For example, press the Home button to display the Home screen, and then tap the Pages icon. Normally, when you launch Pages, the Pages screen appears by default; if a document opens instead, tap the Documents button to display the Pages screen.

2. Tap the Locations button in the upper-left corner of the Pages screen to display the Locations pop-up menu (see Figure 7-29).

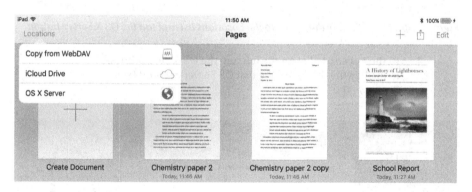

Figure 7-29. *On the Pages screen, tap the Locations button, and then tap the OS X Server item on the Locations pop-up menu*

3. Tap the OS X Server button to display the Browse dialog (see Figure 7-30).

■ **Note**   If tapping the OS X Server button takes you straight to the dialog for a particular location other than the location you want to use, tap the Locations button in the upper-left corner of the dialog to return to the Browse dialog. You can then tap the appropriate location.

Figure 7-30. *In the Browse dialog, go to the Locations list and tap the OS X Server button*

4. In the Locations list on the left, tap the OS X Server button to display the dialog for the macOS Server account (see Figure 7-31).

Figure 7-31. *In the dialog for the macOS Server account, tap the folder you want to open*

5. Tap the folder you want to open. The folder's contents appear (see Figure 7-32).

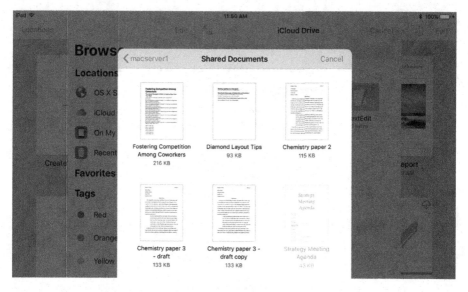

Figure 7-32. Tap the document you want to open from the server

6. Tap the document you want to open. The document opens in Pages.

Setting Up Caching Service on macOS Server to Speed Up Data Delivery

macOS Server includes a Caching service that you can turn on to speed up data delivery on your network. You can configure the Caching service to work for all networks, only local networks, or only specific networks you choose. You can choose whether to share content with other caching servers, and you can specify whether to cache users' personal iCloud data.

To set up the Caching service, follow these steps in macOS Server:

1. In the Server app, go to the Services category in the sidebar. If the Services category is collapsed, move the pointer over the Services heading, and then click the Show button to expand the Services category.

2. Click the Caching item in the Services category to display the Caching pane (see Figure 7-33).

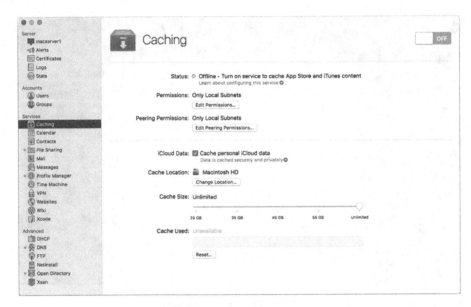

Figure 7-33. *Click the Caching item in the Services category to display the Caching pane, and then set the switch in the upper-right corner to On*

3. Set the switch in the upper-right corner to On. The Status readout shows that the service is available and indicates that devices on the local network will automatically use the Caching service (see Figure 7-34).

Figure 7-34. *The Status readout shows that the Caching service is available*

4. If the Restart Devices to Take Advantage of Caching Immediately dialog opens (see Figure 7-35), select the Do Not Show This Message Again check box, and then click the OK button. You can now restart iPads (or other devices)—or have students and staff restart them—to force the iPads to discover the Caching service sooner rather than later.

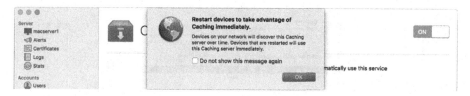

Figure 7-35. *In the Restart Devices to Take Advantage of Caching Immediately dialog, select the Do Not Show This Message Again check box, and then click the OK button*

5. In the Permissions section of the Caching pane, click the Edit Permissions button. The Caching dialog opens (see Figure 7-36).

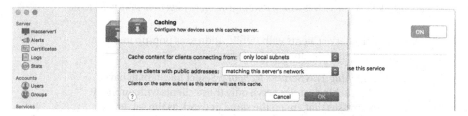

Figure 7-36. *In the Caching dialog, specify the clients for which to cache content and choose how to serve clients with public addresses*

6. Click the Cache Content for Clients Connecting From pop-up menu, and then click the appropriate item:

- *All Networks*: Select this item to enable caching for clients connecting from all networks.

- *Only Local Subnets*: Select this item to limit caching to only clients that connect from local subnets.

- *Only Some Networks*: Select this item to specify the networks for which caching is available. The Caching dialog expands to show a box for the networks (see Figure 7-37). The Private Networks item appears in the list automatically and is selected at first; you can remove this item by clicking the Remove (–) button or by clicking the Add (+) button and then clicking the This Mac item. Alternatively, add another network you've already defined by clicking the Add (+) button and then clicking the network's item on the pop-up menu, as with the Building 2 network shown in the example. You can set up a new network by clicking the Create a New Network button, entering the name, starting IP address, and ending IP address in the Create a New Network dialog (shown in Figure 7-17, earlier in this chapter), and then clicking the Create button.

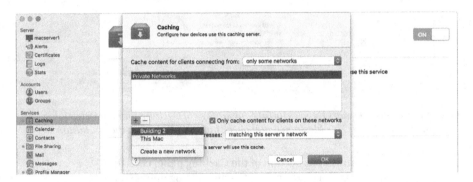

Figure 7-37. *When you select the Only Some Networks item in the Cache Content for Clients Connecting From pop-up menu, you can choose among Private Networks, This Mac, networks you've already created, and one or more new networks you create*

7. Click the Serve Clients with Public Addresses pop-up menu, and then click the appropriate item:

   - *Matching This Server's Network*: Select this item to have the Caching service serve only those clients with public IP addresses that are on the same network as the server.

   - *On Other Networks*: Select this item to have the Caching service serve clients with public IP addresses on other networks as well.

8. Click the OK button to close the Caching dialog and return to the Caching pane.

9. In the Peering Permissions section, click the Edit Peering Permissions button. Another Caching dialog opens (see Figure 7-38).

Figure 7-38. *In this Caching dialog, choose the other caching servers this server's Caching service should share content with*

10. Click the Share Content with Other Caching Servers Connecting From pop-up menu, and then click the appropriate item:

    - *All Networks*: Select this item to allow sharing with caching servers on all networks.

430

- *Only Local Subnets*: Select this item to limit sharing to caching servers on local subnets.

- *Only Some Networks*: Select this item to specify the networks to share cached content with. When you select this item, the dialog expands to show a box for the networks. Add networks as needed by clicking the Add (+) button and then either clicking an existing network's item on the pop-up menu or clicking the Create a New Network item and then working in the Create a New Network dialog. If you need to remove a network from the box, click the network, and then click the Remove (-) button.

11. Click the OK button to close the Caching dialog and return to the Caching pane.

12. In the iCloud Data section, select the Cache Personal iCloud Data check box if you want the Caching service to cache users' personal iCloud data.

13. In the Cache Location section, look at the readout showing the cache's current location. If you need to store the cache elsewhere, click the Change Location button, select the appropriate volume in the Choose the Storage Volume for Cached Content dialog (see Figure 7-39), and then click the Choose button.

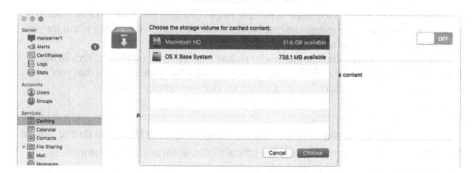

Figure 7-39. *In the Choose the Storage Volume for Cached Content dialog, select the storage volume on which to place the cache, and then click the Choose button*

■ **Note** When you move the cache to a different volume, the Caching service stops caching temporarily so that it can copy its current cache to the new volume. Once copying is complete, caching resumes.

---

14. In the Cache Size area, drag the slider to set the amount of space dedicated to the cache.

15. Look at the Cache Used readout if you need to see how much of the cache is currently in use.

16. If you need to reset the cache, erasing all the data it currently contains, click the Reset button, and then click the Reset button in the Reset Cache Content? dialog that opens (see Figure 7-40).

Figure 7-40. *You can wipe the contents of the cache by clicking the Reset button in the Caching pane and then clicking the Reset button in the Reset Cache Content? dialog*

Accessing Files on Online Storage

If your iPads stay within the school's confines, you may need only local storage, not online storage. If so, great—local storage is not only almost always faster than online storage, but also doesn't burden your school's Internet connection.

But if your school has a one-to-one deployment of iPads, you'll likely need to keep at least some files on online storage so that students can access them as easily when they're outside the school as when they're at school.

In this section, we'll look at four major online storage services: iCloud, OneDrive, Dropbox, and Google Drive. Each online storage service has pros and cons that you'll likely want to evaluate before deciding which service—or services—to use.

Note An alternative way of providing students with access to files when they're outside the school is to enable them to access the school's internal servers across the Internet connection, preferably using a virtual private network (VPN) for security. But unless your school has a heroically fast Internet connection or you're dealing with very small numbers of students, this means of access is likely to be slow or hamstring the school's Internet connection, or both.

Comparing iCloud Drive, OneDrive, Dropbox, and Google Drive

The iCloud Drive, OneDrive, Dropbox, and Google Drive online storage services can all be effective solutions for schools that deploy iPads. Here's what you need to know about each of them:

- *iCloud Drive*: Apple's iCloud Drive should be the first online storage service you evaluate because iOS includes built-in support for it. The iCloud Drive app included in most installations of iOS 10, and the Files app built into iOS 11, connect seamlessly to iCloud, and any app that includes the iOS document-management features can connect to iCloud and store data in it. If your school uses Apple's Pages, Numbers, and Keynote productivity apps, iCloud is usually the best online storage service. Microsoft's Office apps can also store data on iCloud as well as on OneDrive. Each free iCloud account includes 5 GB of storage; as of this writing, you can upgrade to 50 GB ($0.99 per month), 200 GB ($2.99 per month), or 2 TB ($9.99 per month).

- *OneDrive*: Microsoft's OneDrive is a natural fit if your school uses the Office apps, but it also offers strong all-round performance for storing everything from data files to photos and videos online. You can access OneDrive through the OneDrive app for iOS. Each OneDrive account provides 5 GB of storage for free. If you need more space, you can get a 50 GB storage-only OneDrive account for $1.99 per month or pay for an Office 365 account that includes more storage.

- *Dropbox*: Dropbox can be a great way to sync your documents, photos, and videos automatically across multiple devices and platforms—for example, to sync your files across an iPad, an iPhone, and one or more PCs. A free Dropbox account, called Dropbox Basic, provides 2 GB of storage for free—less than the other services mentioned here—but you can earn additional storage by encouraging other people to sign up for Dropbox accounts. You can also pay for extra space by getting a Dropbox Plus account, which provides 1 TB of space for $9.99 (monthly) or $99.99 (yearly).

■ **Note** Higher-educational institutions can also sign up for a Dropbox Education account, which gives 15 GB of storage per user but encourages the use of teams. For a team, each user's 15 GB of storage is pooled, allowing individual team members to have more than 15 GB of files as long as the team's total stays below its limit.

- *Google Drive*: Google's online storage service, Google Drive, is likely to be the best choice if your school uses Google Apps rather than Microsoft Office or Apple's apps for productivity. Google Drive offers 15 GB of space for free, but you can upgrade to 1 TB for $9.99 per month or 10 TB for $99.99 per month; Google Drive even offers 20 TB and 30 TB plans for seriously heavy users. You access Google Drive using the Google Drive app.

The downside to these online storage services is that most require you to install an app to access them—the OneDrive app for OneDrive, the Google Drive app for Google Drive, the Dropbox app for Dropbox, and so on. To help you deal with multiple online storage services, we'll also look at an app that lets you access multiple online storage services—and that can even copy files from one online storage service to another.

Accessing Files on iCloud Drive

Each iPad comes fully equipped to access files on iCloud, so you (or the user) need only set up the appropriate Apple ID on the iPad. When configuring the iPad directly, you can choose settings on the iCloud screen to control which apps can store data in iCloud; when configuring the iPad via policy, you can choose whether to allow iCloud documents and data and whether to allow managed apps to store data in iCloud.

To browse folders and files stored in the iCloud account the iPad is connected to, you can use the iCloud Drive app on iOS 10 (see Figure 7-41) or the iCloud category in the Files app in iOS 11 (see Figure 7-42).

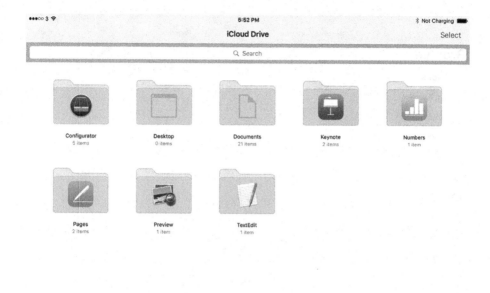

Figure 7-41. On iOS 10, use the iCloud Drive app to browse folders and files stored in the iCloud account the iPad is connected to

---

■ **Tip** In iCloud Drive, you can pull down a short way on the screen to display tab buttons for browsing by date, name, or tags, plus a button for switching between a list layout and a grid layout.

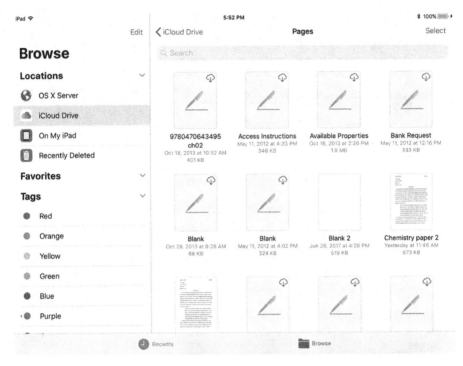

Figure 7-42. *On iOS 11, use the iCloud Drive category in the Files app to browse folders and files in iCloud*

When working within an app, you can tap the iCloud Drive button on the Locations pop-up menu to display the dialog for browsing iCloud Drive.

Accessing Files on OneDrive

To access files on OneDrive, install the Microsoft OneDrive app either manually from the App Store or via policy. Once the app is installed, launch it, and follow the prompts to enter the details of the Microsoft account.

■ **Note**   You can also access files on OneDrive directly from Microsoft Office apps such as Word, Excel, and PowerPoint.

After signing in to OneDrive, you can browse your files, folders, and account details easily by tapping the five tabs at the bottom of the screen:

- *Files tab*: This tab (see Figure 7-43) displays the folders and files in your OneDrive account. As usual, tap a folder to open it so that you can see its contents.

Figure 7-43. *The Microsoft OneDrive app gives you easy access to your files and folders via the five tabs at the bottom of the screen*

- *Photos tab*: This tab lets you browse your photos all together, by albums, or by tags you've applied to the photos. You can also enable or disable the Camera Upload feature, which automatically uploads photos you take with the Camera app.

- *Recent tab*: This tab displays a list of the files you've used recently. This list is often the most convenient way to resume work on a file.

- *Shared tab*: This tab displays the list of items that you're sharing and lists of items that other OneDrive users are sharing with you. You can tap the Enable Notifications link to control whether you receive notifications when other people share items with you.

- *Me tab*: This tab enables you to add other Microsoft accounts to OneDrive, mark files for offline usage (storing them on your iPad and your other devices), see how much storage space you've used and how much remains available, retrieve files from the Recycle Bin, and choose settings for OneDrive.

Accessing Files on Dropbox

To access files on Dropbox, install the Dropbox app either manually from the App Store or via policy. After installing the app, launch it, and tap the Sign In button to start the process of signing in to the Dropbox account. You can then choose setup options, such as uploading some photos or backing up all the photos in the iPad's Camera Roll folder.

Once you've signed in to Dropbox, you can use the four tabs at the bottom of the sidebar to navigate among your files and folders:

- *Recents*: Tap this tab to see a list of recent files and folders arranged in reverse chronological order, so the most recent ones appear first. You can tap a button to open that file or folder, or tap the down-arrow button to display a pop-up panel containing actions you can take with the file or folder. For example, for a document file, the pop-up panel contains the Share, Make Available Offline, Rename, Copy, Move, and Delete buttons.

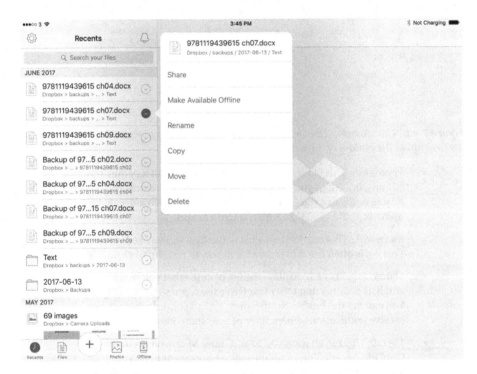

Figure 7-44. The Recents tab in the sidebar of the Dropbox app gives you quick access to files you have used recently. You can tap a file's or folder's down-arrow button to display a pop-up panel of actions you can take with that file or folder.

- *Files*: Tap this button to display an alphabetical list of folders in your account. You can then tap a folder to display its contents.

- *Photos*: Tap this button to display the photos you've uploaded.

- *Offline*: Tap this button to display the list of files you've made available offline.

Accessing Files on Google Drive

To access files on Google Drive, install the Google Drive app either manually from the App Store or via policy. After installing the app, launch it and follow the prompts to connect the Google account. If Two-Step Verification is enabled on the Google account, the account holder must verify the connection via another means, such as by entering on the iPad a one-time verification code sent to the mobile phone number listed in the Google account.

■ **Note**   You can also set up a Google account via policy. For example, in Apple Configurator, create a Google Account payload specifying the account. However, this means of setting up an account is somewhat labor intensive, because you must set up a separate payload (and thus a separate profile containing the payload) for each Google account. You can't specify general parameters for the payload and have the user fill in the e-mail address for the Google account.

Once the account is connected, Google Drive displays the contents of the My Drive folder by default (see Figure 7-45). You can then configure and navigate your account using these moves:

- *Get Notified About New Files prompt*: If this prompt appears, tap the Turn On button or the No Thanks, button, as needed.

- *Folders*: In this area, tap the folder you want to open.

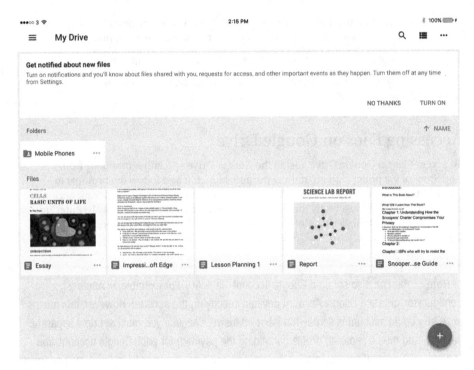

Figure 7-45. *If Google Drive displays the Get Notified About New Files prompt, tap the Turn On button or the No Thanks button, as needed*

- *Files*: In this area, tap the file you want to open.

- *New (+)*: Tap this button to display the New panel (see Figure 7-46). From here, you can create a new folder, upload one or more files, upload a photo you take with the camera, or create a new Google Docs document, Google Sheets workbook, or Google Slides presentation.

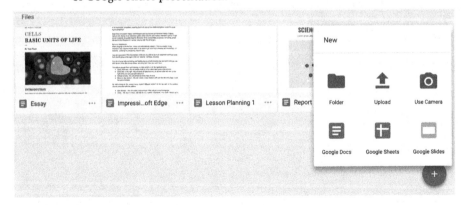

Figure 7-46. *The New panel enables you to create a new folder, create a new document, workbook, or presentation, upload a photo you take with the iPad's camera, or upload a file*

- *Menu panel*: To navigate from folder to folder, choose settings, or manage your notifications, tap the Menu button (the icon showing three horizontal lines) in the upper-left corner of the screen. Alternatively, simply swipe right from the left side of the screen. On the Menu panel (see Figure 7-47), tap the folder you want to access, tap the Notifications button to view notifications, tap the Settings button to display the Settings dialog, where you can review and change settings, or tap the Storage button to display the Storage dialog, which shows how much space you're using and how much you have left.

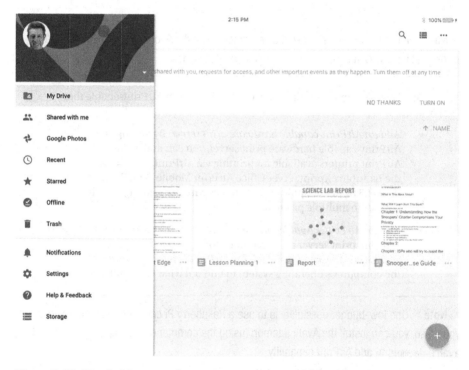

Figure 7-47. Use the Menu panel to navigate among your folders, choose settings, and manage your storage

▪ **Note** You can also access files on Google Drive directly through the Google Docs apps.

Printing from iPads

Despite the contribution that iPads can make to keeping down the number of schoolbooks your students need, the paperless school remains a dream rather than a reality, and your students will likely need to print at least some documents from their iPads.

441

This section discusses which printers you can use for printing from iPads and other iOS devices, how to make those devices available via policy, and how to print.

Which Printers Can You Use?

Each iPad comes equipped to connect easily to—and print on—printers that support the AirPrint standard developed by Apple. Most current printers and many recent printers from major brands such as Brother, Canon, Epson, Konica-Minolta, Lexmark, Ricoh, and Samsung support AirPrint. If your school has relatively new printers, there's a good chance at least some of them will have AirPrint.

■ **Note**   For a full list of AirPrint-capable printers, visit the About AirPrint page on Apple's website at https://support.apple.com/en-us/HT201311.

If your school's printers don't support AirPrint, you can AirPrint-enable them in a couple of ways:

- *Add an AirPrint-capable hardware print server*: By adding an AirPrint-capable hardware print server, you can make non-AirPrint printers available for printing via AirPrint. For example, the Lantronix XprintServer Office AirPrint Mobile Print Server ($199.95 from the Apple Store) enables wireless printing from iOS devices to multiple printers.

- *Add an AirPrint-capable software print server*: You can run a software print server on a computer connected to the network to add AirPrint capability. Search for *AirPrint printer software* and the computer's operating system to find out what's available.

■ **Note**   One low-budget possibility is to use a Raspberry Pi computer as a print server. If you do so, you can install the Avahi daemon (using the command sudo apt-get install avahi-daemon) to add AirPrint capability.

Making Printers Available to iPads via Policy

Once you've gotten your AirPrint-capable printers or printing system, you can use policy to connect the iPads to the printers. For example, in Apple Configurator, you create an AirPrint payload that specifies the hostname or IP address of the printer and the resource path to it. See the section "Configuring an AirPrint Payload in the Profile" in Chapter 4 for details. Similarly, you can use MDM solutions to connect iPads to printers.

Printing to an AirPrint Printer

When your printers are in place, the iPads can print to them. Here's an example using the Pages app:

1. Open the document you want to print.

2. Give the Print command. How you do this varies depending on the app, but in Pages you tap the More (...) button, and then tap the Print item on the More menu (see Figure 7-48).

Figure 7-48. *Give the Print command to start the printing process. In Pages, you tap the More (...) button, and then tap Print on the More menu.*

3. After you give the Print command, the Printer Options dialog opens (see Figure 7-49).

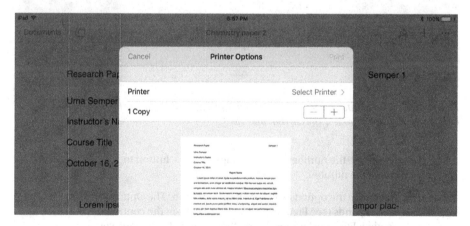

Figure 7-49. *In the Printer Options dialog, see if the Printer button shows the printer you want to use. If not, tap the Printer button to display the Printer dialog.*

4. Look at the Printer button to see if the printer you want to use is already selected. If so, go to step 6; if not, tap the Printer button to display the Printer dialog (see Figure 7-50).

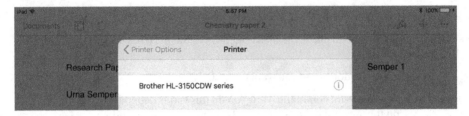

Figure 7-50. *In the Printer dialog, tap the printer you want to use. You can tap the Info (i) button for a printer to display information on its capabilities.*

5. Tap the printer you want to use. The Printer Options dialog appears again, now with the printer listed on the Printer button (see Figure 7-51). The Options button summarizes the options that are selected.

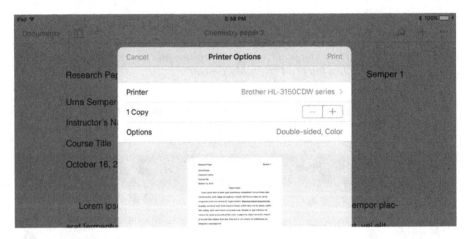

Figure 7-51. *The Printer button in the Printer Options dialog shows the printer, and the Options button summarizes the current options*

6. To change the number of copies, tap the + or – button to adjust the number.

7. To change the options, tap the Options button. The Options area expands (see Figure 7-52), and you can set the controls as needed. For example, for the Brother printer shown here, you can set the Double-Sided switch and the Black & White switch to On or Off, as needed.

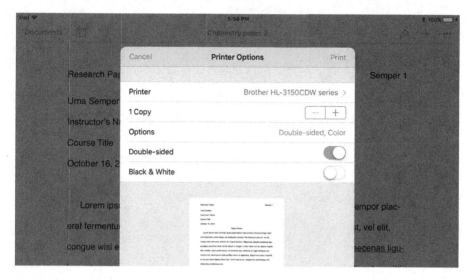

Figure 7-52. *After expanding the Options area in the Printer Options dialog, you can set each option as needed*

8. When you finish choosing options, tap the Print button to print the document.

Summary

In this chapter, you've learned how to connect your school's iPads to shared folders on Windows Server and on macOS Server. You've also learned how to set up macOS Server to handle iOS clients and how to configure the Caching service on macOS Server to speed up network performance by caching data.

Beyond this, we examined how to connect your school's iPads to the four leading online storage services—iCloud Drive, Microsoft OneDrive, Dropbox, and Google Drive— and how you access these services on iPads. We also covered connecting your school's iPads to printers and printing documents.

In the next chapter, we'll go through how to run lessons from an iPad using Apple's Classroom app.

CHAPTER 8

■ ■ ■

Controlling a Lesson with Classroom for iPad

In this chapter, you'll learn to use Apple's Classroom app to manage your students' iPads directly from your own iPad. Classroom is a great tool for running iPad-based lessons, giving you the power to do everything from launching the app the students will use for the class to monitoring what each student is viewing—or doing—on screen at any moment.

Classroom includes capabilities such as launching the app or navigating the whole class—or selected parts of it—to the web page or book page students will start work on, muting or locking iPads, and displaying an iPad's screen on the monitor connected to an Apple TV.

Understanding What Classroom Is and What It Does

Classroom is an iPad app that you and your fellow teachers or administrators use to organize and control students' iPads in the classroom and to guide the students' learning.

Classroom enables you to perform a wide range of actions, of which the following are typically the most useful:

- Managing classes that have already been set up in your school's MDM solution or in macOS Server

---

■ **Note** Just a quick reminder—here, the *class* is the group of students meeting to study a subject, not the room in which they meet.

- Setting up classes manually

- Creating and managing groups of students during a class

- Launching the apps you want the students to use

© Guy Hart-Davis 2017
G. Hart-Davis, *Deploying iPads in the Classroom*,
https://doi.org/10.1007/978-1-4842-2928-6_8

- Making students' iPads display the website, the page in an iBooks book, or the iTunes U course that you want the students to view

- Monitoring the screen of a student's iPad to see what's happening

- Locking an iPad's screen

- Locking an iPad itself to prevent a student from taking further actions on it

- Displaying an iPad's screen on a TV or monitor connected to an Apple TV

Getting Started with Classroom

Only your instructor iPads—the iPads the teachers will use—need the Classroom app. If you haven't installed Classroom already, go ahead and install it by using either the App Store app on the iPad itself or your mobile device management (MDM) solution.

Meeting the Welcome to Classroom Splash Screen

When you launch Classroom, the Welcome to Classroom splash screen appears (see Figure 8-1), announcing these four key areas of functionality:

- *Screen View*: Classroom lets you view the screen of any iPad in the class.

- *The Big Screen*: Classroom enables you to project a student's work onto a monitor or TV connected to an Apple TV.

- *Remote Control*: You can launch apps, websites, or books on each student's iPad, or on the iPads used by a particular group of students.

- *Peace and Quiet*: You can mute any iPad in the class.

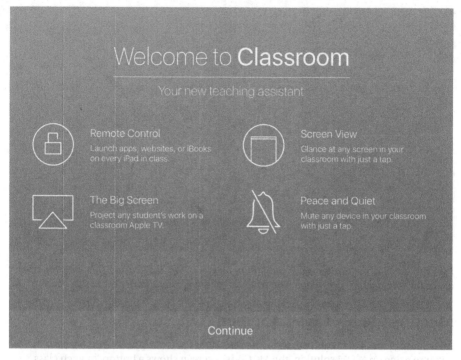

Figure 8-1. *Tap the Continue button on the Welcome to Classroom splash screen to start working with Classroom*

Tap the Continue button to dismiss the splash screen and get to work.

Setting Your Teacher Information

When you first launch Classroom, the My Classes screen appears automatically, and the Teacher Information dialog opens so that you can enter your details (see Figure 8-2). Type your name, and then tap the photo placeholder and add a photo by either tapping the Take Photo button and taking a photo or tapping the Choose Photo button and selecting an existing photo from your photo library. Tap the Done button after filling in your information.

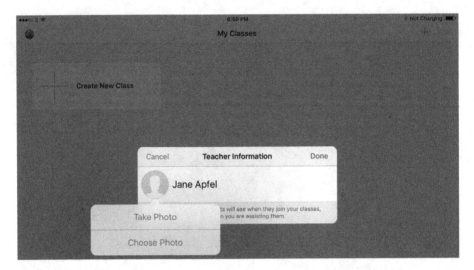

Figure 8-2. *The first time you run Classroom on your iPad, the Teacher Information dialog opens for you to enter your name. You can add a photo to help students identify you*

Meeting the My Classes Screen

After setting your teacher information, the My Classes screen appears (see Figure 8-3). If you're using an MDM solution, the My Classes screen shows a button for each class assigned to you in the MDM solution. (MDM here includes macOS Server systems.) This screen contains only two other controls:

- *Account icon*: This is the icon in the upper-left corner of the screen that bears your photo, the picture assigned to your account, or a placeholder graphic showing a head outline. You can tap the Account icon to display the Teacher Information dialog. Here, you can change your name by tapping the field and typing the changes. You can change the picture by tapping the thumbnail and then tapping Take Photo to take a new photo with the camera or tapping Choose Photo and selecting an existing photo. If you simply want to get rid of the photo, tap the thumbnail and then tap Delete Photo.

- *Edit button*: Tap this button to switch the My Classes screen to Edit mode, in which you can rearrange the class buttons. Drag a button to where you want it to appear, and then drop it there—just like rearranging icons on the Home screen in iOS. Tap the Done button (which replaces the Edit button) when you finish.

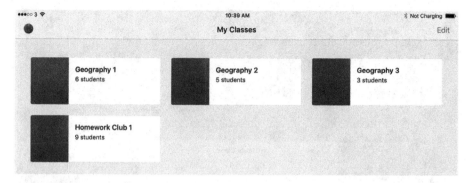

Figure 8-3. *At first, the My Classes screen shows all the classes for which you are assigned as instructor in your MDM solution*

If your school isn't using MDM, you'll see only classes that you've created manually—in other words, none yet—and a Create New Class button to encourage you to get started. Figure 8-4 shows an example of this screen.

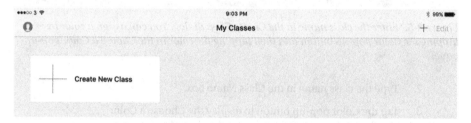

Figure 8-4. *If the Create New ClassClassroom: button and the + button in the upper-right corner appear on the My Classes screen, your school's system is set up for you to create your own classes as needed*

Setting Up Your Classes in a Non-MDM System

If your school isn't using MDM to control the iPads, you can create new classes from within Classroom—and delete classes if necessary.

Creating a New Class

Follow these steps to create a new class:

1. On the My Classes screen, tap the Create New Class button or the + button. The Create Class dialog opens (see Figure 8-5).

451

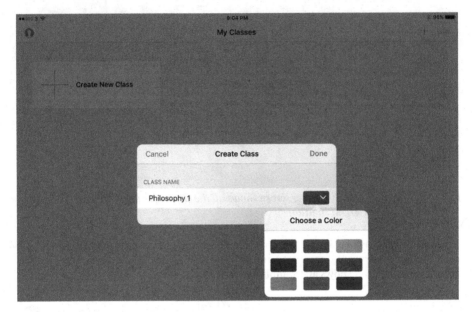

Figure 8-5. *Enter the class name in the Create Class dialog. You can assign a color by tapping the Color pop-up button and then tapping the color in the Choose a Color pop-up panel*

2. Type the class name in the Class Name box.

3. Tap the Color pop-up button to display the Choose a Color panel, and then select the color for the class's buttons and backgrounds.

4. Tap the Done button. The class appears on the My Classes screen.

You can then add other classes as needed by repeating these steps.

■ **Note**   You can edit the details for a class by tapping the Info (i) button that appears next to the class on the My Classes screen.

Adding Students to a Class

After creating a new class, you can add students to it. You add students by opening the class and then having the students enter an identifying code on their iPads. The students' iPads must be connected to the same Wi-Fi network as the teacher's iPad.

To add students to a class, follow these steps:

1. On the My Classes screen, tap the class to open it. The screen for the class appears (see Figure 8-6).

No Students

Add Students

Figure 8-6. *On the screen for the class, tap the Add Students button to start adding students*

2. Tap the Add Students button. The Add Students to This Class dialog opens (see Figure 8-7), showing an identifying code, a four-digit number.

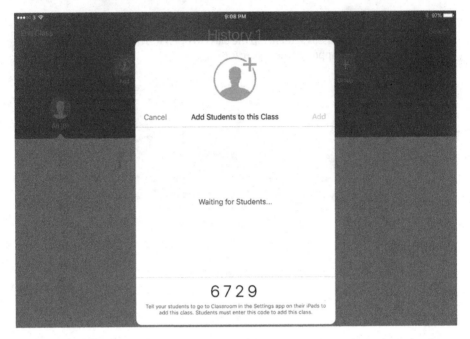

Figure 8-7. *After opening the Add Students to This Class dialog, tell the students the class number and wait for them to accept the invitation*

3. Tell the students the class name and the code, and have them enter it on their iPads like this:

    a. Tap the Settings icon on the Home screen to open the Settings app.

    b. Tap Classroom in the left column to display the Classroom screen (see Figure 8-8).

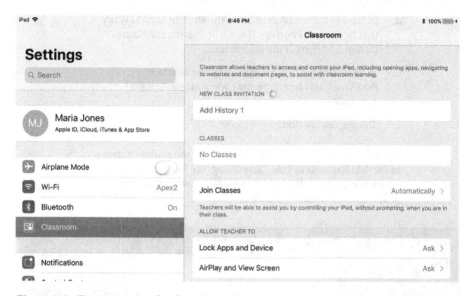

Figure 8-8. *To start joining the class, the student taps Settings, taps Classroom, and then taps the appropriate class button, such as the Add History 1 button shown here*

    c.   Tap the button for the class they're joining. A dialog opens, showing the name of the class in the title bar (see Figure 8-9).

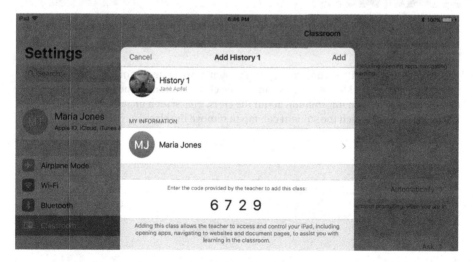

Figure 8-9. *In the Add dialog for the class, the student types the code for the class, adjusts her information as needed, and then taps the Add button*

455

    d.   In the My Information section, the student should verify that her name is correct. If not, she can tap the Name button and correct the information.

    e.   In the Enter the Code Provided by the Teacher to Add This Class box, type the code you (the teacher) announce.

    f.   Tap the Add button.

4.   Once the student has done this, a button for the student appears in the Add Students to This Class dialog (see Figure 8-10). When your students have all joined, tap the Add button to close the dialog and start running the class.

Figure 8-10. *A button for the student appears in the Add Students to This Class dialog. When you've lined up your students, tap the Add button to close the dialog.*

On the student's iPad, the class now appears in the Classes list on the Classroom screen (see Figure 8-11). The student can tap the class's button, or the Info (i) button, to display the screen with information about the class. This screen includes the Remove This Class button, which the student can tap to remove the class.

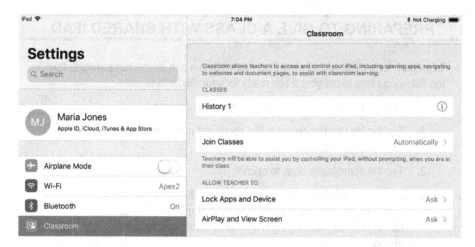

Figure 8-11. After the student joins the class, the class appears in the Classes list on the Classroom screen

In the Allow Teacher To box, the student may be able to control two settings, depending on how the iPads are configured:

- *Lock Apps and Devices*: Tap this button to display the Lock Apps and Devices screen, and then choose the appropriate setting to control whether the teacher can lock apps on the iPad and the iPad itself. The choices are Always, Ask (ask the student for permission), and Never.

- *AirPlay and View Screen*: Tap this button to display the AirPlay and View Screen screen, and then choose the appropriate setting to control whether the teacher can use AirPlay to display the iPad's screen on a TV or monitor connected to an Apple TV and whether the teacher can view the iPad's screen. Here, too, the choices are Always, Ask, and Never.

Running a Class with Classroom

In this section, we'll go through how to run a class with Classroom, from opening the class at the start of the lesson to ending the class session. Along the way, we'll examine how to work with existing groups and groups you create on the fly, how to get your students to the right starting point for a lesson, and the tools Classroom offers to help you keep the students and their iPads under control.

PREPARING TO GIVE A CLASS WITH SHARED IPAD

To prepare for a class with Shared iPad (rather than a one-to-one deployment), take the following steps to get your iPads ready for your students to use:

1. Launch the Classroom app if it's not already running.

2. Tap the My Classes button in the upper-left corner of the screen to display your classes.

3. Tap the appropriate class to open it.

4. Choose the students you want to assign to the class by tapping the All button, tapping a group button, or tapping the Select button and then tapping each individual student you want to include.

5. Tap the Assign button on the Action bar.

6. Tap the iPad group you want to use. Classroom assigns an iPad to each student.

■ **Note** When you assign a student group to an iPad group with Shared iPad enabled and the students using Managed Apple IDs, Classroom checks to see if any of the iPads in the iPad group have been assigned to the students in the student group before. If so, wherever possible, Classroom assigns a student to an iPad he or she has used before in order to reduce the amount of files the iPad needs to download before the student can use it.

Starting a Class

To start a class, tap the button for the class on the My Classes screen. The screen for the class appears, such as the Geography 1 screen shown in Figure 8-12. As you can see, the screen contains the following features:

- *End Class button*: Tap this button in the upper-left corner of the screen when you're ready to end the class.

- *Select button*: Tap this button in the upper-right corner of the screen to select students whom you want to group or take other actions on. (We'll get to groups and the actions you can take a little later in this chapter.)

- *Add button*: In non-MDM classes, this button appears to the left of the Open button on the toolbar. You can tap it to start adding students to the class.

- *Open button*: Tap this button to open a dialog that enables you to launch an app on the students' iPads, locking it if necessary.

- *Navigate*: Tap this button to display the Navigate dialog, which enables you to steer students to a page in an iBooks book or to a web page in Safari.

- *Lock button/Unlock button*: Tap the Lock button to lock students' iPads; tap the Unlock button (which replaces the Lock button) to unlock them again.

- *Mute*: Tap this button to mute the audio output on students' iPads.

- *Screens*: Tap this button to view the screens of students' iPads.

- *Group*: Tap this button to start creating a new group of iPads.

- *All group button*: Tap this group button at the left end of the group bar to see the list of all the students in the class. For each student whose iPad is online, Classroom displays a label indicating the app or screen the iPad is showing, such as "Home Screen" if the iPad is at the Home screen or "Settings" if the Settings app is displayed. For each student whose iPad is offline, Classroom displays the label "Offline."

- *Buttons for other groups*: The group bar also displays a button for each other group; you can tap the button to display the students in the group. We'll get to the different types of groups in just a moment.

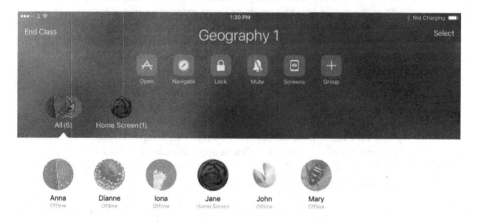

Figure 8-12. *On the screen for a class, you can see which students are online and which are offline. You can also see which app or screen each online student is viewing*

We'll look at how to use all these features in the remainder of this chapter. Before that, we'll look at Classroom's groups and how you choose the students you want to affect by an action you're taking.

Understanding and Using Groups

For much of your work with Classroom, you'll use groups. Classroom automatically creates a group that contains all the students assigned to a class, but it also creates groups based on the apps or screens the students are viewing. Better yet, Classroom enables you to create custom groups as needed.

Understanding Classroom's Three Types of Groups

Classroom supports three types of groups:

- *All*: This group contains all the students in the class.

■ **Note**   In a class organized via MDM, the All group contains all the students assigned to the class in the system, whether their iPads are online or not. In a class you set up on your iPad, the All group contains all the students who have joined the class by typing the class's ID code on their iPads.

- *Manual group*: A *manual* group contains only those students you add to the group. You can create as many manual groups as you need, and you can remove them when you no longer need them. For example, if you have teams of students working on different projects, you might create a separate manual group for each project.

- *Dynamic group*: A *dynamic* group is a group that Classroom creates automatically to help you manage the iPads. Classroom creates a group for students who are on the Home screen and a group for each app the students are using. For example, if some of your students are using the iBooks app, Classroom creates a dynamic group called iBooks that enables you to work with only those students who are using the app.

Creating a Manual Group of Students

Sometimes, you may need to create a small group of students during a class so that you can temporarily manage their iPads separately from the rest of the class. For example, if you assign a handful of students to work on a group project, you may want to be able to treat those students as a separate group from the rest of the class.

To create a manual group, follow these steps:

1. Tap the Select button in the upper-right corner of the screen to switch to Selection Mode. The Select Students prompt appears at the top of the screen (see Figure 8-13).

Figure 8-13. *When you switch Classroom to Selection Mode, the Select Students prompt appears at the top of the screen*

2. Tap each student you want to add to the group. A blue check circle appears on each student you tap (see Figure 8-14).

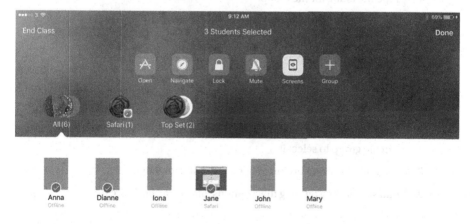

Figure 8-14. *Tap each student you want to add to the group*

3. Tap the Group (+) icon in the Actions list. Classroom adds a new group icon to the Group bar, selects its default name (Group), and displays the keyboard (see Figure 8-15).

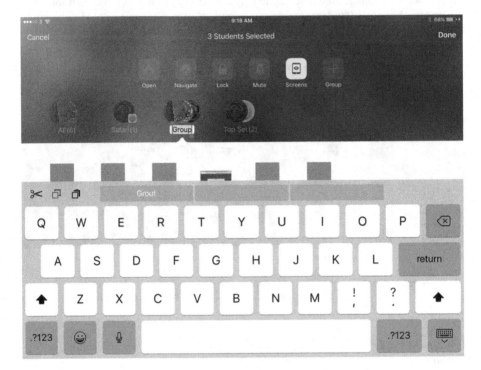

Figure 8-15. *Type the name for the new group, and then tap the Done button*

4. Type the name for the group.

5. Tap the Done button in the upper-right corner of the screen to finish creating the group.

Classroom continues to display the members of the new group.

Changing the Members of a Manual Group

Once you've created a manual group, you can change its members easily like this:

1. Tap the group to select it.

2. Tap the Edit Group button to open the group for editing.

3. Add students by tapping their buttons, placing a check circle on them.

4. Remove students by tapping their buttons, removing the check circle from them.

. 5. Tap the Done button in the upper-right corner of the screen when you finish editing the group.

Removing a Manual Group of Students

When you no longer need a manual group, remove it by tapping and holding the group name, and then tapping the Remove button on the pop-up panel (see Figure 8-16).

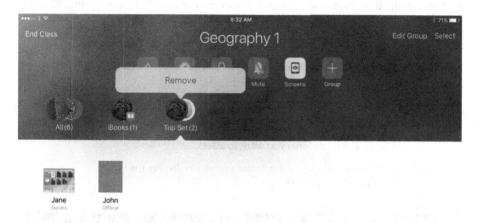

Figure 8-16. *To remove a manual group of students, tap and hold the group name, and then tap the Remove button*

Choosing Which Students to Affect

You can take most of the actions in Classroom either for the entire class, for a group of students, for an individual student, or for multiple students. You select the group or the student before giving the command.

Here's how to choose whom an action affects:

- *Entire class*: Tap the All button, and then tap the button for the action. For example, if you want to open an app for all the students, tap the Open button.

- *Dynamic group or manual group*: Tap the button for the group, and then tap the button for the action. For example, to mute all the iPads that are running GarageBand, tap the GarageBand group button, and then tap the Mute button.

- *Individual student*: Tap the button for the student in the All group or in another group in which the student appears.

463

- *Multiple students*: Tap the Select button in the upper-right corner of the screen, and then tap each student, placing a check circle on each. You can do this in the All group or any other group.

Opening an App on Your Students' iPads

Often, the quickest way to get the students started on a task is to open the app needed for the task on the students' iPads. By opening the app centrally from your iPad, you can ensure that the students start in the right place with a minimum of messing about.

You can open the same app for each student in the class, for an existing group of students, or for students in a new group that you create manually. When opening the app, you can lock it in place if necessary, or let the students switch to other apps as needed.

■ **Note** As you'd imagine, the app must be installed on each iPad for you to be able to open it.

To open an app on your students' iPads, follow these steps:

1. Choose which students you want to affect.

2. Tap the Open button in the Actions group to display the Open dialog (see Figure 8-17).

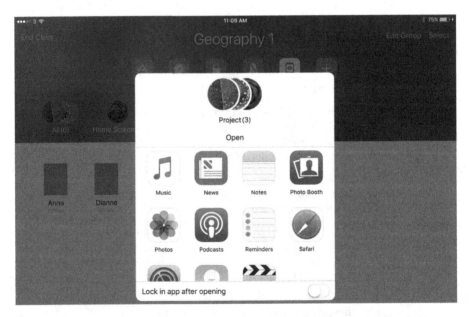

Figure 8-17. *In the Open dialog, tap the app you want to open for the students. Set the "Lock in app after opening" switch to On if you want to lock the students in the app*

3. Tap the app you want to open. The Open dialog shows the result of the action, such as "Opened Notes on 2 iPads" (see Figure 8-18).

Figure 8-18. *The Open dialog shows the result of the action and a button for opening the app on your teacher iPad*

■ **Note**   If some of the students' iPads don't contain the app you try to open, you'll see a message such as "Failed to open Keynote on 2 iPads" and a list of the iPads (identified by student name) with details of the problem, such as "Keynote not installed."

4. Tap the Open App on this iPad button if you want to open the same app on your iPad. Otherwise, tap the Done button to dismiss the Open dialog.

If you've just opened an app for only some students in the class, repeat the process for each other group that needs a different app launched.

Locking an App to Prevent Students from Changing It

When launching an app on students' iPads, you can choose to lock the app in position after opening it. Locking the app in position prevents the students from closing the app or from switching to another app.

465

To lock the app, set the "Lock in app after opening" switch in the Open dialog to On. When you dismiss the Open dialog, a padlock icon appears next to the app's name under the student's name (see Figure 8-19).

Figure 8-19. *When you lock students into an app, the padlock icon appears by the app icon under the student's name. Tap the Unlock button to set the students free again*

■ **Caution**   Before locking students into an app, warn them about the locking. Otherwise, students may think that the Home buttons on their iPads have stopped working, because there's no visual indication of the locking. Similarly, tell students when you've unlocked them from an app—otherwise, they won't know unless they press the Home button or use app-navigation gestures.

When you are ready to give the students freedom of movement again, unlock the app:

- *Unlock the app for all students*: Tap the Unlock button on the Action bar. The Unlock dialog opens, confirming the unlocking (see Figure 8-20); tap the Done button to close it.

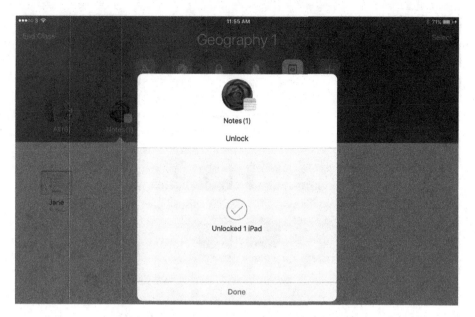

Figure 8-20. *The Unlock dialog confirms the unlocking action and shows the number of iPads that Classroom has unlocked*

- *Unlock the app for a group*: To unlock the app for a group, tap the group's button, and then tap the Unlock button. Again, the Unlock dialog opens to confirm the action.

- *Unlock the app for multiple students*: To unlock the app for multiple students, tap the Select button, and then tap each student you want to affect. With the students selected, tap the Unlock button. Again, the Unlock dialog opens.

- *Unlock the app for a single student*: To unlock the app for a single student, tap that student's button. In the Actions dialog that opens (see Figure 8-21), tap the Unlock button.

467

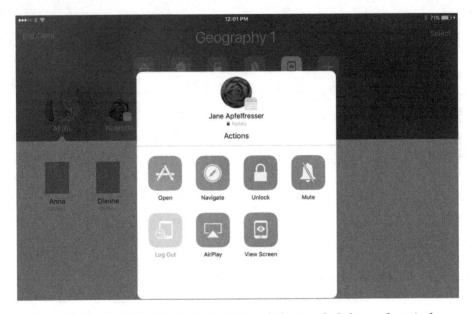

Figure 8-21. *Tap the Unlock button in the Actions dialog to unlock the app for a single student*

Navigating to a Web Bookmark, iBook, or PDF

Classroom enables you to navigate students to a bookmarked web page in Safari, to a particular page in an e-book, or to a PDF file in the iBooks app.

To navigate students, follow these steps:

1. Choose which students you want to affect.

2. Tap the Navigate button on the Action bar to display the Navigate dialog box (see Figure 8-22).

Figure 8-22. *In the Navigate dialog, tap the iBooks button or the Safari button, as appropriate*

468

3. Tap the Safari button to navigate to a web page for which you have created a bookmark on your iPad, or tap the iBooks button to navigate to an e-book or a PDF file. This example uses Safari.

4. In the dialog that opens, navigate to the bookmark or file, and then tap it. Figure 8-23 shows an example using a bookmark. Classroom opens the web page, e-book, or PDF on the students' iPads, and displays a dialog showing the number of iPads navigated (see Figure 8-24).

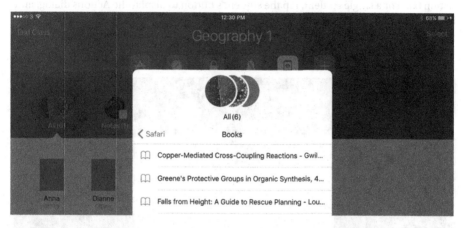

Figure 8-23. *Tap the bookmark for the web page you want to open in Safari*

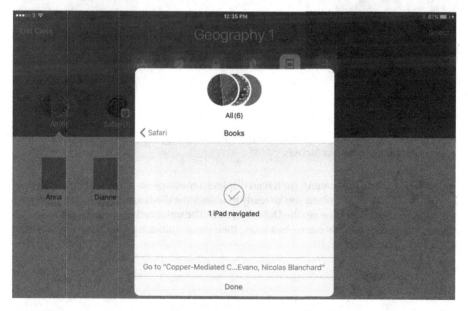

Figure 8-24. *In the confirmation dialog box, either tap the Go to button to go to the bookmark, book, or PDF yourself, or tap the Done button*

469

5. Tap the Go to button if you want to display the same item on your iPad. Otherwise, tap the Done button.

Locking and Unlocking the iPad Screen

When you need to focus your students' attention on something other than their iPad screens, such as unmissable live instruction you're delivering, you can lock the screens. To do so, select the students you want to affect, and then tap the Lock button on the Action bar. For a single student, tap the student's button to display the Actions dialog, and then tap the Lock button.

Classroom displays the Lock dialog (see Figure 8-25) to confirm the locking action. Tap the Done button to dismiss it.

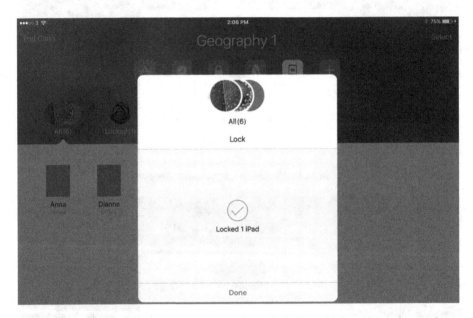

Figure 8-25. *Tap the Done button to dismiss the Lock dialog, which confirms the number of iPads that Classroom has locked*

When you lock the screens, each iPad displays a message saying it has been locked by you (see Figure 8-26). When you're ready to unlock the iPads again, select the students you want to affect, and then tap the Unlock button. The unlocked iPads show the lock screen, which the students can unlock using their usual unlock method, such as entering a passcode or using Touch ID.

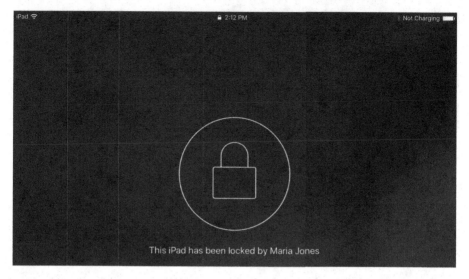

Figure 8-26. Each iPad you've locked displays a lock icon and a message identifying the culprit

Muting a Student's iPad

You can mute your students' iPads as needed when you need to quieten the classroom. Simply choose the group or the individual students to affect, and then tap the Mute button on the Action bar. The Mute dialog opens, confirming the number of iPads muted; tap the Done button to close the dialog.

Viewing Your Students' iPad Screens

When you need to see what your students are doing, you can view thumbnails of their screens. To do so, tap the Screens button on the Action bar. The thumbnails appear (see Figure 8-27), showing whether each iPad is in portrait orientation or landscape orientation.

Figure 8-27. *Tap the Screens button on the Action bar to display a thumbnail of each student's iPad screen*

To see more detail, tap the thumbnail of the appropriate iPad, and then tap the View Screen button in the Actions dialog. The student's screen appears in a frame (see Figure 8-28), allowing you to monitor exactly what the student is doing. Tap the Done button when you finish.

Figure 8-28. *You can view a student's screen in a frame*

■ **Note** The status bar across the top of the student's screen goes blue to indicate that a teacher is viewing the screen.

Depending on how your school's iPads have been configured, a student may need to give permission for you to view the screen. If students are allowed to make this decision, the Allow Teacher To box appears under the Classes box on the Classroom screen in the Settings app (see Figure 8-29). The student can tap the AirPlay and View button to display the AirPlay and View screen (see Figure 8-30), and then tap the Always button, the Ask button, or the Never button, as appropriate.

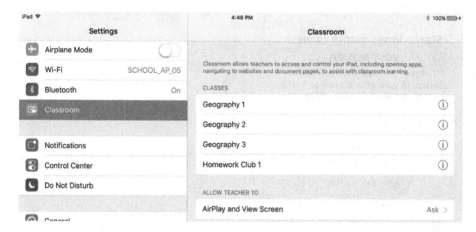

Figure 8-29. *If the Allow Teacher To box appears on the Classroom screen in Settings, the student can control whether teachers can use AirPlay to view the screen*

Figure 8-30. *On the AirPlay and View screen, the student can choose Always, Ask, or Never, as needed*

Depending on the Classroom configuration, the Classroom screen in the Settings app may also contain the Lock Apps and Devices button. Tap this button to display the Lock Apps and Devices setting, and then tap the Always, Ask, or Never button, as appropriate.

If the student has chosen the Ask setting, the *Teacher* Wants to View Your Screen dialog (see Figure 8-31) opens when you (the teacher) give the View Screen command. The student can tap the Allow button to allow this instance, the Always Allow button to select the Always item on the AirPlay and View screen, or the Deny button to select the Never item on the AirPlay and View screen.

Maria Jones wants to view your screen

"Always Allow" will allow any of your teachers to view your screen or AirPlay your iPad. This can be configured in Settings.

Allow

Always Allow

Deny

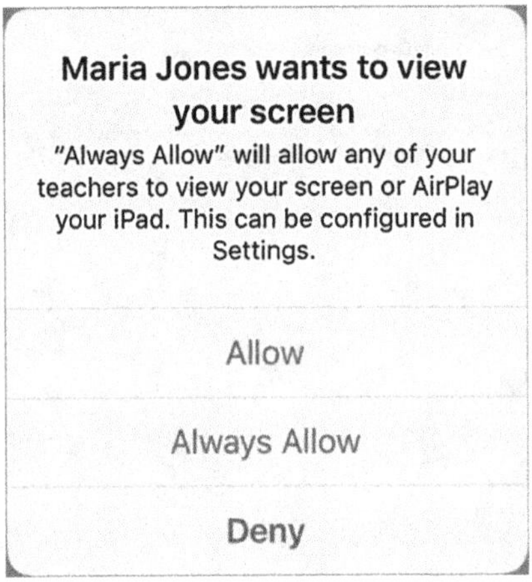

Figure 8-31. The Teacher Wants to View Your Screen dialog lets the student control whether you (the teacher) can view the iPad's screen

Displaying an iPad's Screen via Apple TV

Classroom enables you to display an iPad's screen on a TV or monitor connected to an Apple TV. For example, you might need to display an iPad's screen on a monitor to share a student's document or presentation with the whole class.

■ **Note**   Depending on how your school's iPads are configured, AirPlay may also be controlled by the student's choice of setting on the AirPlay and View screen in the Settings app.

To allow an iPad to display its screen via Apple TV, follow these steps:

1. Tap the appropriate student's iPad. The Actions dialog opens.

2. Tap the AirPlay button. The AirPlay screen appears, showing the list of available Apple TVs (see Figure 8-32).

■ **Note** The iPad must be connected to the same Wi-Fi network as the Apple TV. So if the AirPlay screen doesn't show the Apple TV you want to use, verify that the iPad is connected to the right Wi-Fi network, and change Wi-Fi networks if necessary.

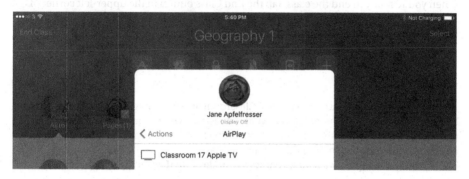

Figure 8-32. *In the AirPlay dialog, tap the Apple TV on which you want to display the student's screen*

3. Tap the button for the appropriate Apple TV. The AirPlay Code dialog opens (see Figure 8-33).

Figure 8-33. *In the AirPlay Code dialog, type the code displayed on the Apple TV's monitor*

4. Type the code displayed on the monitor connected to the Apple TV.

5. Tap the OK button. Classroom directs the output from the student's iPad to the Apple TV. The AirPlay dialog shows the message "iPad is AirPlaying," and the AirPlay icon appears on the status bar of the student's iPad.

6. Tap the Done button to dismiss the AirPlay dialog. An AirPlay symbol appears on the student's button as a reminder.

When it's time to stop playback, tap the student's button to display the Actions dialog, and then tap the Stop AirPlay button.

Ending the Class

When you're ready to end the class, tap the End Class button in the upper-left corner of the screen. Classroom ends the class and displays the My Classes screen again, where you can tap the next class you need to teach.

Summary

In this chapter, you've learned to use the Classroom app to manage an iPad-based lesson. You now know what Classroom is and what it does; you've installed Classroom on your teaching iPad, and you know how to do everything from starting a class, through opening apps and managing the students, to ending the class.

In the next chapter, we'll look at how to troubleshoot iPads in the classroom.

CHAPTER 9

■ ■ ■

Troubleshooting iPads in the Classroom

In this chapter, I'll show you how to troubleshoot the problems you're most likely to experience with iPads in the classroom. We'll start by looking at how to locate a missing iPad—and how to erase it remotely if necessary. We'll then move on to resetting an iPad in different ways, which can clear up everything from minor ailments to lost passwords. After that, we'll go over troubleshooting apps, network connections, Bluetooth issues, display issues, audio problems, and problems connecting to AirPort devices and Apple TVs.

As you'll know from your experience with computers and devices, many different things can go wrong with hardware, software, or both. Some problems have quick and easy fixes, whereas other problems—even if they initially appear trivial—may require involved steps and take plenty of time to troubleshoot.

This chapter assumes that you'll be troubleshooting iPads deployed in your classroom and that your priority is to keep the iPads running and your classroom functioning smoothly. This means you likely won't have time to dig into the specifics of each problem the moment it occurs; instead, you'll want to work around problems as far as possible. To this end, the chapter begins by suggesting a troubleshooting approach that assumes you have multiple iPads—preferably more than you need at any one point—that you can swap in and out as necessary.

Two Moves to Streamline Troubleshooting Your iPads

When something goes wrong with a desktop computer in the classroom, you'll normally need to troubleshoot it soon—if not immediately—in order to keep the classroom functioning usefully. Unless your iPads are secured with mounts or stands you can't unlock, you'll likely have more flexibility in troubleshooting. This means you may be better off using a restart-and-replace approach to troubleshooting any problem that you can't instantly resolve.

© Guy Hart-Davis 2017
G. Hart-Davis, *Deploying iPads in the Classroom*,
https://doi.org/10.1007/978-1-4842-2928-6_9

Restarting as a Troubleshooting Move

As you no doubt well know, you can clear up many problems with end-user electronics—from smartphones and tablets to laptops and desktops—by restarting them. The speed and simplicity of restarting an iPad means that a restart is often a sensible place to start troubleshooting any problem that doesn't have an immediate fix. A restart usually takes less than a minute, and any student can perform it—unless you've configured the iPads to prevent restarts.

You'll find that many of the sections in this chapter suggest restarting the iPad either as a first move in troubleshooting a problem or as a subsequent move if other options fail.

Replacing an iPad as a Troubleshooting Move

If a restart doesn't clear up a problem that will prevent the iPad from functioning as needed in the classroom, your best bet is to replace the iPad with a spare—as long as you have a spare.

If possible, plan and maintain your iPad fleet so that you have one or more spare devices that you can swap in when an iPad suffers problems or gets broken.

■ **Tip** Replacement as a troubleshooting move works best when your iPads have a standard configuration and you keep all your important files on the network rather than on the iPads themselves.

Locating and Dealing with Missing iPads

If an iPad goes missing, you can use Find My iPhone to locate it. Find My iPhone is an Apple service that enables you to track not just the iPhone but also the iPad, the iPod touch, and Macs. The service is called Find My iPhone because Apple debuted the service for the iPhone, but on the iPad the feature is called Find My iPad; on the iPod touch, it's called Find My iPod; and on the Mac, it's called Find My Mac.

Find My iPhone works via the Apple ID associated with the iPad (or other device). You must first enable the feature on the iPad. Then, if the iPad goes missing, you can use Find My iPhone to determine where it is. You can then play a sound on the iPad, lock the iPad and display a message on it, or erase the iPad and display a message on it.

Turning On the Find My iPad Feature on an iPad

To be able to locate an iPad using the Find My iPhone service, you need to enable the Find My iPad feature on the iPad. This section shows you how to enable the Find My iPad feature by working on the iPad manually. You can also turn on the Find My iPad feature by using Apple Configurator (see Chapter 4), Apple School Manager (see Chapter 5), or mobile device management (MDM) tools (see Chapter 6).

To turn on Find My iPad manually, follow these steps:

1. From the Home screen, choose Settings ➤ Apple ID ➤ iCloud ➤ Find My iPad to display the Find My iPad screen (see Figure 9-1). Apple ID is the button that shows your Apple ID name.

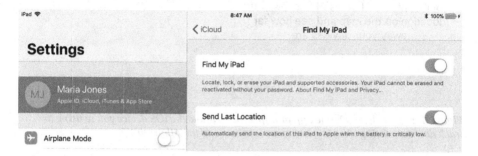

Figure 9-1. On the Find My iPad screen, set the Find My iPad switch to On to activate the Find My iPad feature. You may also want to set the Send Last Location switch to On to make sure you can track down the iPad even if its battery runs flat

2. Set the Find My iPad switch to On.

3. If you want the iPad to send its current location to the Find iPhone service when its battery is critically low, set the Send Last Location switch to On. Enabling this feature is normally a good idea, because it may help you track down a misplaced iPad whose battery has run out.

Locating a Missing iPad

To locate a missing iPad, you use another computer, tablet, or phone. How you use the Find My iPhone service depends on the type of computer or device you're using:

- *iOS device*: If you're using another iOS device (an iPhone, iPad, or iPod touch) to locate the missing iPad, use the Find iPhone app on that device. This app is normally included in an installation of iOS; look for it in the Extras folder or simply search for it. The app presents a similar interface to that of the Find My iPhone feature on the iCloud website. If iOS prompts you to allow the Find iPhone app to access your location while you use the app (see Figure 9-2), tap the Allow button to enable the app to work fully.

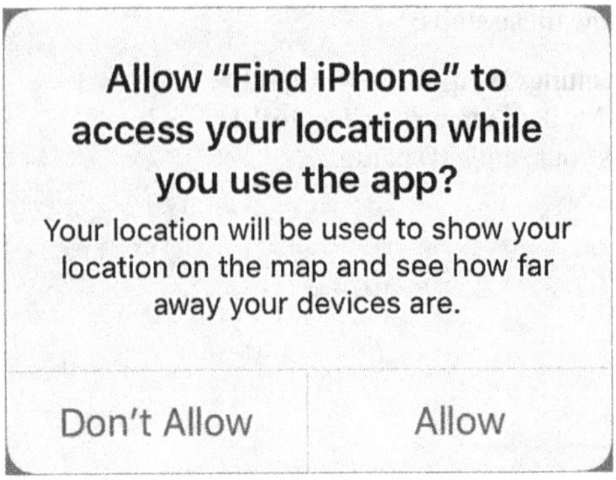

Allow "Find iPhone" to access your location while you use the app?

Your location will be used to show your location on the map and see how far away your devices are.

Don't Allow   Allow

Figure 9-2. If the Find iPhane app prompts you to allow the iOS device you're using to track down a missing iPad to access your location, tap the Allow button

- *Mac, PC, or other computer or device*: If you're using a computer or any device other than an iOS device, use the Find iPhone app on the iCloud website. Point your web browser at www.icloud.com, sign in using your Apple ID and password, and then click the Find iPhone icon on the main iCloud screen. (If the iCloud website displays an app rather than the main screen, click the app's name in the upper-left corner of the screen to display the Apps panel, and then click the Find iPhone icon.)

■ **Note**   If the Update Your Apple ID dialog opens when you sign in to the iCloud website, follow the prompts to update your Apple ID by choosing new security questions. These security questions—such as "Where did you go the first time you flew on a plane?"—used to be optional, but Apple has made them compulsory to help keep users' sensitive data secure.

Figure 9-3 shows the Find iPhone app running on an iPad, and Figure 9-4 shows the Find iPhone app on the iCloud website. As you can see, the iOS app and the website app have similar interfaces, and they work in much the same way. On iOS, the Find iPhone app displays a sidebar containing the list of available devices, whereas on the iCloud website, the app provides a pop-up panel for selecting the device you want to track. Click the All Devices button or the current device's button in the middle of the toolbar to display the pop-up panel, and then tap the appropriate device.

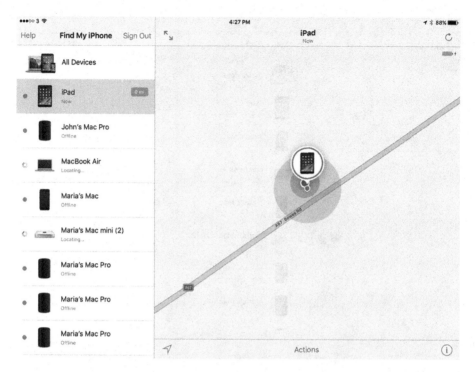

Figure 9-3. *The Find iPhone app runs on the iPhone, iPad, and iPod touch and enables you to locate iOS devices, Macs, and Apple Watches registered to the Apple ID you log in with*

■ **Note**   You may see duplicate devices in the Find My iPhone list—the service seems to err on the side of caution when it has stored what may be multiple records for the same device or multiple devices with similar names. Usually, any spurious devices will be marked as being offline, so you can ignore them easily enough.

Figure 9-4. *The Find My iPhone app on the iCloud website uses a pop-up panel for selecting the device you want to track. Tap the All Devices button or the button bearing the name of the current device to open the panel, and then tap the appropriate device*

Choosing the Map Type and Zooming as Needed

In either the iOS app or the iCloud app, you can choose the map type you want to view. If you've used Apple's Maps app on an iOS device or on a Mac, you'll already be familiar with the three map types:

- *Standard map*: This map shows the road layout, with labels on places and landmarks.

- *Satellite map*: This map shows a satellite photo of the area without labels on places and landmarks. The satellite photo may be several years old, but it may still help you identify a location.

- *Hybrid map*: This map shows the satellite photo with labels on places and landmarks. The hybrid map is usually more useful than the satellite map for tracking lost devices.

Here's how to choose which map type the app displays:

- *iOS app*: Tap the Information (i) button in the lower-right corner to display the Information dialog, and then tap the Standard, Hybrid, or Satellite button.

- *iCloud app*: Click the pop-up menu button in the lower-right corner of the screen, and then click the Standard, Hybrid, or Satellite item. The pop-up menu button shows the name of the current map type.

You can also zoom the map in and out as needed:

- *iOS app*: Place two fingers (or finger and thumb) on the screen and pinch out to zoom in, or pinch in to zoom out.

- *iCloud app*: Click the + button in the upper-left corner of the screen to zoom in; click the – button to zoom out.

Selecting the Missing iPad

Once you've gotten the map type and zoom to your satisfaction, select the missing iPad by tapping it in the sidebar in the iOS app or by tapping the All Devices pop-up menu button (or the button showing the name of the current device) and then tapping the iPad on the pop-up panel.

■ **Note**   After selecting the device on the iOS app, you can tap the Full Screen button (the one with two diagonal arrows pointing apart) to expand the map area to full screen, hiding the sidebar. Tap the Back button (the < button in the upper-left corner of the screen) when you want to display the sidebar again.

Once Find My iPhone has located the iPad, you can display the controls for taking actions with it:

- *iOS app*: Tap the device's icon, making the app show a circle around it. Then tap the Actions button at the bottom of the screen to display the bar of actions (see Figure 9-5).

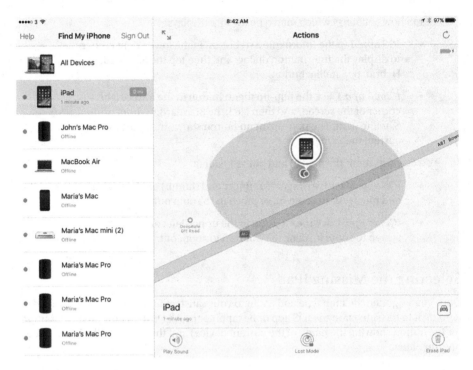

Figure 9-5. In the iOS app, tap the iPad and then tap the Actions button to display the bar of actions at the bottom of the screen

- *iCloud app*: Click the iPad's icon to select it, and then click the Information (i) icon to display the dialog shown in Figure 9-6.

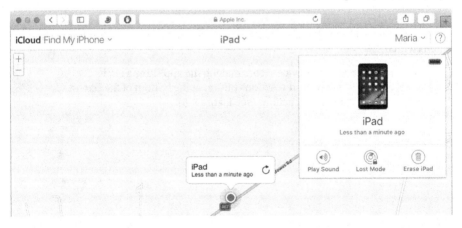

Figure 9-6. On iCloud, click the icon for the found iPad to display the dialog of actions you can take. The battery indicator in the upper-right corner of the dialog shows the state of the iPad's battery

■ **Note** The Find My iPhone service displays an Old Location flag in the dialog of actions if the location the service has for the iPad is an old location rather than a current one. In this case, you can check the "Notify me when found" check box to have the Find My iPhone service notify you via a pop-up message when it locates the iPad. The Old Location flag also appears when the iPad is out of power or has been powered off.

Playing a Sound on the Missing iPad

The Find My iPhone service enables you to play a sound on the missing device. If you see from the Find My iPhone information that the missing iPad is somewhere nearby, you may want to play a sound to help you locate the iPad. If the Find My iPhone information shows the Old Location flag, the iPad likely isn't able to play a sound.

To play a sound, tap the Play Sound button on the bar of actions in the iOS app or in the dialog of actions on iCloud. The sound is an echoing beep at full volume, and continues for a minute; if you locate the iPad, you can stop the sound by swiping its alert and then tapping the Clear button (if the iPad is locked) or by tapping the OK button in the Find My iPad Alert dialog box (see Figure 9-7) if the iPad isn't locked.

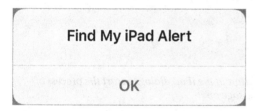

Figure 9-7. Tap the OK button in the Find My iPad Alert dialog to stop the sound playing once you locate the iPad

Locking the Missing iPad and Displaying a Message on It

After finding out approximately where a missing iPad is, you may need to make sure it's locked. You can do this by enabling the Lost Mode feature of Find My iPhone. Lost Mode also enables you to display a message on the missing iPad. Displaying a message is useful for letting somebody who finds it know how to arrange the return of the iPad to you. In a pinch, you can also use this feature as a way to identify an iPad among many others in a classroom.

The Lost Mode feature works slightly differently on iOS and on iCloud. The following subsections cover iOS and iCloud separately.

Using Lost Mode on iOS

On iOS, follow these steps to use Lost Mode to lock an iPad and display a message on it:

1. Tap the Lost Mode button on the bar of actions. The iPad dialog opens (see Figure 9-8).

Figure 9-8. *Tap the Turn On Lost Mode button in the iPad dialog to start the process of locking a missing iPad and displaying a message on it*

2. Tap the Turn On Lost Mode button. The Step 1 of 3 dialog opens (see Figure 9-9), prompting you to enter a passcode to lock the iPad.

Figure 9-9. *In the Step 1 of 3 dialog, type the passcode with which you want to lock the iPad*

3. Type a six-digit passcode. The Step 1 of 3 dialog then prompts you to type the passcode again for confirmation.

■ **Note** The passcode for locking the iPad must be numbers rather than symbols or letters, even though the iPad enables you to display the letters keyboard while the Step 1 of 3 dialog is open.

---

4. Type the passcode again. The Step 2 of 3 dialog then opens (see Figure 9-10), prompting you to enter a contact phone number.

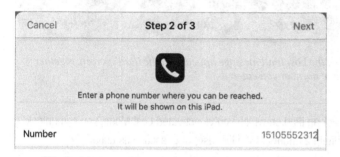

Figure 9-10. *In the Step 2 of 3 dialog, type your contact phone number for the return of the iPad, and then tap the Next button*

5. Type the phone number at which you can be contacted by someone who finds the iPad.

6. Tap the Next button. The Step 3 of 3 dialog opens (see Figure 9-11), suggesting a boilerplate message to someone who finds the iPad.

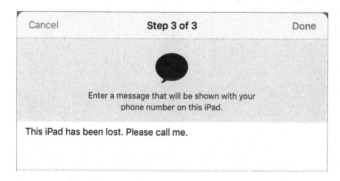

Figure 9-11. *In the Step 3 of 3 dialog, customize the boilerplate messages as needed, and then tap the Done button*

7. Customize the message as needed. For example, you might add your name and the school's name, or a suggestion of how to return the iPad to you.

8. Tap the Done button. The Find My iPhone service locks the iPad and displays the message and phone number (if any) on it. Figure 9-12 shows an example.

Lost iPad

This iPad has been lost. Please call me.
(510) 555-1234

Figure 9-12. In Lost Mode, the Lost iPad message appears on the iPad's screen, together with any text and any phone number you entered

■ **Note** When you recover an iPad on which you've activated Lost Mode, you can unlock it using your fingerprint (within 24 hours of the last use) or passcode as usual.

Using Lost Mode on iCloud

On iCloud, follow these steps to use Lost Mode to lock an iPad and display a message on it:

1. Tap the iPad's location to display the dialog of actions.

2. Tap the Lost Mode button in the dialog of actions for the iPad. The first Lost Mode dialog opens (see the left screen in Figure 9-13).

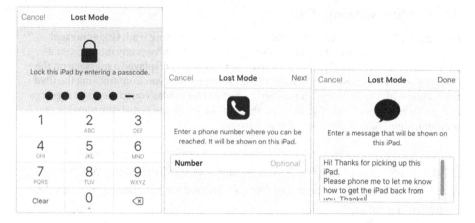

Figure 9-13. *In the first Lost Mode dialog (left), type a locking passcode and then confirm it. In the second Lost Mode dialog (center), type your contact phone number and click the Next button. In the third Lost Mode dialog (right), type a message and then click the Done button*

3.   Type a six-digit passcode to lock the iPad. The first Lost Mode dialog then prompts you to re-enter the passcode.

4.   Type the passcode again. The second Lost Mode dialog then opens (see the center screen in Figure 9-13).

5.   Optionally, type your contact phone number. Normally, entering the phone number is a good idea unless you're certain it's not needed—for example, because you can see that the iPad is in the school buildings and you'll specify the physical location where it should be returned.

6.   Click the Next button. The third Lost Mode dialog opens (see the right screen in Figure 9-13).

7.   Optionally, type a message to the person who finds the iPad. Again, you'll normally want to do this.

8.   Click the Done button. The Find My iPhone service locks the iPad and displays the message and phone number (if any) on it.

Erasing the Missing iPad

The Find My iPhone service also enables you to erase a missing iPad. Under normal circumstances, you'd want to erase a missing iPad only if you've pretty much given it up for lost—for example, if you've activated Lost Mode and displayed a message on the iPad, but you've received no response. The erasure prevents you from tracking the iPad any further with the Find My iPhone service, but it still enables you to display a message and phone number on the iPad's screen after it's erased, so the possibility remains that someone might find the iPad and return it to you.

■ **Tip** You can also use the Find My iPhone service to erase an iPad that you haven't lost but whose passcode has been forgotten. See the next section, "Dealing with Forgotten Passcodes," for details.

■ **Note** The main reason for erasing a missing iPad is to prevent anybody who finds it from gaining access to sensitive information it contains. If the missing iPad is one of your classroom devices and you've followed the advice in this book to keep all valuable data on the network rather than on the iPads, the iPad may contain little sensitive information in the normal sense. But it's still likely to contain information that might help a malefactor to connect to your school's network or attack it in other ways, so you will usually want to erase the iPad if it seems unlikely that you will be able to recover it.

The Erase iPad feature works slightly differently on iOS and on iCloud. The following subsections cover iOS and iCloud separately.

■ **Note** If the Find My iPhone service doesn't have the iPad's current location, it sets up the erase operation to run the next time the iPad connects to the Internet.

Erasing a Missing iPad on iOS

To erase a missing iPad using the Find iPhone app on iOS, follow these steps:

1. Tap the Erase iPad button. The iPad dialog opens (see Figure 9-14), warning you that the iPad's contents and settings will be erased and that you won't be able to locate or track it.

Figure 9-14. This iPad dialog warns you that you can't locate or track an erased iPad. Tap the Erase iPad button if you're sure you want to proceed

2. Tap the Erase iPad button. The Apple ID Password dialog opens.

3. Type the password for the Apple ID you're using to track the iPad.

4. Tap the Erase button. The Find My iPhone service instructs the iPad to erase its contents.

HOW DOES AN IPAD ERASE ITS CONTENTS?

Like other iOS devices, the iPad stores its data in an encrypted format that requires an encryption key to decipher. When you give the command to erase its contents, the iPad deletes its encryption key, rendering the data unreadable.

Deleting the encryption key takes only a moment. By contrast, "old-school" methods of erasing data involved writing zeroes over all the blocks in the storage. This could take several hours, depending on the device's capacity, and if the process were interrupted (either by a human or by power loss, such as the battery running flat), some data might remain readable.

Erasing a Missing iPad on iCloud

To erase a missing iPad using the Find iPhone app on iCloud, follow these steps:

1. Click the Erase iPad button in the dialog of actions. The Erase this iPad? dialog opens (see Figure 9-15).

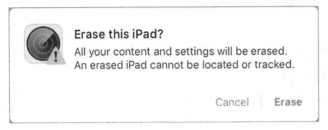

Erase this iPad?

All your content and settings will be erased.
An erased iPad cannot be located or tracked.

Cancel   Erase

Figure 9-15. *On iCloud, the Erase this iPad dialog warns you that an erased iPad can't be located or tracked. Click the Erase button if you're determined to erase the device*

2. Click the Erase button. The first Erase iPad dialog opens, prompting you for your Apple ID password.

3. Type your password.

4. Click the Next button. The second Erase iPad dialog opens (see the left screen in Figure 9-16).

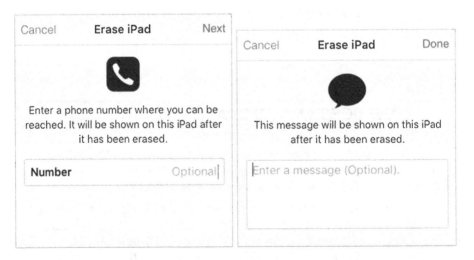

Figure 9-16. *When erasing an iPad via iCloud, you can enter a phone number in the second Erase iPad dialog (left) and a message in the third Erase iPad dialog (right)*

5. Optionally, type the contact phone number to display on the iPad after it has been erased.

6. Click the Next button. The third Erase iPad dialog opens (see the right screen in Figure 9-16).

7. Optionally, type a message encouraging the person who finds the iPad to contact you.

8. Click the Done button. The Find My iPhone service instructs the iPad to erase its contents. The Erased readout appears in the dialog of actions (see Figure 9-17), as does the Remove from Account button, which you can click to remove the iPad's association to your Apple account.

Figure 9-17. *The Erased readout appears in the dialog of actions, confirming that the Find My iPhone service has instructed the iPad to erase its contents. You can click the Remove from Account button if you want to remove the iPad from your Apple account*

■ **Note** Erasing an iPad triggers Apple's Activation Lock feature, which locks an iOS device to a particular Apple ID to prevent an unauthorized person from setting up the device. See the section "Erasing and Restoring an iPad via iCloud," later in this chapter, for coverage of setting up an iPad on which Activation Lock has been triggered.

Dealing with Forgotten Passcodes

As you know, iOS uses a passcode as a last line of defense for devices even if you enable Touch ID. So if you forget the passcode for an iPad—or if one of your students or your colleagues forgets the passcode—you have to do some work to get the iPad operational again.

To get the iPad working again, you need to erase it. If the iPad has been backed up to iTunes, or if it's been backed up to iCloud and you've enabled the Find My iPad feature in iCloud, you should be able to restore data to the iPad after erasing it. If the iPad hasn't been backed up, you won't be able to restore the data.

Erasing and Restoring an iPad via iTunes

If the iPad with the forgotten passcode is one that you've backed up to iTunes, you can use iTunes to restore the iPad. This is the best way of getting the iPad fully operational again, so use it if you have the option. One limitation is that you must be able to turn off the Find My iPad feature on the iPad if it's enabled. See the sidebar "Turning Off Find My iPad on the iPad," later in this chapter, for instructions on turning off Find My iPad.

Erasing and restoring an iPad via iTunes is straightforward, but it may take a while, because iTunes may need to download an operating system image to install on the iPad. An *operating system image* is a file that contains the operating system for reinstallation.

Here's how to erase and restore an iPad using iTunes:

1. Connect the iPad to your Mac or PC via USB.

2. If iTunes doesn't launch (or become active) when you connect the iPad, launch or activate iTunes as usual from the Dock or Launchpad (on the Mac) or from the Start menu or taskbar (on Windows).

■ **Note** If iTunes prompts you for a passcode for the iPad, it means you're using a different computer than the one with which the iPad was last synced. Connect the iPad to the right computer instead. If you can't identify the right computer, you'll need to erase the iPad using Recovery Mode. See the section "Erasing an iPad Using Recovery Mode," later in this chapter, for details.

---

3. If iTunes automatically starts backing up the iPad after you connect it, allow the backup to finish. If not, run a backup manually by following these steps:

    a. Click the iPad button on the navigation bar at the top of the iTunes window to display the iPad's control screens.

    b. In the sidebar, click the Summary icon if it's not already selected. The Summary screen appears (see Figure 9-18).

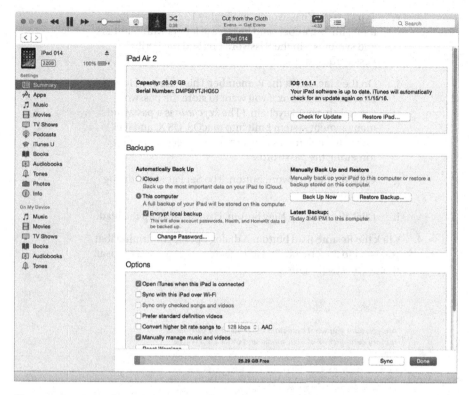

Figure 9-18. *From the Summary screen for an iPad, you can back up the iPad and restore it*

    c.   In the Backups box, make sure the This Computer option
           button is selected.

    d.   Select the Encrypt Local Backup check box. The Set
           Password dialog opens (see Figure 9-19).

Figure 9-19. *In the Set Password dialog, type a strong password to protect the iPad
backup. On the Mac, you can select the Remember This Password in My Keychain check
box to store the password securely in your keychain.*

e.   Type a strong password—preferably 12 characters or more, mixing upper- and lowercase letters with numbers and symbols—in the Password box and the Verify Password box.

f.   On the Mac, select the Remember This Password in My Keychain check box if you want to store the password securely in your keychain. (The *keychain* is a password-management system built into macOS, OS X, and iOS.) This is a good move to ensure you can recover from forgetting the password.

g.   Click the Set Password button. The Set Password dialog box closes.

h.   Click the Back Up Now button. iTunes backs up the iPad.

4.   Click the Restore iPad button. A dialog opens, confirming that you want to restore the iPad to its factory settings and erase all its contents (see Figure 9-20).

Figure 9-20. *In this dialog, click the Restore button to confirm that you want to restore the iPad to factory settings and erase all its contents*

TURNING OFF FIND MY IPAD ON THE IPAD

If iTunes displays a dialog saying that Find My iPad must be turned off before the iPad can be restored, click the OK button. Unlock the iPad via Touch ID, go to the Home screen, and choose Settings ➤ iCloud ➤ Find My iPad to display the Find My iPad screen. Set the Find My iPad switch to Off. In the Apple ID Password dialog that opens, type your password, and then tap the Turn Off button.

This is easy enough, but it relies on the iPad having Touch ID—and on you (or an available colleague or student) having a registered fingerprint. If the iPad doesn't have Touch ID, or if you don't have access to a registered fingerprint, you'll need to erase the iPad instead. See the section "Erasing an iPad Using Recovery Mode," later in this chapter, for details.

5. Click the Restore button. iTunes extracts the software from its existing archive, restores it to the iPad, and then displays the Welcome to Your New iPad screen (see Figure 9-21).

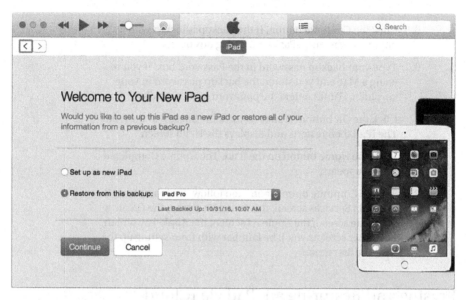

Figure 9-21. *On the Welcome to Your New iPad screen, select the Restore from This Backup option button and then select the backup in the pop-up menu*

■ **Note** iTunes stores the most recent system image file for each iOS device you sync with the computer. On the Mac, iTunes stores the latest system image file for iPad in the ~/Library/iTunes/iPad Software Updates folder, where the tilde (~) represents your Home folder. On Windows, iTunes stores the file in the \Users\username\AppData\ Roaming\Apple Computer\iTunes folder, where *username* is your username. When iTunes downloads a new file, it deletes the old one without putting it in the Trash (on the Mac) or the Recycle Bin (on Windows). So if you want to keep any of the files in order to be able to revert to earlier versions of the iPad firmware, copy the file from this location to somewhere else. To make sure you don't forget to copy a system image file, copy the file immediately after iTunes downloads it.

6. Select the Restore from This Backup option button.

7. Open the pop-up menu to the right of the Restore from This Backup option button, and then click the backup you want to use.

8. Click the Continue button. If the backup is locked with a password, the Enter Password dialog box opens.

9. Type your backup password in the Password box. If you're using a Mac and you stored the backup password in your keychain, iTunes enters the password automatically.

10. Click the OK button. iTunes restores the backup to the iPad. The iPad then restarts and displays the Hello screen.

11. Press the Home button on the iPad. The Update Completed screen appears.

12. Tap the Continue button, and then follow the prompts on the Location Services screen, the Touch ID screen, the Create a Passcode screen, the Apple ID screen, the Apple Pay screen, and other screens you'll be familiar with from setting up the iPad the first time.

Erasing and Restoring an iPad via iCloud

Your second option for dealing with a forgotten passcode is to use iCloud to erase and restore the iPad. This works well as long as you've backed up the iPad to the iCloud account that you'll use for the restoration.

Follow the steps in the section "Erasing a Missing iPad on iCloud," earlier in this chapter, to erase the iPad's contents.

Once you've done that, follow these steps to restore the iPad from iCloud:

1. Turn the iPad on. The Hello screen appears, just like when you first set up an iOS device.

2. Follow through the setup routine, choosing the display language and connecting to a Wi-Fi network, until you reach the Activation Lock screen (see Figure 9-22).

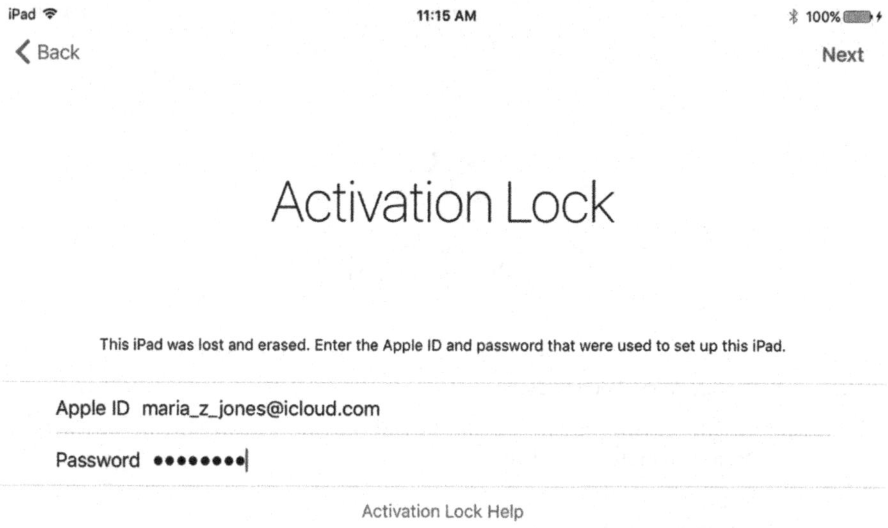

❮ Back   **Next**

Activation Lock

This iPad was lost and erased. Enter the Apple ID and password that were used to set up this iPad.

Apple ID maria_z_jones@icloud.com

Password ••••••••|

Activation Lock Help

Figure 9-22. *On the Activation Lock screen, enter the Apple ID and password associated with the iPad, and then tap the Next button*

3.   Type the Apple ID used to set up the iPad.

4.   Type the password for that Apple ID.

5.   Tap the Next button. The iPad contacts the activation server system and verifies the information.

6.   Continue with the setup routine, registering a Touch ID fingerprint (optional) and setting a passcode (mandatory), until you reach the Apps & Data screen (see Figure 9-23).

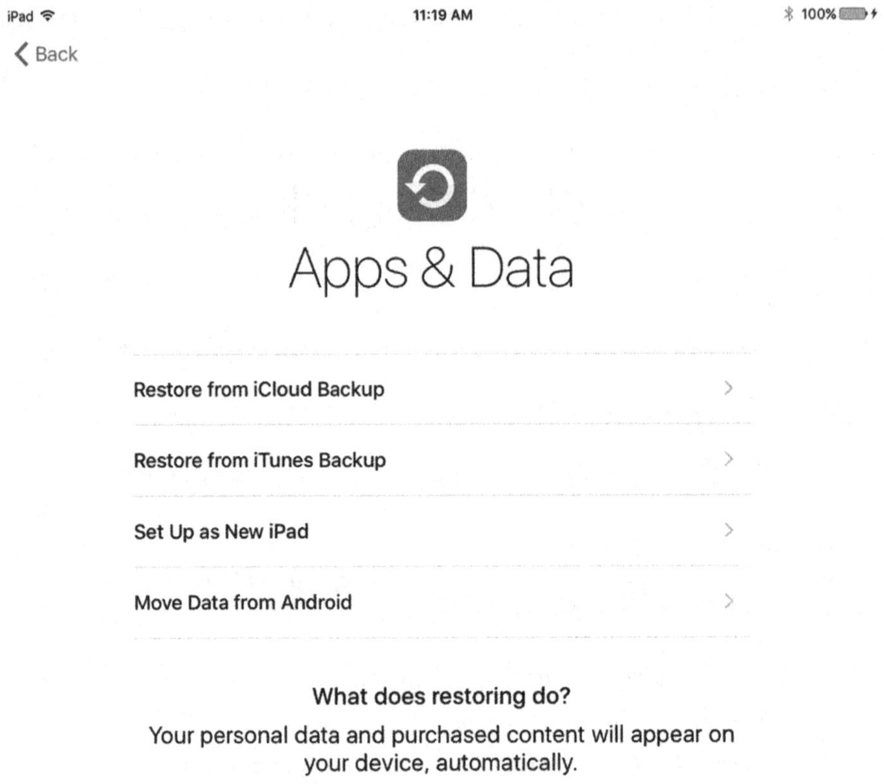

iPad 🤝   11:19 AM   ⚡ 100% 🔋 ⚡

❮ Back

Apps & Data

Restore from iCloud Backup	>
Restore from iTunes Backup	>
Set Up as New iPad	>
Move Data from Android	>

What does restoring do?

Your personal data and purchased content will appear on
your device, automatically.

Figure 9-23. On the Apps & Data screen, tap the Restore from iCloud Backup button

7. Tap the Restore from iCloud Backup button. The iCloud Sign
    In screen appears.

8. Enter your Apple ID.

9. Enter your passcode.

10. Tap the Next button. The Terms and Conditions screen
    appears.

11. Tap the Agree button. The iPad updates your iCloud settings,
    and then displays the Choose Backup screen (see Figure 9-24).

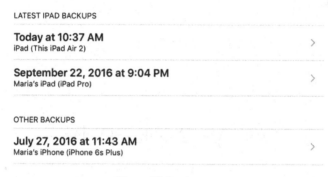

iPad 🛜   11:33 AM   ✳ 100% 🔋⚡

❮ Back

Choose Backup

LATEST IPAD BACKUPS

Today at 10:37 AM
iPad (This iPad Air 2)   ⟩

September 22, 2016 at 9:04 PM
Maria's iPad (iPad Pro)   ⟩

OTHER BACKUPS

July 27, 2016 at 11:43 AM
Maria's iPhone (iPhone 6s Plus)   ⟩

Show All Backups

Figure 9-24. On the Choose Backup screen, tap the button for the backup you want to restore

12. In the Latest iPad Backups list, tap the backup you want to use. Normally, you'll want to use the latest backup unless you know there's something wrong with it.

■ **Note**   If the Latest iPad Backups list doesn't show the backup you want to use, tap the Show All Backups button to force the iPad to list all available backups. You can also use a backup from another device, such as one from an iPhone, by tapping the appropriate button in the Other Backups list on the Choose Backup screen.

---

13. If the backup includes items purchased on a different Apple ID than the one you're using to set up the iPad again, the iPad prompts you to enter the Apple ID used for purchases on the App Store, iTunes Store, and iBook Store. Type the Apple ID and password and tap the Next button.

■ **Tip** If the Apple ID used for store purchases isn't yours and you don't have access to this information, tap the Skip This Step button to defer the decision for now.

---

14. If you've enabled two-step verification for the Apple ID, the Verify Your Identify screen appears (see Figure 9-25). Tap the appropriate trusted device in the Trusted Devices list, and then tap the Send button to send the verification code to that device. Then type the code on the Verification Code screen on the iPad.

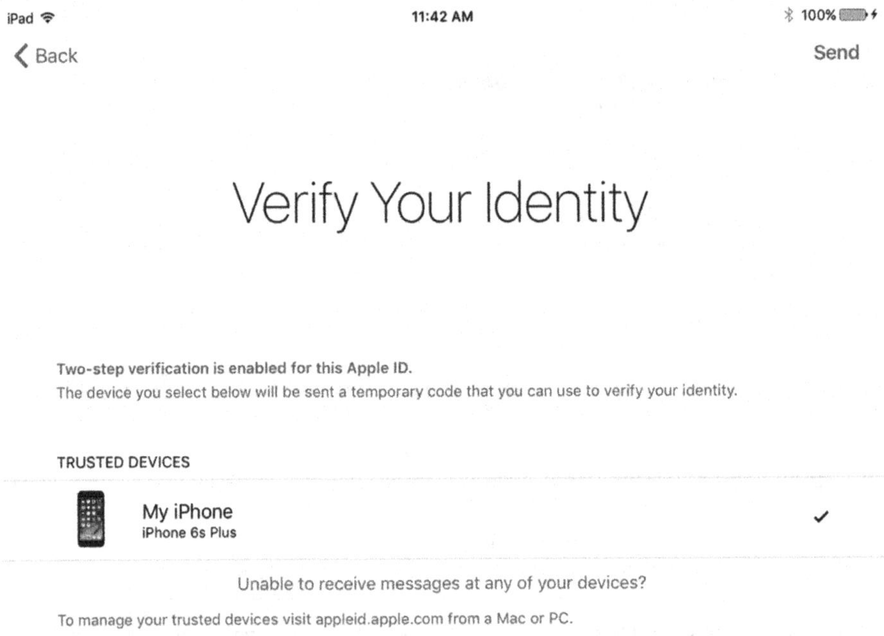

iPad 🛜   11:42 AM   ⚡ 100% ▭◖

❮ Back   Send

Verify Your Identity

Two-step verification is enabled for this Apple ID.
The device you select below will be sent a temporary code that you can use to verify your identity.

TRUSTED DEVICES

 My iPhone
iPhone 6s Plus   ✓

Unable to receive messages at any of your devices?

To manage your trusted devices visit appleid.apple.com from a Mac or PC.

Figure 9-25. On the Verify Your Identity screen, tap the trusted device on which you want to receive the verification code, and then tap the Send button

15. Wait while the iPad restores the data from iCloud. The Restore from iCloud screen shows you a progress readout (see Figure 9-26).

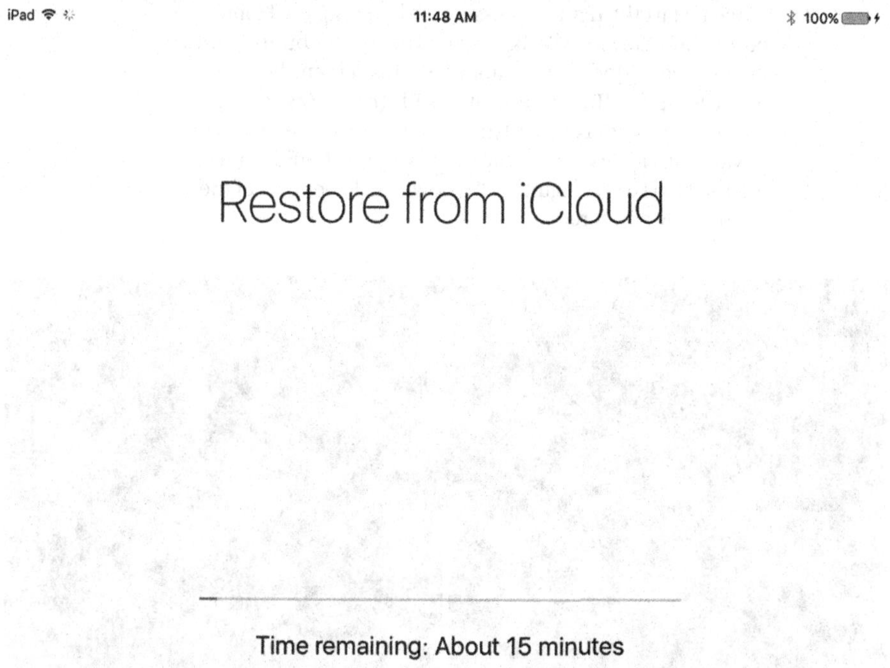

Restore from iCloud

Time remaining: About 15 minutes

Figure 9-26. *The Restore from iCloud screen displays a progress readout as the iPad restores data from iCloud*

16. After the restoration completes and the iPad restarts, enter your passcode to unlock the iPad. You'll then need to follow through a short setup routine, much the same as when you install an update to iOS.

Erasing an iPad Using Recovery Mode

Your third option for dealing with a forgotten passcode is to use Recovery Mode to erase the iPad using Recovery Mode. You can then set it up again from scratch, but you won't be able to restore data to the iPad unless you have a backup for it in it iTunes—in which case you would normally follow the procedure explained in the section "Erasing and Restoring an iPad via iTunes," earlier in this chapter.

Here's how to erase an iPad using Recovery Mode:

1. Connect the iPad to your Mac or PC via USB.

2. If iTunes doesn't launch (or become active) when you connect the iPad, launch or activate iTunes as usual from the Dock or Launchpad (on the Mac) or from the Start menu or taskbar (on Windows).

3. Force restart the iPad by pressing and holding the Home button and the Sleep/Wake button (the power button) until the Recovery Mode screen appears. This screen shows the Apple Support URL for restoring iPads (http://support. apple.com/ipad/restore) and a Lightning cable reaching toward the iTunes logo, indicating that you should connect the iPad to iTunes. Figure 9-27 shows the lower part of the Recovery Mode screen.

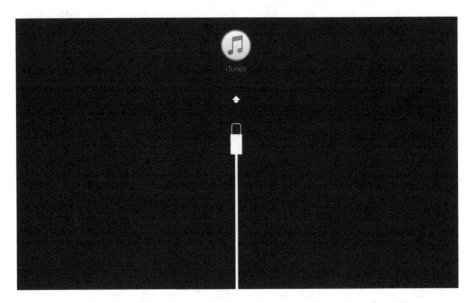

Figure 9-27. The Recovery Mode screen indicates that you've put the iPad into Recovery Mode. This is the lower part of the screen

■ **Caution** When force-restarting the iPad, don't release the Home button and the Sleep/Wake button when the Apple logo appears on screen. Wait for a few more seconds until the Recovery Mode screen appears.

4. When iTunes notices the iPad in Recovery Mode, it displays the There Is a Problem with the iPad That Requires It to Be Updated or Restored dialog (see Figure 9-28). Click the Restore button. This causes iTunes to start downloading the latest operating system image for the iPad.

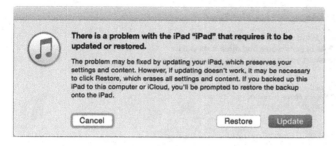

Figure 9-28. *Click the Restore button in the There Is a Problem with the iPad That Requires It to Be Updated or Restored dialog to erase the iPad using Recovery Mode*

■ **Tip** When you click the Restore button in the There Is a Problem with the iPad That Requires It to Be Updated or Restored dialog, you may see an alert dialog telling you that software for this iPad is not currently available and advising you to make sure you have the latest version of iTunes and try again. If this happens, you'll need to update iTunes to the latest version by using Software Update.

An iPad system image is around 2–3 GB in size, so it takes a few minutes to download even if your school has a fast Internet connection. iTunes displays a readout saying that it's downloading the iPad software, but it doesn't give you a useful progress readout, so you'll need to check periodically to see if it's finished the download.

In the meantime, the iPad stays in Recovery Mode for only 15 minutes and then times out. When iTunes finishes downloading the iPad system image, follow these steps:

1. If you disconnected the iPad from the Mac or PC, connect it again.

2. If iTunes doesn't launch (or become active) when you connect the iPad, launch or activate iTunes as usual from the Dock or Launchpad (on the Mac) or from the Start menu or taskbar (on Windows).

3. Put the iPad back into Recovery Mode by pressing and holding the Home button and the Sleep/Wake button until the iPad displays the Recovery Mode screen again. When iTunes recognizes the iPad, it displays an alert dialog to confirm that you want to restore the iPad to its factory settings (see Figure 9-29). This alert contains either the Restore and Update button or the Restore button, depending on whether the system image that iTunes has downloaded contains an update or the same version of iOS as the iPad is currently running.

Figure 9-29. *In this alert dialog, click the Restore and Update button or the Restore button to confirm that you want to erase the iPad's contents*

4. Click the Restore and Update button or the Restore button (whichever appears). The first iPad Software Update dialog opens (see Figure 9-30).

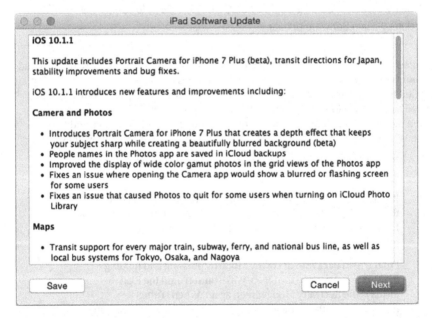

Figure 9-30. *The first iPad Software Update dialog summarizes any changes in an updated version of iOS that you're installing*

5. If you want to save the details of the changes, click the Save button and specify where to save the file.

6. Click the Next button. The second iPad Software Update dialog opens, showing terms and conditions for using the software.

7. If you want to save the terms and conditions, click the Save button and specify where to save the file.

8. Click the Agree button if you want to proceed. iTunes restores the software on the iPad. The Activation Lock screen then appears (see Figure 9-31), prompting you for the Apple ID and password used to set up the iPad.

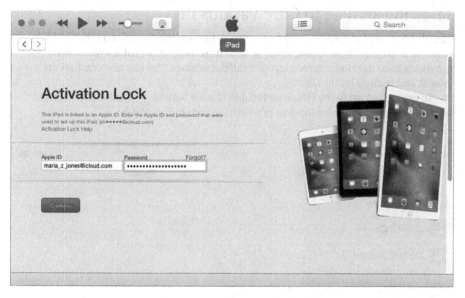

Figure 9-31. *On the Activation Lock screen, enter the Apple ID and password used to set up the iPad*

9. Type the Apple ID in the Apple ID box.

10. Type the password in the Password box. If you've forgotten the password, click the Forgot? link to have a password-reset link sent to you via e-mail.

11. Click the Continue button. The Welcome to Your New iPad screen appears (refer to Figure 9-21).

12. Select the Set Up as New iPad option button.

■ **Note** On the Welcome to Your New iPad screen, you can select the Restore from This Backup option button and then choose the appropriate backup in the pop-up menu. This enables you to restore the iPad using a backup from another device. (In this section, I'm assuming that you're erasing the iPad because you don't have a backup of it.)

---

13. Click the Continue button. iTunes displays the Sync with iTunes screen, and you can click the Get Started button to set up syncing. Alternatively, you can disconnect the iPad from the computer and set it up manually from scratch.

Resetting an iPad to Cure Various Ills

If an iPad isn't responding normally, or seems to be running slowly, you may be able to restore it to health by resetting some or all of its settings. iOS enables you to reset everything from the Home screen layout to all the settings. You can also erase all the content and settings on the iPad.

To get started, go to the Home screen and choose Settings ➤ General ➤ Reset to display the Reset screen, the top part of which appears in Figure 9-32.

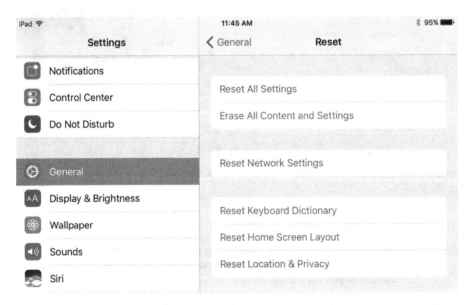

Figure 9-32. *From the Reset screen in the Settings app, you can reset various aspects of the iPad's configuration, such as the Home screen layout, the network settings, or the entire range of settings*

From the Reset screen, you can perform six different reset operations: Reset All Settings, Erase All Content and Settings, Reset Network Settings, Reset Keyboard Dictionary, Reset Home Screen Layout, and Reset Location & Privacy. Table 9-1 explains what each reset operation does and when you'd use it.

Table 9-1. *Reset Operations on the Reset Screen in the Settings App*

Reset Setting	What It Does	When You'd Use It
Reset All Settings	Resets all the iPad's settings to their defaults but doesn't erase the iPad's contents.	To recover from problems that are preventing the iPad from running normally. In some cases, you'd use another Reset command, such as the Reset Network Settings command or the Reset Location & Privacy command, before resorting to this command.
Erase All Content and Settings	Erases all the iPad's content and restores it to factory settings.	To prepare the iPad for selling, giving to someone else, or otherwise disposing of it. Erasing wipes the iPad and restores it to factory settings, so someone else can set it up from scratch.
Reset Network Settings	Restores the network settings to their default values. The iPad forgets the Wi-Fi networks to which it has connected, and deletes their passwords. It deletes any VPN connections you have set up. On a cellular iPad, this command also deletes any custom APN (Access Point Names) you've set up.	The iPad's network settings have become corrupted, so it can't connect to networks or the Internet consistently.
Reset Keyboard Dictionary	Resets the keyboard dictionary to its default settings. The effect of this is to delete all the custom words you've added to the dictionary by typing them on the keyboard and rejecting suggestions.	When you've accidentally added incorrect or unsuitable words to the keyboard dictionary and the Auto-Correction feature is suggesting them as you type text.
Reset Home Screen Layout	Resets the Home screen icons to their default settings.	After someone has customized the Home screen.
Reset Location & Privacy	Resets the Location Services commands and the Privacy commands to their default values.	After someone has customized the Location Services settings or the Privacy settings. This command gives you a quick way to restore the default settings without having to adjust individual settings manually.

When you give one of these commands, you'll see one or more dialogs:

- *Enter Passcode dialog*: For any reset operation except Reset Home Screen Layout, the Enter Passcode dialog opens so you can authenticate yourself by entering your passcode. This check helps avoid unauthorized users performing reset operations.

- *Enter Passcode dialog for Restrictions passcode*: If you've applied restrictions to the iPad, and the reset is a type that will change or remove them, iOS next prompts you for the Restrictions passcode. This check makes sure users can't use a reset operation to remove restrictions.

- *Confirmation dialog or dialogs*: Once you've passed the security checks, a Reset dialog (such as the Reset Settings dialog box shown in Figure 9-33) opens to confirm the reset operations. Tap the Reset button if you want to go ahead. The Reset All Settings command and the Erase All Content and Settings command then display a second confirmation dialog to make doubly sure, because these commands have extensive effects.

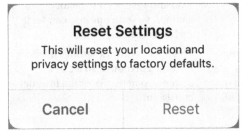

Figure 9-33. *The iPad displays a Reset dialog, such as this Reset Settings dialog, to confirm the reset operation you've chosen. Tap the Reset button to proceed*

Here's a bit more detail on two of the Reset commands:

- *Erase All Content and Settings*: This is the heaviest-duty of all the reset commands. To execute this command, you need to be able to enter the passcode. Also, if the Find My iPad feature is enabled, you'll need to enter the iCloud password for the Apple ID associated with the iPad. Neither of these requirements is surprising, but together they mean that you can't use the Erase All Content and Settings command to recover from a forgotten passcode on an iPad even though one of the Touch ID registered fingerprints is available.

- *Reset Location & Privacy*: This command resets your Location Services settings (including the System Services settings) and Privacy settings to their default values. Table 9-2 explains what the default Privacy settings are, and Table 9-3 lists the default Location Services and System Services settings.

***Table 9-2.** Default Privacy Settings for an iPad*

Setting	Value
Location Services	On (see Table 9-3 for details).
Contacts, Calendars, Reminders, Photos, Bluetooth Sharing, Microphone, Speech Recognition, Camera, HomeKit, Media Library, Motion & Fitness	No apps have permission to request data from these apps.
Twitter, Facebook	No apps have permission to request data from your social networking accounts.
Diagnostics & Usage	Don't Send.
Advertising	The Limit Ad Tracking switch is set to Off.

***Table 9-3.** Default Location Services and System Services Settings for an iPad*

Setting	Value
Share My Location	Share My Location switch set to Off
Compass Calibration	On
Find My iPad	On
HomeKit	On
Location-Based Alerts	On
Location-Based Apple Ads	On
Location-Based Suggestions	On
Setting Time Zone	On
Share My Location	On
Wi-Fi Networking	On
Frequent Locations	On
Diagnostics & Usage	On
Popular Near Me	On
Routing & Traffic	On
Improve Maps	Off
Status Bar Icon	Off

Troubleshooting Power Issues

Much of the space inside each iPad is devoted to the battery, which—under good conditions—provides enough power for a full day's use. The problem you're most likely to encounter is that the battery doesn't provide as much runtime as you need, so we'll start by looking at the settings you can configure to reduce the iPad's power draw. We'll then move on to the second most common power problem: the iPad failing to charge.

Reducing Power Draw on the Battery

As with most electronic devices, the amount of runtime the battery delivers depends on how you're using the iPad. For example, shooting video and editing video consume far more battery power than working in an Office app. But no matter what you're doing with the iPad, you can reduce the power draw by configuring settings the right way.

Reducing Power Draw Quickly from Control Center

When you need to reduce the power draw quickly, open Control Center by swiping up from the bottom of the screen. On iOS 10, if the iPad Controls card doesn't appear at first, swipe left or right as needed to display it. You can then make as many of the following changes as needed to reduce the iPad's power consumption:

- *Brightness*: Drag the Brightness slider to the left to turn the brightness down.

- *Airplane Mode*: Tap this button if you want to shut down all the iPad's communications.

- *Wi-Fi*: Tap this button to turn Wi-Fi off.

- *Bluetooth*: Tap this button to turn Bluetooth off.

- *AirDrop*: Tap this button to display the AirPlay dialog, and then tap the Receiving Off button to turn AirPlay off.

■ **Note**   Turning on Airplane Mode saves a decent amount of power, but in most classroom situations, you'll want to keep Wi-Fi turned on so that the iPads can access the network and the Internet. Unless you're using Bluetooth, turn it off and keep it turned off.

Reducing Power Draw from the Settings App

When you want to make more extensive power savings, dig into the settings in the Settings app. This section explains the changes you can make and which changes to make when. To get started, tap the Settings button on the Home screen.

- *Airplane Mode*: Set the switch at the top of the left column on the Settings screen to On if you need to turn off all communications.

- *Wi-Fi*: If you can dispense with Wi-Fi, tap the Wi-Fi button in the left column, and then set the Wi-Fi switch at the top of the Wi-Fi screen to Off.

- *Bluetooth*: Unless you need Bluetooth, tap the Bluetooth button in the left column, and then set the Bluetooth switch at the top of the Bluetooth screen to Off.

- *Notifications*: Notifications take up only a modest amount of power, but to minimize distractions, it's a good idea to tap the Notifications button in the left column and then review all the apps allowed to raise notifications. Chances are, you can slim down the list of allowed apps without causing the iPad's user to miss any important notifications.

- *Display & Brightness*: Tap the Display & Brightness button in the left column to show the Display & Brightness screen, and then drag the Brightness slider as far left as you can while still leaving the screen at a usable brightness. Set the Auto-Brightness switch to On if you want the iPad to adjust the brightness to suit the ambient brightness that its sensors detect. Tap the Auto-Lock button to display the Auto-Lock screen, and then tap the button for the appropriate time interval. You'll want to strike a balance between shutting off the screen when the iPad isn't being used and having the screen go off while students are listening to instructions or pondering their next move. Your choices are 2 Minutes, 5 Minutes, 10 Minutes, 15 Minutes, or Never; Never is a useful setting for iPads you're using to display information without user interaction, but it's a killer for battery runtime.

- *Privacy*: The Privacy settings might seem to have no connection to battery runtime, but this is where you can disable the Location Services feature or simply prune the number of apps and services that are allowed to use Location Services. On the Privacy screen, tap the Location Services button to display the Location Services screen (see Figure 9-34). You can then set the Location Services switch to Off if you want to turn off Location Services altogether, but since this prevents the Find My iPhone service from working, you probably won't want to do this. Instead, review the list of apps that can use Location Services; if an app doesn't need Location Services, tap the app's button to display the screen for controlling the app's access, and then tap the Never button. You should also review the list of system services that are using Location Services: tap the System Services button on the Location Services screen to display the System Services screen (see Figure 9-35), and then set the switch to Off for any service for which the iPad doesn't need Location Services.

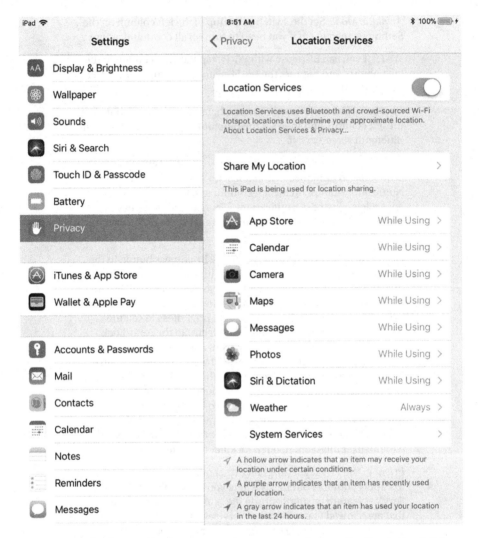

Figure 9-34. *On the Location Services screen, you can set the Location Services switch to Off if you want to disable the feature entirely. Otherwise, review the apps in the lower box, disabling any that don't need Location Services, and then tap the System Services button and review the list of system services as well*

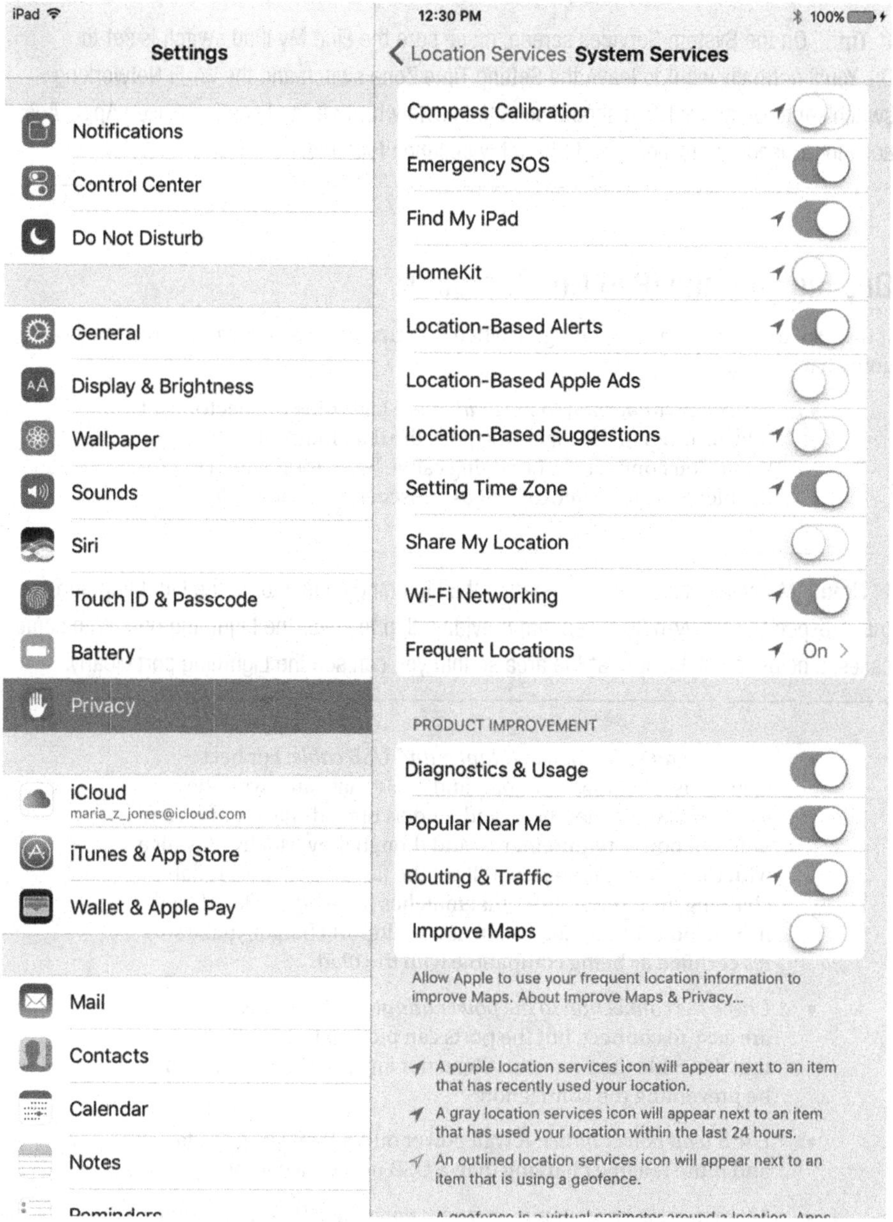

iPad 🛜	12:30 PM	☀ 100% 🔋 ⚡
Settings	‹ Location Services **System Services**	

Settings
📷 Notifications
🎛 Control Center
🌙 Do Not Disturb
⚙️ General
AᴀA Display & Brightness
🌸 Wallpaper
🔊 Sounds
🌊 Siri
👆 Touch ID & Passcode
🔋 Battery
✋ Privacy
☁️ iCloud maria_z_jones@icloud.com
Ⓐ iTunes & App Store
💳 Wallet & Apple Pay
✉️ Mail
👤 Contacts
📅 Calendar
📝 Notes
Reminders

System Services	
Compass Calibration	➤ ⚪
Emergency SOS	🔵
Find My iPad	➤ 🔵
HomeKit	➤ ⚪
Location-Based Alerts	➤ 🔵
Location-Based Apple Ads	⚪
Location-Based Suggestions	➤ ⚪
Setting Time Zone	➤ 🔵
Share My Location	⚪
Wi-Fi Networking	➤ 🔵
Frequent Locations	➤ On ›

PRODUCT IMPROVEMENT

Diagnostics & Usage	🔵
Popular Near Me	🔵
Routing & Traffic	➤ 🔵
Improve Maps	⚪

Allow Apple to use your frequent location information to improve Maps. About Improve Maps & Privacy...

➤ A purple location services icon will appear next to an item that has recently used your location.

➤ A gray location services icon will appear next to an item that has used your location within the last 24 hours.

➤ An outlined location services icon will appear next to an item that is using a geofence.

A geofence is a virtual perimeter around a location. Apps

Figure 9-35. *On the System Services screen, set the switch to Off for any system service that you want to prevent from using Location Services*

■ **Tip**   On the System Services screen, make sure the Find My iPad switch is set to On. You'll normally want to leave the Setting Time Zone switch and the Wi-Fi Networking switch set to On as well. You should be able to safely turn off the Location-Based Apple Ads, Location-Based Suggestions, and Share My Location features.

Dealing with the iPad Not Charging

If the iPad doesn't seem to be charging when it's plugged in to a power source, start by going back to basics:

- *Check the connection to the iPad:* If the Lightning connector isn't fully inserted in the Lightning port, the iPad may not charge. When you connect the Lightning cable, listen for the iPad to give the bleep of electronic delight as it discovers the power feed.

■ **Note**   Many iPad cases make inserting the Lightning connector in the Lightning port tricky, especially heavy-duty cases that provide a flap to cover the Lightning port. With some cases, it helps to point a light at the area so that you can see the Lightning port clearly.

- *Use the iPad's USB power adapter and USB cable*: For best results, use the power adapter and cable that came with the iPad. Different generations and models of iPads have somewhat different power requirements, and though they usually play nice with the power adapters, you'll get the fastest and most reliable charging from the adapter that matches the iPad model. If you're using a power accessory, such as a multiport charger, make sure it's certified as being compatible with the iPad.

- *Check the connection to the power adapter*: USB cables and ports are easy to connect, but the ports can pick up lint or other gunk that the cable then rams in. Clean out any dirt or debris that may be preventing the connection.

- *Use a wall power outlet*: A wall power outlet typically gives faster and more reliable charging than a USB port on a computer.

- *Make sure the computer is on and is not asleep*: When charging from a computer, make sure it's powered on and not asleep.

If the battery won't charge when the iPad is connected to its own power adapter, and that power adapter is plugged into a wall power outlet that you know is working, the battery may need replacing. To find out, get the battery checked out by a technician at an Apple Store or an Apple Authorized Service Provider.

DEALING WITH THE LOW-BATTERY SCREEN

If the iPad's battery has been run very nearly flat, you may see a black screen with a red battery icon when you plug the iPad into power. When this happens, give the iPad half an hour or more to charge to a usable level before trying to power it on. After half an hour, the iPad should be displaying the Charging screen, the one that shows a battery gradually being filled.

If—after that half-hour—the Charging screen hasn't appeared, check the Lightning port, the USB cable, and the power adapter for dirt or damage. If the charging hardware seems okay, force a restart on the iPad by holding down the Sleep/Wake button and the Home button simultaneously for around 20 seconds, releasing the buttons when the Apple logo appears on the screen. Try another half-hour of charging.

If the Charging screen still doesn't appear, you'll need to get the battery checked out by a technician.

Troubleshooting Apps

If an app stops responding, you can usually close it by using the App Switcher: double-click the Home button to display the App Switcher, and then swipe the thumbnail for the problem app upward off the screen.

Once you've closed the app, try running it again. If the app stops responding again, close it by using the App Switcher once more. Then restart the iPad and try again.

If the app continues to give trouble after you restart the iPad, try deleting the app and then reinstalling it. Follow these steps:

1. On the Home screen, tap and hold the app's icon until the apps start jiggling.

2. Tap the Delete (X) button at the upper-left corner of the app's icon.

3. In the dialog that opens, tap the Delete button.

4. Press the Home button to stop the apps jiggling.

5. Tap the App Store button to launch the App Store app.

6. Tap the Purchased button at the bottom of the screen to display the Purchased list, which shows the apps you've purchased.

7. Tap the Not on This iPad tab to display its contents.

8. Locate the app—search if necessary—and the tap the Download icon (the cloud icon).

Once the download and installation finish, try running the app again.

■ **Note**   If the app *still* crashes after you reinstall it, contact the app's developer. From the Purchased screen in the App Store app, tap the app's button to display the dialog containing its information. Tap the Reviews tab to display its contents, and then tap the App Support link.

Troubleshooting Wi-Fi and Network Connections

To get the most out of your school's iPads, you'll need to connect them to the school's network and to the Internet via Wi-Fi. These days, Wi-Fi generally works pretty well—but plenty of things can still go wrong. This section shows you the moves you'll need to keep the iPads connected to the network.

Turning Wi-Fi Off and Then On Again

If an iPad can't connect to a Wi-Fi network, your first move should be to turn Wi-Fi off and then on again. Doing so forces the iPad to scan again for Wi-Fi networks.

You can toggle Wi-Fi on and off either from Control Center or in the Settings app:

- *Control Center*: Swipe up from the bottom of the screen to open Control Center. In iOS 10, make sure the iPad Controls card is displayed; if not, swipe left to display it. Look to verify that Wi-Fi is on; if not, tap the Wi-Fi icon to turn Wi-Fi on. Assuming Wi-Fi is on, tap the Wi-Fi icon to turn Wi-Fi off, wait a moment, and then tap the Wi-Fi icon again to turn Wi-Fi back on.

- *Settings app*: From the Home screen, choose Settings ➤ Wi-Fi, and then set the Wi-Fi switch to Off. Wait a few seconds, and then set the switch back to On.

Once Wi-Fi is running again, see if the iPad can connect to the Wi-Fi network. If not, continue with the following sections.

Renewing the Lease on a Wi-Fi Connection

If the iPad is using DHCP to get its IP address, your next troubleshooting move is to renew the lease. When a DHCP server assigns an IP address to a client device, it does so not forever but for a specific length of time, called a *lease*. The length of the lease depends on how the DHCP server is configured—you won't be able to see the length of the lease on the iPad.

Normally, if the client stays connected to the network, the client and the DHCP server automatically renew the lease. But sometimes that doesn't happen, and you may need to renew the lease manually.

To renew the lease, follow these steps:

1. From the Home screen, choose Home ➤ Settings ➤ Wi-Fi to display the Wi-Fi screen.

2. Tap the Info (i) button to display the screen for the network. Figure 9-36 shows an example of this screen, which is titled with the network's name.

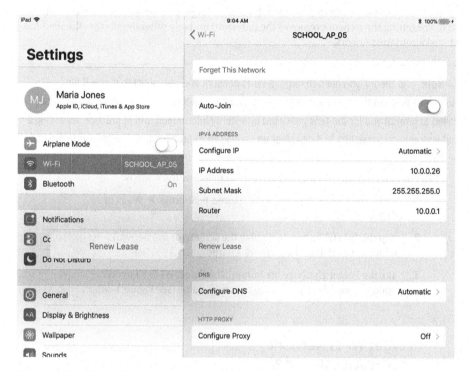

Figure 9-36. *Tap the Renew Lease button on the screen for the Wi-Fi network to try renewing the lease*

3. Tap the Renew Lease button. On iOS 11, a pop-up panel opens showing another Renew Lease button, as shown in Figure 9-36; on iOS 10, the Renew Lease dialog opens (see Figure 9-37).

Figure 9-37. *Tap the Renew button in the Renew Lease dialog*

4. Tap the Renew Lease button on iOS 11 or the Renew button on iOS 10. The iPad requests a new lease from the DHCP server.

Wait a few seconds and see if the iPad is able to connect to network resources or the Internet again.

Forgetting a Wi-Fi Network and Reconnecting to It

Your next troubleshooting step is to tell the iPad to forget the network, and then reconnect to it. Forgetting the network removes the password and any other details that the iPad has stored about the network.

■ **Note** In theory, you need to forget a Wi-Fi network and reconnect to it only if the network's password or other security mechanism has changed and iOS has for some reason failed to prompt you for the new password or security information. But in practice, forgetting a network and reconnecting to it can clear up various Wi-Fi problems, so it's well worth trying.

To forget a Wi-Fi network and reconnect to it, follow these steps:

1. From the Home screen, choose Home ➤ Settings ➤ Wi-Fi to display the Wi-Fi screen.

2. Tap the Info (i) button to display the screen for the network, which is titled with the network's name.

3. Tap the Forget This Network button. The Forget Wi-Fi Network? dialog opens, also showing the network's name (see Figure 9-38).

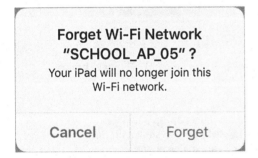

Figure 9-38. Tap the Forget button in the Forget This Network? dialog to forget a Wi-Fi network's information so that you can try reconnecting the iPad to the network

4. Tap the Forget button. The iPad forgets the information for the Wi-Fi network.

5. Tap the Wi-Fi button in the upper-left corner of the network's screen to return to the Wi-Fi screen.

6. Tap the button for the network you've just forgotten. The Enter Password dialog opens.

7. Type the password.

8. Tap the Join button. The iPad connects to the network, and the network's name appears with a check mark at the top of the Wi-Fi screen.

Turning Off Wi-Fi Assist on a Cellular iPad

On a cellular iPad, you may sometimes need to turn off the Wi-Fi Assist feature to sort out problems with a Wi-Fi network. Wi-Fi Assist automatically uses the cellular network to transfer data if the available Wi-Fi networks are unreliable or not working.

To turn off the Wi-Fi Assist feature, follow these steps:

1. From the Home screen, choose Home ➤ Settings ➤ Cellular Data to display the Cellular Data screen.

2. On the right side of the screen, swipe up to scroll all the way down to the bottom of the screen (see Figure 9-39).

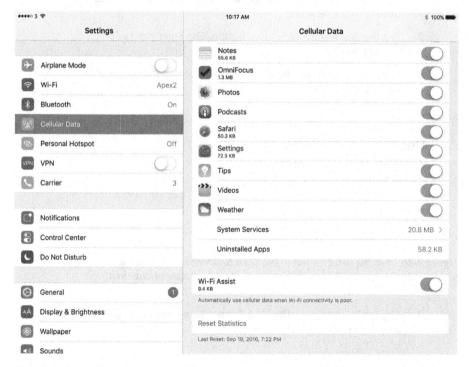

Figure 9-39. *To clear up Wi-Fi problems, you may need to turn off the Wi-Fi Assist feature by setting the Wi-Fi Assist switch at the bottom of the Cellular Data screen in Settings to Off*

3. Set the Wi-Fi Assist switch to Off.

Restarting the iPad

If you've worked through the troubleshooting steps in the previous sections, but the iPad still won't connect to the Wi-Fi network, your next move is to restart the iPad. As usual, press and hold the Sleep/Wake button until the Slide to Power Off screen appears, and then slide the Slide to Power Off slider to the right.

Once the iPad has powered down, press and hold the Sleep/Wake button for a couple of seconds until the Apple logo appears on the screen. When the lock screen appears, type your passcode to unlock the iPad. Then try connecting to the Wi-Fi network again.

Resetting the Network Settings

If even restarting the iPad doesn't clear up the problem with the Wi-Fi network, you may need to reset the iPad's network settings. This move wipes the network settings clean; afterward, you must set up each network again from scratch, either manually or by using a profile.

To reset the network settings, follow these steps:

1. From the Home screen, choose Settings ➤ General ➤ Reset to display the Reset screen.

2. Tap the Reset Network Settings button. The Enter Passcode dialog opens.

3. Type your passcode. The Reset Network Settings dialog opens (see Figure 9-40).

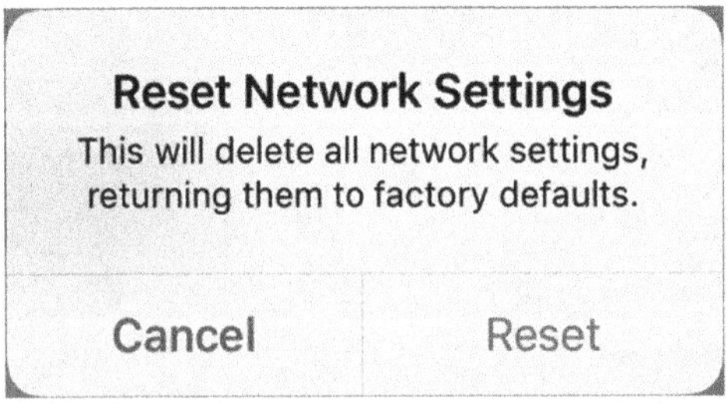

Reset Network Settings
This will delete all network settings, returning them to factory defaults.

| Cancel | Reset |

Figure 9-40. Tap the Reset button in the Reset Network Settings dialog to delete all the network settings on the iPad so that you can set up each network again afresh

4. Tap the Reset button. The iPad deletes the network settings and then restarts.

5. When the lock screen appears, type your passcode to unlock the iPad.

6. From the Home screen, choose Settings ➤ Wi-Fi to display the Wi-Fi screen. You can then set up each Wi-Fi network as needed. See the section "Connecting to Wi-Fi Networks" in Chapter 3 for details.

■ **Note**   Resetting the network settings removes any trusted relationships you have set up between the iPad and Windows or Mac computers. When you connect the iPad to a Windows PC or to a Mac, the iPad and iTunes prompt you to set up a trust relationship between the two.

Managing a Network with AirPort Utility

If you've installed Apple's AirPort Utility app on an iPad, you can launch AirPort Utility by tapping the Manage This Network button on the screen for a Wi-Fi network, which you access from the Wi-Fi screen in the Settings app. This works only for Wi-Fi networks created by Apple's AirPort devices, because these are the only wireless access points that AirPort Utility can manage.

■ **Note**   Apple's AirPort range includes three main types of device. The AirPort Extreme is a business-class wireless access point. The AirPort Time Capsule is an AirPort Extreme with one or more built-in hard drives for backup or sharing files. The AirPort Express is a consumer-class device that includes the ability to play audio streamed from iOS devices and from iTunes. However, as of this writing, Apple has disbanded the AirPort development team and appears to not be updating the devices.

The first time you tap this button, iOS displays a dialog telling you that "'Settings' wants to open 'AirPort Utility.'" Tap the Open button, and iOS launches and displays the AirPort Utility app. As you can see in Figure 9-41, you can tap one of the items shown to display information about it.

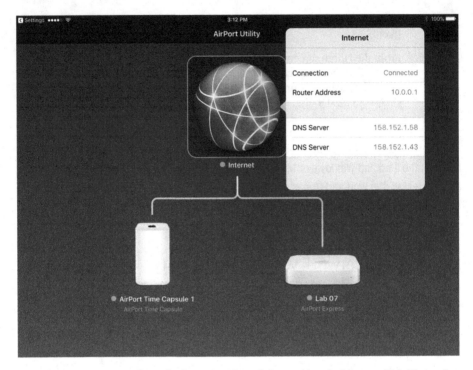

Figure 9-41. *AirPort Utility, which you can launch by tapping the Manage This Network button on a Wi-Fi network's screen in the Settings app, displays information about the AirPort devices and their configuration.*

Once you're using the AirPort Utility app, you can start configuring an AirPort device in AirPort Utility by tapping the device's icon to display its Information window, and then tapping the Enter Password button in the Device Password dialog. You can then tap the Edit button to display the dialog for managing the device (see the example in Figure 9-42). The contents of this dialog depend on the AirPort device and model, but may include the following items:

- *Base Station*: Tap this button to display the Base Station dialog, where you can change the name assigned to the AirPort device and set its password.

- *Network*: Tap this button to display the Network dialog, which enables you to set the Wi-Fi mode (your options are Create a Wireless Network, Extend a Wireless Network, or Off), specify the security method (such as WPA/WPA2 Enterprise), set the SSID, and set the password. You can also set the Hidden Network switch to On if you want to create a closed network rather than an open network.

- *Guest Network*: For an AirPort Extreme or AirPort Time Capsule model, you can turn on the Guest Network feature, assign a name to the guest network, and choose a security method.

- *Internet Connection*: Tap this button to display the Internet dialog, where you can configure DHCP, static IP, or PPPoE settings.

- *Advanced*: Tap this button to display the Advanced dialog, which includes items such as IPv6, DHCP and Network Address Translation (NAT), and access control.

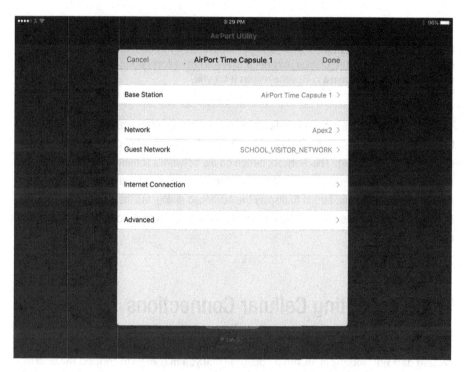

Figure 9-42. *From AirPort Utility's main dialog, which shows the name of the AirPort device, you can configure the base station, Wi-Fi network, guest network (on some devices), Internet connection, and advanced features.*

> ■ **Note** The guest network on an AirPort Extreme or AirPort Time Capsule enables Wi-Fi devices to access the Internet but not any local network resources. The access point limits the guest network to a modest amount of bandwidth to prevent it from hogging the Internet connection. For convenience, you may choose not to implement a security method for the guest network or to use an easy-to-remember password that you give out freely to visitors.

Changing the DHCP or Static IP Settings on the iPad

To sort out other problems with the network settings on an iPad, you may need to manually configure its DHCP settings, static IP settings, or proxy settings. See the sections "Configuring DHCP Settings," "Configuring Static IP Settings," and "Configuring Proxy Settings" in Chapter 3 for coverage of these topics.

Restarting the Access Point if Possible

If you establish that multiple iPads—and perhaps other Wi-Fi computers or devices—are suffering network problems, you may need to restart the access point that's providing the wireless network, or have a colleague restart it for you.

> ■ **Note** If the access point in question is an Apple AirPort device, you can restart it by using AirPort Utility on an iPad. To do so, launch AirPort Utility either from the Home screen or by tapping the Manage This Network button on the network's screen in the Settings app, tap the icon for the AirPort device, and then tap the Edit button. In the dialog for the AirPort device, tap the Advanced button to display the Advanced dialog, tap the Restart Base Station button, and then tap the Restart button in the Restart Base Station dialog that opens to confirm the action.

Troubleshooting Cellular Connections

If you have cellular iPad models rather than Wi-Fi–only models, you may sometimes need to troubleshoot the cellular connection. The problem you're most likely to face is cellular data not working at all, but it's possible that you may need to connect the iPad to a different cellular access point.

Troubleshooting Cellular Data Not Working

If an iPad is unable to transfer data over the cellular connection, follow these steps to troubleshoot the problem:

- *Toggle Airplane Mode*: Toggle Airplane Mode to make the iPad refresh the cellular connection. You can toggle Airplane Mode either from Control Center (tap the Airplane Mode icon so that it goes orange, wait a few seconds, and then tap it again so that it goes gray) or in the Settings app (move the Airplane Mode switch at the top of the left column to On, wait a few seconds, and then move the switch back to Off).

- *Ensure cellular data is on*: From the Home screen, choose Settings ➤ Cellular Data to display the Cellular Data screen (see Figure 9-43). Then make sure the Cellular Data switch at the top of the screen is set to On.

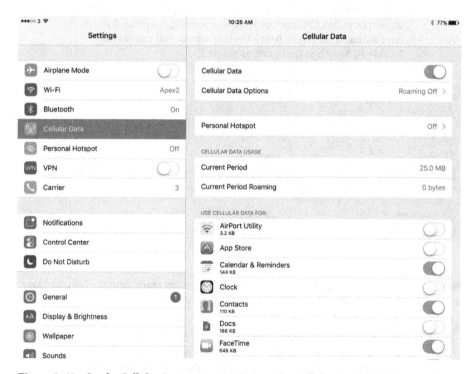

Figure 9-43. *On the Cellular Data screen, make sure the Cellular Data switch is set to On. Then go to the Use Cellular Data For box and make sure the switch is set to On for each app you need to use via the cellular network*

- *Make sure cellular data is enabled for the apps you're using*: Still on the Cellular Data screen in the Settings app, look at the Use Cellular Data For box and make sure the switch is set to On for each app you want to be able to use cellular data.

■ **Tip** Usually the problem with the apps in the Use Cellular Data For box on the Cellular Data screen is the other way around—rather than useful apps having cellular disabled, all the switches are set to On, even for apps you'd seldom (if ever) need cellular data for, such as the built-in Tips app or AirPort Utility (for managing Apple's AirPort Wi-Fi devices). Take a minute to review the apps and make sure that only the apps for which you need cellular data are set to use it.

- *Enable or disable 4G, as needed*: From the Cellular Data screen, tap the Cellular Data Options button to display the screen that should be called Cellular Data Options but at this writing doesn't have a name (see Figure 9-44). On this screen, you can set the Enable 4G switch to On or Off, as needed.

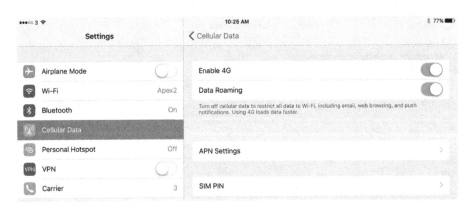

Figure 9-44. *On this screen, which has no title but which you reach from the Cellular Data screen, you can enable or disable 4G (or LTE) and data roaming, as needed*

- *Enable or disable data roaming, as needed*: On the same unnamed screen, set the Data Roaming switch to Off or On, as needed. Data roaming usually involves paying extra to the carrier involved, so normally, you'll want to keep Data Roaming turned off all the time unless you go somewhere that requires it.

- *Turn off Wi-Fi Assist*: At the bottom of the Cellular Data screen, set the Wi-Fi Assist switch to Off unless you need the cellular connection to kick in when your current and available Wi-Fi networks have limited connectivity.

Connecting a Cellular iPad to a Different Access Point Name

Another move you may be able make to resolve cellular problems is to connect the iPad to a different access point name (APN) rather than the default APN. Whether you can do this depends on the carrier that provided your iPad's SIM card and the type of cellular network the carrier provides. The APN is the identifier for the gateway between a cellular network (your carrier's network, in this case) and another network (in this case, the Internet).

Normally, the iPad's SIM card controls which APN the iPad connects to. You don't normally need to change the APN, but here are a couple of circumstances when you might need to change it:

- *Your school's IT department provides a special APN for cellular devices to use*: Usually, this happens only in large schools, institutions, or enterprises. In this case, you'd get the details you need—APN name, username, and password—from the IT department.

- *Your carrier is altering its infrastructure and needs to move you to a different APN*: This is relatively unusual. In this case, you'd get the APN name, username, and password from the carrier's support staff.

You can connect to a different APN either manually, as described here, or by applying a configuration profile that includes the APN) information. Connecting manually works only if your carrier allows the settings to be changed on the iPad; if not, you can't reach the settings. Applying a configuration profile works whether your carrier permits the change or not.

■ **Caution**   If you change the APN manually, you'll need to change it again after updating iOS, because updates restore the default APN settings.

To connect the iPad to a different APN, follow these steps:

1. From the Home screen, choose Settings ➤ Cellular Data to display the Cellular Data screen.

2. Tap the Cellular Data Options button to display the unnamed screen that might be called Cellular Data Options.

3. Tap the APN) Settings button to display the APN Settings screen (see Figure 9-45).

Figure 9-45. *The APN Settings screen enables you to connect a cellular iPad to a different APN (access point name) than the default APN for the iPad's SIM card. Connecting to a different APN is a specialized move that you're unlikely to need to perform*

4. Tap the APN) field and type the APN name your IT department or carrier has given you.

5. Tap the Username field and type the username.

6. Tap the Password field and type the corresponding password.

The iPad saves the data automatically—there's no Save button to tap.

To determine whether the iPad has connected to the cellular network with the new settings, tap the Wi-Fi button in the left column in the Settings app, and then set the Wi-Fi switch to Off. Then look at the status bar to see whether the cellular icon (such as the 3G icon, the 4G icon, or the LTE icon) appears toward the left end.

When you need to restore the default APN settings for your iPad's carrier, tap the Reset Settings button on the APN Settings screen, and then tap the Reset button in the Reset dialog that opens (see Figure 9-46).

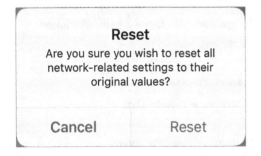

Figure 9-46. *Tap the Reset button in the Reset dialog to reset an iPad's cellular settings to the carrier's default settings*

Troubleshooting Bluetooth Issues

On the iPad, as on many other devices, Bluetooth generally works pretty well as long as the device is compatible with the iPad. Normally, you'll discover any compatibility problems when you first try to use the device with the iPad. If you can't get the iPad to recognize the device, or if the device and the iPad won't pair, the device may well not be compatible.

■ **Note**   See the section "Connecting Bluetooth Devices" in Chapter 3 for instructions on pairing a Bluetooth device with an iPad.

Follow these general steps to troubleshoot Bluetooth issues with devices that you've previously paired and used successfully:

- *Turn the device off and then on again*: How you do this depends on the device, so you may need to consult the documentation. If the device has only a single button, try holding it down for five or more seconds to turn the device off. If that works, release the button for a moment, and then hold it down for a few more seconds to turn the device back on.

- *On the iPad, turn Bluetooth off and then on again*: The easiest way to do this is to open Control Center, tap the Bluetooth icon to turn Bluetooth off, and then tap the Bluetooth icon again to turn it back on. (On iOS 10, you'll need to make sure the iPad Controls card in Control Center is displayed.) Alternatively, choose Settings ➤ Bluetooth from the Home screen, and then set the Bluetooth switch at the top of the Bluetooth screen to Off and then back to On.

- *Restart the iPad*: As usual, press and hold the Sleep/Wake button for a few seconds until the Slide to Power Off slider appears, and then move the slider to the right. After the iPad powers off, press and hold the Sleep/Wake button for a couple of seconds until the Apple logo appears on the screen.

- *Forget the Bluetooth device and then pair with it again*: From the Home screen, choose Settings ➤ Bluetooth to display the Bluetooth screen. Tap the Information (i) button for the device to display its screen, tap the Forget This Device button, and then tap the OK button in the Forget dialog that opens. Then put the device into pairing mode and try pairing it again.

■ **Tip**   If you can't pair the iPad with the device, make sure the device isn't paired with another iPad or other device.

UNDERSTANDING WHICH BLUETOOTH PROFILES THE IPAD MODELS SUPPORT

If you're having trouble pairing an iPad with a Bluetooth device, or getting a paired device to work consistently, you may want to check that the iPad you're using supports the Bluetooth profile that the device requires.

In the Bluetooth standards for wireless communication, a *Bluetooth profile* is a specification that gives details for a particular type of communication—for example, the Human Interface Device Protocol (HID for short) gives details of how input devices such as keyboards, mice, and game controllers can communicate via Bluetooth.

The iPad 2 and all subsequent iPad models support the following Bluetooth profiles, described with iPad-specific examples:

- *Hands-Free Profile (HFP 1.6)*: This profile enables Bluetooth headsets and hands-free kits to communicate with the iPad.

- *Advanced Audio Distribution Profile (A2DP)*: This profile enables the iPad to stream high-quality audio to a Bluetooth headset, Bluetooth speakers, or a car audio system.

- *Audio/Video Remote Control Profile (AVRCP 1.4)*: This profile enables the iPad to control playback of audio or video files on a compatible Bluetooth device. The iPad can browse the selection of files available and can give five playback commands: Play, Pause, Stop, Next, and Previous.

- *Personal Area Networking Profile (PAN)*: This profile enables the iPad to send files to other Bluetooth-equipped devices and receive files from them.

- *Human Interface Device Profile (HID)*: This profile enables input devices such as keyboards, mice, and game controllers to communicate with the iPad.

The first-generation iPad supports the Advanced Audio Distribution Profile, Audio/Video Remote Control Profile, Personal Area Networking Profile, and Human Interface Device Profile, but it doesn't support the Hands-Free Profile.

Troubleshooting Display Issues

On the iPad, the display does double duty, functioning as not only the main output device but also the main input device via its touch component. So when the display malfunctions, your means of communicating with the iPad are severely limited.

In this section, we'll look at how to deal with color problems, screen-rotation problems, and problems with the screen being blank, unresponsive, or both. We'll also touch on what to do if an iPad's screen gets cracked.

Dealing with Colors Being Inverted, Grayscale, or Wrong

Normally, the iPad's screen displays vivid colors, at least if you've got the brightness turned up far enough. So, if there are problems with the colors—such as the colors being muted, inverted, missing, or just plain wrong—you'll likely notice soon enough.

All these problems are ones that can be produced by the Display Accommodations features in the iPad's Accessibility settings, so start by opening the Settings app and seeing if this is the problem. From the Home screen, choose Settings ➤ General ➤ Accessibility to display the Accessibility screen, and then tap the Display Accommodations button in the Vision box to show the Display Accommodations screen (see Figure 9-47).

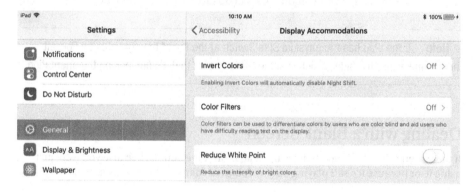

Figure 9-47. *Visit the Display Accommodations screen in the Accessibility section of the Settings app to troubleshoot problems with missing or inverted colors, or colors that otherwise look wrong*

Once you're at the Display Accommodations screen, you can resolve color problems quickly enough:

- *Invert Colors*: On iOS 11, if this button shows On, tap it to display the Invert Colors screen, set the Smart Invert switch or the Classic Invert switch to Off, and then tap the Display Accommodations button to return to the Display Accommodations screen. On iOS 10, the Invert Colors switch appears on the Display Accommodations screen; if this switch is set to On, set it to Off to restore inverted colors to normal.

533

- *Color Filters*: If the readout at the right side of this button says On, tap this button to display the Color Filters screen. Here, you can see which color filter is applied—Grayscale, Red/Green Filter, Green/Red Filter, Blue/Yellow Filter, or Color Tint. Set the Color Filters switch at the top of the screen to Off to turn off the filtering.

- *Reduce White Point*: If this switch is set to On, set it to Off to restore the intensity of bright colors.

Troubleshooting the Screen Rotation Being Stuck

If the screen seems to be stuck in portrait orientation or landscape orientation, first make sure the app you're using supports rotation. Some apps are permanently portrait, while others are permanently landscape. Most of the built-in apps rotate, so if you need to check whether the screen is stuck, try an app such as Notes, Clock, or Settings—or just display the Home screen and try turning the iPad.

Once you've determined that the screen won't rotate, look at the right side of the status bar to see if the Orientation Lock icon is displayed. (The Orientation Lock icon is a padlock with an arrow curling clockwise around it.) If the Orientation Lock icon does appear, open Control Center (on iOS 10, display the iPad Controls card if it doesn't appear at first), and then tap the Orientation Lock icon to turn off Orientation Lock.

■ **Note**   If the iPad has the physical Side Switch at the top of the right side (in Portrait mode), make sure the Side Switch is set to Off to ensure that it's not locking the orientation.

Dealing with a Blank Screen

If the screen is blank but you believe the iPad is on (for example, because you were just using it, or because it's still playing audio), follow as many of these steps as necessary:

- Press the Home button.

- Press the Sleep/Wake button a couple of times.

- Hold down the Sleep/Wake button for five seconds to try to display the Slide to Power Off slider. If it appears, drag the slider to the right to power the iPad down. Once it's powered down, press and hold the Sleep/Wake button for a couple of seconds to start the iPad again.

- Hold down the Sleep/Wake button and the Home button for about 25 seconds to force the iPad to restart. When the Apple logo appears on the screen, release the buttons, and let the iPad continue restarting.

Dealing with No Response to the Touchscreen

If the touchscreen fails to respond to fingers (or thumbs), your first move should be to restart the iPad. Hold down the Sleep/Wake button for five seconds to display the Slide to Power Off slider, and then see if the touchscreen registers you moving the slider to the right. If so, wait for the iPad to power down, and then press and hold the Sleep/Wake button for a couple seconds to restart the device.

If the Slide to Power Off slider doesn't appear, or if the iPad doesn't respond to you moving the slider, force a restart by holding down the Sleep/Wake button and the Home button for about 25 seconds. Release the buttons when the Apple logo appears on the screen. Let the iPad finish restarting, and then see if the touchscreen is responding again.

If the touchscreen is still not responding, remove any case or screen protector from the iPad and try again. Clean the screen with a lint-free cloth, dampening it slightly with water if you need to remove gunk.

If the touchscreen still doesn't respond after your tender, loving care, you'll need to have a technician look at the iPad.

Dealing with Cracks in the Screen

As you likely know from experience, the screen is typically the most vulnerable hardware component of a tablet such as the iPad. So, even if you've armored up your school's iPads with heavy-duty cases (as recommended in Chapter 2) or fixed them in position using secure mounts or stands (same chapter), some screens may still get cracked.

When this happens, you should plan to get the screen replaced:

- If the iPad is under an AppleCare plan, have Apple or an Apple-certified repair establishment replace the screen.

- If the iPad doesn't have AppleCare coverage, you may be able to save money by using less formal services.

- If you have technician-level skills, you can replace the screen yourself.

■ **Note** If the screen suffers minor cracks rather than full-on crazy paving, you may be able to smooth over the damage temporarily by applying a thick screen protector. Even if you do this, the damage will typically get worse with use, so plan to get the iPad repaired as soon as is practicable.

Troubleshooting Audio Issues

Normally, an iPad can output good-quality audio through its speakers at a decent volume—perhaps louder than you'll want if students are using the iPads in the classroom. An iPad can also output audio to speakers or headphones through its headphone socket, to Bluetooth speakers or headphones via the Bluetooth wireless protocol, or to AirPlay speakers or an Apple TV via the AirPlay protocol.

This section discusses how to troubleshoot the audio issues your iPads are most likely to suffer. These issues include the following:

- *No audio output*: There's no audio output at all.

- *No audio output from speaker*: There is no audio output from the speaker, although headphones work fine.

- *Audio volume is too low*: The audio volume is too low, and you can't turn it up far enough.

- *Audio is distorted*: The sound plays back through the speaker or headphones, but it's distorted.

- *iPad can't play audio via AirPlay*: The iPad is unable to play through AirPlay speakers or speakers connected to Apple TV.

- *iPad can't play audio via Bluetooth*: The iPad can't play audio to Bluetooth speakers or headphones.

The following subsections show you how to deal with each of these audio issues in turn, except for AirPlay, which is covered in the section "Troubleshooting AirPlay and Apple TV," later in the chapter.

Troubleshooting No Audio Output at All

If you're not getting any audio output at all from the iPad, start by making sure that the audio isn't muted. Usually, the easiest way to check is by pressing the physical Volume Up button on the iPad. When you do so, the Volume pop-up should appear briefly in the middle of the screen, indicating the current volume (see Figure 9-48).

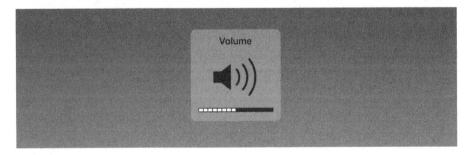

Figure 9-48. *The Volume pop-up enables you not only to see the current volume but also to verify that the Volume Up button and Volume Down buttons are working*

■ **Note** If the iPad is a model that has the Ring/Silent switch at the top of the right side, make sure the switch is set to the Ring setting. (The Silent setting shows orange underneath the switch, so if you see orange, move the switch to the opposite position.)

Alternatively, or as your next move if you get no response from the Volume Up button, open Control Center and check that the Mute icon isn't red (which indicates that muting is turned on). In iOS 10, the Mute icon is on the iPad Controls card, so if the Music card appears at first, swipe left to display the iPad Controls card.

After making sure muting isn't the problem, see which audio output device the iPad is using:

- *iOS 11*: Tap and hold the Music box (see the left screen in Figure 9-49) until it expands (see the center screen in Figure 9-49), and then tap the AirPlay icon in the upper-right corner. In the AirPlay dialog that opens (see the right screen in Figure 9-49), see which audio output device bears a checkmark; tap the iPad button to use the iPad's speakers.

Figure 9-49. *In iOS 11, tap and hold the Music box (left) to expand it (center), then tap the AirPlay icon in the upper-right corner to display the AirPlay dialog (right). You can then see which audio output device the iPad is using*

- *iOS 10*: After opening Control Center, swipe left to display the Now Playing card (see Figure 9-50), and then look at the box on the right side to see which audio output device the iPad is using. If necessary, tap the iPad button to switch the output back to the iPad's speakers.

Figure 9-50. *In iOS 10, look at the box on the right side of the Now Playing card in Control Center to see which audio output device the iPad is using*

MAKING SURE THE PORTS ARE DRY AND CLEAN

Make sure the iPad's headphone port is dry, because moisture in the port can trick the sensors into detecting headphones when none is plugged in.

If the headphone port is visibly wet—for example, if you can see a drop of water protruding from it—use a cotton bud to remove as much water as possible, and then use warm air to remove the rest. If the problem is that the iPad has been in a steamy environment, try inserting a headphone plug and see if the headphones produce sound. If so, try inserting and removing the headphone plug a few times to try to clear the problem.

If the iPad is an older model that has the Dock connector port rather than the Lightning port, make sure the Dock connector port doesn't have dust, dirt, or debris in it. The Dock connector port is a digital audio output for older models of iPad (and iPhone, and iPod), and "foreign objects" in the Dock connector port may make the iPad try to output audio through that port instead of through the speakers or the headphone port.

Troubleshooting Low Sound Volume

If the iPad is producing only a low volume of sound, the problem may simply be that the output volume is turned down. If not, the iPad may have a volume limit imposed. This volume limit may have a Volume Limit restriction applied to prevent the limit from being changed.

■ **Note** If the iPad is connected to speakers via a cable plugged into its headphone socket, make sure the 3.5 mm jack on the cable is fully inserted and that both the jack and the headphone socket are free of lint or dirt.

Troubleshooting Low Sound Volume

If the iPad is producing only a low volume of sound, first press the physical Volume Up button on the iPad to increase the volume. When you do so, the Volume pop-up should appear briefly in the middle of the screen, indicating the current volume.

If you don't see the Volume pop-up, the Volume Up button may be stuck. Try pressing the Volume Down button instead.

■ **Tip** Barring straightforward damage, the Volume Up button and Volume Down button are usually more likely to stick if the iPad is in a case. The case's buttons may themselves become stuck, or they may not be aligned correctly with the iPad's buttons. So, if the iPad you're troubleshooting is wearing a case, try removing the case so that you can manipulate the buttons directly.

If pressing the Volume Down button doesn't display the Volume pop-up, open Control Center. On iOS 10, swipe left to display the Now Playing card (unless the iPad displays it at first). Then drag the Volume slider to adjust the volume.

Troubleshooting Low Sound Volume Because of a Volume Limit

If the volume controls on the iPad seem to be working correctly, but you still can't get enough volume even if you crank the volume up all the way, chances are that the iPad has a volume limit set. The volume limit may simply be set on the Music screen in the Settings app, but it's likely to be imposed with a Volume Limit restriction.

To find out whether a restriction is in place, choose Settings ➤ Music to display the Music screen in the Settings app. Tap the Volume Limit button to display the Volume Limit screen, and then see if you can move the Max Volume slider. If you can't move it, a restriction is in place.

To lift the restriction so you can change the volume, follow these steps:

1. Scroll back up the left column in the Settings app, and then tap the General button to display the General screen.

2. Tap the Restrictions button. The Enter Passcode dialog opens.

3. Type the Restrictions passcode. The Restrictions screen appears.

4. Scroll down to the bottom of the screen.

5. In the Allow Changes box, tap the Volume Limit button to display the Volume Limit screen.

You can now go back to the Music screen in the Settings app and drag the Max Volume slider to increase the volume as needed.

Troubleshooting Distorted Audio Output

If the audio output from the iPad's speakers is distorted, you need to look into several potential causes. The problem may simply be the playback volume, it may be physical, or it may be in the iPad's configuration.

Take the steps in the following subsections to troubleshoot distorted audio output.

Checking the Playback Volume

First, make sure the iPad isn't playing back at full or near-full volume. As usual, either press the Volume Down button and look at the Volume pop-up that appears in the middle of the screen, or swipe up from the bottom of the screen to open Control Center—on iOS 10, swipe left (if needed) to display the Now Playing card—and then check the setting of the Volume slider.

Checking for Physical Damage and Foreign Bodies

Once you've determined that volume isn't the problem, look at the speakers to see if they've sustained physical damage or what doctors and technicians call "foreign bodies." Remove any case the iPad is wearing, and then pick any dust bunnies, gum, or debris off the speakers. If necessary, use a can of compressed air to blow dust out of the speaker grille.

Restarting the iPad

If the speakers seem okay but the sound is still distorted, it's worth restarting the iPad at this point. Restarting can clear up a wide variety of problems and normally takes less than a minute, so even if it doesn't work, you have little to lose.

Resetting All Settings

If restarting the iPad fails to remove the distortion from the audio output, you may need to reset all settings on the iPad. To do so, follow these steps:

1. From the Home screen, choose Settings ➤ General ➤ Reset ➤ Reset to display the Reset screen.

2. Tap the Reset All Settings button. The Enter Passcode dialog opens.

3. Type your main passcode (the one you use to unlock the iPad). The first Reset All Settings dialog opens.

■ **Note** If you've applied restrictions to the iPad, the Enter Passcode dialog box opens again, prompting you to enter your Restrictions passcode. This security check prevents a user from using the Reset All Settings move to remove restrictions.

---

4. Tap the Reset button. The second Reset All Settings dialog opens, double-checking that you want to reset all the settings.

■ **Note** After resetting all settings, you'll need to configure each Wi-Fi network the iPad uses, together with other settings, such as restrictions. See the section "Resetting an iPad to Cure Minor Ills," earlier in this chapter, for more detail on the various types of reset you can perform on an iPad.

---

5. Tap the Reset button. The iPad restarts, taking longer than usual because it wipes the settings clean.

6. Once the iPad has restarted, unlock it, choose Settings ➤ Wi-Fi, and then connect to the local Wi-Fi network.

Troubleshooting Mono Audio

If an iPad has stereo speakers but plays audio through only one channel, the problem is usually that mono audio has been enabled or that the left-right sound balance has been switched to one side. Both these settings belong to the Accessibility settings.

To see if either mono audio or the left-right balance is the problem, follow these steps:

1. From the Home screen, choose Settings ➤ General ➤ Accessibility to display the Accessibility screen.

2. Scroll down to the Hearing section if you can't see it at first.

3. Make sure the Mono Audio switch is set to Off.

4. Make sure the L–R slider is set to its midpoint.

If this move doesn't fix the problem, it's possible that the nonplaying speaker has been damaged and needs to be replaced.

Troubleshooting the iPad Being Unable to Play Audio via Bluetooth

If the iPad can't play audio to a Bluetooth speaker or headset, first verify that the Bluetooth speaker or headset appears in the list of devices and that it's selected for playback. Here's how to do this on iOS 11 and iOS 10:

- *iOS 11*: Swipe up from the bottom of the screen to open Control Center. Tap and hold the Music box until it expands, and then tap the AirPlay icon in the upper-right corner. In the AirPlay dialog that opens, make sure the Bluetooth speaker or headset has a checkmark next to it; if not, tap its button to select it.

- *iOS 10*: Swipe up from the bottom of the screen to open Control Center. If the iPad Controls card appears, swipe left to display the Now Playing card, and then look at the box on the right side to see which audio output device the iPad is using. If necessary, tap the button for the Bluetooth speaker or headset to switch audio output to that device.

Once you've checked the device, follow the steps in the "Troubleshooting Bluetooth Issues," earlier in this chapter, to resolve the problem.

Troubleshooting AirPlay and Apple TV

AirPlay can be a great way to share audio and video in the classroom. If you run into problems with it, you need to make sure the AirPlay device or Apple TV is on and is connected to the network, check whether the iPad can see the device, and ensure that AirPlay is enabled. The following subsections give you the details.

Making Sure the AirPlay Device or Apple TV Is On

First, make sure that the AirPlay device or Apple TV is powered on and that it's not signaling a problem. For example:

- *AirPort Express*: The AirPort Express displays a green light when it's on and all is well. If you see a yellow light or orange light, try restarting the AirPort. You may also need to reconfigure it.

- *Apple TV*: The Apple TV displays a solid white light when it's on and happy. If the LED is flashing, restart the Apple TV, and then reconfigure it if necessary.

If you're trying to play audio, check that the speakers, monitor, or TV are powered on and that the volume isn't set to zero or otherwise muted.

If you're trying to play video, verify that the monitor or TV is connected to the Apple TV and powered on.

Checking the Network Connection

Next, check the network connection on the AirPlay device or Apple TV. For example:

- *AirPort Express:* If the AirPort Express uses a wired connection, make sure a network cable is plugged into its Ethernet port.

- *Apple TV:* Look at the monitor and TV to make sure it's not displaying the message "Your Apple TV is not connected to the network." If this message does appear, either plug a network cable into the Ethernet port or choose Settings ➤ General ➤ Network and connect to the appropriate Wi-Fi network.

Checking Whether the iPad Can See the AirPlay Device or Apple TV

Once you're sure the AirPlay device or Apple TV is powered on and is connected to the network, open Control Center on the iPad and see whether the device or Apple TV appears in it. As usual with Control Center, this is different in iOS 11 and iOS 10:

- *iOS 11:* Swipe up from the bottom of the screen to open Control Center. For an Apple TV, tap the Screen Mirroring button and see if the Apple TV appears in the Screen Mirroring dialog. For an AirPlay device, tap and hold the Music box until it expands, tap the AirPlay icon in the upper-right corner to open the AirPlay dialog, and then see if the device appears.

- *iOS 10:* Swipe up from the bottom of the screen to open Control Center. For an Apple TV, tap the AirPlay Mirroring button on the iPad Controls card and see if the AirPlay dialog lists the Apple TV. For an AirPlay device, swipe left to display the Now Playing card, and then see if the list on the right side includes the device.

If the device appears, you're in business.

Checking the Wi-Fi Network

For AirPlay to work, the iPad and the AirPlay device or Apple TV must be on the same Wi-Fi network. To check, choose Settings ➤ Wi-Fi from the Home screen and see which Wi-Fi network the iPad is on. If it's the wrong network, connect to the right one.

Making Sure AirPlay Is Enabled

If you've checked that the iPad and the AirPlay device or Apple TV are on the same Wi-Fi network, but the iPad still can't see the device or Apple TV, make sure that AirPlay is enabled on the device or Apple TV. For example:

- *AirPort Express:* Run the AirPort Utility app and tap the icon for the AirPort Express. Tap the Edit button to open the main dialog for configuring the AirPort, and then tap the AirPlay button to display the AirPlay dialog (see Figure 9-51). Set the Enable AirPlay switch to On, and then tap the Done button.

Figure 9-51. *Set the Enable AirPlay switch in the AirPlay dialog to On to enable AirPlay on an AirPort Express.*

- *Apple TV*: Choose Settings ➤ AirPlay, and then set the AirPlay option to On.

Summary

In this chapter, you've learned to deal with a variety of the problems you're most likely to encounter when running a fleet of iPads in the classroom. You now know how to locate a missing iPad, lock it and display a message on it, and erase it if necessary. You've seen how to use iOS' various reset operations to clear up assorted problems, and how to troubleshoot apps, network connections, Bluetooth issues, display issues, and problems with audio and with connecting to AirPort devices and Apple TVs.

Index

■ N

■ O

■ P, Q

■ R

■ S

Get the eBook for only $5!

Why limit yourself?

With most of our titles available in both PDF and ePUB format, you can access your content wherever and however you wish—on your PC, phone, tablet, or reader.

Since you've purchased this print book, we are happy to offer you the eBook for just $5.

To learn more, go to http://www.apress.com/companion or contact support@apress.com.

Apress®

Printed in the United States
By Bookmasters